PRAISE FOR *AGILE*

Adam Gibson provides us with a guide to agile workforce planning for professionals at all levels. This is a go-to handbook on how to plan for the future that I will be using many more times for its wealth of case studies and examples.
Erik van Vulpen, Founder, Academy to Innovate HR

In *Agile Workforce Planning*, Adam Gibson has delivered the definitive book on workforce planning. As businesses navigate uncertainty and complexity, this book shows how workforce planning will need to be agile and built upon solid principles of business, economics and risk. It is a must-read for practitioners in this space.
Nicholas Garbis, former leader of SWP at General Electric and Allianz SE

At last a comprehensive and practical guide to workforce planning! Whilst organizations are realizing the value of strategic workforce planning, as a relatively new discipline within the HR profession and wider business, there hasn't been the corresponding capability to capitalize on their interest. Staying true to Adam's 7Bs of workforce planning, if there is no internal supply and a scarcity of skill in the market then organizations need to build this capability. Adam's book takes significant steps in providing the resource for organizations to build a workforce planning capability for themselves. It enables people to become SWP professionals, providing them with the knowledge, tools and approach to form a solid foundation as an SWP practitioner.
Kath Soole, Strategic Workforce Planning Lead, Ministry of Defence

Adam has woven together his considerable experience, detailed academic research, organizational case studies and fascinating military anecdotes to convey the 'what', the 'how' and critically the 'why' behind agile workforce planning. I believe all HR professionals, not just those devoted to workforce planning, will find the framework and insights provided of real practical value in shaping, building and delivering the workforces their organizations require.'
Steven Scott, Global Head and Managing Director, Workforce Management and Analytics, Standard Chartered Bank

Agile Workforce Planning

How to align people with organizational strategy for improved performance

Adam Gibson

Publisher's note
Every possible effort has been made to ensure that the information contained in this book is accurate at the time of going to press, and the publishers and authors cannot accept responsibility for any errors or omissions, however caused. No responsibility for loss or damage occasioned to any person acting, or refraining from action, as a result of the material in this publication can be accepted by the editor, the publisher or the authors.

First published in Great Britain and the United States in 2021 by Kogan Page Limited

Apart from any fair dealing for the purposes of research or private study, or criticism or review, as permitted under the Copyright, Designs and Patents Act 1988, this publication may only be reproduced, stored or transmitted, in any form or by any means, with the prior permission in writing of the publishers, or in the case of reprographic reproduction in accordance with the terms and licences issued by the CLA. Enquiries concerning reproduction outside these terms should be sent to the publishers at the undermentioned addresses:

2nd Floor, 45 Gee Street	122 W 27th St, 10th Floor	4737/23 Ansari Road
London	New York, NY 10001	Daryaganj
EC1V 3RS	USA	New Delhi 110002
United Kingdom		India
www.koganpage.com		

© Adam Gibson 2021

The right of Adam Gibson to be identified as the author of this work has been asserted by him in accordance with the Copyright, Designs and Patents Act 1988.

ISBNs
Hardback 978 1 78966 607 6
Paperback 978 1 78966 605 2
Ebook   978 1 78966 606 9

British Library Cataloguing-in-Publication Data

A CIP record for this book is available from the British Library.

Library of Congress Control Number

2020948770

Typeset by Hong Kong FIVE Workshop, Hong Kong
Print production managed by Jellyfish
Printed and bound by CPI Group (UK) Ltd, Croydon, CR0 4YY

For Katy and Thomas

CONTENTS

Lists of figures and tables xii
About the author xiv
Foreword xv
Preface xviii
Acknowledgements xix

PART ONE
Introduction to workforce planning 1

01 What is workforce planning? 3
Introduction 3
Three levels of the organization 3
Seven rights of workforce planning 5
Three horizons of workforce planning 14
Summary 17
References 17

02 Evolution of workforce planning 20
Introduction 20
History 20
Evolution 21
Current state 25
Summary 27
References 27

03 The value and limitations of workforce planning 30
Introduction 30
Value of workforce planning 30
Limitations of workforce planning 36
Summary 42
References 43

04 The agile approach 46

Introduction 46
Agile origins 47
Contemporary agile thinking 50
The principles of agile workforce planning 56
Six-stage agile workforce planning framework 59
Summary 61
References 62

PART TWO
Baseline 65

05 Analysing the strategic context 67

Introduction 67
Types of organization 68
Strategic alignment 73
Environmental scanning 76
Summary 77
References 78

06 Understanding the workforce 80

Introduction 80
Data gathering 81
Making assumptions 83
Workforce segmentation 85
Workforce analytics 92
Summary 94
References 95

07 Gaining buy-in 97

Introduction 97
How are decisions made? 98
Stakeholder mapping 99
Engaging with stakeholders 101
Agree terms of reference 102
Summary 106
References 106

PART THREE
Supply 109

08 Understanding workforce evolution 111

Introduction 111
Organizational churn 111
Modelling and forecasting 114
The impact of megatrends 119
Workforce performance 124
Skill decay 128
Summary 129
References 130

PART FOUR
Demand 135

09 The nature of demand 137

Introduction 137
What is demand? 138
Calculating demand 143
Summary 148
References 149

10 Forecasting demand 150

Introduction 150
The impact of change 150
Changing demand trends 155
Quantitative methods 160
Qualitative methods 162
Determining the seven rights 165
Summary 169
References 169

PART FIVE
Gap analysis 175

11 Establishing the gap 177
Introduction 177
Assessing the gap 177
The gap in the seven rights 181
Re-engaging stakeholders 185
Summary 189
References 190

PART SIX
Action plan 191

12 The planning approach 193
Introduction 193
The seven Bs of action planning 194
Collaborating with key partners 197
Cost–benefit analysis 201
Summary 203
References 204

13 Demand optimization 205
Introduction 205
Balance 206
Bot 232
Summary 240
References 241

14 Talent management 248
Introduction 248
Buy 248
Build 259
Borrow 274
Bind 282
Bounce 289

Summary 295
References 295

15 Creating the plan 301

Introduction 301
Tasting the plan 301
Aspects of the plan 306
The plan of plans 309
Summary 311
References 311

PART SEVEN
Deliver 313

16 Implementing the plan 315

Introduction 315
Managing a living plan 315
Embedding the process 321
Summary 324
References 324

PART EIGHT
Conclusion 327

17 Becoming a workforce planning professional 329

Index 331

LIST OF FIGURES AND TABLES

FIGURES

Figure 0.1 Blueprint of Agility xvi
Figure 1.1 Three levels of the organization 4
Figure 1.2 Seven rights of workforce planning 5
Figure 1.3 Three horizons of workforce planning 15
Figure 2.1 Harmonized unemployment rates 2005–2015 24
Figure 3.1 The Global Goals for Sustainable Development 37
Figure 4.1 The waterfall chart 47
Figure 4.2 Principles of modern agile 55
Figure 4.3 Agile workforce planning framework 60
Figure 5.1 Economic sectors 68
Figure 5.2 Strategic framework 73
Figure 6.1 Capability segmentation framework 89
Figure 6.2 Gaussian and Paretian distributions of performance 90
Figure 6.3 Decomposition tree to analyse turnover 93
Figure 7.1 Example of RAPID® matrix for training change 99
Figure 7.2 Power vs interest stakeholder map 100
Figure 8.1 The organizational churn model 112
Figure 8.2 The workforce performance model 125
Figure 9.1 The input–output model of processes 138
Figure 9.2 Product of labour curves 144
Figure 11.1 Traditional and agile gap analyses 178
Figure 11.2 Scenario-based gap analysis 180
Figure 12.1 Workforce planning levers 195
Figure 13.1 Demand fluctuation against maintained supply 215
Figure 13.2 Time fences 217
Figure 13.3 The Greiner Curve 218
Figure 13.4 The competing values framework 223
Figure 13.5 The PDCA cycle 226
Figure 14.1 Talent lakes, pools and streams 251
Figure 14.2 Speed to competence 262
Figure 14.3 The performance to value model 283
Figure 15.1 Strategic alignment of workforce plans 305

TABLES

Table 8.1 Transition probability matrix 116
Table 8.2 Retirement model 118

ABOUT THE AUTHOR

Adam Gibson is a global leader in workforce planning, creator of the Agile Workforce Planning methodology and a popular keynote speaker. Having successfully implemented and transformed workforce planning and analytics in businesses across multiple industries, he continues to advise company executives on how to create a sustainable workforce that increases productivity and reduces cost. Now a consultant in the professional services, has held senior roles in workforce planning, workforce analytics and talent management in a number of prominent public and private sector organizations. Prior to his current career in business, he served in the British Army as a commissioned officer in the infantry; he deployed on multiple operational tours, serving on the front lines of Afghanistan and Iraq, and received the Joint Commander's Commendation in the 2007 Operational Honours and Awards.

Adam is Founder and Director of Agile Workforce Planning Ltd and leader of the Strategic Workforce Planning Faculty of the Chartered Institute of Personnel and Development (CIPD). He holds a Bachelor of Arts degree (with Honours) in Politics from the University of Sheffield and a Post-Graduate Diploma in Strategic Management and Leadership from Stratford Business School. He is a Chartered Fellow of the Chartered Institute of Personnel and Development (Chartered FCIPD) and a Fellow of the Chartered Management Institute (FCMI).

FOREWORD

In a recent television interview, the guest was asked about some unexpected current event and what it meant. With a sly grin, the guest simply responded 'It's 2020!' The year 2020 may become a meme for unparalleled change with cumulative calamities:

- Global coronavirus pandemic affecting 7 billion people on earth with nearly 40 million infected and over one million deaths
- Racial and civil unrest reflected in Black Lives Matter protests and movement
- Global immigration, refugee and humanitarian challenges
- Natural disasters of fires, earthquakes, hurricanes, floods and even locusts
- Economic decline in many industries
- Political squabbles and diatribes
- Personal and emotional malaise with increased rates of anxiety and stress and decreased rates of well-being

Whew! Some have said it is time to apply the neuralyzer from *Men in Black* and erase the year 2020.

Of course, we cannot erase 2020, or even pretend it did not exist.

Individuals and organizations need to learn to not merely survive, tolerate, or endure the uncertainty that these crises create, but to harness the uncertainty and find opportunities in it.

The good fortune for individuals and organizations is that there has been a lot of focus the last few years around creating agility. Agility, or the capacity to anticipate and respond quickly, has become a key concept to help both individuals cope with change and organizations harness uncertainty. Clearly agility matters in this unprecedented 2020 world.

In our work, we have defined laid out a roadmap for agility (Figure 1). This roadmap has three fours: (1) four dimensions to define agility (create a future, anticipate opportunity, adapt quickly, learn always; (2) four stakeholders where agility applies (strategy, organization, leader, and individual); (3) four HR practices to drive agility (people, performance, communication, work). This overview of agility offers leaders a blueprint to build a learning organization that can adapt to what is not yet known.

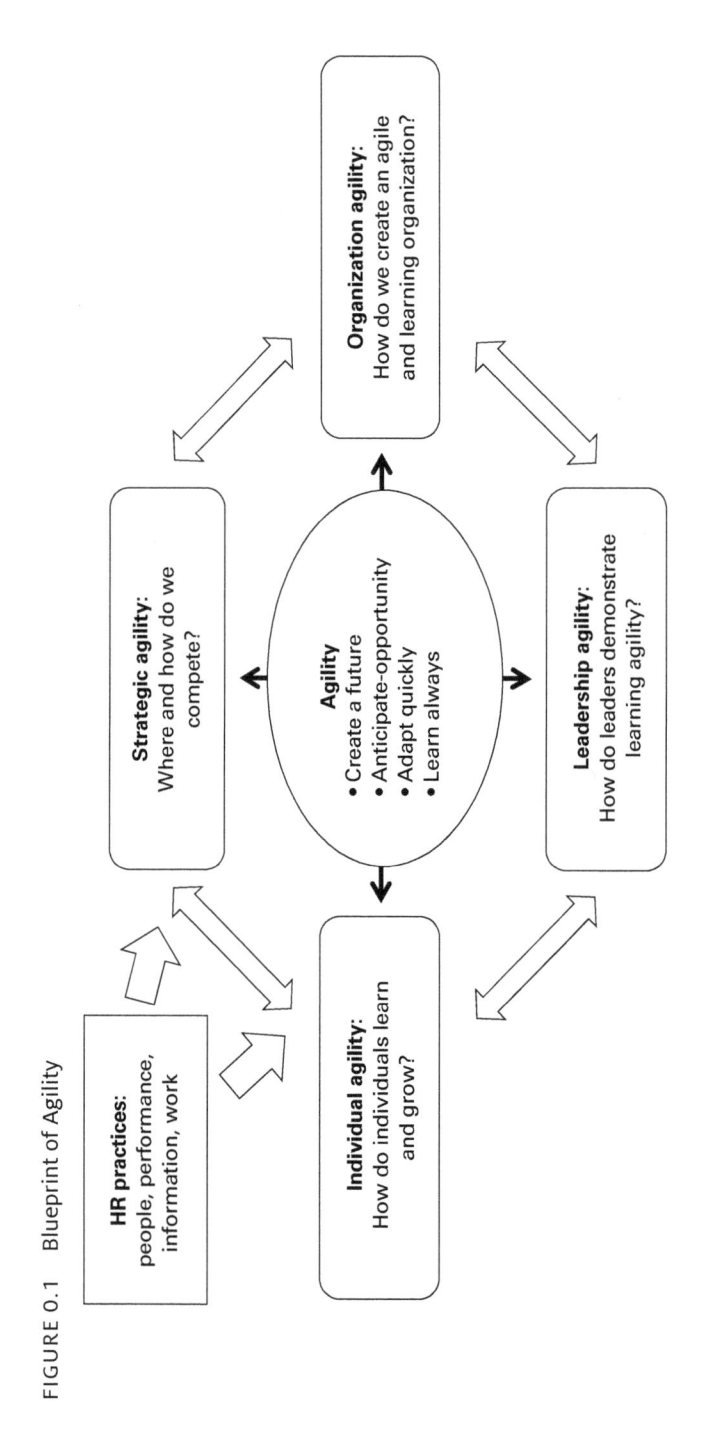

FIGURE 0.1 Blueprint of Agility

For agility to become a central capability and element of an organization's culture, individuals have to become nimble, deft, and change-able. To ensure individual agility, an organization needs to create a more agile workforce planning process.

Adam Gibson's ideas in this book offer unique and relevant guidance for creating this agile workforce planning process. His work does a superb job capturing and synthesizing the rich and diverse literature on workforce planning so that the seven rights of workforce planning can occur: shape, size, location, time, cost, risk, and capability.

His framework with six stages for doing agile workforce planning (baseline, supply, demand, gap analysis, action plan, deliver) are relevant, timely and useful. For each of these six stages, he provides conceptual insights, useful tools and specific actions that will enable a business or HR leader to make agile workforce planning happen.

With the ideas and insights in this book, the threats and fears of 2020 may be replaced with opportunity and confidence in how to better manage talent in times of uncertainty.

Dave Ulrich
Rensis Likert Professor
Ross School of Business
University of Michigan Partner
The RBL Group

PREFACE

Throughout my younger years I was fascinated by history. Perhaps it was the study, on three separate occasions (such was British education in the 1990s), of German history between the two world wars that drove my interest in political history. I was interested in the romantic and utopian notions of an ideal state of politics and of duty, espoused by Plato and Aristotle, concepts that would lead me into military service. Equally, I had an interest in *realpolitik*, the way things are, characterized by the likes of Thomas Hobbes and Niccolò Machiavelli. My career in the army was similarly demarcated: enemies were fought, and hearts and minds won, through realpolitik; however, the conduct of the army was based on duty. I recall being on parade, early in my service, and we were addressed by a senior officer: *do what you ought, not what you want*. It was a phrase that stuck with me as all of us were directed through the use of terms such as *should*, *will* and *must*. They were phrases that worked; the military acted on those terms and were punished when they failed.

When I left the military, I found that much of the civilian world used the same phraseology: managers said that *people should*, processes said that *people will*, and leaders said that *people must*. Except, often people could not, would not and did not; and that is usually why plans take longer than expected, run over budget, or fail. The same has been true with workforce planning: either plans are based on organizations assuming people *should*, or plans themselves rely on an expectation that people *will*. As I have practised workforce planning, I have done so on a mantra I continue to preach: **people can or they cannot, they will or they will not, they have or they have not: plan on that basis.** The agile workforce planning approach has evolved out of a necessity of realpolitik, an approach that works rather than existing as an academic exercise.

I have written this book with the same things in mind: to be able to take those with an interest in businesses and the people within them, those with experience in workforce planning and those who may have never heard of it, and those from both junior and senior levels within organizations, and help us all create the workforce we need.

ACKNOWLEDGEMENTS

Going right back to the start of this journey, I would like to thank Warren Howlett, who made the initial introductions to Kogan Page and made this book a possibility. Then there is the team at Kogan Page, whose support was vital, particularly Anne-Marie Heeney and Lucy Carter. The many who provided an invaluable contribution along the way: the Searchologist, Katrina Collier, for her early advice on writing, and Matthew Mee, from Emsi, who was invaluable in making the introductions that resulted in a number of the great case studies in the book. Toni Richards from Impellam Group and Lorna Bunnell from Cordant Group, for their kind support and permission to use case studies from their businesses. The SDG team at the United Nations, who kindly granted permission to include their sustainable development goals, and Brenda Blowman, who graciously gave permission to include the fierce lion, Sam Blowman, within this book. Also, a huge thanks to Nicholas Garbis, James Poletyllo, Kath Soole, Tanya Thomas and Sarah Weber for their support, encouragement, cheerleading and detailed review of early drafts.

This book would not have been what it is, without the direct input of many who agreed to be interviewed and provided many of the fantastic case studies and examples that illustrate the art of agile workforce planning: Dr Max Blumberg, Katy Bowers, Charlotte Brownlee, Peter Cheese, Antony Ebelle-ebanda, Simon Fanshawe OBE, Keith Halliwell, Phillip Knight, Mark Lawrence, Rob McCargow and Kevin Porter. Each and every one of you has my immense thanks. I am very grateful for the support of Professor Dave Ulrich who provided the foreword to the book, and also to Mihaly Nagy for initiating that introduction back in Nice.

Finally, a heartfelt thank you to my family, who have not only sacrificed a great deal, but whose love and support have allowed me to write and bring this book to you all.

PART ONE

Introduction to workforce planning

01

What is workforce planning?

Introduction

In early 2019 I was a member of a panel at PAFOW London (People Analytics Future of Work) discussing workforce planning; the organizer and a global figure in people analytics, Al Adamsen, was chairing the panel. In recognition of the challenge in understanding workforce planning, he posed a quotation: 'The beginning of wisdom is to call things by their proper name' (Confucius, 1979). Workforce planning is known by many different names, including people planning, headcount planning, manpower planning, human capital planning, and human resource planning. The director of research and consultancy at the Institute for Employment Studies, Peter Reilly, provides the following opening definition: 'A process in which an organization attempts to estimate the demand for labour and evaluate the size, nature, and sources of the supply which will be required to meet that demand' (Reilly, 1996). In this chapter, we will go deeper into the definition and explore the way we look at organizations when thinking about workforce planning, the specifics of what workforce planning aims to achieve, and the timelines we consider when planning.

Three levels of the organization

By their very etymology, the concepts of workforce and organization are inextricably linked: a business organization is a workforce that is structured and managed to pursue a collective goal. Organizations vary in scale and complexity and, with this, the considerations and implications of workforce planning vary. Organizations can be viewed as existing at three levels

FIGURE 1.1   Three levels of the organization

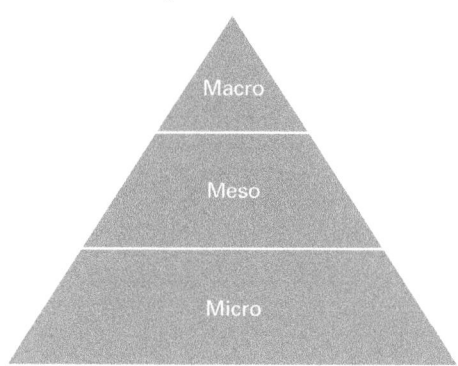

(Wagner and Hollenbeck 2015), lenses through which we will view workforce planning throughout this book.

Macro

This is the level of the organization as a whole; for example, the Acme Corporation featured in Warner Bros' *Looney Tunes* is the macro level.

Meso

These are the component levels within an organization. For example, the Acme Corporation may be subdivided by its central product departments, including explosives and vehicles. Those departments may be divided further into lines of specific products: the Acme 'Little Giant' Firecracker and Acme Self-Guided Aerial Bomb production lines within the explosives department, and the Acme Rocket Sled and Acme Spring-Powered Shoes production lines within the vehicles department. Each of these departments and lines can be considered the meso level.

Micro

This is the level of the individual teams, for example, the team on a product line who box up the Acme Birdseed.

Workforce planning sets out to achieve the following seven Rights at each of those levels of the organization.

Seven rights of workforce planning

FIGURE 1.2 Seven rights of workforce planning

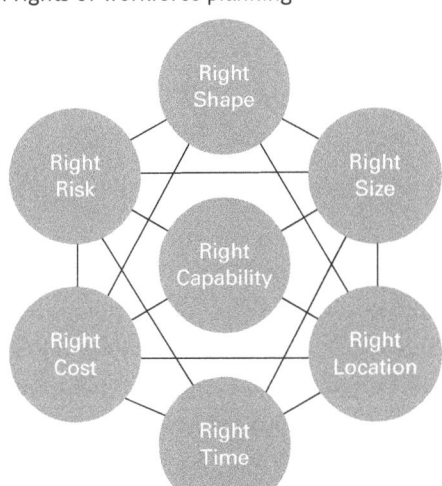

In the most commonly quoted definition, workforce planning 'strives to have the right number and the right kinds of people, at the right places, at the right time, doing things which result in both the organization and the individual receiving maximum long-run benefit' (Vetter, 1967). From those first four rights, this section will cover the expanded seven rights that are key aims of workforce planning.

Right capability

Capability is the extent of an ability to achieve a particular outcome and both combines and transcends the traditional categorizations of *right people* and *right skills* (eg Sinclair, 2004; Lambert, 2009). As we will discuss further in Chapter 6, the modern workforce is a hybrid of people and technology. Also, both people and technology are inextricably linked to activity, leaving capability as a more accurate descriptor.

When we consider a workforce, we can view capability as a construct of five components (Matthews, 2014): knowledge, skills, mindset, physiology and environment. Knowledge is the internally memorized information required to complete a particular task. It is derived from a learning experience, either active in the form of training or passive through having direct exposure. Knowledge is distinct from having access to knowledge, which is an element of the environment. Indeed, the growing ease of access to information and the increasing use of intuitive systems has corresponded with a reduction in the requirement for knowledge to complete tasks.

Skills are practised techniques that enable the achievement of an outcome. These skills can be viewed as considering ideas (cognitive), doing things (technical) or relating to people (interpersonal). Competency is often used interchangeably with the word skill. However, a competency is created when skills combine with specific knowledge and physiology (and, where necessary, accreditation). To that extent, competency can exist in individuals and only translates into capability within the context of the organization alongside mindset and environment.

The mindset comprises the mental aspect that both enables skills and knowledge to be achieved and for them to become action. It can be said to comprise three distinct elements: emotional, how we feel about something; cognitive, how we think about something; and behavioural, how we react to something. The range of these elements is often considered as a range from positive to negative; it is probably more helpful to recognize mindset within the Aristotelian concept of virtues and vices. In this sense, virtue is the positive element itself (such as courage) and vices are the negative excesses (rashness) or deficit (cowardice) (Aristotle, 1980). Elements within mindset, such as self-belief or courage, are often referred to as competencies; more accurately, these are situational and better reflected as part of capability.

Physiology refers to those characteristics required to achieve knowledge, skills, and mindset, and also the ability to translate that into action in a particular circumstance. It comprises mental (eg intelligence) and physical (eg appearance and strength); health and well-being, both mental and physical, are key elements. Physiology can also be said to relate to natural ability that can enable knowledge and skills to be attained quicker or executed to a higher degree of performance. Throughout time, technology has continued to bridge physiological limitations, both enabling competency attainment and execution for the first time in some and pushing the boundaries of human possibility for others.

Environment is the factors independent of a worker that promote, enable, restrict or prevent a competency from translating into the desired outcome. This can include hygiene factors (eg noise, temperature and comfort), hard factors (eg technology, processes and resources) and soft factors (eg culture and leadership). Environment is a critical factor that both impacts mindset (positive and negative) and can overcome limitations of physiology.

To the five components proposed by Matthews, I add a sixth: accreditation. Even with all the above five components, which theoretically translate into action, accreditation is the increasingly common requirement to translate action into reality. At a basic level, most workers are subject to some form of screening or basic background check. Roles in government, defence and law enforcement typically require varying degrees of security clearance. Regulated professions necessitate accreditations either on the basis of a single qualification, such as barristers passing the bar, or a time-limited certification, as is the case with gas engineers. Those regulated professions with exacting standards around safety require declarations around personal health and intoxication, or logbooks confirming hours worked in advance. For both these professions and the vast majority of workers, accreditation will take the form of a licence or pass that must be carried. Indeed, even basic capabilities in the modern workplace are inextricably linked to the completion of mandatory training, regardless of whether or not that training translates into knowledge.

Fundamentally, workforce planning is about ensuring an organization has the *right capability* to achieve its business objectives. More important is how that capability connects across six additional dimensions.

Right size

Size is often used as a synonym for capacity; though they are related, they are distinct and capacity will be covered in greater depth in Chapter 9. Size is simply about the numbers: is there a sufficient quantity of a capability within an organization to achieve an outcome? It is a concept requiring some care as the compound, to *rightsize*, has negative connotations as a euphemism for layoffs (Kokemuller, 2014). Indeed, an article in the *New Yorker* satirizes it with a discussion of a Cubicle Inhabitant Reduction Program and says, 'Rightsizing simply refers to our commitment to optimizing our head count after discovering that we are, in fact, wrong-sized. I want to reassure you that this is very different from downsizing, which is something we haven't done since before the word "rightsizing" was invented' (Nissan, 2014). Amongst HR thinkers, however, the concept of rightsizing is correctly recognized as a positive approach to ensure there are the right number of workers to do the work:

> A work force may indeed be too small for the task. And the work then suffers, if it gets done at all. But this is not the rule. Much more common is the workforce

that is too big for effectiveness, the workforce that spends, therefore, an increasing amount of time *interacting* rather than working (Drucker, 1985)

Right shape

If size is about the numbers of a capability, then shape is the mix of those capabilities within a workforce: is there the right shape of capabilities to achieve an outcome? We can break down shape into four components:

INTRA-CAPABILITY

We acknowledge that a capability is derived from an individual mix of knowledge, skills, mindset and physiology, further intertwined with organization-specific environment and accreditation. From the purest perspective, therefore, there can be no two capabilities that are the same; each capability would be as unique as a fingerprint. In reality, we recognize capabilities within broad categories (eg project management, and human resources). The intra-capability components are the sub-levels or degrees within capabilities; it is easiest to understand capabilities as ranging from foundation, to intermediate and then advanced (perhaps with the final dimension of expert for the truly exceptional). When we look at the right shape at an intra-capability level, we are looking for that mix of foundation, intermediate and advanced capabilities. Work tends to require a mix of capability levels and is subject to the phenomenon of *regression to the mean* (Galton, 1889), so that the majority of work requires an intermediate level of capability. That being the case, too much capability at foundation level will result in a substandard outcome, whilst too much capability at an advanced level will result in a wasted capability (and impact *right cost*).

As we recognize that an intra-capability mix is a necessity, it provides the additional benefit that capabilities being used actively can be expected to develop over time. Just like a muscle, a capability that hinges heavily upon skill will develop based on continued practising of that skill. Similarly, those capabilities that rely on knowledge should expect to grow that knowledge as more relevant information becomes internally memorized. It is important to appreciate that foundation, intermediate and advanced levels are not absolute: not only do they change over time, largely on the basis of increasing global knowledge, but they are viewed differently between organizations (eg consider how a small bookkeeping firm might determine an intermediate level of computer literacy when compared to a technology giant).

INTER-CAPABILITY

If intra-capability is about the mix of levels *within* capabilities, then the inter-capability component is concerned with the mix *of* capabilities. Whereas an intra-capability view cannot exist at the lowest micro level of an organization (a worker cannot be both foundation level and advanced level at project management), the inter-capability view exists at all three organizational levels. At the micro level, this might refer to the mix of programme management and team management capabilities within a worker. At a meso and macro level, this is the mix of capabilities within teams, business areas and across the organization.

CHARACTERISTIC

The characteristic component relates to those dimensions of a workforce that are not inextricably linked to capabilities and can be subdivided as sentient, physiological and non-physiological. The sentient component refers to the extent that a capability is a conscious being (Nagel, 1974) and can be considered as human, artificial intelligence (where robotics can mimic human cognitive function), animal (consider the continuing use of working animals in transportation, guarding, searching, hunting and assisting), automated (non-intelligent machines) and inanimate (capabilities that are either stationary or move only through interaction with one of the other types of sentience). As explained earlier, the physiological component of a capability is directly related to the ability to achieve knowledge, skills, and mindset, and also the ability to translate that into action in a particular circumstance. The physiological component of a characteristic does not, in and of itself, enhance or limit the ability to create an outcome. Take for example someone who needs to use a wheelchair for mobility. That physiological component becomes a factor limiting the attainment of a capability in an environment without a wheelchair ramp; in an environment with a wheelchair ramp, this is simply a physiological characteristic. The most recorded physiological characteristics in the workplace are age, sex, ethnicity, disability and physical dimensions (consider the provision of uniforms). The non-physiological element encompasses the myriad characteristics that make us what we are, including our heritage (eg nationality, socio-economic background and previous employment), our life circumstances (eg personal relationships, parenthood and caring responsibilities) and our lifestyle (eg politics, propensities and activities).

Whilst there are many physiological and non-physiological characteristics that can rightly be considered beyond the scope of the workplace, it must be recognized that the cultural fabric of an organization is a complex mixture of these characteristics and they are increasingly recorded and monitored to improve the diversity of thought (the mindset element of capability) and promote inclusivity.

CONTRACT

The contractual position of capabilities is closely interlinked to some characteristic components. The difference is that whilst a characteristic does not impact a capability, the contractual component does impact the way that a capability can be used. For example, a capability related to a permanent employee cannot necessarily be leveraged in the same way as an identical capability related to a consultant.

CASE STUDY
NATO

The military has used the concept of *command states* for decades to differentiate these relational elements of capabilities that match the contractual position. In doing so, it allows senior commanders to delegate authorities to more junior levels and increase the speed of decision making, which, in turn, delivers outcomes faster. NATO (2013) use the following:

- **Operational Command (OPCOM)**
  The authority to assign and reassign specific tasks and to redeploy all capabilities. This could be considered to be equivalent to the authority a CEO wields within a business.

- **Operational Control (OPCON)**
  The authority to assign and reassign specific tasks to units and to redeploy those units. The authority does not extend to those capabilities *within* units. This could be seen as similar to a business working with a matrix structure: a senior manager may ask their finance manager to focus on a particular issue, but that does not allow that leader to direct the way that finance task is done.

- **Tactical Command (TACOM)**
  The authority to assign specific tasks to all capabilities for the duration of a particular mission. This is similar to a project lead directing a project team and that ability being limited to the scope and duration of that project.

- **Tactical Control (TACON)**
  The localized direction of a capability whose task has already been assigned. This could be viewed as a junior manager working with an assigned consultancy

service; they would have a limited ability to direct when and where the work takes place, but not how it is done.

The importance of this contractual position cannot be understated; it tends to be inextricably linked to the concepts of *right time*, *right cost* and *right risk*.

Right location

Is a capability in the right location to achieve an outcome? It can be considered within two specific dimensions: geographic and structural. Depending on the meso level of the organization, the geographic element could be viewed as an economic region level (eg EMEA – Europe, Middle East and Africa), at a national level, an intra-national level (eg states, counties or cities) or at a locale level (eg offices or plants). There are strong views that location is no longer important (Friedman, 2007) due to the rise of technology-enabled globalization. Technology has certainly impacted global supply chains and connectivity is increasingly overcoming physical locations. Accordingly, it is important to recognize cyberspace as a geographic location. That said, 'location does matter and will continue to matter' (Hagel and Seely Brown, 2010) as activity happens in a location, be that physical or cyber.

The structural location relates to the business hierarchy in which a capability exists, usually a team. In simple terms, if a finance team requires a finance capability, it is of limited value if that capability is otherwise employed within the marketing team. Whilst it is not unusual for some capabilities to be dispersed within a structure, it requires some form of business structure to bring it together at scale, even only on a temporary basis. Consider, for example, a fire and evacuation capability; these are usually dispersed around locations with emergency procedures to enable that capability.

Right time

Just as activity always happens in a place, it also always happens at a time. The right time is considered across two dimensions: firstly, is a capability available at the point it is needed? A capability too early may result in wasted value, a capability too late may delay an outcome and waste value in related capabilities. Consider the wasted value of an aircraft, of ground crew and aircrew, just through the delay of a pilot. Secondly, is a capability available for the duration it is needed? Every task takes time and even the shortest of tasks have a duration where a capability is needed. A capability that cannot be provided for the duration can result in delay and wasted value. Consider both a capability required for three days, but only provided for one, and a capability provided for three days but borrowed elsewhere for the second day. In addition, after the duration of a task a capability is surplus and, unless reassigned, again results in wasted value. Time is often the most overlooked aspect within the field of workforce planning: 'The output limits of any process are set by the scarcest resource. In the process we call *accomplishment*, this is time... one cannot rent, hire, buy or otherwise obtain more time' (Drucker, 1985). To ensure the right workforce at the right time is to ensure that time is not wasted.

Right cost

Are we paying the right cost for the capability? This goes beyond the concept of a budget and if an organization can afford a cost, but is more importantly seen as a question of *value for money*. The cost can be considered in three different ways: accounting, opportunity and external. The accounting cost is the sum of funds spent on an activity. This is typically understood as fixed costs that do not vary with output (eg factories) and variable costs that do change with output (eg raw materials). At a macro level, human capabilities are semi-variable as a workforce is always needed to keep the lights on. At a meso level, however, the cost of human capabilities can be distinguished as either fixed or variable; this will be covered in greater detail within Chapter 11. The opportunity cost is the cost of employing a capability in one activity rather than another and captures imputed costs where factors of production are already owned by an organization. For example, whilst employing a team would be considered as an accounting cost, reassigning them from one activity to another would be considered an opportunity cost. In addition to the accounting and opportunity cost, usually grouped together as the economic cost, is the external cost. The external costs are those imposed on a third party; the commonly cited example is the external cost of passive smoking that results from the tobacco industry. In relation to the workforce, this cost is typically associated with decisions around *offshoring* (relocating a business process from one country to another) to satisfy an economic cost. The resulting layoffs can devastate local communities (Bottini *et al*, 2007) and must be recognized as an organization may wish to take a different choice once the *true cost* is established.

Right risk

Risk is concerned with two things: the potential impact of a negative event and the likelihood of that event taking place. The workplace has myriad risks that will need to be accepted or mitigated. Mitigations come at cost, such as:

CAPABILITY DEFICIT

This is the risk that at a future point in time there will be insufficient levels of capability to deliver an output, which might result in lost revenue for an organization. It can be separated into two elements: non-delivery and capability loss. If you are reading this book, you probably work in an organization that has learnt to accept the risk of non-delivery of capability, which typically manifests as vacancies. It is important to recognize the distinction between a vacancy (a current gap in the workforce) and a requirement (eg the requirement to hire an employee to fill a future vacancy). Vacancies typically arise when a capability is lost and there is no immediate replacement. Non-delivery also manifests where a capability fails to keep pace with market requirements; consider the pace of change in digital skills, for example. In this sense, having the right capability now that is inflexible to change may increase the risk of a future capability deficit.

The concept of workforce loss is inextricably linked to non-delivery; as the likelihood of losing a capability increases, so too does the risk of non-delivery to replace that capability. Capability loss tends to relate to the contract component of *right shape*; contracts of permanent employment with a three-month notice period have a far lower risk of capability loss than a one-week notice period. The fear of capability loss can lead to a reluctance to invest in training; that reluctance to invest in training can lead simply to not having the capability at all.

CAPABILITY SURPLUS

At the opposite end of a capability deficit is having more capability than is needed. The key element is that the standard mitigations for capability surplus, such as the use of contract workers and limited notice periods for staff, directly increase the risk of capability deficit. Balancing this risk is a key challenge, one example being the apocryphal tale of the chief financial officer asking of employees, 'What happens if we train them and they leave?', to which the chief executive officer replies, 'What happens if we don't train them and they stay?' This is played out in boardrooms globally as organizations try to balance deficit through non-delivery against cost through capability surplus.

FRAUD AND CRIMINALITY

It is estimated that a typical organization loses 5 per cent of revenues annually as a result of fraud (ACFE, 2016). The risks of fraud and criminality tend to be heavily mitigated within organizations, not only during employment but also in advance of it. A famous article by the Governor of New York State and the CEO of Ben & Jerry's claimed that one in every three Americans had a criminal record. Organizations will often mitigate the risk of fraud and criminality through not hiring those with certain criminal records. They went on to highlight that joblessness was the single biggest predictor of reoffending (an *external cost* to taxpayers of a hiring decision), therefore employment of those individuals that could reduce reoffending by just 10 per cent would result in an annual saving of $635 million to the United States (Cuomo and Solheim, 2017).

Three horizons of workforce planning

Having understood the seven rights, we circle back to the concept of *right time* and establish *when* the right time is. In workforce planning, we talk about those time periods as three horizons: resource planning, operational workforce planning and strategic workforce planning. These horizons relate to the time frame when the seven rights are achieved, not the point where planning or indeed execution of plans takes place.

Horizon one – resource planning

Resource planning, also known as resource management or capacity planning, focuses on the period of the current financial year. The aim is to manage the workforce against the fluctuations of demand and the natural evolution of employees (eg absence and turnover). At the most basic level, this is what line managers do on a daily basis: they ensure they have sufficient staff to meet the need, they manage their workforce and work

FIGURE 1.3 Three horizons of workforce planning

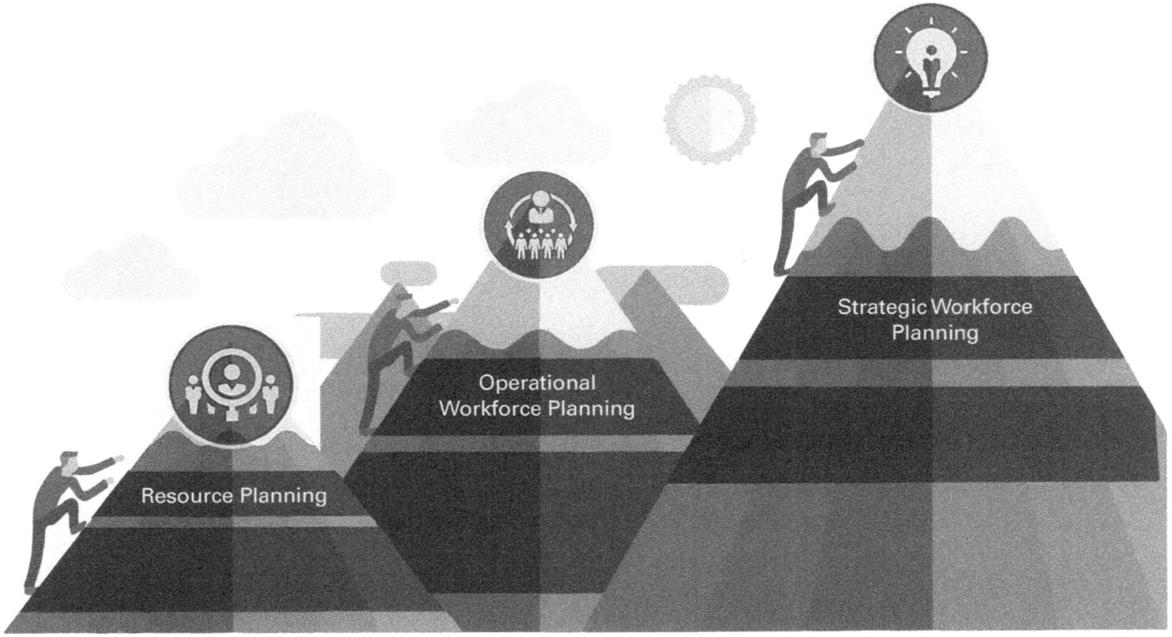

accordingly when additional work arrives or an employee is sick. In many organizations, this planning translates into a rota or schedule detailing when employees are expected in the workplace, or to be at a particular location. Most of the time, these schedules can be provided in advance, in others an advanced schedule can be accompanied by real-time resource management (eg taxicab drivers). Resource planning, unlike operational and strategic workforce planning, takes a *bottom-up* approach that starts at the micro level with the resources required to do the work and then rolls upwards to the meso and macro levels. At advanced levels, resource planning delves into the detail of productivity and utilization, which we will explore in Chapter 9.

Horizon two – operational workforce planning

Operational workforce planning focuses on the period of the next financial year. The aim is to plan a workforce that will achieve the business objectives for the coming year. Operational workforce planning is often run by finance functions as part of a budgetary planning process and, as a result, is the most common approach to workforce planning. This approach tends to result in a focus more around workforce costs at macro and meso levels and less on *how* that workforce will be achieved.

Horizon three – strategic workforce planning

Strategic workforce planning focuses beyond the next budgetary cycle and across multiple years. As Peter Cheese, CEO of CIPD, says, 'strategic workforce planning has never been more important' (Cheese, 2020). There are myriad definitions of the practice; one of the better definitions is provided by Rob Tripp, workforce planning manager at Ford Motor Company, that strategic workforce planning is 'a disciplined business process that ensures that current decisions and actions impacting the workforce are aligned with the strategic needs of the enterprise' (Tripp, 2013).

Though approaches to strategic workforce planning vary as much as the definitions, they all follow a path similar to that articulated by consultant and thought leader in workforce planning and analytics, Tracey Smith:

- determine the roles of interest;
- establish the current state and historical trends;
- determine desired forecasting scenarios;

- perform gap assessments (in headcount and skill sets);
- establish action plans (Smith, 2012).

As a result, it is an approach that typically starts at the macro level and trickles down to the meso level.

Summary

The concepts of workforce planning can appear impenetrable at first glance. The reality is that many subjects that claim to be different are simply workforce planning by another name. Moreover, many subjects claiming to be workforce planning but with different approaches are constituent parts of workforce planning that differ based on organizational levels and planning horizons. Workforce planning practitioners will continue to provide different definitions and approaches for their craft, but all those successful practitioners will agree on the organizational lenses we look through (the levels of the organization), what workforce planning aims to achieve (the seven rights) and the timelines we consider (the three horizons).

> This chapter serves as the basis for the rest of the book. When you practice workforce planning, ask yourself:
> - Which level of the organization are we thinking about?
> - Which planning horizon are we looking at?
> - Does this approach deliver each of the seven rights of workforce planning?

References

ACFE (Association of Certified Fraud Examiners) (2016) *Report to the Nations on Occupational Fraud and Abuse*, www.acfe.com/rttn2016/docs/2016-report-to-the-nations.pdf (archived at https://perma.cc/QXN5-499N)

Aristotle (1980) *The Nicomachean Ethics*, Oxford University Press, Oxford

Bottini, N, Ernst, C and Luebker, M (2007) *Offshoring and the Labour Market: What are the issues?* International Labour Organization, Geneva, www.ilo.org/public/english/employment/download/elm/elm07-11.pdf (archived at https://perma.cc/SYC4-BNW9)

Cheese, P (2020) In-person interview, 8 January

Confucius, ed (1979) *The Analects*, Penguin Books, London

Cuomo, A M and Solheim, J (2017) Employers are often unwilling to hire someone convicted of a crime. That's a problem – and it needs to change [Blog] *LinkedIn*, www.linkedin.com/pulse/employers-often-unwilling-hire-someone-convicted-crime-andrew-cuomo/ (archived at https://perma.cc/GFH4-YZGK)

Drucker, P F (1985) *The Effective Executive*, HarperCollins, New York

Friedman, T L (2007) *The World is Flat*, Picador, New York

Galton, F (1889) *Natural Inheritance*, Macmillan, London

Hagel, J and Seely Brown, J (2010) The increasing importance of physical location, *Harvard Business Review*, 27 October, www.hbr.org/2010/10/the-increasing-importance-of-p (archived at https://perma.cc/9D76-98R7)

Kokemuller, N (2014) What is organizational rightsizing? [Blog] *Chron.com*, https://smallbusiness.chron.com/organizational-rightsizing-78217.htm (archived at https://perma.cc/7B8K-JRYU

Lambert, P (2009) Tomorrow's workforce: Right people, right place, right skills? [Blog] *HR Zone*, 19 May, www.hrzone.com/lead/strategy/tomorrows-workforce-right-people-right-place-right-skills (archived at https://perma.cc/K39L-C5TK)

Matthews, P (2014) *Capability at Work: How to solve the performance puzzle*, Three Faces Publishing, Milton Keynes

Nagel, T (1974) What is it like to be a bat? *The Philosophical Review*, 83 (4), pp 435–50, www.jstor.org/stable/2183914 (archived at https://perma.cc/P4CG-CL99)

NATO (2013) *NATO Glossary of Terms and Definitions*, AAP-06, www.academia.edu/10269177/AAP-6_NATO_Glossary_of_Terms_and_Definitions_2013_ (archived at https://perma.cc/64FP-VQ9J)

Nissan, C (2014) Rightsizing our workforce, *The New Yorker*, 13 March, www.newyorker.com/humor/daily-shouts/right-sizing-workforce (archived at https://perma.cc/Y6FT-SR5M)

Reilly, P (1996) *Human Resource Planning: An introduction*, IES, Brighton, www.employment-studies.co.uk/system/files/resources/files/312.pdf (archived at https://perma.cc/3VZS-HY3U)

Sinclair, A (2004) *Workforce Planning: A literature review*, IES, Brighton, www.employment-studies.co.uk/system/files/resources/files/mp37.pdf (archived at https://perma.cc/BG7G-WX7F)

Smith, T (2012) *Strategic Workforce Planning: Guidance and back-up plans*, CreateSpace Independent Publishing Platform, South Carolina

Tripp, R (2013) Current practices, in D L Ward and R Tripp (eds) *Positioned: Strategic workforce planning the gets the right person in the right job*, AMACOM, New York

Vetter, E W (1967) *Manpower Planning for Hight Talent Personnel*, University of Michigan, Ann Arbor

Wagner, J A and Hollenbeck, J R (2015) *Organizational Behavior: Securing competitive advantage*, Routledge, New York

02

Evolution of workforce planning

Introduction

This short chapter will cover the origins and evolution of workforce planning to its current state. This is not only important from a historical perspective, it also helps to build understanding of how much of the thinking has been gradually fragmented and subsumed into separate areas. In addition, this will help provide insight into the opinions of stakeholders towards workforce planning, whose views have been shaped by the experiences this chapter will cover. Stakeholder views on workforce planning may be impacted adversely by a *negativity bias* where unpleasant memories have a higher psychological impact than positive ones (Kanouse and Hanson, 1972). Of equal value for practitioners in workforce planning is the knowledge that their craft is grounded in the history of civilization, regardless of the surfeit of thinkers who may claim inventorship.

History

Many consider that workforce planning began in the middle of the 20th century and chart the origins of the term *manpower planning* to the 1960s. The concept certainly existed in the Second World War; a British short film entitled *Manpower* claimed, 'the nation that wins a war is the one that plans best its use of manpower' (Ministry of Information, 1943). Economist Alfred Marshall recognized the necessity of planning workforce needs in the late 19th century when he added the factor of organization and entrepreneurship to the existing three factors of production in classical economic theory: land, capital and labour (Marshall, 1890). Researchers have been able to track its existence to an entire century before Marshall and point to actuary John Rowe, who 'as early as 1779 had been engaged on a study of the career structures, wastage rates and promotion prospects in the Royal Marines' (Smith and Bartholomew 1988).

In the warring states period in China, nearly two-and-a-half centuries before, Samuel Griffith writes in the introduction to his translation of Sun Tzu's *The Art of War*, 'conscription and direction of the labour forces needed to carry out the grandiose schemes of the rulers, who attempted to outdo one another in the magnificence of their palaces, terraces, parks, and towers, posed complicated administrative problems. As these were solved a science of organization was created' (Sun, 1963). Indeed, Sun Tzu himself wrote, 'Order or disorder depends on organization'.

Well before the partition of the Jin state in the 5th century BC, which was the precursor to the warring states period, we have the construction of the pyramids in Egypt. Records from Deir el-Medina, home to the artisans who built the Valley of the Kings from the 16th to the 11th century BC near modern-day Luxor, are the most informative. Workers were split into shifts called *phyles*, which were each split into two divisions; within these were 120-strong *gangs*, containing different categories of workmen. Drawing the term from boat crews, these *gangs* were split into a left and right side; the *chief of the gang* retained responsibility for reassignment of workers between these sides (David, 1986).

Though the ability to plan and organize a workforce is clear within our history, I would arguably pinpoint the start of modern thinking to 1776 and the publication of *An Inquiry into the Nature and Causes of the Wealth of Nations* by Adam Smith. In it he introduces the concept of the three factors of production (land, capital and labour), inputs that create outputs in the form of economic goods (Smith, 1776). This input–output model, where increasing a factor of production to create a corresponding increase in the output, begins the evolution to current thinking.

Evolution

Sixties boom

From Adam Smith we fast-forward past Alfred Marshall a century later, beyond the two world wars that conducted this planning on an unfathomable scale, to the 1960s and the use of *material requirements planning* (MRP). This enabled organizations to schedule manufacturing and the workforce needed to deliver it. This technology-enabled approach would be slowly adopted over the next 20 years.

The end of the 1960s saw the publication of *Manpower Planning for High Talent Personnel* by Eric Vetter (1967). In it, he details a four-step process that has become the basis for modern thinking:

- data collection and analyses of the workforce;
- identification of goals and solutions;
- implementation of solutions;
- control and evaluation of those solutions.

This thinking would be bolstered by the publication, by Elmer Burack and James Walker, of a compendium of essays and articles from education and industry on the subject of manpower planning (Burack and Walker, 1972). Walker would proceed to co-found the Human Resource Planning Society (HRPS) a few years later and publish the seminal *Human Resource Planning* in 1980. The second edition drew out the critical emphasis on aligning resources with the business strategy and priorities (Walker, 1992).

Longer-term workforce planning as a practice began to falter over the course of the mid-1970s to early-1980s when the ability to forecast demand was shocked during the energy crisis. Major industrial economies were impacted by the surge in oil prices and the combination of stagnant growth and price inflation was categorized by the term *stagflation* (Cappelli, 2008).

Eighties decline

Centralized planning functions began to be dismantled from the early 1980s. Henry Mintzberg cites 1984 as a time of intensification in the criticism of business planning. The CEO of General Motors was quoted as saying, 'We got these great plans together, put them on the shelf and marched off to do what we would be doing anyway'. Similarly, CEO and Chairman Jack Welch purged scores of planners from General Electric (Mintzberg, 1994).

The decline of workforce planning continued into the following decade after the end of the Cold War, The subsequent shock to oil prices that accompanied the invasion of Kuwait by Iraq saw consumer and business confidence decline and a recession take hold. Increasing unemployment meant that a shortage of workers was not a problem and businesses saw a decreasing need for proactive planning. This was accompanied by a growing trend in decentralized decision making and a shift in the HR agenda towards qualitative issues such as performance improvement and flexible working, and away from quantitative issues such as sufficiency of workers (Reilly, 1996).

The war for talent

The game would change when McKinsey & Company partner Steven Hankin coined the term 'the war for talent' in the seminal article of the same name (Chambers *et al*, 1998). This painted the picture of a declining supply of executive talent that would continue until 2015 and created a burning platform for strategic workforce planning. By the early 2000s, surveys of HR leaders saw 'workforce planning... consistently listed among their top five issues' (Sullivan, 2002). The period also saw the release of *Strategic Staffing* by Thomas Bechet (2002), which shaped the craft of strategic workforce planning and includes approaches still relevant today.

Extensive literature from the time points to 'significant skill imbalances and a loss of institutional memory' (Pegnato, 2003) following the downsizing of US government agencies as a result of the recession in the early 1990s. That same year, the US House of Representatives would hear sworn testimony from USAID on the impact of existing approaches to budgeting and planning that were complicating its ability to build the workforce it needed and the critical role that strategic workforce planning would have in overcoming that (United States Congress, 2003). The drum of the war for talent would be beaten again later in the decade with *Workforce Crisis*, which supported Employment Policy Foundation projections of 'a shortage of several million workers… [by 2010, and] 10 million by 2015' in the US market (Dychtwald *et al*, 2006).

Global financial crisis

The resurgence of workforce planning would have probably continued unabated, had it not been for the burst of the United States real estate bubble between 2006 and 2007. Financial systems, which were highly leveraged against US real estate, resulted in a global recession. As economies contracted many businesses failed, and those that survived could only do so with significant workforce layoffs; in the United States, the unemployment rate nearly doubled within a year. As organizations focused on their immediate survival, planning for the long term all but ceased.

FIGURE 2.1 Harmonized unemployment rates 2005–2015

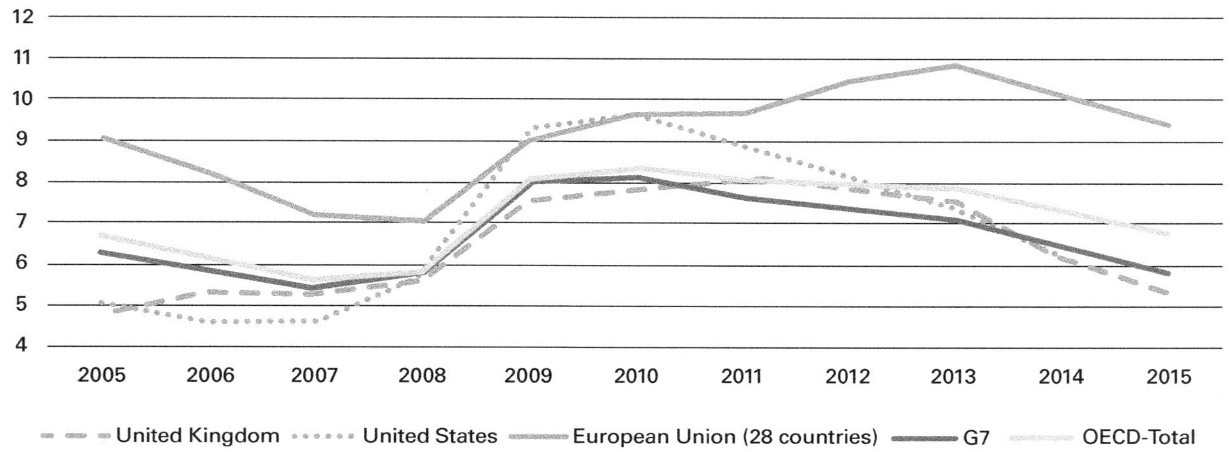
12
11
10
9
8
7
6
5
4
2005
2006
2007
2008
2009
2010
2011
2012
2013
2014
2015
United Kingdom
United States
European Union (28 countries)
G7
OECD-Total

SOURCE OECD

Government intervention, such as the US $700 billion Troubled Asset Relief Program (TARP), provided bailouts and liquidity that would start the road to recovery in 2010 for G7 nations. In Europe, decreased liquidity coupled with the collapse of the Icelandic banking system and high levels of sovereign debt in Portugal, Ireland, Italy, Greece and Spain (the PIIGS), triggered a subsequent crisis that would prolong the impact on organizations.

Current state

Resurgence

The crisis was recognized as a 'black swan event', a phrase coined by statistician and scholar Nassim Nicholas Taleb. The three characteristics are that the event is 'an outlier', 'it carries an extreme impact' and, 'in spite of its outlier status, human nature makes us concoct explanations for its occurrence after the fact, making it explainable and predictable' (Taleb, 2007).

The current state of workforce planning flows directly from the ashes of the global financial crisis as it forced businesses to recognize that they were now existing in a *VUCA* world; to survive, organizations needed to adopt a new way of thinking.

VUCA

An acronym to describe conditions of change:

Volatility

- When change takes place, the degree and frequency of change cannot easily be determined.

Uncertainty

- A lack of predictability about the future, meaning that change could take place at any time and without warning.

Complexity

- Issues have a multiplicity of factors and components, which makes it difficult to identify cause and effect.

> *Ambiguity*
> - With all available information, the current and future picture remains unclear.

With the early green shoots of recovery starting to show, influential HR thinker Dr John Boudreau published *Retooling HR*, which gave considerable focus to strategic workforce planning as 'a tool for considering multiple futures and designing the optimum talent mix to meet them' (Boudreau, 2010). Less than four years after the start of the crisis, a survey of US organizations showed two-fifths of businesses had 'conducted strategic workforce planning assessments to identify their future workforce needs for the next five years' (SHRM, 2012). By the middle of the decade, a survey in APAC concluded that workforce planning was 'the #1 key ingredient for organizational success' and 63 per cent of respondents were planning to increase investment in workforce planning (HRBoss, 2015).

Workforce analytics

The current state of workforce planning cannot be discussed accurately without reference to the growth in analytics accompanied by the prenominal of *HR*, *workforce* or *people*. Many thinkers on the subject recognize the interchangeability (and geographical propensities) of these terms to refer to the same activity (van Vulpen, 2016). Tracy Layney, Chief Human Resource Officer for personalized photo-gift company Shutterfly Inc, made a differentiation in an interview:

- Workforce analytics is the approach of measuring behaviours in an organization and knitting them together to improve business performance.
- HR analytics are the metrics and performance indicators of the HR function (Guenole *et al*, 2017).

Brief interviews with leading thinkers and practitioners David Green, Andy Campbell, Jouko van Aggelen, Luk Smeyers, Dirk Jonker and Tom Haak all pointed towards people analytics as the prevalent term: organizations are about people. That said, David Green admitted that both he and Jonathan Ferrar were increasingly convinced that *workforce analytics* was possibly the more appropriate term (AIHR, 2018).

The increase in workforce analytics tools and techniques has enabled workforce planning to leverage better information and insight in creating success for businesses. That said, the increasing democratization of workforce analytics products has convinced some business leaders that the creation of workforce plans rests solely in new analytics tools. Melissa Cummings, then strategic workforce planning lead for managed healthcare company Aetna, said in an interview:

> Analytics has thrown a veil over what passes for workforce planning... data is about what happened in the past. Forecasting is a static vision of the future. We take data and forecasts and build on them with *what ifs* to create a richer vision. That's the qualitative piece that the enterprise needs (Hansen, 2009).

Summary

Today's business leaders have been shaped by these experiences: they will have seen some of this first-hand and will have been mentored by those who had earlier encounters. Their views on workforce planning are similarly intertwined with these experiences and, for many, will be impacted adversely by a negativity bias.

The world we inhabit, and the ancient world before it, is a product of the ability to plan a workforce. As we will cover in the next chapter, workforce planning can bring immense benefit to organizations, people and the wider economy. However, the traditional approaches are also beset with significant limitations, which highlight the need for the new approach outlined in this book.

References

AIHR (Academy to Innovate HR) (2018) Should we use HR analytics or people analytics? [Online video] youtu.be/2VvLctbyzgQ (archived at https://perma.cc/R4VY-2XRG)

Bechet, T P (2002) *Strategic Staffing: A practical toolkit for effective workforce planning*, AMACOM, New York

Boudreau, J (2010) *Retooling HR: Using proven business tools to make better decisions about talent*, Harvard Business School Publishing, Boston

Burack, E H and Walker, J W (1972) *Manpower Planning and Programming*, Allyn & Bacon, Boston

Cappelli, P (2008) *Talent on Demand: Managing talent in an age of uncertainty*, Harvard Business School Publishing, Boston

Chambers, E G et al (1998) The war for talent, *The McKinsey Quarterly* (3), https://www.researchgate.net/publication/284689712_The_War_for_Talent (archived at https://perma.cc/U6BP-4BS7)

David, A R (1986) *The Pyramid Builders of Ancient Egypt*, Routledge, London

Dychtwald, K, Erickson, T J and Morison, R (2006) *Workforce Crisis: How to beat the coming shortage of skills and talent*, Harvard Business School Publishing, Boston

Guenole, N, Ferrar, J and Feinzig, S (2017) *The Power of People*, Pearson, London

Hansen, F (2009) Strategic workforce planning in an uncertain world, Workforce.com, 9 July, www.workforce.com/2009/07/09/strategic-workforce-planning-in-an-uncertain-world/ (archived at https://perma.cc/SB9P-W9JJ)

HRBoss (2015) Workforce Planning Survey Report 2015: Rethinking workforce planning in Asia, https://hrboss.com/whitepapers/rethinking-workforce-planning-asia-2015 (archived at https://perma.cc/8ENT-GGGL)

Kanouse, D E and Hanson, L (1972) *Negativity in Evaluations, Attribution: Perceiving the causes of behaviour*, General Learning Press, Morristown

Marshall, A (1890) *Principles of Economics*, Prometheus Books, New York

Ministry of Information (1943) Manpower, https://www.iwm.org.uk/collections/item/object/1060006327 (archived at https://perma.cc/5V52-EXMP)

Mintzberg, H (1994) *The Rise and Fall of Strategic Planning*, The Free Press, New York

OECD (2020), Harmonised unemployment rate (HUR) (indicator) doi: 10.1787/52570002-en

Pegnato, J A (2003) Federal workforce downsizing during the 1990s, *The Public Manager*, 32 (4), www.questia.com/library/journal/1G1-119744197/federal-workforce-downsizing-during-the-1990s-a-human (archived at https://perma.cc/4ZZN-8G2M)

Reilly, P (1996) *Human Resource Planning: An introduction*, IES, Brighton, www.employment-studies.co.uk/system/files/resources/files/312.pdf (archived at https://perma.cc/3VZS-HY3U)

Smith, A (1776) *The Wealth of Nations*, 1982 reprint, Penguin, London

SHRM (Society for Human Resource Management) (2012) SHRM survey findings: SHRM-AARP strategic workforce planning, www.shrm.org/hr-today/trends-and-forecasting/research-and-surveys/Pages/StrategicWorkforcePlanning.aspx (archived at https://perma.cc/84ZA-7MCN)

Smith, A R and Bartholomew, D J (1988) Manpower planning in the United Kingdom: An historical review, *Journal of the Operational Research Society*, 39 (3), pp 235–48, www.doi.org/10.1057/jors.1988.41 (archived at https://perma.cc/7CZE-KCTM)

Sullivan, J (2002) Why workforce planning is hot [Blog] 29 July, www.ere.net/why-workforce-planning-is-hot/ (archived at https://perma.cc/LJ5P-Z7WT)
Sun, T (1969) *The Art of War*, Oxford University Press, Oxford
Taleb, N N (2007) *The Black Swan*, Penguin, London
United States Congress (2003) *Strategic Workforce Planning at USAID: Hearing before the Subcommittee on National Security, Emerging Threats and International Relations of the Committee on Government Reform*, House of Representatives, 23 September, www.govinfo.gov/content/pkg/CHRG-108hhrg92392/pdf/CHRG-108hhrg92392.pdf (archived at https://perma.cc/74LQ-BVYB)
Walker, J W (1992) *Human Resource Strategy*, McGraw-Hill, New York
van Vulpen, E (2016) *The Basic Principles of People Analytics*, Analytics in HR, Rotterdam
Vetter, E W (1967) *Manpower Planning for High Talent Personnel*, University of Michigan, Ann Arbor

03

The value and limitations of workforce planning

Introduction

I have a vision of engaged people connected with meaningful work. Effective workforce planning achieves that vision; it is achieved in a way that creates both sustainable growth and the best possible margins through improved productivity. It is because of this that I remain passionate about workforce planning and the difference it can make to organizations and society.

However, many exercises in workforce planning have either been unable to create this value or have resulted in unintended consequences. Indeed, common reasons for failures of traditional approaches to workforce planning (Sullivan, 2002a, 2002b) are still prevalent today.

This chapter will cover both the value of workforce planning and also the limitations of traditional approaches, which together prompt a change in direction for the practice to a more agile approach.

Value of workforce planning

Why plan?

In the early 20th century, French mining engineer and executive Henri Fayol distilled management into five key elements: planning, organizing, command, coordination and control (Fayol, 2013). *The Rise and Fall of Strategic*

Planning (Mintzberg, 1994) sets out four reasons for planning, which I will put into a workforce context:

'ORGANIZATIONS MUST PLAN TO COORDINATE THEIR ACTIVITIES'
When new work lands, but there is an insufficient level of capability to service that work, the failure is usually attributed to a lack of effective planning. With increasing complexity and scale, coordination of effort becomes a critical task, which requires planning to ensure that neither value nor opportunities are wasted.

'ORGANIZATIONS MUST PLAN TO ENSURE THAT THE FUTURE IS TAKEN INTO ACCOUNT'
'We think about our future in order to anticipate our needs and reduce our risks' (Ward, 2013). Being future-focused is critical for all businesses. Threats and opportunities all exist in the future: 'this is a common failing of mankind, never to anticipate a storm when the sea is calm' (Machiavelli, 1532). Consideration of the future can be done in line with the principles of the *three-point estimation* or *programme evaluation and review technique* (PERT): *planning* for the most likely scenario, *preparing* for the best-case scenario, and *pre-empting* the worst-case scenario (Department of the Navy, 1958). No employee generates value *before* the decision to hire them. It follows, therefore, that all workforce decisions would take place in relation to the future and can only benefit from planning.

'ORGANIZATIONS MUST PLAN TO BE RATIONAL'
To quote directly from Mintzberg (1994), 'formalized decision making is better than nonformalized decision making'. Nobel prize winner Daniel Kahneman (2011) had a different approach when he talked of fast, automatic thinking (system one) and slow, effortful thinking (system two). System one thinking is quick and automatic, driven by habit and emotion; system two thinking is more complex and rational. As system one thinking is based around normality and bias, it is suitable for dealing with simple decisions in the immediate space (eg which apple to pick from a bowl, where to step when walking). System two thinking exists for more complex decisions that require mental effort and several steps to come to a conclusion, ie planning. Therefore, this would certainly apply to anything in relation to the workforce; proper planning would prevent decisions being made on the basis of system one thinking.

'ORGANIZATIONS MUST PLAN TO CONTROL'

The aim of control is to protect organizations from 'careless, costly, or uninformed decisions or behaviours' (Finkel, 2015). At a basic level, checklists operate as a visual control; surgeon and author Dr Atul Gawande has written extensively on the importance of checklists to effect immediate improvements in performance (Gawande, 2010). From checklists to improve patient safety in clinical areas (Pronovost et al, 2003) to a checklist to ensure a new starter is onboarded successfully, all controls require advance planning to understand the path to success. All degrees of planning maturity, from basic financial planning to strategic management, are geared around the ability to 'exercise effective control over most factors affecting their businesses' (Gluck et al, 1980).

Benefits of workforce planning

The workforce is typically the biggest cost within an organization; advisory firm Willis Towers Watson state it is typically 70 per cent of opex (operating expenses) within large organizations (Tandon, 2018). If organizations accept the premise of planning, the logic follows to make plans for the largest cost base: the workforce. Beyond this, we will examine some specific benefits of workforce planning:

GUIDING THE BUSINESS FORWARD

Workforce planning is critical to guiding businesses towards their objectives by connecting strategy to execution, as 'a business strategy cannot be executed without the available skills and capability in the workforce' (Stanford, 2013). Then Global Head of Resourcing for steel and mining giant ArcelorMittal, Ali Gilani, was quoted as saying that an effective strategic workforce plan delivered the following benefits:

- a plan which maintains focus on strategy;
- a year-by-year action plan that executes that strategy;
- avoidance of bad tactical decisions that could result in long-term problems;
- a degree of preparedness for unforeseen situations;
- a securing of core jobs and key skills (Brooks, 2012).

This aspect we will cover in greater detail throughout this book.

PROVIDING BUSINESS INSIGHT

A 2019 survey by professional services firm Capita cited that business leaders viewed HR and recruitment as the least effective area of their business at collecting, analysing and using data to drive business outcomes (Capita, 2019). A report from *Harvard Business Review* Analytic Services stated that whilst two-thirds of CEOs received basic metrics from their HR departments, just 24 per cent said they also received analytics that 'connect their people metrics to business metrics' (Harvard Business Review, 2017). The ability to connect the two hinges on workforce plans that link capability to successful business outcomes. This will be a recurring theme throughout this book and detailed specifically in Chapter 15.

LEADING HUMAN RESOURCES FUNCTIONS

Workforce planning is a key component of successful HR. In a *Forbes* article calling workforce planning 'the War Room of HR', human capital management thought leader Sylvia Vorhauser-Smith was clear:

> As the cornerstone of strategic human resources, the workforce plan certifies that human capital and talent management strategies run parallel to the business goals. As workforce plans hinge on effective forecasting, analysis and preparation, the failure to craft and implement an effective one will almost certainly deliver an adverse impact to a company's ability to acquire, inspire and retain talent (Vorhauser-Smith, 2015).

If implemented correctly, workforce planning drives the activity of human resources functions; this will be covered in greater detail within Part Six.

BECOMING RESILIENT AND ANTIFRAGILE

Events such as the global financial crisis and the Covid-19 pandemic have demonstrated the fragility of organizations, economies and nations; with the increased acceptance of a VUCA world, organizations are increasingly sensing their fragility and looking towards building resilience. This approach is based on the misconception that resilience is the opposite of fragile. In fact, resilience is simply a point on the continuum between being fragile and antifragile: 'Resilient resists shocks and stays the same; the antifragile gets better' (Taleb, 2013). The approaches we take throughout this book are geared towards building resilience and antifragility and solidified in Parts Six and Seven of this book.

OVERCOMING PREVAILING TRENDS

Notwithstanding the challenges of a VUCA world, organizations are facing a number of prevailing trends that workforce planning can mitigate and overcome:

> In the past 20 or 30 years, where perhaps the pace of change wasn't quite what it is now, maybe we could kind of get away with [a lack of workforce planning]. But the reality, and the reason why I think strategic workforce planning has become so critical, is because it is very evident that we're in a very fast-changing world. It isn't just about technology. Technology [is] going to impact in the coming years, at a faster rate, the kinds of jobs and [capabilities] that we need… in ways that we have not seen in the past… We've also got… social and demographic change [and] skills shortages… You cannot build a business strategy without an understanding of the nature of your [changing] workforce (Peter Cheese, CEO of the Chartered Institute for Personnel and Development, 2020).

MULTI-GENERATIONAL WORKFORCE

Some organizations are trying to manage a generational gap of over 50 years between their oldest and youngest workers. As life expectancy increases, so will the length of working lives; the 2020s will see the first occasion of five different generations in the workplace at the same time:

- traditionalists/the silent generation (born 1927 to 1945);
- baby boomers (born 1946 to 1964);
- generation X (born 1965 to 1980);
- generation Y/millennials (born 1981 to 1996);
- generation Z (born 1997 to 2012).

Though the differences between the generations are often overstated, workforce plans can draw the greatest value from behavioural tendencies and capability mixes within those generations, alongside management of the health and well-being implications of older workers in particular. This trend will continue as the end of the decade will see the traditionalists leave the workforce as a new generation, likely *Generation Alpha*, begin their working lives. This subject will be covered in Chapter 8 of this book.

DIVERSITY AND INCLUSION

In addition to increasing diversity of age within the workforce, organizations are continuing to experience increasing diversity across the spectrum of workforce characteristics discussed in Chapter 1. Organizations, many prompted by legislated reporting requirements, are making proactive steps towards increasing diversity. This strategic choice of a new, different, *right shape* requires workforce planning to be successful. Moreover, increasing diversity necessitates greater inclusion of difference, which in turn requires planning of the interventions to build an inclusive culture and behaviours.

AUTOMATION

In *The Future of Jobs Report 2018*, the World Economic Forum estimates that 75 million current workers will be displaced from their roles due to the rise in automation, yet 133 million new roles may emerge at the same time. Founder and Executive Chairman, Klaus Schwab, said, 'to prevent an undesirable lose–lose scenario – technological change accompanied by talent shortages, mass unemployment and growing inequality – it is critical that businesses take an active role in supporting their existing workforces through reskilling and upskilling' (WEF, 2018). With a 2019 survey indicating that almost half of organizations rely on 'instinct and gut feel' when assessing current workforce skills and future skills requirements (Capita, 2019), workforce planning has a critical part to play in data-led analysis and execution and will be covered in greater detail in Part Six of this book.

THE SKILLS GAP

PwC's *22nd Annual Global CEO Survey* called out the skills gap as a continuing pain point for organizations. Over half of CEOs said they were 'not able to innovate effectively' and that 'people costs are rising more than expected'. Just 4 per cent of CEOs said there was no impact from the availability of key skills on their own organization's growth and profitability (PwC, 2019). A study by the Society for Human Resource Management showed that 83 per cent of HR professionals had had difficulty recruiting suitable candidates within the previous year and over half said the skills shortage had worsened over the past two years (SHRM, 2019). With organizations desperate to both retain their own talent and bring in new talent, workforce planning provides visibility of the drivers of both and an approach to create the desired workforce. This will be covered in further detail in Part Six of this book.

THE PRODUCTIVITY CHALLENGE

The Bank of England's Chief Economist, Andy Haldane, said 'the slowdown of productivity growth has clearly been a global phenomenon... From 1950 to 1970, median productivity growth averaged 1.9 per cent per year. Since 1980, it has averaged 0.3 per cent per year' (Haldane, 2017). This view is reinforced by the OECD: 'Since 2010, annual growth in labour productivity [in OECD countries] has slowed to 0.9 per cent, about half the rate recorded in the pre-crisis period.' It also notes that organizations in some countries (eg US, UK and Canada) have tended towards increased headcount, rather than capital investment, to increase growth since the financial crisis (OECD, 2019). This means that, rather than investing in technology and development, organizations have simply recruited increasing numbers of workers in order to grow. The need to pivot back to a more sustainable approach to investment is highlighted by survey findings that 77 per cent of CEOs expected to use operational efficiencies to drive revenue growth (PwC, 2019). Understanding the components of workforce productivity and improving upon that is a key component of workforce planning and will be covered in Chapter 8 and Part Six of this book.

CHANGING THE WORLD

In 2015 the United Nations created 17 goals for sustainable development, available from www.un.org/sustainabledevelopment/ (archived at https://perma.cc/FWJ2-AXAW).

Effective workforce planning is at the heart of the eighth goal, to 'promote sustained, inclusive and sustainable economic growth, full productive employment and decent work for all'. Economic growth and work are the catalysts for many of the 16 other development goals. With decent work comes 'gender equality' and 'reduced inequalities for all'; it achieves 'no poverty' and 'zero hunger', which are critical to delivering 'good health and well-being'. Workforce planning supports 'industry, innovation and infrastructure', which leads to 'responsible consumption and production' and 'quality education'. The pathway to changing the world sits within a complex ecosystem, but workforce planning is able to make a significant impact on the UN's goals for 2030.

Limitations of workforce planning

The benefits that workforce planning can bring to organizations and their people can fall short due to the limitations of traditional approaches. The overarching limitation of the traditional approach to workforce planning is

FIGURE 3.1 The Global Goals for Sustainable Development.

THE GLOBAL GOALS
For Sustainable Development

1 NO POVERTY	2 ZERO HUNGER	3 GOOD HEALTH AND WELL-BEING	4 QUALITY EDUCATION	5 GENDER EQUALITY	6 CLEAN WATER AND SANITATION
7 AFFORDABLE AND CLEAN ENERGY	8 DECENT WORK AND ECONOMIC GROWTH	9 INDUSTRY, INNOVATION AND INFRASTRUCTURE	10 REDUCED INEQUALITIES	11 SUSTAINABLE CITIES AND COMMUNITIES	12 RESPONSIBLE CONSUMPTION AND PRODUCTION
13 CLIMATE ACTION	14 LIFE BELOW WATER	15 LIFE ON LAND	16 PEACE, JUSTICE AND STRONG INSTITUTIONS	17 PARTNERSHIPS FOR THE GOALS	THE GLOBAL GOALS For Sustainable Development

SOURCE globalgoals.org (archived at https://perma.cc/42GQ-5TL7). Reproduced with permission from the United Nations, the content of this publication has not been approved by the United Nations and does not reflect the views of the United Nations or its officials or Member States.

that the three horizons have, unfortunately, led to silo approaches to the subject.

Horizon one – resource planning

The main limitation of resource planning is that it tends to focus on efficiency (doing things right) rather than effectiveness (doing the right things). Capacity models, based on the current operation and mapped against demand forecasts, are often not attuned to the organizational strategy, changes in workforce trends or issues impacting the wider enterprise.

CASE STUDY
UK Government

In April 2017 an apprenticeship levy came into effect in the UK, which was payable by all employers with an annual wage bill of over £3 million. The levy was payable to a digital account at a rate of 0.5 per cent of the total wage bill and earned a 10 per cent contribution from the government. This fund can be used by the employer to fund apprenticeship training; any funds that remain unspent after 24 months are immediately reclaimed by the government. It was projected to impact 1.3 per cent of employers and raise £2.675 billion for employee apprenticeships in its first year of operation (Department for Education, 2016).

Since April 2019, when funds have started to expire, tens of millions have been lost each month. Kemi Badenoch MP, Parliamentary Under-Secretary of the Department for Education, admitted that in two months alone (July and August 2019) a total of £96 million expired in employers' digital accounts (Hansard, 2019).

One impacting factor is the requirement for those on the schemes to spend 20 per cent of their time in off-the-job training (NAO, 2019). This requirement has dissuaded many responsible for resource planning from the use of apprenticeships as uneconomical within their planning models at a meso level, despite the impact of lost levy finances at a macro level.

Horizon two – operational workforce planning

In isolation, operational workforce planning tends to be the approach that is most fraught. Planning in this horizon not only tends to be conducted outside HR, but it is also sufficiently removed from the workforce that it fails to connect with the reality of workers and their work.

BUDGETING APPROACH

The method of workforce budgeting itself can result in damaging implications for the organization. The three most common approaches to budgeting are zero-based, incremental and activity-based. Zero-based, or zero-sum budgeting is a bottom-up approach that assumes a department starts with no budget and must therefore justify each individual item of expense. This bakes in the same risk: the prioritization of efficiency over effectiveness. Where a resource planning model has not been used, it is common for zero-based budgets to take place as a one-off exercise in cost reduction. As a result, the skill of zero-based budgeting tends to be lacking (as it is not regularly practised) and the outputs are weak by comparison. Incremental budgeting, the practice of starting with the previous budget and adding or subtracting a percentage, is the quickest and most common form of budget. It does, however, perpetuate the status quo and the existing inefficient or ineffective practices. In addition, it is the least attuned to the market as it ignores specific changes in cost drivers. The opposite of the zero-based approach, activity-based budgeting is a top-down method that starts with the objective to be achieved and then works through the inputs required to achieve that objective. This approach tends to be the most effective; however, it can ignore non-financial and longer-term objectives that we will cover in the next section.

IMPROPER FINANCIAL LENS

As operational workforce planning is often a finance-led exercise, the result is structured based on how the finance department operates rather than the way that work is done. Budgets are apportioned based on profit or cost centres and decisions are often made on that basis, rather than with a view to business objectives. In many organizations, changes to the overhead costs for shared capabilities tend to be offset against cost centres as a percentage of their own budgets. That means that a department that benefits heavily from a shared postal function, and another that does not, would each have to absorb a 1 per cent budgetary reduction as a result of an increase in the cost of the postal function. Equally damaging, wider budgetary pressures tend to be apportioned on a similar basis; a department generating £10 million in revenue and one generating £500,000 in revenue may each have to reduce costs by 5 per cent, placing far more revenue at risk in the first department. The greatest damage results from typical methods of reducing costs. *Salami slicing* or *penny shaving*, the application of small incremental cuts in cost can cause significant damage to longer-term growth through the gradual erosion of quality and service levels.

DAMAGING BEHAVIOURS

As mentioned above, the main limitation of operational workforce planning is that it tends to be focused primarily on financial inputs and outcomes, rather than the totality of what an organization seeks to achieve. It is common for longer-term growth to suffer as a result of declines in quality and service as a result of trying to achieve annual budgets. Conscious of these pressures, budget holders may attempt to gain some budgetary slack either by overstating the budgetary requirements or understating revenue estimates. At the end of the year, it is equally common for departments to authorize the spend of this budgetary slack in an ineffective way in order to avoid losing the funds and this potentially impacts the budget for the following year.

POOR INVESTMENT CHOICES

David Brussin had experience of running three businesses before he co-founded Monetate, the e-commerce software provider, in 2008. As the executive chairman, having taken the company from start-up to passing a milestone in 2019 of $2 billion in influenced revenue, he is clear that annual planning is 'broken and suboptimal' (Brussin, 2015). In his experience, planning on a purely annual basis discourages investment in anything beyond the next financial year. Unless it will deliver a return in the coming year, it is overlooked: 'If you're all about hitting a number, you won't make choices that might distract from that goal, or that won't immediately help you achieve it'.

DEBILITATING RIGIDITY

As one of the key outputs from operational workforce planning is a budget, it is, by definition, a method of restriction: the purpose of a workforce budget is to prevent over-hiring. This can lead to two problems: shifting risk and unresponsiveness. The rigidity of a budget can result in under-hiring in the early part of the year in order to create budgetary slack. Having insufficient workers will directly impact operational delivery and the achievement of both in-year and future-year objectives, shifting the risk to a later point in time. In addition, the limitations of the budget can lead an organization to become unresponsive and ignore shifts in the market that can result in both unintended costs and lost opportunities.

Horizon three – strategic workforce planning

THE FIVE DS

The key limitation of traditional strategic workforce planning rests in the way the craft has been deployed and the standard models used to do so. Practitioners of strategic workforce planning operated as consultants, either independently or as part of larger firms, and were a key contributor to the post-2010 growth. Using approaches similar to that detailed in Chapter 1, many statements of work were undertaken to create a strategic workforce plan for organizations, which typically followed a pathway called the *five Ds*: digest, deliver, depart, disrupt and disregard. At first, an engagement commences between the consultant and their client, the organization, and the consultant *digests* the business strategy, objectives and workforce data. The consultant creates a strategic workforce plan and *delivers* it to the client. On submission of the strategic workforce plan, the engagement ends and the consultant *departs*. The organization is subsequently *disrupted*, typically in one of two forms: internal and external. Internal disruptions are typically where operational changes are dependencies of the strategic workforce plan, but these transformations are late, different or cancelled. These tend to be due to underestimations on budgets, underappreciation of the need for the capability to deliver both transformation and daily business operations, or a culture that fails to realize the benefits of a change. External disruptions are the ones most apparent in the wider market and could be in the form of market shocks (eg recession), legal (eg regulatory changes) or competitive forces (eg downloads and streaming in the music industry). As a result of disruption, the strategic workforce plan is deemed no longer fit for purpose and is *disregarded*. The organization has the choice of re-engaging with the consultant, attempting to come up with a new plan, or simply doing without a plan and chalking it up to experience.

STRATEGIC DISCONNECT

A very common issue, which we will cover in more detail in Chapters 5, 13 and 15, is that the plan often fails to account for a fundamental disconnect between the strategy (either business or workforce strategy) and the *way* that work is done. Strategies are often highly fragmented: not only can a strategy document become dated by new thinking, but there tend to be a multiplicity of strategies, objectives and priorities at the macro and meso levels of the organization. Not only are there conflicting narratives, but the approaches themselves often do not appreciate the complexity of business operations. This results in strategic workforce plans that, even without disruption, can never be realized.

TECHNOLOGICAL OVERRELIANCE

In a clear step away from the *five Ds* approach, consultancies are leveraging varying degrees of workforce analytics as a vehicle for strategic workforce planning. Either as part of an enterprise resource planning (ERP) platform, or as a standalone tool, these technology solutions have become exceedingly popular with the allure of democratizing workforce planning. Whilst a number of analytics tools masquerading as strategic workforce planning solutions are little more than multi-year incremental budgets, the better tools can provide game-changing insights. The limitation, as Ross Sparkman, then Head of Strategic Workforce Planning at Facebook, writes, 'While workforce analytics is an important aspect of [strategic workforce planning]... there is much more to it than just the analytics' (Sparkman, 2018). Simply put, workforce planning requires more than being competent in the use of an analytics tool.

Summary

The benefits that workforce planning can bring to organizations and their people are clear; indeed 'workforce planning is taking on new urgency as the complexion of the workforce changes and different skill sets emerge, evolve and expire' (Johnson, 2019). The tragedy is that these benefits can be eroded and the impact can fall short due to the limitations of traditional approaches. Silos have grown within each of the three horizons: on the one hand, resource planners can be planning against an existing way of working and be unaware of a strategic cliff-edge; on the other hand, strategic workforce planners can be ignorant of the current operational challenges that will prevent longer-term success.

The agile approach we will cover in the next chapter moves away from this silo thinking and, as McKinsey & Company did with growth, demonstrates how to plan and execute across all three horizons at once (Baghai *et al*, 1999).

References

Baghai, M, Coley, S and White, D (1999) *The Alchemy of Growth*, Perseus Publishing, New York

Brooks, S (2012) The emerging discipline of strategic workforce planning [Blog] *HR Zone*, 9 February, www.hrzone.com/talent/development/blog-the-emerging-discipline-of-strategic-workforce-planning (archived at https://perma.cc/VLW6-9C9G)

Brussin D (2015) Annual planning is killing your growth – try this plan instead [Blog] *First Round Review*, 29 January, www.firstround.com/review/Annual-Planning-is-Killing-Your-Growth-Try-This-Instead/ (archived at https://perma.cc/D9FE-62TN)

Capita (2019) How data and insight can deliver the skills needed in a hybrid workforce, 21 June, https://content.capitapeoplesolutions.co.uk/whitepapers/insight-edge-talent-acquisition (archived at https://perma.cc/ZP45-ES4B)

Cheese, P (2020) In-person interview, 8 January

Department for Education (2016) Information on apprenticeship levy, August, https://assets.publishing.service.gov.uk/government/uploads/system/uploads/attachment_data/file/545145/Apprenticeships_-expected_levy_and_total_spend_-_Aug_2016.pdf (archived at https://perma.cc/AZW6-WARJ)

Department of the Navy (1958) *Program Evaluation Research Task: Summary report phase 1 (July)*, apps.dtic.mil/dtic/tr/fulltext/u2/735902.pdf

Fayol, H (2013) *General and Industrial Management*, Martino Fine Books, Eastford

Finkel, D (2015) The 3 types of business controls [Blog], *Inc.com*, www.inc.com/david-finkel/the-3-types-of-business-controls.html (archived at https://perma.cc/H2NQ-5UEL)

Gawande, A (2010) *The Checklist Manifesto*, Profile Books, London

Gluck, F W, Kaufman, S P and Walleck, A S (1980) Strategic management for competitive advantage, *Harvard Business Review* (July), hbr.org/1980/07/strategic-management-for-competitive-advantage (archived at https://perma.cc/3ECA-CEE7)

Haldane, A (2017) *Productivity Puzzles* [speech], 20 March, www.bankofengland.co.uk/-/media/boe/files/speech/2017/productivity-puzzles.pdf (archived at https://perma.cc/N69Y-PKKP)

Hansard (2019) Apprentices: Taxation: Written question – 284461, 5 September, www.parliament.uk/business/publications/written-questions-answers-statements/written-question/Commons/2019-09-02/284461/ (archived at https://perma.cc/4NAQ-Z23T)

Harvard Business Review (2017) *How CEOs and CHROs can Connect People to Business Strategy*, Harvard Business School Publishing, https://hbr.org/resources/

pdfs/comm/visier/HowCEOsandCHROsCanConnect.pdf (archived at https://perma.cc/HF5H-UFRK)

Johnson, L (2019) Gartner top 3 priorities for HR leaders in 2019, *HR & Digital Trends*, 15 January, www.hrdigitaltrends.com/story/14124/gartner-top-3-priorities-hr-leaders-2019 (archived at https://perma.cc/4FHC-9U7D)

Kahneman, D (2011) *Thinking, Fast and Slow*, Allen Lane, London

Machiavelli, N (1532) *The Prince*, 1995 reprint, Penguin, London

MacLean, P D (1990) *The Triune Brain in Evolution: Role in paleocerebral functions*, Plenum, New York

Mintzberg, H (1994) *The Rise and Fall of Strategic Planning*, The Free Press, New York

NAO (National Audit Office) (2019) The Apprenticeships Programme, 28 February, www.nao.org.uk/wp-content/uploads/2019/03/The-apprenticeships-programme.pdf (archived at https://perma.cc/N8PD-7JVH)

OECD (Organisation for Economic Co-operation and Development) (2019) Compendium of productivity indicators, https://www.oecd-ilibrary.org/industry-and-services/oecd-compendium-of-productivity-indicators-2019_b2774f97-en (archived at https://perma.cc/629X-HZ33)

Pronovost, P, Berenholtz, S, Dorman, T, Lipsett, P A, Simmonds, T and Haraden, C (2003) Improving communication in the ICU using daily goals, *Journal of Critical Care*, **18** (2), pp 71–75, www.sciencedirect.com/science/article/abs/pii/S088394410370001X (archived at https://perma.cc/MPX9-ZMWW)

PwC (2019) *22nd Annual Global CEO Survey*, www.pwc.com/gx/en/ceo-survey/2019/report/pwc-22nd-annual-global-ceo-survey.pdf (archived at https://perma.cc/YP2B-CEUA)

SHRM (Society for Human Resource Management) (2019) *The Global Skills Shortage: Bridging the talent gap with education, training and sourcing*, www.shrm.org/hr-today/trends-and-forecasting/research-and-surveys/Documents/SHRM%20Skills%20Gap%202019.pdf (archived at https://perma.cc/8SC4-YAZE)

Sparkman, R (2018) *Strategic Workforce Planning: Developing optimized talent strategies for future growth*, Kogan Page, London

Stanford, N (2013) in D L Ward and R Tripp (eds) *Positioned: Strategic workforce planning the gets the right person in the right job*, AMACOM, New York

Sullivan, J (2002a) Before you try it, understand why workforce planning fails [Blog] 12 August, *ERE*, www.ere.net/before-you-try-it-understand-why-workforce-planning-fails (archived at https://perma.cc/R2PQ-3UFG)

Sullivan, J (2002b) Why workforce planning fails, part 2 [Blog] 19 August, ERE, www.ere.net/why-workforce-planning-fails-part-2 (archived at https://perma.cc/32YW-8EFV)

Taleb, N N (2013) *Antifragile*, Penguin, London

Tandon, N (2018) Total cost of workforce: The new magic word for CFOs, *CFO Connect*, February, cfo-connect.com/2018/april2018/insight2.php (archived at https://perma.cc/45SP-W456)

United Nations (2019) *The Sustainable Development Goals Report*, unstats.un.org/sdgs/report/2019/The-Sustainable-Development-Goals-Report-2019.pdf (archived at https://perma.cc/3BGU-LSGC)

Vorhauser-Smith, S (2015) Workforce planning: The war room of HR, *Forbes*, 25 May, www.forbes.com/sites/sylviavorhausersmith/2015/05/25/workforce-planning-the-war-room-of-hr (archived at https://perma.cc/HKN8-GV3R)

Ward, D L (2013) How long has this been going on? in D L Ward, D L and R Tripp (eds) *Positioned: Strategic workforce planning the gets the right person in the right job*, AMACOM, New York

WEF (World Economic Forum) (2018) *The Future of Jobs Report 2018*, http://www3.weforum.org/docs/WEF_Future_of_Jobs_2018 (archived at https://perma.cc/QYE4-RFHZ)

04

The agile approach

Introduction

In my time as an infantryman in the Iraq War, it was a life of daily patrols and a constant threat of roadside bombs, suicide vests, firefights and rocket and mortar attacks. It was in Al Basrah Province from 2006 to 2007, at the height of the conflict for British forces in southern Iraq fighting against the *Jaysh al Mahdi* (the Mahdi Army), that I found myself as a young infantry platoon commander.

In early 2007 I led a small team in two unarmoured Land Rovers to an area called R'as al Bishah, on the farthest tip of the Al Faw peninsula, to intercept a small boat expected to be smuggling 107 mm rockets from Iran across the Shatt al Arab river. Driving down a single track in the twilight, with open plains of thick mud to our right, we were caught in an ambush. Outnumbered eight to one, a heavy rain of bullets came from our front and left, pinning us down. If we had planned to attack, we would aim to outnumber the enemy three to one; if we expected to survive a direct confrontation, we would want to be at least evenly matched. Fourteen kilometres from our own patrol base and over 100 kilometres from our nearest support, the odds were not in our favour. Long, hard training had indoctrinated the concept of the OODA loop: *observe, orientate, decide* and *act* (Boyd, 1976). This agility, being able to move to action faster than the enemy, is critical to being able to survive and win. With just 100 metres to the enemy's front line, we needed time and space to withdraw; unable to move left and restricted to my right, I took half my team and attacked forward.

I have nothing but pride and admiration for my team's spirit and action that night as we faced overwhelming odds. Our counterattack caught the enemy by surprise and gave us the space to turn our vehicles around; Lance

Corporal Sam Blowman's direct hit on an enemy truck with a 40 mm grenade prevented their pursuit and we withdrew without casualties.

Agility, being able to adapt and act at speed, kept us alive that day and is the basis of the principles I have used in business ever since. 'Learning agility is a mindset and corresponding collection of practices that allow leaders to continually develop, grow, and utilize new strategies that will equip them for the increasingly complex problems they face in their organizations' (Burke *et al*, 2016). This chapter will focus on agile thinking and how that translates into the agile workforce planning methodology.

Agile origins

The waterfall approach to project management

Dr Winston Royce, a computer scientist and director at aerospace company Lockheed, gave a speech at a convention of the Institute of Electrical and Electronics Engineers (IEEE) in 1970, where he described the implementation steps to develop a large computer program for a customer.

FIGURE 4.1   The waterfall chart

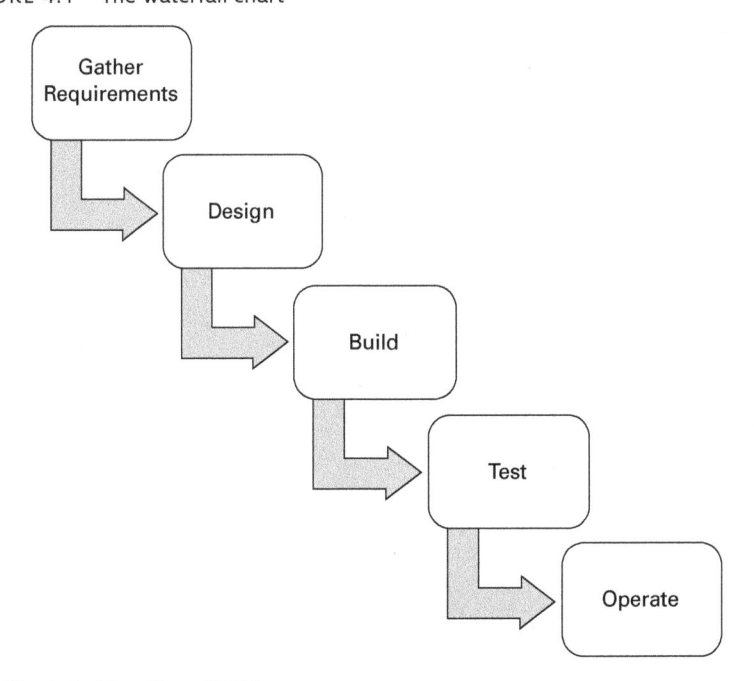

Gather Requirements → Design → Build → Test → Operate

SOURCE Adapted from Royce (1970)

This linear process, later dubbed a *waterfall process*, was to become the standard for software development for decades. The approach would attract criticism for being inflexible; customers often did not know their requirements and, upon seeing the finished product, would add new requirements that resulted in increased costs and delays.

The Agile Manifesto

In 2001, 17 independent thinkers on software development agreed on the *Manifesto for Agile Software Development*, commonly known as the *Agile Manifesto*.

MANIFESTO FOR AGILE SOFTWARE DEVELOPMENT

'We are uncovering better ways of developing software by doing it and helping others do it.

Through this work we have come to value:

Individuals and interactions over processes and tools.
Working software over comprehensive documentation.
Customer collaboration over contract negotiation.
Responding to change over following a plan.

That is, while there is value in the items on the right, we value the items on the left more.

Kent Beck
Mike Beedle
Arie van Bennekum
Alistair Cockburn
Ward Cunningham
Martin Fowler
James Grenning
Jim Highsmith
Andrew Hunt
Ron Jeffries
Jon Kern
Brian Marick
Robert C Martin
Steve Mellor

> Ken Schwaber
> Jeff Sutherland
> Dave Thomas
>
> © 2001, the authors. This this declaration may be freely copied in any form, but only in its entirety through this notice' (Agile Alliance, 2001).

Applying this to workforce planning leads to the following considerations:

- It is more important to have workforce planners who understand the methodology, principles and techniques and can interact with each other and their stakeholders, than it is to have particular processes or workforce planning software.
- It is more important to deliver the seven rights of workforce planning than it is to create a glossy workforce plan.
- It is more important to be collaborating directly with stakeholders on an enduring basis, and translating business needs into the required workforce, than it is to have business stakeholders define the exact future state of the workforce.
- It is more important to create a plan that is flexible, iterating and responding to change, than it is to stay wedded to the execution of a plan based on assumptions that have subsequently changed.

AGILE SOFTWARE DEVELOPMENT PRINCIPLES

This manifesto was based upon 12 principles:

1. Customer satisfaction by early and continuous delivery of valuable software.
2. Welcome changing requirements, even in late development.
3. Deliver working software frequently (weeks rather than months).
4. Close, daily cooperation between business people and developers.
5. Projects are built around motivated individuals, who should be trusted.
6. Face-to-face conversation is the best form of communication (co-location).
7. Working software is the primary measure of progress.
8. Sustainable development, able to maintain a constant pace.

9 Continuous attention to technical excellence and good design.
10 Simplicity – the art of maximizing the amount of work not done – is essential.
11 Best architectures, requirements, and designs emerge from self-organizing teams.
12 Regularly, the team reflects on how to become more effective, and adjusts accordingly (Agile Alliance, 2001).

Though this may sound contradictory to the notions of planning and methodology, Jim Highsmith, co-author of the manifesto, noted:

> The Agile movement is not anti-methodology, in fact, many of us want to restore credibility to the word methodology. We want to restore a balance. We embrace modeling, but not in order to file some diagram in a dusty corporate repository. We embrace documentation, but not hundreds of pages of never-maintained and rarely used tomes. We plan, but recognize the limits of planning in a turbulent environment (Agile Alliance, 2001).

Contemporary agile thinking

Since the publication of the manifesto, the concept of agile quickly made its way into the zeitgeist. This new way of thinking permeated beyond software and quickly became a powerful movement, which generated further developments in the agile approach.

Cynefin

A Welsh word meaning habitat, cynefin (pronounced ku-NEV-in) is a framework that recognizes the multiple factors within our environment. Created by management consultant Dave Snowden (1999), then at IBM, he spoke of five domains of decision making:

COMPLEX

To restate the definition from Chapter 1, issues in the complex domain have a multiplicity of factors and components, which makes it difficult to identify cause and effect. This intractability is what then US Secretary of Defense, Donald Rumsfeld, famously called 'unknown unknowns' (Rumsfeld, 2002). When there is a failure to acknowledge complexity, those engaged in planning can fall victim to optimism bias: underestimating the cost and overestimating the benefit of an initiative. This bias, also known as the *planning fallacy*, exists because the complexity will typically prevent the use of existing benchmarks when creating plans and forecasts (Kahneman and Tversky, 1982).

This state of 'constant flux… is the domain to which much of contemporary business has shifted' (Snowden and Boone, 2007). The cynefin model points to the ability to identify, in retrospect, cause and effect within a complex environment; the solution to complexity, therefore, is one of experimentation, 'probe first, then sense, and then respond' (Snowden and Boone, 2007). This approach we will revisit in Chapter 16.

COMPLICATED

Complication is the realm of 'known unknowns' (Rumsfeld, 2002); cause and effect can be established only with analysis and expertise. It is often analysis, increasingly enabled by technology, that has shifted environments once considered to be complex into a position of complication. The approach to the complicated is 'sense–analyse–respond'; establish the facts, conduct analyses and respond appropriately with 'good practice' (Snowden and Boone, 2007). This is the starting point for the analysis of the workforce we will discuss in Chapters 6 and 16; the response to this analysis may include moving into the complex domain.

SIMPLE

The simple domain represents 'known knowns… things we know we know' (Rumsfeld, 2002); the processes or 'best practice' (Snowden and Boone, 2007). The approach of 'sense–categorize–respond' (Snowden and Boone, 2007) captures most business and HR processes: best practice dictates an employee who submits a timely request for a holiday will have that request granted. Equally, such simplicity can evolve. Since the mid-1950s, when the concept of *management by objectives* (MBO) was created by leading management theorist Peter Drucker (2007), HR has seen a gradual evolution towards the annual performance review. Organizations holding tight to this best practice can become complacent in the process, which can result in a shift from simple to chaotic:

> 12% of the Fortune 1000… have abandoned the traditional performance review, recognizing that the process looks backward rather than forward and is primarily concerned with grading people rather than helping them achieve their best (Elliot and Corey, 2018).

CHAOTIC

The domains of simple, complicated and complex all exist within the realms of the Cartesian theory espoused by René Descartes. This theory held that applying rational reasoning to situations will allow us to understand the link between cause and effect (Descartes, 1641). Chaos breaks from such thinking. In a chaotic domain, not only are the relationships between cause and effect completely unclear, but 'searching for right answers would be pointless'; the realm is 'unknowable' (Snowden and Boone, 2007). The basis of this thinking is in deterministic nonperiodic flow, or chaos theory, 'a simple system… is solved numerically… [in a system of chaos all solutions are] unstable, and almost all of them are nonperiodic' (Lorenz, 1963).

In such a circumstance, the approach is, 'act to establish order, then *sense* where stability is present and from where it is absent, and then *respond* by working to transform the situation from chaos to complexity, where the identification of emerging patterns can both help prevent future crises and discern new opportunities' (Snowden and Boone, 2007).

This approach is no better demonstrated than by the story of Cyril Richard 'Rick' Rescorla. He was a former British Army paratrooper, who served in the Cyprus emergency from 1957 to 1960 and later served as a platoon leader with the 7th Cavalry Regiment in the Vietnam war; his heroism was detailed in the book, *We Were Soldiers Once… And Young* (Moore and Galloway, 1992). He was the vice president of security for Morgan-Stanley on 11 September 2001, a day that was the very definition of chaos. Ignoring the Port Authority announcement for people to remain at their desks, Rescorla began a systematic evacuation of the South Tower and WTC 5. Grabbing his bullhorn, he directed the staff down the long staircase; he continued to encourage them when the building shook as the second plane hit the South Tower and sang loudly to keep them calm. He is credited with saving the lives of 2,700 employees and was last seen on the 10th floor of the South Tower heading upwards, shortly before it collapsed (Stewart, 2002). His name is located on panel S46 of the south pool at the National September 11 Memorial.

DISORDER

Disorder is the context that applies when it is unclear which of the other four domains is dominant. In between the ordered domains of simplicity and complication, and unordered domains of complexity and chaos, disorder is marked by the jostling of multiple perspectives. In this state, all a decision maker can do is break down the disorder into its constituent parts and attempt to assign those to one of the other four domains and intervene accordingly. It is within this domain that Taleb's assessment of forecasters is most appropriate: 'You are not trying to gauge their knowledge but rather their evaluation of their own knowledge' (Taleb, 2007).

Three laws of agile

In his book *The Age of Agile* (2018), management thinker Stephen Denning referenced three laws of agile, which I will overlay with the application within workforce planning:

THE LAW OF THE SMALL TEAM

Teams are not a new concept; Aristotle believed that it was natural to associate and organize into groups rather than to exist solely as individuals (Aristotle, 1981). Denning cites management thinkers throughout the 20th century who have continued to point to the benefits of working in teams. Indeed, leadership theorist John Adair was clear that teams and organizations are created to 'achieve a task which an individual or small group cannot do on its own' (Adair, 2010). However, over time, the tendency has evolved towards bureaucratic teams that centre on top-down management of individual responsibilities, rather than interacting as a team, and the team is simply a method of organizing accountabilities.

Conversely, the agile law of the small team returns to the concepts of earlier thinkers: autonomous cross-functional groups that form and interact for the purpose of achieving a goal. In Chapters 7 and 14, we will discuss the use of agile teams in creating workforce plans, rather than workforce planning practitioners operating in a silo.

THE LAW OF THE CUSTOMER

The customer-centric priority draws heavily from the first of the agile principles, 'customer satisfaction by early and continuous delivery of valuable software' (Agile Alliance, 2001). The competitive marketplace has seen organizations shift from selling *what they had* to selling *what the customer wants*. The complexity of modern organizations means that, for many, 'they do what they can for the customer – but only within the limits of their own internal systems and processes' (Denning, 2018).

From a workforce planning perspective, this law translates into two things: first, that it starts with the business problem and not the potential solution. It is common for HR departments to be aware of initiatives in other organizations, with illusory correlation to workforce challenges, and seek to implement them within their own organization without any real understanding of the cost or benefit. This activity, which I refer to as *stealing other people's artificial grass*, is exemplified by businesses that deck out their offices with bean bags because they saw high-growth technology companies do the same. This perhaps accounts for the valuation of the global bean bag market at $110 million (Grand View Research, 2019). Workforce planning translates the business problem into workforce requirements before identifying appropriate solutions that are tailored specifically to the organization.

Secondly, the law of the customer changes the dynamic to identifying the *true* customer. Projects often become unstuck because customer interaction starts and ends with someone often called a *product owner* or *relationship manager*. 'Who were these product owners and how did they figure out what the customer wanted or needed?' (Denning, 2018). Workforce planning has often found customer interaction channelled through HR's ersatz relationship partner, the Business Partner; this results in business challenges partly translated into HR speak. The agile approach forces workforce planning to engage directly with the customers who are experiencing the challenge, the senior stakeholders within the organization, to accurately define problem statements and agree on approaches. We will focus on this heavily within Chapter 7 and return to it throughout this book.

THE LAW OF THE NETWORK

'Agile practitioners view the organization as a fluid and transparent network of players that are collaborating toward a common goal of delighting customers' (Denning, 2018). This view may find an obvious tension in the more common bureaucratic structures within many large organizations. For workforce planning, the law is tied closely with the law of the customer; practitioners seek those stakeholders who can add value in collaborating towards a successful workforce initiative. Too often, those trying to solve problems work in isolation rather than seeking solutions from the wider network; in Chapter 12, for example, we will discuss this in detail in relation to action planning.

Modern agile

Founder and CEO of Industry Logic, Joshua Kerievsky, took the manifesto and translated it into a more universal approach he dubbed 'modern agile'. It is defined by four guiding principles, as seen in Figure 4.2.

FIGURE 4.2 Principles of modern agile

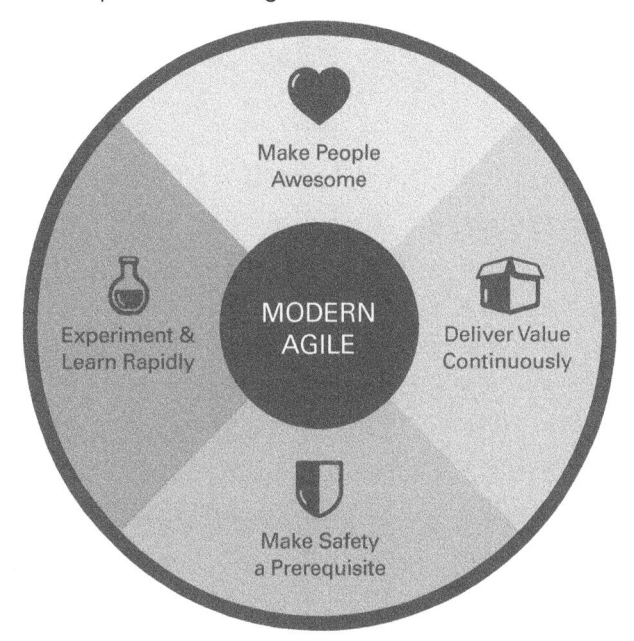

Principles diagram: Modern Agile at centre, surrounded by four quadrants — Make People Awesome (top), Deliver Value Continuously (right), Make Safety a Prerequisite (bottom), Experiment & Learn Rapidly (left).

SOURCE modernagile.com (archived at https://perma.cc/HX3N-N999), reproduced under Creative Commons licence

MAKE PEOPLE AWESOME

'In modern agile we ask how we can make people in our ecosystem awesome?' (modernagile.org (archived at https://perma.cc/2VEL-S8PH)). This principle ties to my own vision of engaged people connected with meaningful work and is the basis of my approach to workforce planning. Not only is this a key aim of workforce planning, it is the aspiration for all those involved in workforce planning.

MAKE SAFETY A PREREQUISITE

Some professions, like those involving heavy machinery, are rightly regarded as hazardous and have stringent safety procedures. However, all work contains elements of hazard that modern agile seeks to protect from, including time, reputation, information and money. Safety is a prerequisite of sustainability, which is a key aspect when we consider the concept of *right time*. Not only does workforce planning actively seek safety for the workforce, it also does so in relation to the interactions of workforce planning itself. Insights developed through workforce planning can challenge the preconceived notions of senior business leaders and the agile approach aims to tell these stories in a way that protects the reputations of all parties. Moreover, the action planning we will discuss in Part Six will rely upon those involved having the safe space to innovate in solving workforce challenges.

EXPERIMENT AND LEARN RAPIDLY

Inextricably linked to safety is the concept of being safe to fail:

> The best… practitioners I've met are highly intelligent, naturally curious and have an insatiable appetite to learn and broaden their horizons. They are not afraid to fail (occasionally!) and understand that not every research project will produce insights and not every insight will be actioned. They learn from their failures, refine their approach where necessary, remain resilient and continue to be focused on delivering actionable insights on issues that are the most important to the business (Green, 2017).

Workforce planning rarely has the luxury of operating in the simple domain of the cynefin framework, therefore all approaches require an element of experimentation. This approach necessitates what Stanford University psychologist Carol Dweck called a 'growth mindset'; this shifts the perspective from believing everything is *known* to accepting the reality of the *unknown* and continuing to develop knowledge. The elements of the workforce planning methodology covered in Part Seven deal specifically with experimentation, assessment and response.

DELIVER VALUE CONTINUOUSLY

'In modern agile we ask ourselves, *how could valuable work be delivered faster?*' (modernagile.org (archived at https://perma.cc/HX3N-N999)). We experience the impact of continuous delivery in the continuous incremental changes to the software on our phones and computers directly. This approach places vendors on the leading edge as it enables them to experiment and learn directly from users. We take a similar approach in workforce planning: we share insight early rather than keeping it hidden until there is a perfect solution and a grand reveal; we pilot and utilize early adoption to deploy faster intervention; we target areas of higher value to generate a substantial return on investment with the primary stages of an initiative.

The principles of agile workforce planning

Drawing from contemporary thinking on agile, my approach to agile workforce planning is based on seven principles:

Start with why

One of the first questions military planners ask is: why? Mission statements are always appended with the why, the *unifying purpose*, with the words *in order to* (eg seize the hill in order to prevent enemy overwatch of our movements). The phrase *start with why* was coined by organizational consultant Simon Sinek and popularized by his book of the same title (Sinek, 2011). In it, he highlights the ability to define *why* as the key differentiator of great leaders and companies. We will talk about establishing the *why* in the next chapter and it will remain a golden thread throughout the book.

Be flexible

One of the biggest limitations cited in Chapter 2 was the lack of flexibility in the approach to planning. The agile approach to workforce planning has flexibility at the core, which allows it to be utilized within all organizations and applied across all horizons. Traditional approaches to workforce planning are based on the waterfall approach; a critical pathway of gathering specific datasets into tables and conducting defined analyses to create generic outputs. These fixed processes are often not aligned to the *why* of the organization, as a quotation from global HR industry expert, Josh Bersin, accurately captures:

> After a recent speech, an attendee came up to me and said, I can predict attrition for my firm to 92 per cent accuracy. I said, Wow! That's great. Is attrition a problem for your company? And she said, No, not really' (Guenole *et al*, 2017)

Generic processes may provide insight, but they are unlikely to help an organization to achieve its goals. The agile approach is grounded in principles and methods that allow it to be executed across all organizations, rather than being a slave to processes that will at best provide limited value and, at worst, frustrate stakeholders and damage your reputation. The agile approach is also designed to be applicable across all three horizons of workforce planning, rather than being fixed to one specific time period. Continuous delivery principles entail bringing value within the current financial year in addition to providing value in future years.

A team of teams

'Perhaps the most critical success factor in building a high-powered SWP function is creating a team with the right mix of skills, competencies and experience required to support that function's vision' (Sparkman, 2018). Much has been made over the years around functional design; I prefer to think of it as what General Stanley McChrystal called a 'team of teams' (McChrystal *et al*, 2015). Throughout this book we will see that success in workforce planning needs to be more than a *them* (stakeholders) and *us* (workforce planning) ideology. Chapter 12 specifically deals with how we approach this in workforce planning and in Part Seven we will see the possibilities that can be achieved through approaching this as a capability rather than as a function.

Iterative planning

Otto von Bismarck's Chief of the General Staff, Field Marshall Helmuth von Moltke, said 'no plan of operations extends with certainty beyond the first encounter with the enemy's main strength' (Moltke, 1993); this is often paraphrased as 'no plan survives contact with the enemy'. This was not a cry against planning, but an acceptance of the need to have flexibility as the situation changes. The agile approach executes plans based on the most likely scenario and creates contingency for the best and worst cases; as circumstances change and the domains of complication, complexity and chaos become clearer, plans are revised in sufficient time to enable action. This approach to iteration is covered in Chapter 16.

Incremental problem solving

Many organizations thinking about workforce planning for the first time become quickly unstuck; resolving the complexities of their workforce appears to be an intractable problem as they try to *boil the ocean*. Agile workforce planning examines problems incrementally, first dealing with those that will have the greatest return or are easiest to understand and resolve. This approach can often start to illuminate drivers of other business challenges, enabling an increased tempo of resolution. This approach is detailed specifically in Chapter 16.

Always be learning

This is unashamedly adapted from Alec Baldwin's line 'Always be selling' in *Glengarry Glen Ross* about about the central tenet of successful sales professionals. Equally, always be learning is the same for workforce planning.

Those engaged in workforce planning must continue to learn about their workforce, their organization, their customers, their market, their industry and the wider landscape intertwined within it. Just as most articles about workforce planning are rarely titled as such, neither are business problems immediately attached to workforce planning. It is only through a mantra of *always be learning* that workforce planning professionals can expect to make an enduring impact. As Leo Tolstoy wrote, 'We can know only that we know nothing, And that is the highest degree of human wisdom' (1869).

It's about the workforce

The aim of workforce planning is not to create a workforce plan; the aim of workforce planning is to create the right workforce to deliver the desired business outcomes. Traditional approaches have failed because the requirement was a plan that could be shared with stakeholders. As we will cover in Chapter 15, the concept of a standalone workforce plan is something of a misnomer. The workforce plan is a concept that comprises many different plans and sub-plans, from specific projects to enduring portfolios of activity, all focused on creating the workforce that is needed now and in the future.

> Organization is, to a large extent, a means of overcoming the limitations mortality sets to what any one man can contribute. An organization that is not capable of perpetuating itself has failed. An organization therefore has to provide today the men who can run it tomorrow. It has to renew its human capital. It should steadily upgrade its human resources (Drucker, 1985).

Six-stage agile workforce planning framework

My application of agile principles to the contemporary workforce planning approaches led to the development of the agile workforce planning methodology and creation of the agile workforce planning framework, which I first shared in early 2017, and is shown in Figure 4.3.

The framework is the basis of the methodology and comprises six stages:

Baseline

Covered in Part Two, the baseline is where we establish the nature of the organization: what does it look like, what is it trying to achieve and why?

FIGURE 4.3   Agile workforce planning framework

This critical first stage provides the arc for all subsequent activity conducting workforce planning for the organization.

Supply

Covered in Part Three, supply is where we establish the forecast for the workforce. We examine historical workforce trends, which informs our subsequent modelling and forecasting of the future workforce.

Demand

Part Four considers the other side of the coin from supply: demand. At this stage, we delve into the concept of *work* and how that translates into a demand for a workforce. We establish how demand is structured and what drives demand at all levels of the organization. We use that understanding to create a forecast for the future.

Gap analysis

In Part Five we discuss how we take the forecasts of supply and demand and establish the gap between the two.

Action plan

In Part Six we examine the action plan, the best way to close the gap between supply and demand. It is here that we cover the seven Bs of action planning, leading us into approaches of demand optimization and talent management.

Deliver

The final stage of the methodology, covered in Part Seven, is to deliver. This stage focuses on how to execute a successful workforce plan that delivers the workforce and achieves organizational objectives.

As a cycle, this final stage launches us back into a baseline where we continue to iterate the plan.

Summary

The agile workforce planning approach has been developed over many years based on my experience of planning and executing operations using agile approaches. This has been overlaid with traditional and contemporary approaches to agile and workforce planning, which results in an approach that works in organizations. Though the framework has remained unchanged since it was released in 2017, agile thinking and a growth mindset have enabled the methodology to evolve with changes in the wider business landscape and advanced in technology.

In the three years since its inception, the methodology has grown in popularity. Already, as a result of this methodology, hundreds of thousands of workers around the globe are moving closer to engagement and meaningful work. The approach now forms the basis for workforce planning approaches recommended and taught by the Chartered Institute of Personnel and Development (CIPD).

Remain mindful of these agile approaches as you continue through each of the parts of this book: I wish you every success on your journey.

When you practise workforce planning, ask yourself:

- Am I starting with why?
- Am I being flexible in my approach?

- Am I working with the people who are best placed to understand or solve this challenge?
- Am I planning in a way that creates value in the best speed and iterating as I go, or am I trying to capture every possibility before I move onto the next stage?
- Am I solving problems incrementally or am I trying to accomplish everything in one go?
- Am I open to new ways of thinking and am I continuing to learn about the workforce, the organization, the industry, the craft of workforce planning and myself?
- Am I focused on creating the plan or creating the right workforce?

References

Adair, J (2010) *Strategic Leadership*, Kogan Page, London

Agile Alliance (2001) Manifesto for Agile Software Development, agilemanifesto.org (archived at https://perma.cc/9DPK-GPNK)

Aristotle (1981) *The Politics*, Oxford University Press, Oxford

Boyd, J R (1976) Destruction and creation, 3 September, US Army Command and General Staff College, www.goalsys.com/books/documents/DESTRUCTION_AND_CREATION.pdf (archived at https://perma.cc/K4HX-XDN9)

Burke, W, Roloff, K and Mitchinson, A (2016) *Learning Agility: A new model and measure*, Columbia University, New York

Denning, S (2018) *The Age of Agile*, AMACOM, New York

Descartes, R (1641) *Discourse on Method and Meditations on First Philosophy*, 1998 reprint, Hackett Publishing Company, Cambridge

Drucker, P F (1985) *The Effective Executive*, HarperCollins, New York

Drucker, P F (2007) *The Practice of Management*, Butterworth-Heinemann, London

Dweck, C (2017) *Mindset – Updated edition: Changing the way you think to fulfil your potential*, Random House, New York

Elliot, G and Corey, D (2018) *Build It: The rebel playbook for world-class employee engagement*, Wiley, Chichester

Glengarry Glen Ross (1992) [Film] Zupnik Enterprises, USA

Grand View Research (2019) Bean Bag Chairs Market Size, Share & Trends Analysis Report By Product (Indoor, Outdoor), By Distribution Channel (Offline, Online), By Region, And Segment Forecasts, 2019 – 2025, www.grandviewresearch.com/

industry-analysis/bean-bag-chairs-market (archived at https://perma.cc/8Q95-A6WD)

Green, D (2017) What constitutes best practice in people analytics? [Blog] *LinkedIn*, 16 January, www.linkedin.com/pulse/what-constitutes-best-practice-people-analytics-david-green/ (archived at https://perma.cc/VR5F-GXH4)

Guenole, N, Ferrar, J and Feinzig, S (2017) *The Power of People*, Pearson, London

Kahneman, D and Tversky, A (1982) Intuitive prediction: Biases and corrective procedures, in A Tversky (ed) *Judgment Under Uncertainty: Heuristics and biases*, Cambridge University Press, New York

Lorenz, E N (1963) Deterministic nonperiodic flow, *Journal of the Atmospheric Sciences*, 20 (2), pp 130–44, eaps4.mit.edu/research/Lorenz/Deterministic_63.pdf (archived at https://perma.cc/MZ4D-KFDU)

McChrystal, S et al (2015) *Team of Teams: New rules of engagement in a complex world*, Penguin, New York

Moltke, H v (1993) in D J Hughes (ed) *Moltke on the Art of War: Selected writings*, Presidio Press, New York.

Moore, H G and Galloway, J L (1992) *We Were Soldiers Once... And Young*, Random House, New York

Royce, W W (1970) Managing the development of large software systems, Proceedings IEEE WESCON (August), pp 1–9, http://www-scf.usc.edu/~csci201/lectures/Lecture11/royce1970.pdf (archived at https://perma.cc/76LY-V93R)

Rumsfeld, D H (2002) Department of Defense news briefing (12 February) archive.defense.gov/Transcripts/Transcript.aspx?TranscriptID=2636 (archived at https://perma.cc/8T6J-KX5V)

Sinek, S (2011) *Start With Why: How great leaders inspire everyone to take action*, Penguin, London

Snowden, D, ed (1999) *Liberating Knowledge*, CBI Business Guide (October) Caspian Publishing, London

Snowden, D J and Boone, M E (2007) A leader's framework for decision making, *Harvard Business Review*, November, hbr.org/2007/11/a-leaders-framework-for-decision-making (archived at https://perma.cc/LRY8-C28F)

Sparkman, R (2018) *Strategic Workforce Planning: Developing optimized talent strategies for future growth*, Kogan Page, London

Stewart, J B (2002) The real heroes are dead, *The New Yorker*, 3 March, www.newyorker.com/magazine/2002/02/11/the-real-heroes-are-dead (archived at https://perma.cc/6WJD-85HE)

Taleb, N N (2007) *The Black Swan*, Penguin, London

Tolstoy, L (1869) *War and Peace*, Penguin, London

PART TWO

Baseline

*What does the organization look like,
what is it trying to achieve and why?*

05

Analysing the strategic context

Introduction

In the summer of 2013, my wife and I took a holiday around the sites of ancient Greece. As we made our way south-east to the capital, Athens, we stopped at Delphi, a small town, overshadowed by the dark limestone of the Phaedriades. There, at the edge of the town, were remains of the Sanctuary of Apollo, the temple once the home of Pythia, the high priestess commonly known as the Oracle of Delphi. The most famous of her maxims, inscribed in the forecourt of the temple, is 'know thyself'.

For organizations, 'know thyself' is encapsulated within the business model. The first thing those engaged in workforce planning need to know is: what is the organization, what does it do and why does it do those things? This is critical both as the anchor for the organization, but also because of the 'need to consider how to connect... [workforce] questions to the frameworks that business leaders already know, use and trust' (Boudreau, 2010).

The next thing to know is where the organization is going, the direction or destination, and why. The final things to understand, before we consider the workforce, are those things that might change that journey or impact what we are. What is the wider ecosystem and how might it impact our organization?

The answers to these questions will lie outside HR and the 'true institutional difficulty is in bringing all the agencies together to answer all the questions' (Smith, 2005). Much like my journey around Greece, answering these questions will involve a voyage of discovery in our organizations.

Types of organization

Economic sectors

FIGURE 5.1   Economic sectors

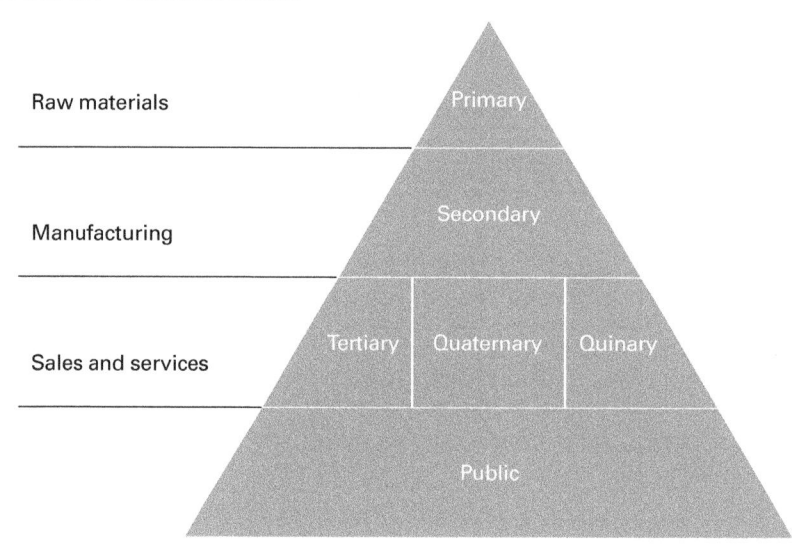

Raw materials

Manufacturing

Sales and services

Primary
Secondary
Tertiary | Quaternary | Quinary
Public

Our organizations will fall into one of the following economic sectors, of which Fisher (1939) breaks down the economy into the first three:

PRIMARY
The primary sector is concerned with raw materials; it includes both the extraction of natural resources, such as mining, and cultivation and collection of resources, such as agriculture.

SECONDARY
The secondary sector of the economy is based on manufacturing, the creation of useable goods. The initial stage is the conversion of raw materials from the primary sector into products. Further stages are the combining of components into further products; consider, for example, the different components that will be combined to create a mobile device.

TERTIARY
The tertiary sector is concerned with two elements: sales and services. This includes both the services to provide products from the primary and

secondary sectors to the end user, for example transportation, and the eventual sale.

The tertiary element of the three-sector model has since evolved to incorporate two further sectors and acknowledge the parallel 'public' sector:

QUATERNARY

This is the knowledge economy, a term popularized by Peter Drucker (1969) and best described as 'production and services based on knowledge-intensive activities that contribute to an accelerated pace of technical and scientific advance, as well as rapid obsolescence' (Powell and Snellman, 2004). The sector is aimed at future growth and development, and includes knowledge-driven services, such as information technology and pharmaceuticals; professional services, such as consulting and financial services; and in addition the knowledge-centric activities of media, entertainment and education.

QUINARY

The quinary sector is an expansion of the highest levels of the quaternary sector. Often referred to as 'gold collar workers' (Kelly, 1985), the inhabitants of this sector have the strongest base of power and are focused on control. Common examples are the highest echelons of the legal, media, financial and professional services firms.

Whilst the three-sector model helped define the operating environment of organizations in the past, modern businesses will find themselves straddling multiple sectors. In addition to the extraction of raw materials (primary), an oil firm may also construct its own operating rigs (secondary), distribute and sell its products (tertiary), conduct research and development (quaternary) and have key figures responsible for managing the eminence of the firm (quinary).

PUBLIC

Strictly speaking, the concepts of private and public are centred around ownership rather than sectors. However, whilst a public (or state) sector organization can straddle all five sectors, it is important to draw it out as distinctive. Organized at three levels (national, regional and local), the public sector may either be run directly by government or delivered through an agency. The sector delivers public goods such as military, law enforcement and the creation and maintenance of infrastructure. In addition, the sector may include state-owned enterprises that deliver private goods, such as transportation, power and mining. Finally, the sector operates public administration: the policymaking for services and the taxation to fund those services.

The voluntary, or third, sector is not called out separately in the model as it is more closely aligned to the first five sectors (though most commonly service based).

Business model

All organizations exist to create value and the business model describes the way an organization creates and captures value. Success is determined largely by the ability to generate margin, that is to create a higher degree of value than the cost to produce it. In neo-classical economic theory, value equates to the price a product or service would bring in a competitive and open market (Marshall, 1997). Contemporary thinking recognizes more normative views; key amongst these is that there is a subjective value placed on a product or service, which is higher than the price paid. Creating this *utility* is the focus for modern organizations and is a critical concept in understanding both the way it operates in relation to the external market, and the internal operation at a meso level.

One perspective is that all organizations are based around one or more of the '12 standard forms of value' (Kaufman, 2012):

- **Product** – create a tangible item to sell, like a book.
- **Service** – provide support or assistance and then charge a fee, like dog walking.
- **Shared resource** – create an asset that can be used by many people and charge for access, like a gym.
- **Subscription** – offer an ongoing benefit and charge a recurring fee for access, like a video streaming service.
- **Lease** – acquire a product and allow another party to use it for a fee, like renting property.
- **Agency** – market and sell something on behalf of a third party and collect a commission, like a real-estate agent.
- **Audience aggregation** – curate an audience with common characteristics and sell access to them, like a trade fair.
- **Loan** – lend money and collect payments over time, like a property mortgage.

- **Option** – provide the ability to take an action within a specific timeframe, like a train ticket.
- **Insurance** – take on the financial risk of an event, like home insurance.
- **Capital** – purchase a stake in a business and collect either an ongoing dividend or one-off payment.
- **Resale** – acquire a product or capital and resell it, like buying a book from a publisher and reselling it in a bookshop.

These concepts are of crucial importance as each is unique in the way value is created and requires different approaches in order to be successful, particularly when combining multiple value forms, or *bundling*.

CASE STUDY
Nintendo

A joint study by professors at Harvard Business School and Carnegie Mellon University pointed to mixed success for gaming giant Nintendo (Derdenger and Kumar, 2011).

Between 2001 and 2005, prior to the release of Sony's PlayStation Portable, Nintendo monopolized the portable video game market. In that period, Nintendo released two hardware products, the Game Boy Advance and Game Boy Advance SP, alongside multiple software products. Over a two-year period, Nintendo released bundles of these consoles with Mario software titles.

The study showed that bundled products were viewed by consumers as less valuable than the sum of their component parts. However, bundling was particularly useful in generating sales to those consumers who may have waited a longer period before buying, which led to greater software sales over time. A strategy of *mixed bundling*, selling hardware and software as either a bundle or as separates, would generate over 100,000 additional hardware sales and over a million additional software sales.

However, in *pure bundling*, where the hardware was only available as a bundle, the effects would be disastrous. Hardware unit sales dropped by millions and software sales fell by over 10 million. In total, revenues decreased by 20 per cent as a result.

This distinction in fortunes may seem counter-intuitive, as choice has been limited to a more expensive bundle. However, consumers know that the price for computer hardware drops significantly over time; they postpone purchase until the price is in better relation to the value they place on it.

THE VALUE CHAIN

The concept of the value chain was first described by business strategist Michael Porter in his book *Competitive Advantage* (1985) as a method of articulating the business model. The model is based on a number of value activities, the distinct activities performed by an organization that are the building blocks to a form of value (eg a product) that would generate revenue. These value activities are categorized as: primary, those that comprise the business operations; and support, those that enable the business operations. Around these activities there is a final wrap of margin to ensure the value chain is viable.

The primary activities are: inbound logistics; operations; outbound logistics; marketing and sales; and service. Inbound logistics are the elements concerned with receiving, storing and disseminating inputs. For a product or resale, this might include warehousing and managing an inventory. Operations are the activities that take those inputs and transform them into the final form of value; for a product this might be the manufacturing process, for a service it would be the specific delivery of that service. Outbound logistics is the storage and distribution of forms of value, like the technology systems that process the orders, packaging and delivery. Marketing and sales are the means of purchasing a form of value, advertising, pricing and channel management. In the context of the value chain model, service includes the post-sale activities to enhance and maintain value, such as installation, helpdesks and repair.

The supporting activities are procurement, technology development, human resource management and firm infrastructure. Procurement is the function of purchasing inputs used in the value chain; technology development utilizes technological advancement to provide competitive advantage; human resource management to recruit, develop and compensate workers; and the firm infrastructure to provide overall planning and management.

THE BUSINESS MODEL CANVAS

The business model canvas is a more recent approach created by business theorist Alexander Osterwalder. He describes a canvas of nine building blocks (Osterwalder, 2005). At the centre is the value proposition, the tangible benefits to the customer of a specific form of value. Connecting to this value proposition are two ecosystems: one contains the key activities of the business model, the essential resources needed for the business model and the network of partners who participate in the business model; these elements all come with an associated cost. The second ecosystem connects the value proposition to the client segments addressed by the proposition, the communication and distribution channels to those clients, and finally the relationship with those clients; this ecosystem is then contained within a wrap of the revenue stream that the model generates.

Strategic alignment

Having established what the business is, the next stage is to understand why an organization exists and where it is going. 'Workforce plans must flow from, and be consistent with, the overall business and HR strategies' (Cascio, 2006).

Framework of strategic alignment

Effective organizations are able to connect their *why* to the way that work is done; this is called strategic alignment.

FIGURE 5.2 Strategic framework

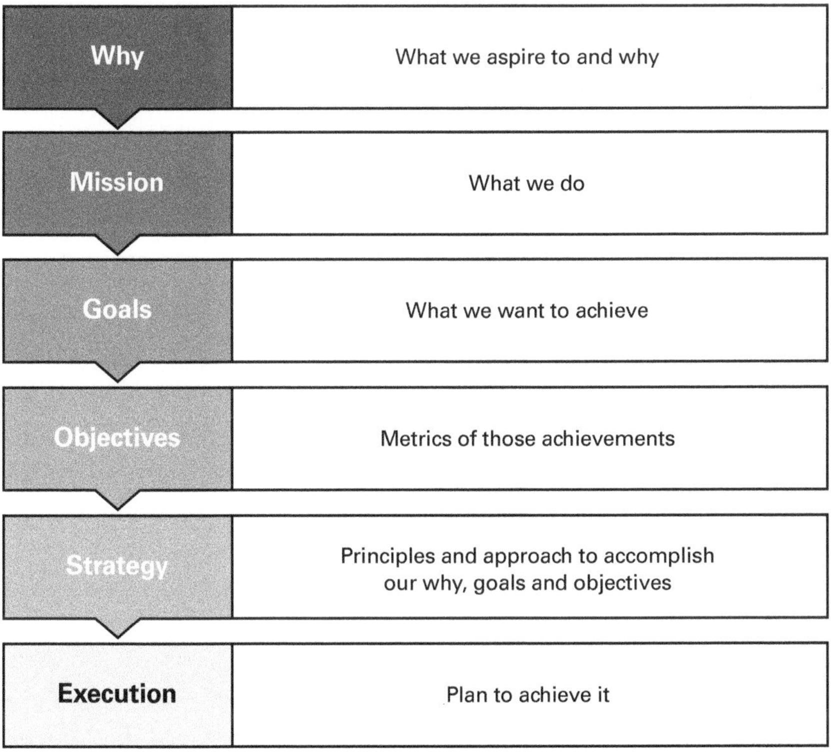

Why	What we aspire to and why
Mission	What we do
Goals	What we want to achieve
Objectives	Metrics of those achievements
Strategy	Principles and approach to accomplish our why, goals and objectives
Execution	Plan to achieve it

WHY

In line with the first principle of agile workforce planning, we begin with Sinek's call to start with why: why did the organization come into existence, why does it continue to exist? The 'why' is most often framed as one of two things: vision or purpose. Vision is an imagined future state of what the organization, the marketplace or the world will look like; for example, my personal vision is *engaged people connected with meaningful work*. Purpose is the enduring objective to be achieved, which is inextricably linked to the vision; for example, my personal purpose is *to connect engaged people with meaningful work*.

MISSION

This is the 'what' to the 'why': what do we do? Also known as 'economic mission' (Gilmore and Brandenburg, 1962) it concerns the kind of business the organization should be in; this might be manufacturing cars or conducting workforce planning.

GOALS

These are the broad aims to be achieved. Goals may be the first instance where a broader consideration is given to timeframes. Fundamentally, a goal is something that can be achieved by the 'mission'.

OBJECTIVES

These are the goals framed in specific metrics to measure achievement within a timeline. A goal might be to increase profits, whereas the objective may be a 20 per cent profit growth within three years.

STRATEGY

This is the 'way', the principles and broad approach to achieve those objectives. If a 'goal', by itself, does not contribute to the 'why', then the 'strategy' is what makes that connection. It defines 'the right product-market-sales approach combination' to achieve the objectives (Gilmore and Brandenburg, 1962). Successful strategy hinges on creating difference; it means 'deliberately choosing a different set of activities to deliver a unique mix of value' (Porter, 1996). A company with a vision around a stronger local community may well have a goal of profit growth and their strategy may stipulate that there should be no layoffs to achieve that growth, as doing so would damage the local community. Strategies are often framed around timeframes (eg a strategy around cost reduction would not be enduring) and longer-term strategies are often framed as policy.

> ### THE WORKFORCE STRATEGY
>
> In organizations there is a cascade of strategic alignment amongst departments and functions. For example, in car manufacturing the objectives of the sales department would be different to the objectives of the repair department. However, these all need to be complementary both laterally at the meso level and vertically at the macro level, otherwise the result is silos and a damaging strategic disconnect.
>
> For the purposes of a function with the mandate for the workforce (eg HR), the *workforce strategy* is a blueprint or design for our people to accomplish our organizational strategy. It is about **who** we want our people to be, focusing on ambitions (eg greater diversity) and broad concepts (eg flexibility) and sets the framework for workforce planning. 'The employment or workforce strategy is not always articulated in one or more written documents, but covers the dimensions, sources and supply and any changes required to the size, shape and nature of the workforce and its contractual and psychological relationship with the organization' (Brown et al, 2019).

EXECUTION

These are the specific plans to achieve the *objectives*. Plans are always framed in timeframes (eg short-term operational plans and long-term strategic plans) and are either *business as usual* (BAU) or *ad-hoc*, sometimes referred to as *run* and *change*. The execution of BAU activity is often framed as processes, whereas the execution of ad-hoc activity is typically within a programme or project.

The operating model is the representation of how the organization is run: both how the organization conducts that *execution* and the way it determines all other elements of strategic alignment. The operating model signified a shift away from a traditional hierarchical viewpoint to more of a systems-based approach. The most common operating model approach evolved from the diamond model for creating organizational change (Leavitt, 1965): structure, tasks, people and technology. This is now more commonly recognized as a triangle of people, process and technology.

Since then, more advanced approaches have come to the fore when formulating the operating model. One of the most prevalent is McKinsey's 7-S framework of strategy, structure, systems, style, staff and skills which are all interlinked with superordinate goals (Waterman *et al*, 1980). The superordinate goals, since renamed shared values, sit at the core of the model and are what the organization wants to achieve. The strategy is the high-level plan to achieve those goals, the structure represents the structure of the organization and the systems are the processes and procedures. These *hard S* factors contrast with the *soft S* factors: style, the way the organization is managed; staff, the numbers of employees; and skills, the capabilities of those employees.

Environmental scanning

If we have a destination and a direction of travel, the process of environmental scanning allows us to identify the opportunities and threats along the journey. One of the best approaches was originally conceived as ETPS: economic, technical, political and social (Aguilar, 1967). Over time, this model has evolved a number of different variations; I tend towards PESTLE: political, economic, social, technological, legal and environmental. The political factors relate to the following: political stability; the regulatory framework of the government, including taxation, trade restrictions and tariffs; and governmental policy, including investment in health, education and infrastructure. Economic factors include both the internal aspects of growth, inflation and interest rates, in addition to the comparative external factors of exchange rates and purchasing power. The social aspects include both the cultural norms of society and the demographic trends of the population. The technological factors relate to both the pace of technological change and the levels of investment in research and development, automation and digitization. The legal factors include those that protect workers (eg discrimination, employment law, health and safety), those that protect consumers (eg false advertising claims and refunds) and those that protect businesses (eg antitrust, theft and fraud). Other factors in variations of ETPS include: demographic, which I incorporate in *social*; ethical, which I incorporate into *sociological* and *environmental*; and regulatory, which I incorporate in *political* and *legal*.

This scanning enables an organization to do two things: firstly, to establish the threats to the strategic ambition and the additional opportunities that may exist. The second is derived from a common viewpoint on control: 'inside' factors are controlled by the organization (eg those discussed under types of organization and strategic alignment) and 'outside' factors sit outside the control of the organization (Pfeffer and Salancik, 1978). This perhaps overlooks the reality of organizational influence, so environmental scanning allows us to establish those aspects that sit firmly outside the control of the organization and those factors that an organization may be able to influence (eg lobbying for a regulatory change). It is common for thinkers on environmental scanning to consider the external environment before the internal aspects of the organization (eg Hax and Majluf, 1990). This approach can result in an exhausting exercise of attempting to capture every facet of the external environment and *boil the ocean*. In my experience, it is far better to understand the internal context of the organization and use that to frame the scanning of the external environment.

Summary

Whenever I conduct analysis of the strategic context, I am always reminded of the following exchange from *Alice in Wonderland*:

'Would you tell me, please, which way I ought to go from here?'

'That depends a good deal on where you want to get to,' said the Cat.

'I don't much care where – ' said Alice.

'Then it doesn't matter which way you go,' said the Cat.

' – so long as I get *somewhere*,' Alice added as an explanation.

'Oh, you're sure to do that,' said the Cat, 'if you only walk long enough.'

Without a direction or destination, all we can guarantee is that the organization will get somewhere, and that will likely be the wrong place at significant cost. Understanding the nature of the organization, its ambition and the factors that may impact it, are the essential first steps in baselining the organization. 'The critical issue is not the individual talent that you have; the competitive advantage is what you do with the talent once you have it. And that is an organizational issue' (Ulrich *et al*, 2017).

When you practise workforce planning, ask yourself:

- In which economic sectors does the organization operate?
- How does the organization create value?
- Why does the organization do what it does?
- What is the organization's mission, goals, objectives and strategy?
- How does the organization execute to achieve those strategic ambitions?
- What are the external factors related to the organization and what threats and opportunities are presented by those factors?

References

Aguilar, F J (1967) *Scanning the Business Environment*, Macmillan, New York

Boudreau, J (2010) *Retooling HR: Using proven business tools to make better decisions about talent*, Harvard Business School Publishing, Boston

Brown, D, Hirsh, W and Reilly, P (2019) *Strategic Human Resource Management in Practice: Case studies and conclusions – from HRM strategy to strategic people management*, IES, Brighton

Cascio, W F (2006) *Managing Human Resources*, McGraw-Hill, New York

Derdenger, T and Kumar, V (2011) The dynamic effects of bundling as a product strategy, Harvard Business School Working Paper 12-043, www.andrew.cmu.edu/user/derdenge/dynamicbundling.pdf (archived at https://perma.cc/BZN8-ZUWN)

Drucker, P F (1969) *The Age of Discontinuity: Guidelines to our changing society*, Pan Books, London

Fisher, A G B (1939) Production, primary, secondary and tertiary, *Economic Record*, **15** (1), pp 24–38, https://onlinelibrary.wiley.com/doi/abs/10.1111/j.1475-4932.1939.tb01015.x (archived at https://perma.cc/64AH-34X6)

Gilmore, F F and Brandenburg, R G (1962) Anatomy of corporate planning, in H I Ansoff (ed) (1969) *Business Strategy*, Penguin, Harmondsworth

Hax, A C and Majluf, N S (1990) The use of industry attractiveness – business strength matrix in strategic planning, in R G Dyson (ed) *Strategic Planning: Models and analytical techniques*, John Wiley & Sons, Chichester

Kaufman, J (2012) *The Personal MBA*, Penguin, London

Kelly, R E (1985) *The Gold Collar Worker: Harnessing the brainpower of the new workforce*, Longman Higher Education, London

Leavitt, H J (1965) Applied organisational change in industry: Structural, technological and humanistic approaches, in J G March (ed) *Handbook of Organisation*, Rand McNally and Company, Chicago

Marshall, A (1997) *Principles of Economics*, Prometheus Books, New York

Osterwalder, A (2005) What is a business model? [Blog] *Business Model Chemist*, 5 November, http://businessmodelalchemist.com/blog/2005/11/what-is-business-model.html (archived at https://perma.cc/9STB-KGDN)

Pfeffer, J and Salancik, R (1978) *The External Control of Organizations: A resource dependence perspective*, HarperCollins, New York

Porter, M E (1985) *Competitive Advantage: Creating and sustaining superior performance*, The Free Press, New York

Porter, M E (1996) What is strategy? *Harvard Business Review*, 74 (6), pp 61–78, hbr.org/1996/11/what-is-strategy (archived at https://perma.cc/BT5P-DEM2)

Powell, W W and Snellman, K (2004) The knowledge economy, *Annual Review of Sociology*, 30, pp 199–220, web.stanford.edu/group/song/papers/powell_snellman.pdf (archived at https://perma.cc/MRQ5-BGNM)

Smith, R (2005) *The Utility of Force*, Allen Lane, London

Ulrich, D *et al* (2017) *Victory Through Organization: Why the war for talent is failing your company wan what you can do about it*, McGraw-Hill, New York

Waterman, R, Peters, T J and Phillips, J R (1980) Structure is not organization, *Business Horizons*, 23 (3), pp 14–26, www.sciencedirect.com/science/article/pii/0007681380900270 (archived at https://perma.cc/76S3-WZSZ)

06

Understanding the workforce

Introduction

In 2002, general manager of the Oakland Athletics baseball team, Billy Bean, found himself in the unenviable position of having a salary budget of $44 million, far below those of their competitors. Through *analysing the strategic context*, he established that the metrics of on-base percentage and slugging percentage were not only the best measures of offensive success, but also that those metrics were undervalued by teams and scouts alike. Knowing the measures that were the drivers of success, both he and assistant general manager, Paul DePodesta, evaluated players based on those metrics. In the Major League Baseball draft of that year, they were able to acquire players who were undervalued in the marketplace. Immortalized in the book *Moneyball* (Lewis, 2003) and depicted by Brad Pitt in the film of the same name, Bean took the Oakland As to the playoffs in 2002 and 2003. Once we understand the organization, the next step is to understand the workforce.

I'm always drawn to a quotation attributed to former CEO of Netscape, Jim Barkdale: 'If we have data, let's look at data. If all we have are opinions, let's go with mine.' In the absence of data, organizations tend to converge on the highest-paid person's opinion, or HiPPO. Billy Bean's approach garnered fierce criticism at the time, where opinions were strongly biased towards statistical relics from the 19th century, such as batting average.

> There was but one question he left unasked, and it vibrated between his lines: if gross miscalculations of a person's value could occur on a baseball field, before a live audience of thirty thousand, and a television audience of millions more, what did that say about the measurement of performance in other lines of work? If professional baseball players could be over- or undervalued, who

couldn't? Bad as they may have been, the statistics used to evaluate baseball players were probably far more accurate than anything used to measure the value of people who didn't play baseball for a living (Lewis, 2003).

In this chapter we will cover both the collection of data and the methodologies and models we use to measure the value of the workforce, including those who do not play baseball for a living.

Data gathering

Understanding the workforce is 'a fact-gathering exercise: collecting and examining data that suggests future trends and changes' (Walker, 1992). To conduct a successful exercise in data gathering, we need to answer the following questions.

What data do I need to understand my workforce?

When we consider the size and scale of modern businesses and public-sector organizations, 'it is hard to realize today that government during the American Civil War... meant the merest handful of people' (Drucker, 1985). Fortunately, this increase in scale has been accompanied by the growth in technology, as management theorist John Hinrichs remarked in the late 1960s: 'Machine technologies make it possible for the personnel researcher to explore an infinite number of interrelationships regarding manpower data in the organization in an effort to gain better understanding of the factors affecting this dynamic resource' (Hinrichs, 1972).

The data we need to understand our workforce relates to the seven rights of workforce planning. It is the data that will tell us the current state and the drivers of capability, size, shape, location, time, cost and risk. We will need to be able to see this not only at the macro level, but also at meso levels appropriate to the structure of our organizations.

Where is the data and how do I access it?

Even organizations with high levels of data maturity and the latest technology would consider themselves incredibly lucky to have all this data in a single location and at the touch of a button. In reality, data on the workforce may be stored in multiple systems and varying formats. The advice is to start with what we may already have available: we may have access to information on the workforce either through reports that are *pushed* to us on a regular basis, for example a monthly slide deck on workforce information, or reporting that we may be able to *pull* from a system on a self-service basis. Not only can this provide us with a great deal of the information we need, it can also help us understand the maturity of the workforce data, the way it is structured and the datasets available. The next place to look is with the HR function, the typical 'owner' of the workforce data. HR technology is booming, with almost $2 billion of venture capital invested in 2018 (Bersin, 2019), and the availability of workforce data within organizations is significant.

How do I make sense of the data?

Muhammad Ali, then still known as Cassius Clay, said famously in advance of his 1964 title fight, 'Float like a butterfly, sting like a bee, his hands can't hit what his eyes can't see' (*Float Like a Butterfly, Sting Like a Bee*, 1969). Just like Ali's opponent, world heavyweight champion Sonny Liston, we too need to be able to see the data to make sense of it. The results of *data visualization* continue to evolve in new ways, and we will cover that more in later chapters; the basics for making sense of the data are tables and charts. Tables show information in rows and columns, whilst charts show the information in a pictorial format. Achieving this requires both analysis and analytics, neither of which are as scary as they are often made out to be. Analysis is the practice of translating raw and unorganized facts (data) into organized and structured facts (information) to bring about meaning (insight). Analytics are the frameworks, processes and tools we use to conduct these analyses. With workforce analytics, this can be seen as combining HR, finance and performance data with evolving approaches around data science.

What is the quality and reliability of the data?

'The foundation of talent analytics are *human capital facts* – a single *version of the truth* regarding individual performance and enterprise-level data' (Shapiro and Davenport, 2013). In order to establish our facts, we need to understand the quality and reliability of our data and establish it as the single version of the truth. First, we need to understand the source of the data, how it was recorded and when. A date of birth, entered by a new starter and validated through a background and referencing check, will have the highest level of quality and reliability. People tend to know their own date of birth better than someone else, so a new starter inputting the data directly will add to accuracy. Cross-checking this data against a passport or birth certificate as part of a check reinforces the reliability. As date of birth is not something that ever changes, it reinforces the reliability. Compare date of birth with, for example, body weight (not to suggest this is a common data set in HR systems). Body weight tends to change over time, so accuracy is dependent on how recently the data was input. Equally important is the method of measurement: I know the scales in my bedroom are slightly more forgiving than the scales in the bathroom. I think we can all also appreciate that body weight records can also be impacted by what we might call, euphemistically, user error. Therefore, it is important to appreciate the who, when and how of capturing data.

CASE STUDY
ABC Corporation

A senior HR director was reviewing some diversity data and challenged the accuracy of the report. They claimed the percentage of members of the executive from an ethnic minority was being reported incorrectly. Though the data came from a single established source for workforce data, the HR director's own eyes were also a source of data. Their own judgment on visible ethnicity suggested that there were higher numbers of ethnic minorities in the executive than were indicated in the report. It was established that the deviation was based on members of the executive who had chosen not to declare their ethnicity, as was their right. Therefore, the human capital facts were as the report indicated, not as the HR director had judged them to be.

The final things to understand are data gaps, of which there are two types. There are gaps *in* data, where there are just some instances of date of birth not being recorded, and gaps *of* data, where date of birth is not recorded at all. That is where assumptions come into play.

Making assumptions

'Some organizations think that they cannot implement workforce planning unless they have *all* the data for *all* the people. They spend so much time gathering and managing data that they end up having no time left to use those data to support workforce planning' (Bechet, 2008). Those engaged in workforce planning have a choice to make: collect data or work with the gaps. I advocate working with the gaps and making assumptions. For many business leaders, the idea of making assumptions can appear reckless (even though robust assumptions are far less reckless than their own HiPPO). In reality, everything hinges on assumptions: 'The map is not the territory it represents, but, if correct, has a similar structure to the territory, which accounts for its usefulness' (Korzybski, 1933). The workforce data is not the workforce, it is a representation of various facets of the workforce that are recorded, stored, retrieved and interpreted. In much the same way, an extensive biography of Winston Churchill is not Winston Churchill himself. To make sense of it, we wrap a number of assumptions around the information.

To understand the concept of making decisions based on assumptions, I often ask people to either imagine or recall an expensive one-off purchase, such as buying a house. Unless we happen to be a residential building surveyor, the typical homebuyer is an amateur. First, a homebuyer will be considering their financial situation: the size of their deposit, the size of mortgage available and the affordability of repayments to determine a budget for a house. In identifying a house, a homebuyer may conduct research on the internet to identify a suitable area. They will assess house prices against their budget, and also review transport links, research crime rates and assess local schooling and amenities. If they have not done so already, they are likely to engage the services of a real-estate agent to identify a potential house. A buyer, or their representative, will visit the property and conduct a visual inspection. Thereafter, the services of experts are commissioned to survey the property. After conducting this analysis and assuming a degree of trust in experts, the property is purchased. It is only on moving in that new things are noticed, things about the house and area that were perhaps missed before. Rarely are these catastrophic oversights, but it does illustrate that our single most expensive purchase decision hinges heavily upon assumption. When I do this exercise with people, I find interesting deviations where some have conducted a practice run of their commute, whilst others have investigated neighbours on social media prior to a decision. Each new facet helps illustrate the extent of the quest for data.

The reality is that there is no such thing as perfect data; we make assumptions with every set. There are clearly variations between organizations in their data quality; some have robust and comprehensive data sets, whilst others have significant quality issues. As we look at each data set, we understand the assumptions we are making about the data and record them. Do the same with the assumptions we make with data gaps; is there a heuristic we can use? For example, is there official government data we can use to understand a prevalence of a characteristic? Are there benchmarks available from similar organizations? As Laurie Bassi, analytics thought leader and CEO of McBassi & Company, said, 'Do what you can with what you've got. You can still move forward' (Guenole et al, 2017).

Workforce segmentation

The aim of workforce segmentation is to divide the workforce into groups in order to better understand the workforce and determine roles of interest.

Better understand the workforce

> In most personnel matters, for instance, events are measured in *averages*, such as the average number of lost-time accidents per hundred employees, the average percentage of absenteeism in the whole work force, or the average illness rate per hundred. But the executive who goes out and looks for himself will find that he needs a different measurement. The averages serve the purposes of the insurance company, but they are meaningless, indeed misleading, for personnel management decisions (Drucker, 1985).

From the outside, a workforce looks simply like a collection of heads and, indeed, headcount and budget planning often does not go beyond this average. Two people in a room with a mean net worth of $50 billion is a vastly different story to you or I being in a room with Amazon CEO Jeff Bezos: averages can hide significant differences. The importance of understanding the differences in averages is the origin of segmentation; the building blocks for segmentation are headcount and FTE.

HEADCOUNT AND FTE

Headcount is the total number, the count, of people present at any given point in time. If we have 1,000 employees, our headcount is 1,000. Full-Time Equivalent (FTE), occasionally Whole-Time Equivalent (WTE), is the measure of time for a person in relation to a pre-defined 'full-time' rate: 1.0 is the full-time equivalent of 1 employee, whereas 0.5 is the equivalent of half a full-time employee. If a full-time employee is contracted to work 40 hours, then all other hours are counted in relation to that metric (ie 0.5 FTE = 20 hours).

FTE is quite complex and can be broken down into some specific types; imagine we are looking at the FTE calculation for the month of January.

Target FTE is the number of FTE that the business requires for January.

Budgeted FTE is the number of FTE that the business has allocated in a budget for January.

Contracted FTE is calculated by looking at all employees and calculating the sum of their individual FTE within their contracts (eg 20 employees all contracted to work 20 hours in a 40-hour FTE week, 0.5 FTE, are 10 contracted FTE). It is often the figure that the HR system provides as the FTE figure when we run an HR report for January.

Financial FTE may only be realized some weeks later based on what was actually worked and will take into account any additional paid hours or overtime that are worked, including the time for any casual employees or zero-hours contract workers. In this, a 0.8 *contracted FTE* (four-day week) who worked an additional day each week would be recorded as a 1.0 *financial FTE*.

Forecast FTE is informed by *financial FTE*, whereby the trends in actual paid hours are used to forecast the coming FTE levels. For example, if a 1.0 *contracted FTE* is routinely a 1.2 financial FTE, then they may be considered a 1.2 forecast FTE. In the UK, the forecast FTE level relates to the Bear Scotland ruling in 2014, which requires employers in the UK to use actual pay over a representative period to calculate holiday pay (UKEAT, 2014).

Planned FTE may well not sit in any official systems and, as a result, may be calculated in many different ways. At a first-line manager level this may include all hours expected to be worked by employees in January, including additional and overtime hours and casual staff/zero hours employees, but may well exclude those on annual leave. Whereas the *forecast FTE* for January may have been calculated many months previously, the planned FTE may be calculated as little as days beforehand. Though this provides an indicative direct resource cost of work, or a particular project, the sum totals of planned FTE across an organization typically do not equate to financial FTE.

Through segmenting the workforce based on different dimensions, we start to see how different parts of the organization contrast in their makeup and therefore need different approaches based on the strategic ambition of an organization. The most often used dimensions for the workforce are structures, demography, tenure, competency and contract. Operational and financial structures are the most common approach to workforce segmentation. The financial structures arrange workers based on business-specific financial management and accountabilities; they are typically referred to as profit (for revenue-generating areas) or cost centres (for functional areas). Operational structures will be derived from the basis of the organizational design, which may include a mixture of product lines, geographies and functions; these should flow all the way from the organization or group level, right down to the team level. The main categories that fall under demography are what is commonly referred to as 'diversity data'; the main ones are considered protected characteristics in the UK under the Equality Act 2010, and include age, gender, ethnicity and disability. The additional aspect to demography is the geographic distribution (both in terms of office locations and worker locations). Tenure refers to the various durations within a worker's history, for example employment start date, time in role and time in pay band. As we introduced in the first chapter, a competency is created when skills (how to do something) combine with specific knowledge (what, when and where to do something), mindset (willingness to do something) and, where necessary, accreditation (proof of that skill or knowledge). Those organizations with an effective job family mapping will have a robust framework for competency dimensions.

In the absence of job families, then it can be helpful to capture the following competency heuristics:

- hierarchy: the level of a person within a hierarchy may be captured with titles (eg Manager), levels (eg CEO minus 4) or pay bands (eg £40–50k);
- sector experience: experience within particular industry sectors;
- qualification: attainment of a specific level within an educational framework;
- certification: attainment of a validated standard that is bound by time;
- education and training: participation in learning;
- talent groups: membership of particular groups that are either recognized as having *high potential* for a particular competency or otherwise grouped together, and supported, to progress to attainment of a particular competency;

- skill: a practised technique that enables the achievement of an outcome;
- appetite: a desire for proficiency in a particular field or experience within an industry sector.

The contract dimension is specific elements of a contractual relationship with the organization: are they a permanent worker or a contractor, are there different full-time rates (eg 37 hours vs 40 hours), what is the mix of full-time and part-time workers, are there any who are seconded from another organization or have inherited different contractual rights as a result of a merger or acquisition?

FULL-TIME AND PART-TIME

There are different national definitions of this, ranging from 30 hours upwards. The concept of part-time is something of an anathema in contemporary thinking and has suffered from the negative connotations of it being seen by some as less important than full-time, or a judgement on a worker's level of commitment. In reality, a full-time 40-hour working week is less than a quarter of the 168 hours in a week. My preferred approach is to group together different FTE groups (eg < 0.4, 0.4–0.8 and > 0.8).

The headcount and FTE of these workforce dimensions will indicate the scale of these groups. To determine the uniqueness of these segments requires multivariate analysis against other metrics. Common metrics in HR are: salary; sickness levels; turnover rate; promotion rates and internal mobility; performance; utilization and productivity; and engagement levels.

Determine roles of interest

The second aim of workforce segmentation is to determine roles of interest. At first glance, and particularly with a large organization, workforce planning can appear to be an overwhelming task of *boiling the ocean*. Determining roles of interest 'simplifies the problem by foreshortening the need for a total forecasting model' (Walker, 1972). Indeed, it allows us to make educated decisions based on where a planned workforce intervention will generate the biggest return on investment.

WHOLE WORKFORCE APPROACH

A defining factor of the fourth industrial revolution is that workforce is a loose concept that incorporates not just permanent employees, but temporary employees, contractors, gig workers, consultancies under statements of work, service providers and, increasingly, robots. As such, even an intent to assess an entire workforce will require a considered view on what should be considered in scope. Even at a basic level, an organization will need to take a decision about whether to include those on long-term abstraction (eg career break, parental leave, long-term sick leave, secondment) or include 'employees' such as fixed-term contractors.

When looking at a whole workforce, I find the most useful approach is to use an adapted version of the HR architecture first proposed by Lepak and Snell (1999), which splits the workforce into four quadrants based on the uniqueness of a capability, its scarcity within the industry and wider marketplace, and the value of that capability to the organization, a concept first raised by Nobel laureate Gary Becker (1964).

FIGURE 6.1   Capability segmentation framework

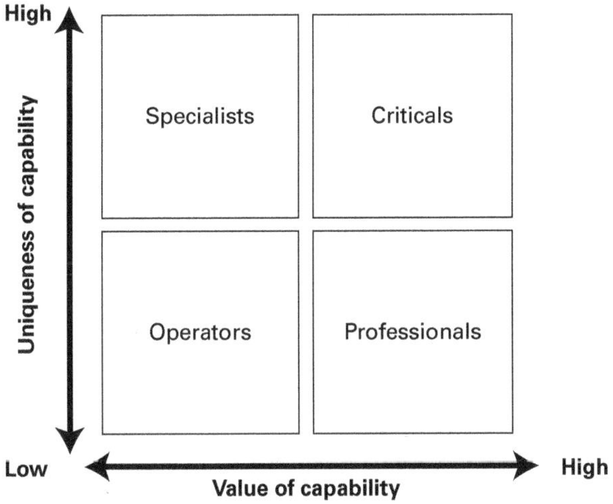

	Value of capability — Low	Value of capability — High
Uniqueness of capability — High	Specialists	Criticals
Uniqueness of capability — Low	Operators	Professionals

SOURCE Adapted from Lepak and Snell (1999)

As the value to the organization increases, there is a shift from a Gaussian distribution (bell curve) of performance to a Paretian distribution (power law relationship). The Gaussian distribution shows that the majority of the workforce are average performers delivering average value and there are a small number of those with comparatively low or high performance and delivering a commensurate level of value. The Paretian distribution follows the principle of Italian economist Vilfredo Pareto that 80 per cent of the workforce delivers 20 per cent of the value and 20 per cent of the workforce delivers 80 per cent of the value (Pareto, 1906). In a Paretian distribution, exceptional performance drives exponential value; this is in sharp contrast to the Gaussian distribution.

FIGURE 6.2 Gaussian and Paretian distributions of performance

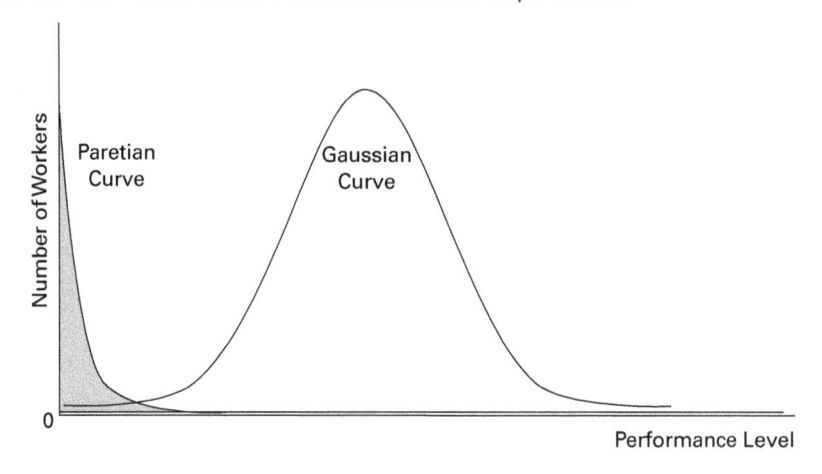

The Gaussian bell curve has been the staple in performance management ever since it was pioneered by former GE chief executive Jack Welch in the 1980s as the 'vitality curve' (Welch, 2001). Leading HR practitioner and CEO of Humu, Laszlo Bock, comments on the bell curve view of performance being outdated compared to a power law view (Bock, 1995). I would argue that, though knowledge workers typically perform on a power law (which was the case at Google, where Laszlo was SVP of People), process workers typically still operate on a bell curve as the system prevents exponential gains.

Specialists are capabilities that are unique and generate a comparatively lower value to the organization. As these capabilities tend to hinge around extremely specific processes, they tend to be concentrated around a particular business or industry. The clear characteristic is that this specialism is typically not in demand from organizations in different industries. I tend to break these down into two types: planned and accidental. Planned specialists usually go through lengthy and vigorous training to achieve their specialism, accompanied by a high initial outlay on training costs. A classic example of these is metro/underground drivers, who cannot be transferred to other modes of transport (trains and planes). Accidental specialists tend to grow over time and are identifiable by long service within the business or industry and have developed a specialism through experience over time. They tend to be the only person who knows how to accomplish a particular task and are likely to slip inadvertently into the critical category.

Professionals are the opposite of specialists, common capabilities across industries that add high value and tend to be characterized by professional accreditation, eg project management, digital skills, finance and HR. This capability tends to be the core of the workforce in a knowledge worker setting.

Operators are generalist capabilities that generate a comparatively lower value to the organization and incorporate manual labour, administrative and entry-level roles that require limited initial training.

Criticals are those capabilities that are both unique within the industry and create considerable value to an organization. They are critical to achieving the business strategy (both in terms of development and execution), they provide an organization's current comparative advantage, and they will provide an organization's future comparative advantage.

Some of the best thinking on the characteristics of critical roles came from Professors Brian Becker, Mark Huselid and Matthew Beatty in what they called 'A Positions' (Huselid *et al*, 2005; Becker *et al*, 2009), which were determined as 'those in which top talent significantly enhances the probability of achieving the business strategy'. They are marked by their ability to create value in revenue enhancement or cost reduction, but also destroy value if mistakes are made. This variability of performance means that the absolute best employees are challenging to attract and retain in the organization.

By identifying critical roles, those conducting strategic workforce planning can focus on areas of the workforce where planning can generate the greatest proportions of return on investment (RoI).

PRIORITY AREAS

Most contemporary thinking around workforce segmentation starts and ends with critical roles; however, there is a final dimension of identifying priority areas, what John Boudreau calls 'vital talent segments' (Boudreau, 2010). These are elements of the workforce that are not behaving in a way that is desirable for example they have a high level of turnover. This will be identified during initial workforce segmentation to understand the workforce, which may immediately indicate these roles of interest with behavioural variation. Finding these may necessitate a degree of workforce curiosity.

Workforce analytics

Curiosity is the basis of workforce analytics, a natural inquisitiveness about the cause and effect within the data. The starting point is the model I first learnt in primary school: who, what, when, where, why and how. Known in some circles as the *5W1H model*, it heralds from Aristotelian thinking (Aristotle, 1980) and is the basis for rational thinking. By asking these questions about data we can start to understand the correlations and causation between data, uncover outliers and identify roles of interest that might be a priority.

The golden rule of correlation and causation is that **correlation does not imply causation**. Correlation is an action or occurrence that has similar characteristics to another, but they may or may not be linked. Numerous instances of factors that have high correlation, but no causal links, are detailed at tylervigen.com (archived at https://perma.cc/P3VB-AJE7), such as per capita cheese consumption and the number of people who have died by becoming tangled in their bedsheets. Causation, however, is an action or occurrence that can result in a separate action or occurrence.

In workforce data there will be numerous linked correlations, for example age and retirement. Where either age, or length of service, mandates retirement (for example, some military and law enforcement professions) then there is cause and effect.

Whilst there are an array of technological tools and solutions that can help identify correlations and causation, I tend towards the *five whys model*: that asking why five times will inevitably find the root cause of a problem. This is best achieved through use of a decomposition tree, a technique that mirrors the fishbone diagram of Kaoru Ishikawa (1986). Take a particular dimension of the workforce and metric, for example a higher level of female voluntary turnover (20 per cent) than the average for an organization (17 per cent – see Figure 6.3).

The next and subsequent steps are to identify the largest population groups that are not contributing to the outlier metric. In this example, we see that females at pay band 5 have a higher level of voluntary turnover (26 per cent). Of those females at pay band 5, the age ranges of 20–30 and 30–40 both trend higher still, at 31.25 and 27.5 per cent respectively. When we look at that first group of 20- 30-year-olds, those who have returned from maternity leave in the last 12 months show a significant spike in voluntary turnover at 60 per cent. This correlation provides three key insights: within that age range, maternity correlates with voluntary turnover and if we investigate the 30- 40-year-old cohort, we may find a similar correlation;

FIGURE 6.3 Decomposition tree to analyse turnover

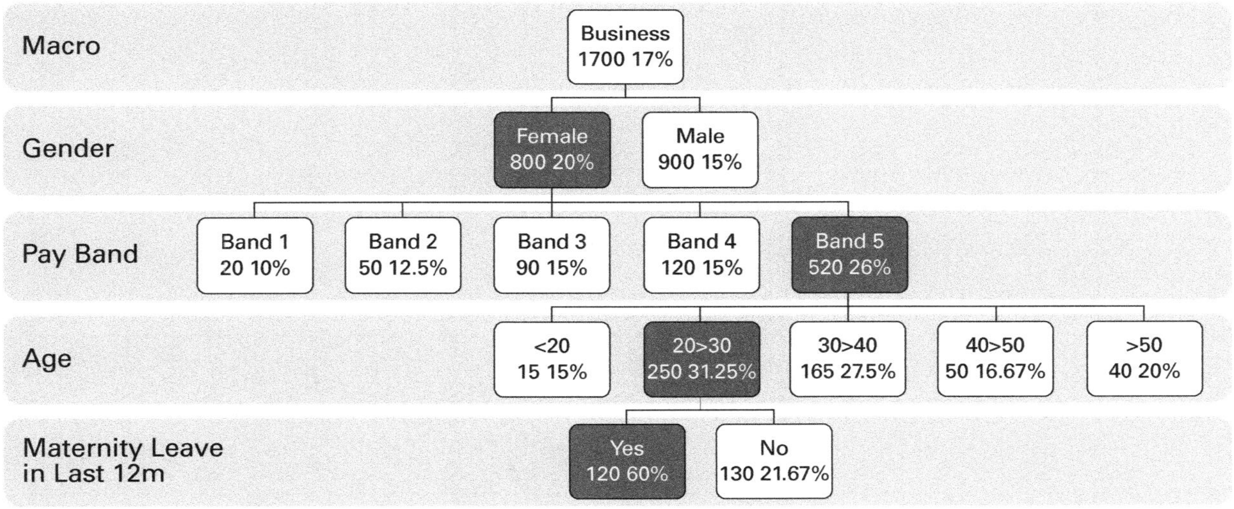

Macro
- Business: 1700 17%

Gender
- Female: 800 20%
- Male: 900 15%

Pay Band
- Band 1: 20 10%
- Band 2: 50 12.5%
- Band 3: 90 15%
- Band 4: 120 15%
- Band 5: 520 26%

Age
- <20: 15 15%
- 20>30: 250 31.25%
- 30>40: 165 27.5%
- 40>50: 50 16.67%
- >50: 40 20%

Maternity Leave in Last 12m
- Yes: 120 60%
- No: 130 21.67%

identifying this correlation will prompt further qualitative and quantitative investigation into the potential cause of this voluntary turnover; and maternity is a leading indicator of voluntary turnover (ie it precedes, and correlates with, voluntary turnover), so it can be used to both predict turnover changes and enable the organization to create an intervention to reduce that voluntary turnover. This is the step that shifts us from descriptive analytics, a statement of where we are, to diagnostic analytics, a statement of why we are.

Summary

Field Marshal Viscount Montgomery, commander of allied ground forces in Normandy during the Second World War, said, 'The raw material of any business is… [people], whether it be soldiering or industry. To succeed, a proper understanding of human nature is essential – whether you want to win battles or have an efficient factory' (Montgomery, 1961). It is the workforce that makes the organization. Once we understand the context of the organization, we must understand the workforce itself and prioritize areas to conduct workforce planning. Data is an essential component of analysing the workforce, but we do not need to wait for perfect data. What matters is that we do what we can to better understand our workforce.

> Know the enemy and know yourself; in a hundred battles you will never be in peril. When you are ignorant of the enemy but know yourself, your chances of winning and losing are equal. If ignorant of both your enemy and yourself, you are certain in every battle to be in peril (Sun Tzu, 1969).

When you practise workforce planning, ask yourself:

- What data do I need to understand my workforce?
- Where is the data and how do I access it?
- How do I make sense of the data?
- What is the quality and reliability of the data?
- What assumptions am I making about the data?
- Which elements of the workforce am I focusing on?
- Where is that workforce and how does it fit into the wider workforce?
- What facets do they have that make them important to consider at this time?

References

Aristotle (1980) *The Nicomachean Ethics*, Oxford University Press, Oxford

Bechet, T P (2008) *Strategic Staffing: A practical toolkit for effective workforce planning*, 2nd edn, AMACOM, New York

Becker, B, Huselid, M and Beatty, D (2009) *The Differentiated Workforce*, Harvard Business Press, Boston

Becker, G S (1964) *Human Capital*, Columbia University Press, New York

Bersin, J (2019) Are we really getting value from all the HR software we buy? [Blog] *JoshBersin.com*, https://joshbersin.com/2019/07/are-we-really-getting-value-from-all-the-hr-software-we-buy/ (archived at https://perma.cc/D9US-XEBZ)

Bock, L (1995) *Work Rules!* John Murray, London

Boudreau, J (2010) *Retooling HR: Using proven business tools to make better decisions about talent*, Harvard Business School Publishing, Boston

Drucker, P F (1985) *The Effective Executive*, HarperCollins, New York

Float Like a Butterfly, Sting Like a Bee (1969) [Documentary] William Klein: USA

Guenole, N, Ferrar, J and Feinzig, S (2017) *The Power of People*, Pearson, London

Hinrichs, J R (1972) Implications of the computer for personnel research, in E H Burack and J W Walker (eds) *Manpower Planning and Programming*, Allyn & Bacon, Boston

Huselid, M A, Becker, B E and Beatty, R W (2005) *The Workforce Scorecard: Managing human capital to execute strategy*, Harvard Business School Press, Boston

Ishikawa, K (1986) *Guide to Quality Control*, Asian Productivity Organization, Tokyo

Korzybski, A (1933) *Science and Sanity: An introduction to non-Aristotelian systems and general semantics*, International Non-Aristotelian Library Publishing Company, New Jersey

Lepak, D P and Snell, S A (1999) The human resource architecture: Toward a theory of human capital allocation and development, *The Academy of Management Review*, 24 (1), pp 31–48, http://citeseerx.ist.psu.edu/viewdoc/download;jscssionid=D5C8E5DF0DD496B2AA84FE07F0196FD2?doi=10.1.1.469.8661&rep=rep1&type=pdf (archived at https://perma.cc/3HJP-F94F)

Lepak, D P and Snell, S A (2002) Examining the human resource architecture: The relationships among human capital, employment, and human resource configurations, *Journal of Management*, 28 (4), pp 517–43, doi.org/10.1177/014920630202800403 (archived at https://perma.cc/M7FC-5DFN)

Lewis, M (2003) *Moneyball: The art of winning an unfair game*, W W Norton & Company, New York

Montgomery, B L (1961) *The Path to Leadership*, Collins, London

Pareto, V (1906) *Manual of Political Economy*, 2014 reprint, Oxford University Press, Oxford

Shapiro, J and Davenport, T H (2013) The rise of talent analytics, in D L Ward and R Tripp (eds) *Positioned: Strategic workforce planning the gets the right person in the right job*, AMACOM, New York

Sun, T ed (1969) *The Art of War*, Oxford University Press, Oxford

UKEAT (UK Employment Appeal Tribunal) (2014) *Bear Scotland Ltd and others vs Mr David Fulton and others*, https://assets.publishing.service.gov.uk/media/592ee0b4ed915d20fb00012c/Bear_Scotland_Ltd_and_Others_v_Mr_David_Fulton_and_Others_UKEATS_0047_13_BI.pdf (archived at https://perma.cc/T5CC-DCH9)

Walker, J W (1972) Forecasting manpower needs, in E H Burack and J W Walker (eds) *Manpower Planning and Programming*, Allyn & Bacon, Boston

Walker, J W (1992) *Human Resource Strategy*, McGraw-Hill, New York

Welch, J (2001) *Jack: Straight from the gut*, Warner Books, New York

07

Gaining buy-in

Introduction

John Donne, the 17th-century poet and cleric, wrote: 'No man is an island, entire of itself; every man is a piece of the continent, a part of the main.'

It is a concept that has been consistently demonstrated by armies throughout history. The Stele of the Vultures, unearthed in Iraq in the 19th century, dates back to 2500 BC and the victory of King Eannatum of Lagash; it depicts Sumerian infantry in the earliest known example of a shield wall (Winter, 1985). The phalanx, interlocking shields to create a shield wall, turns a collection of individual soldiers into a single impenetrable unit. The success of military formations employing the phalanx, such as the Persian sparabara and the Greek hoplite, rested on the shared understanding of what each of them would do. Stakeholders are 'those who depend on the organization for the realization of some of their goal, and in turn, the organization depends on them in some way for the full realization of its goals' (Mitroff and Mason, 1980). It describes perfectly the relationship within the phalanx where the shield would provide protection to a neighbour as well as to the individual.

In what is called intelligence preparation of the battlespace (IPB), modern militaries continue this tradition of understanding those around them. In modern conflict, the stakeholders include not only those forces operating in a coalition, but also the raft of state and civilian actors as well as the population at large. When conducting operations amongst the people, my own success rested heavily upon recognizing those stakeholder groups and conducting key leader engagement (KLE). Hollywood fails to depict that enduring successes in modern conflict often come down to building relationships over a cup of hot chai.

The same is true in the workplace and engaging with stakeholders is a key component of the baselining process. We will have engaged with stakeholders already as part of analysing the strategic context and understanding the workforce. Now, engagement with those stakeholders will be essential in successfully launching workforce planning beyond the baseline. If this is our first attempt at workforce planning, those stakeholders will provide us with the green light. For all of those engaged in workforce planning, this final stage is essential in agreeing the terms of reference for the exercise.

How are decisions made?

In the same way that we look first at the organization in order to create a basis for environmental scanning, so too do we look first at decision making as a basis for stakeholder analysis. For many organizations, they may not recognize how decisions are made. Not only is there likely to be inconsistency in how decisions are made by comparable departments at the meso level, indeed the same types of decisions may be taken in different ways within the same business area. To help clarify decision accountability, Bain and Company created RAPID®, a tool that assigns owners to the five key roles in any decision: recommend, agree, perform, input and decide (Bain, 2011). In the process of making a decision, someone will *recommend* a decision or action; ideally that is us as someone conducting workforce planning. Next are those who provide *input* to that recommendation. In our context this may be through consultation with the workforce planning team prior to the recommendation or later, with stakeholders, following the recommendation. A key concept here is that the view of those providing input may or may not be reflected in the final proposal. If workforce planning is new to our organization, it might be the case that we are providing input to a recommendation made by a senior stakeholder like a chief human resources officer. The recommendation is provided to someone who makes the *decision* and has the authority to commit the organization to action: this is the key stakeholder. Important stakeholders will also be those who have to formally *agree* a decision and their view must be reflected in final proposals. Our operating model will have a significant part to play in determining those who must formally agree: a hierarchical model may have a limited number of stakeholders who need to formally agree, whereas a partnership model may require a significant number of stakeholders to reach a consensus before agreement is reached. Finally, there are those who will *perform* the action once a decision is made.

Not only will the stakeholders in this matrix differ depending on the nature of the decision (eg is it about recruitment or learning), but there may also be tolerances within a scheme of delegation that will allow certain stakeholders to take decisions up to a particular level of cost. Just like in the example below, we will need a broad understanding of the matrix in relation to changes to major workforce operations. Figure 7.1 relates to a recommendation to change the training delivered to employees.

FIGURE 7.1   Example of RAPID® matrix for training change

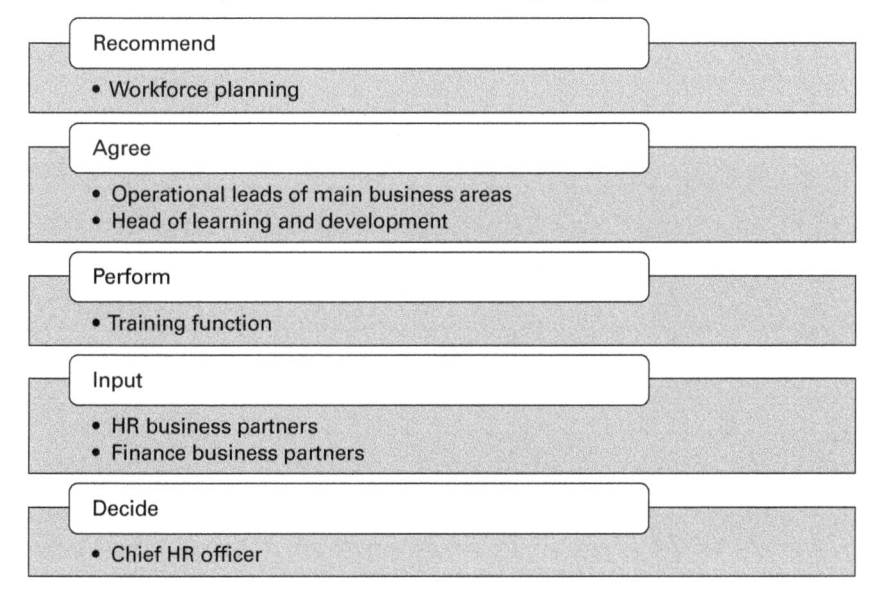

Recommend
- Workforce planning

Agree
- Operational leads of main business areas
- Head of learning and development

Perform
- Training function

Input
- HR business partners
- Finance business partners

Decide
- Chief HR officer

SOURCE Adapted from Bain and Company (2011)

Stakeholder mapping

Following the use of RAPID® to identify some of our stakeholders, we will build on that with a stakeholder map. There are a multiplicity of tools available for stakeholder mapping; during the baselining stage we will focus on just one. Aubrey Mendelow, thinker on management and information systems, created a two-by-two matrix of power and dynamism as a method to support environmental scanning (Mendelow, 1981). Power is an important axis in the model; whilst we tend to recognize stakeholders with power it is important to understand the sources of power in order to be able to compare it against other stakeholders. Power gives stakeholders the ability

FIGURE 7.2 Power vs interest stakeholder map

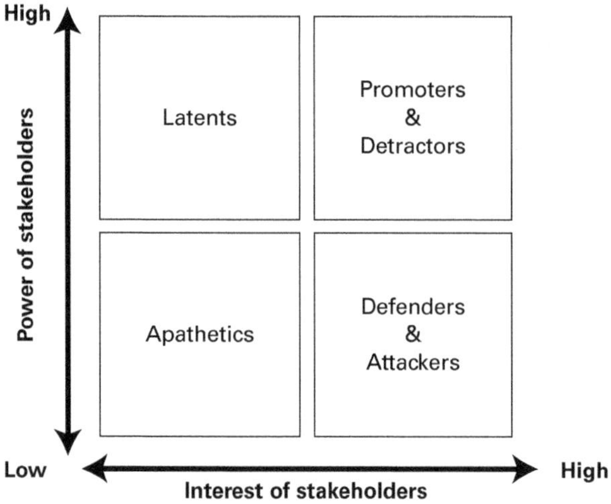

	Low interest	High interest
High power	Latents	Promoters & Detractors
Low power	Apathetics	Defenders & Attackers

SOURCE Adapted from Mendelow (1981)

to restructure situations (Macmillan, 1978) and can arise in four key ways: possession of resources, ability to dictate alternatives, authority, and influence.

Possession of resources provides a significant power base, hence the enduring power of unions in certain industries. Aligned to this possession is the ability to dictate alternatives; the availability of substitute resources reduces the power of the possessor, equally the sole supplier has the greatest of power. A great example is the accidental specialists discussed in Chapter 6; the lack of alternatives provides them with significant power in negotiating pay and conditions. Authority, the right to enforce obedience, has always remained an important source of power. This could be in the form of government and regulatory bodies, but it is equally found in the bureaucracy of organizations in their ability to hire, pay and dismiss workers. The final source of power is influence, the ability to sway those who hold power in other ways. By considering stakeholders on the basis of power, we see them in line with Freeman's stakeholder theory that stakeholders are more than simply the business owners (Freeman, 1984).

Rather than the second axis of dynamism, Mendelow's matrix is adapted to include interest, to create four specific groups: apathetics, latents, defenders with attackers, and promoters with detractors. Apathetics have both low power and low interest, and are those who can be engaged usually through general communications. Latents have low interest but high power, therefore it is essential their needs are met. With this group it is important to engage and consult on areas where they are specifically interested and aim to increase their positive interest. Equally, with activities likely to easily stir angst, it may be more prudent to downplay initiative to reduce the risk of creating attackers. Attackers have low power but high and negative interest; they fall into the same quadrant as defenders, who share low power but have a high positive interest. Defenders are potential supporters and ambassadors. If engaged in the right way, they can be a useful area with which to both consult and potentially involve in low-risk areas. Attackers can reduce the ability of defenders and attract apathetics to their cause, therefore defenders become valuable as ambassadors to neutralize negative opinions. Promoters and detractors are our key stakeholders and are where we need to focus our efforts. Both have high interest and power, but promoters are supportive and detractors are negative. Not only must they be engaged and consulted regularly, but they need to be involved (if they are not already) in the governance and decision making. The aim is to keep promoters onside and to either convert detractors into positivity, or otherwise neutralize them either through the use of promoters or through creating a groundswell by converting latents.

Engaging with stakeholders

The key challenge to overcome at this stage is to convince a stakeholder to let us provide a firm evidence base from which decisions around the workforce can be made. Niccolò Machiavelli said famously that 'Men nearly always follow the tracks made by others and proceed in their affairs by imitation, even though they cannot entirely keep to the tracks of others or emulate the prowess of their models' (1513). The tendency is for stakeholders to favour particular initiatives or courses of action before the evidence is presented or the problem understood fully, a tendency that will be based heavily on cognitive biases. The four main biases we are aiming to overcome are *anchoring, attribute substitution*, the *availability heuristic*, and *pro-innovation bias*. Anchoring is a concept where people depend too heavily on an initial piece of information when making a decision (Sherif *et al*, 1958). If we arrange a meeting with a stakeholder to discuss workforce planning and one of the first things we mention is diversity, then the meeting may well anchor to that specific factor. Attribute substitution is where the complexity of the situation is substituted for a heuristic, either the anchor or some other factor, and then judgement is made based on that substitute (Kahneman and Frederick, 2002). For example, a stakeholder may focus on a specific factor of workforce diversity, like gender balance in the executive board, as a heuristic for the wider challenge of improving the diversity of the workforce. The availability heuristic is a mental shortcut where examples that a stakeholder can recall are viewed more strongly than alternatives (Tversky and Kahneman, 1983). Stakeholders will either recall initiatives that others have implemented, or ones that they themselves have implemented, and promote those. This availability heuristic may well be solidified with a pro-innovation bias, where a stakeholder has such a strong bias in favour of an initiative that they are unable to see the weaknesses or the limitations when applying it in a new situation (Sveiby *et al*, 2009).

All of these biases, either separate or together, will often result in what I call **stealing other people's artificial grass**. Stakeholders have either seen that another organization has taken a particular action, or they themselves have done it in a different organization. Some are unaware of the specific relationship between the action and the effect that is created; others are thinking that the problem the action solves is the same as the challenge they are facing. Depending on our relationship with stakeholders, we can either challenge the bias or pivot. Charlotte Brownlee, the former head of workforce planning at Public Health England, focused heavily on stakeholder engagement during her work with Sierra Leone's National Public Health Agency. She started with the *why* questions to understand what mattered to stakeholders and their areas of greatest concern. She highlighted examples of health systems in Myanmar and Kenya that had developed a more progressive approach to the way they planned their workforce and the success it generated (Brownlee, 2020). A successful pivot can acknowledge that a stakeholder's proposal might be the solution and that the workforce planning exercise can form the basis of a business case for that change. Establish with why this matters to stakeholders; acknowledge and incorporate their thoughts into our planning.

Agree terms of reference

The critical final stage is to agree the terms of reference for the next stage of workforce planning. If we are a well-established workforce planning function, we may have a green light from key stakeholders to continue through to the action plan and possibly to deliver within certain tolerances. If this is a new function, then this stage may simply focus on gaining agreement to proceed to the next stages of supply, demand and gap analysis. Regardless of the aim, it is critical that we have clear agreement from key stakeholders on the following areas.

Organizational levels

Firstly, we need to agree the level of the organization on which we will be conducting workforce planning. The power of our stakeholder is a key determining factor: we will be unable to operate effectively at the macro level if the power of our stakeholder is limited to the meso level. If we are operating at the meso level, be specific around functions and departments.

Roles of interest

In agreeing the organizational levels, we will also need agreement on the roles of interest in this exercise. Be clear around the rationale for those roles: the cohorts need to be of sufficient size that an exercise in workforce planning would be able to achieve a return on the investment of time.

Workforce analytics

Having agreed the roles of interest, we also need to agree the workforce analytics. Crucially, this must include the *counting rules*: the characteristics that determine those who are in or out of scope. These counting rules may relate to the exclusion of contractors or the inclusion of those on secondment. Agree the broad approaches to how we will model and forecast both supply and demand, which we will cover in the next two parts of the book. The importance of this is to avoid surprises at a later point in time; we do not want to be discussing the forecast further down the line and a key stakeholder have a fundamental disagreement with our model.

Horizons

Next, we will need to agree the planning horizon. If this is a new venture, then planning at a minimum of horizon two (the next budgetary year) must be the minimum time period. In my experience, planning in an organization with a low maturity in workforce planning can be slow. Therefore, planning in horizon one may take longer to get to execution than the timeframe of the forecast. As organizational maturity grows, our speed to conduct a workforce planning cycle will increase and allow us to deal with a shorter timeframe. If we are looking at planning in horizon three for the first time, then it is wise counsel to set the limit where are we are able to forecast with an accuracy of plus or minus 20 per cent (Ansoff, 1965).

Scenarios

Finally, we will need to agree the scenarios. Scenarios are a qualitative explanation of how the present might evolve to the future and the plausible variations of that future (Schnaars, 1990). We first broached the subject in Chapter 3 when we talked about the principles of *three-point estimation* or *programme evaluation and review technique* (PERT) (Department of the Navy, 1958): planning for the most likely scenario; preparing for the best-case scenario; and pre-empting the worst-case scenario. It is important to appreciate that 'scenarios are not about predicting the future, rather they are about perceiving futures in the present' (Schwartz, 1991). Therefore, the basis of these scenarios will be the strategic alignment, environmental scanning and understanding of the workforce that we have already conducted within the context of the planning horizon we have agreed. Firstly, what is the organization planning to do: does it plan to grow or maintain its revenue, and is it planning to improve in a different metric (brand advocacy or sustainability, for example)? A consideration at this stage is if the organization already has specific strategies or plans in place that relate directly to the workforce: is there already a commitment to close a workplace or to outsource work? Finally, we consider the future on the basis of the environmental scanning, what Porter calls 'macroscenarios' (1985). Firstly, what do we anticipate might happen in the future regarding our business and what is the likelihood of those events? For example, how attractive do we expect our industry to be and are we vulnerable to disruptive technologies? Secondly, do we anticipate any significant changes that will impact our workforce and what is the likelihood of those events? For example, a political change that could impact the flow of migrant workers.

> Scenarios deal with two worlds: the world of facts and the world of perceptions. They explore for facts but they aim at perceptions inside the heads of decision makers. Their purpose is to gather and transform information of strategic significance into fresh perceptions. This transformation process is not trivial – more often than not it does not happen. When it works, it is a creative

experience that generates a heartfelt *Aha* from your managers and leads to strategic insights beyond the mind's previous reach (Wack, 1985).

Remember that as the length of the planning horizon increases, so too do both the uncertainty of the future and the ambiguity of scenarios. As a result, I recommend adherence to the following 'shirt sleeve' guidelines (Linneman and Kennell, 1990):

- delete variables with both a low probability of occurrence and a low potential impact;
- focus on events likely to have an impact throughout the planning horizon rather than on events that could take place towards the very end of the planning horizon;
- do not include outlier events that would result in total disaster in any given scenario, such as a major nuclear war;
- aggregate multiple factors that contribute towards the same outcome, such as the factors impacting economic growth;
- check for interdependencies and remove dependent variables.

CASE STUDY
MyoKardia

MyoKardia is a biotechnology company that conducted strategic workforce planning as they shifted towards approval by the US Food and Drug Administration (FDA) and the launch of their first therapy. Conscious that they had to anticipate several different possibilities of the future, they conducted scenario planning with the executive team in order to establish the potential forces that could impact the company's future. The start point was to ensure there was a consistent and clear view of the strategic alignment before they focused on the critical areas of uncertainty that could create dramatic disruption within the following five years. Executives were asked searching and open-ended questions about their own perspective on disruptive forces and their optimistic and pessimistic views of the future. They established six critical uncertainties and were able to discount four: one was unlikely to change within the planning horizon, two were contributing factors of another uncertainty, and 'one did not have enough assumed variation to be meaningful in this exercise'. The two remaining forces of change, alliance partnerships and the outcomes of clinical trials, were translated into four scenarios. The executive agreed the most likely scenario and planned on that basis, ensuring they were tracking key metrics on the assumptions they had made (Goldberg and Boyes, 2019).

Summary

Moving beyond ideas and onto execution is a common challenge in the traditional approach to strategic workforce planning. Without buy-in from stakeholders, workforce planning is unable to get as far as ideas, let alone execution. It is critical that we understand who our stakeholders are and recognize them as people in whom we have a vested interest, just as they have a vested interest in us. We need to ensure we have a clear understanding of the nature of power amongst our stakeholders and, where possible, use the interdependencies between stakeholders as leverage in gaining buy-in. HR business partners, for example, can be a fantastic ally if they have influence over other key stakeholders. That allows us to bring them onside to be our advocates with their respective operational areas.

When you practise workforce planning, ask yourself:

- Who are the stakeholders in my organization that I need to consider?
- How do I need to engage and give consideration to them?
- Who are my key stakeholders?
- Do I have agreement from them on how I will proceed?

References

Ansoff, H I (1965) *Corporate Strategy*, McGraw-Hill, New York

Bain and Company (2011) RAPID®: Bain's tool to clarify decision accountability, 11 August, www.bain.com/insights/rapid-tool-to-clarify-decision-accountability (archived at https://perma.cc/PE4E-SGFN)

Brownlee, C (2020) Interview by Telephone, 11 May

Department of the Navy (1958) Program Evaluation Research Task: Summary report phase 1 (July), apps.dtic.mil/dtic/tr/fulltext/u2/735902.pdf

Freeman, R R (1984) *Strategic Management: A stakeholder approach*, Pitman, London

Goldberg, E and Boyes, I (2019) Using scenario planning to facilitate agility in strategic workforce planning, *People & Strategy*, **42** (4), pp 56–61, https://www.questia.com/magazine/1G1-604847455/using-scenario-planning-to-facilitate-agility-in-strategic (archived at https://perma.cc/C7SX-HGHQ)

Kahneman, D and Frederick, S (2002) Representativeness revisited: Attribute substitution in intuitive judgment, in T Gilovich, D Griffin and D Kahneman (eds) *Heuristics and Biases: The psychology of intuitive judgment*, Cambridge University Press, Cambridge, pp 49–81

Linneman, R E and Kennell, J D (1990) Shirt-sleeve approach to long-range plans, in R G Dyson (ed) *Strategic Planning: Models and analytical techniques*, John Wiley & Sons, Chichester

Machiavelli, N (1513) *The Prince*, 1995 reprint, Penguin, London

Macmillan, I C (1978) *Strategy Formulation: Political concepts*, West Publishing, St Paul

Mendelow, A L (1981) Environmental scanning: The impact of the stakeholder concept, ICIS Proceedings, Cambridge, pdfs.semanticscholar.org/3579/ca37344c69961bbc2468ef9addf212200e39.pdf (archived at https://perma.cc/EL53-XC38)

Mitroff A A and Mason, R O (1980) A logic for strategic management, *Human Management Systems*, **1** (1), pp 115–26

Porter, M E (1985) *Competitive Advantage: Creating and sustaining superior performance*, The Free Press, New York

Schnaars, S P (1990) How to develop and use scenarios, in R G Dyson (ed) *Strategic Planning: Models and analytical techniques*, John Wiley & Sons, Chichester

Schwartz, P (1991) *The Art of the Long View*, Doubleday, New York

Sherif, M, Taub, D and Hovland, C I (1958) Assimilation and contrast effects of anchoring stimuli on judgements, *Journal of Experimental Psychology*, **55** (2), pp 150–55, pdfs.semanticscholar.org/fc86/ccdd952b695f3cb3970f9d38775985336512.pdf?_ga=2.116349199.841692985.1575129996-252483930.1575129996 (archived at https://perma.cc/QH7C-4YQ8)

Sveiby, K-E et al (2009) Unintended and undesirable consequences of innovation, Presented at XX ISPIM Conference: The Future of Innovation, Vienna (June), web.archive.org/web/20111008064811/http://sveiby.com/articles/UnintendedconsequencesISPIMfinal.pdf (archived at https://perma.cc/P6PP-DD65)

Tversky, A and Kahneman, D (1983) Extensional versus intuitive reasoning: The conjunction fallacy in probability judgement, *Psychological Review*, **90** (4), psy2.ucsd.edu/~mckenzie/TverskyKahneman1983PsychRev.pdf (archived at https://perma.cc/YLT6-FKLB)

Wack, P (1985) Scenarios: Shooting the rapids, *Harvard Business Review*, November, hbr.org/1985/11/scenarios-shooting-the-rapids (archived at https://perma.cc/H6GT-W5EG)

Winter, I J (1985) After the battle is over: The Stele of the Vultures and the beginning of historical narrative in the art of the ancient near east, in H L Kessler and M S Simpson (eds) *Pictorial Narrative in Antiquity and the Middle Ages*, Center for Advanced Study in the Visual Arts Symposium, 4 (16), pp 11–32

PART THREE

Supply

What are the historical workforce trends and what is the forecast for the future?

08

Understanding workforce evolution

Introduction

The natural world around us is one of wonder. On one axis, the land stretches from the South Pole in Antarctica to the northern tip of Kaffeklubben Island in Greenland; on the other axis, from Attu Island in Alaska to Caroline Island in Kiribati. The elevations range from the highest point of Mount Everest in the Himalayas, to the Challenger Deep in the depths of the Mariana Trench in the western Pacific Ocean. When we look around, the world appears to remain static; yet it is gradually changing, both through natural and human events. It is only in hindsight that we can truly recognize the impact of this change, be it the erosion of a coastal region or the steady urbanization of an area. As the saying goes, often misattributed to C S Lewis, 'Isn't it funny how day by day nothing changes, but when you look back everything is different.' Yet, this is often overlooked by business leaders who frequently consider their workforce as a static capability. It is essential to recognize that what has been recruited is not what we have; an almost imperceptible change results in an evolution of that workforce. The supply part of the process focuses on the factor of production that is labour: what workforce do we have, and will we have, to service organizational demand? In this chapter, we will look closely into this workforce evolution in order to be able to forecast that workforce in the future as part of our planning.

Organizational churn

Much about modern organizations makes them almost unrecognizable in comparison to those of the last century. That said, the basis of organizational churn remains mostly unchanged. To some, the word churn is used interchangeably with concepts such as turnover and attrition; in reality, they are subsets within churn. Organizational churn is the movement of the workforce in, around, and out of the organization.

In the late 1960s, MIT Professor Mason Haire declared that the shifts for a worker were limited to people moving into the organization from outside, people moving out of the organization, people moving up and people moving laterally to an equivalent job. He also accepted that, in some cases, people would move down or be demoted (Haire, 1967). Haire's model of organizational churn can be seen in Figure 8.1. In this chapter we will cover each of these as turnover (inside to outside), recruitment (outside to inside), and internal mobility (up, lateral and down). In addition, Haire recognized that 'some people may change their behaviour and potential' (Haire, 1967). We will consider this as a factor impacting the propensity of a worker to move to a different state.

FIGURE 8.1 The organizational churn model

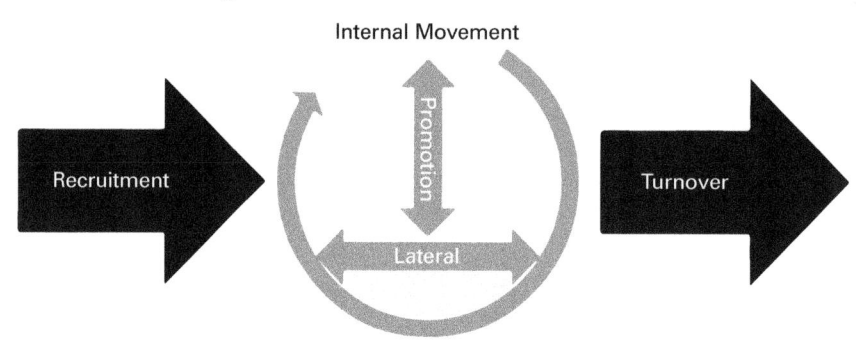

Turnover

The universal truth of the workforce is that, over time, workers will leave the organization. There are finite ways for a worker to leave an organization: resignation, dismissal, mutual severance, end of contract, retirement, and death in service. Resignation is where the worker chooses to terminate a contract of employment. Dismissal is the opposite of resignation, where the organization chooses to terminate a contract of employment. Dismissal requires cause in most jurisdictions; typically this cause is poor performance of the individual or layoffs where the organization is getting rid of roles and is either unable or unwilling to accommodate a worker elsewhere. Mutual severance is a hybrid of resignation and dismissal, where both the worker and the organization agree to sever the contract of employment. It tends to be typified by a disbursement from the organization, hence the term severance pay. Mutual severance is often found in what is termed voluntary redundancy, where layoffs are announced, and a worker volunteers for this offer. It is also found where an organization may wish to dismiss a worker, but either lacks cause (or sufficient evidence of cause) or the worker has leverage (consider employees who have witnessed impropriety and leave with a payoff and a non-disclosure agreement). Despite the term *mutual*, the initiator is typically the organization. End of contract most often relates to temporary workers who are employed on a contract basis. An organization may have the ability to either renew or extend a contract and may choose not to (or a worker may choose to reject the offer of an extension or renewal), and that circumstance would be a revision of an agreement with a specified end date. This categorization can also apply to workers who would be considered permanent, such as the military, who will have specified engagement durations to either compulsory or voluntary active service. The retirement categorization is multi-faceted and can have hallmarks of resignation, mutual severance or end of contract, but differentiated by provisions that allow access to pension benefits. The main type of retirement is age-related; in many countries, such retirement was mandatory at a *retirement age* but has since become a voluntary choice for many workers with the proliferation of legislation against age-based discrimination. Even where such legislation exists, certain professions may still have mandatory retirement; these are often military, law enforcement and airline pilots. Ill-health can often result in retirement if it is sufficiently chronic to warrant access to pension benefits, otherwise ill-health may lead to mutual severance instead.

Recruitment

Recruitment is a catch-all term that covers the myriad ways that a worker may join an organization. It is an activity that results from one of two causes: firstly, a vacancy in an existing base of supply that occurs when the incumbent leaves a role either through turnover or internal mobility; secondly, a new demand that results in the creation of a new role.

Internal movement

Internal movement is a change in either a worker's role or their position within the organizational structure and is either vertical or horizontal.

Vertical movements are promotions and demotions. A promotion is a movement to a role of greater seniority and may involve an application for a more senior role and/or an organization-wide process to determine a cohort for promotion. A demotion, on the other hand, is a movement to a more junior role and likely triggered by the underperformance of a worker. Two further common types of demotion are as a result of a role being made redundant and a worker choosing to accept a more junior, and usually lower-paying, role as an alternative to a layoff. The final type is usually driven by a change in personal circumstances, for example a desire to spend more time with the family. By moving to a more junior role, a worker may perhaps reduce their overseas travel commitments or otherwise achieve a less demanding schedule. Common instances of this may be an element of partial retirement, where a worker at retirement age takes a step back from a senior role but remains in the organization. Horizontal, or lateral, movement takes place where a worker takes a role of similar seniority in a different part of the organization. This is typical when applying for a vacancy in another part of the organization, but may also result from a restructuring exercise, for example the closure of a department and the redeployment of workers to another department.

Modelling and forecasting

The impact of turnover, recruitment and internal movement are plotted against the baseline of the workforce that we created in Chapter 6. As we create the models for our respective workforce segments, it will be helpful if you are able to compare these against the macro levels for the organization and comparator groups. For example, if we were looking specifically at the female segment it will be helpful to compare their churn rates against both those of men and the average for the organization.

Recruitment and internal movement modelling

Recruitment and internal movement are organizational choices, although I appreciate that, depending on our preferences, they are either a Sophie's choice (Styron, 2004) or Kobayashi Maru (*Star Treck II*, 1982). Like those examples from popular culture, the choices to halt recruitment and internal movement are seemingly impossible. Without recruitment, the impact of turnover will gradually wither the organization; without internal movement, the rate of turnover would likely increase. On this basis, the modelling and forecasting of recruitment and internal movement are completed assuming either of two things: first, that there is no recruitment and/or internal movement; second, that the planned level of recruitment and/or internal movement is maintained. Including recruitment and internal movement at the planned rate can help articulate where the organization will go if it continues on the current trajectory. Therefore, the basis of this model would either be a continuation of the existing trends or the inclusion of a new planned level.

Modelling recruitment is straightforward in that we are adding new heads to the organization at our chosen rate:

$$\frac{\textit{Number of new workers}}{\textit{Time period}}$$

For example, 100 new workers every 30 days. Modelling internal movement is a little more complicated and I recommend a stochastic model (Merck, 1965; Dill *et al*, 1966; Vroom and MacCrimmon, 1968) due to the simplicity it can provide. At any given time, each worker has a propensity to move internally; these propensities can be seen as trends in any of our workforce segments. Assume an organization of three divisions (D_a, D_b, D_c) where we are looking at the manager segment. Managers are broken down into three levels (M_1, M_2, M_3), where level three is the highest and the next level is senior manager level 1 (SM_1). If we assume a turnover rate of 10 per cent for all grades, and that a further 4–5 per cent of senior managers move out of their roles, then an analysis of the previous 12 months might produce the transition probability matrix shown in (Table 8.1).

The column on the far left of Table 8.1 shows the distribution of workforce segments by role level and organizational division at the start of the year. The bottom row shows the distribution of workforce segments by role level and organizational division at the end of the year. Those who are managers at the start of the year, and remain in the organization, can find themselves in one of only 12 positions at the end of the year. Each cell shows the percentage of those who were in a role on the *x*-axis at the start of the year and are in a role on the *y*-axis at the end of the year. In this matrix, the majority are still in their role at the end of the year. For example, the cell D_a M_1 shows that 74 per cent of level one managers in division *a* are still in their role at the end of the year. The remainder will have either achieved promotion or moved laterally, either within their own division or to another division.

TABLE 8.1 Transition probability matrix

Distribution of segments (last year)	(this year)										
	D_aM_1	D_aM_2	D_aM_3	D_aSM_1	D_bM_1	D_bM_2	D_bM_3	D_bSM_1	D_cM_1	D_cM_2	D_cM_3	D_cSM_1
1000 $D_a M_1$	0.74	0.10	0.00	0.00	0.01	0.04	0.00	0.00	0.00	0.01	0.00	0.00
600 $D_a M_2$	0.00	0.75	0.10	0.00	0.00	0.03	0.00	0.00	0.00	0.02	0.00	0.00
400 $D_a M_3$	0.00	0.00	0.76	0.06	0.00	0.00	0.04	0.00	0.00	0.00	0.04	0.00
100 $D_a SM_1$	0.00	0.00	0.00	0.85	0.00	0.00	0.00	0.00	0.00	0.00	0.00	0.00
2000 $D_b M_1$	0.00	0.02	0.00	0.00	0.76	0.11	0.00	0.00	0.00	0.01	0.00	0.00
1000 $D_b M_2$	0.00	0.01	0.01	0.00	0.00	0.77	0.10	0.00	0.00	0.01	0.00	0.00
500 $D_b M_3$	0.00	0.00	0.03	0.00	0.00	0.00	0.81	0.06	0.00	0.00	0.00	0.00
300 $D_b SM_1$	0.00	0.00	0.00	0.00	0.00	0.00	0.00	0.85	0.00	0.00	0.00	0.00
500 $D_c M_1$	0.00	0.06	0.00	0.00	0.00	0.02	0.00	0.00	0.70	0.12	0.00	0.00
200 $D_c M_2$	0.00	0.00	0.07	0.00	0.00	0.00	0.03	0.00	0.00	0.72	0.08	0.00
100 $D_c M_3$	0.00	0.00	0.00	0.09	0.00	0.00	0.00	0.06	0.00	0.00	0.71	0.04
30 $D_c SM_1$	0.00	0.00	0.00	0.00	0.00	0.00	0.00	0.00	0.00	0.00	0.00	0.86
Distribution of segments (this year)	740	564	388	100	1540	970	490	291	350	178	83	27

Creating a model without recruitment and internal movement is the most critical version as these are controllable actions. As a result, modelling the workforce without controllable actions provides the clearest view of our workforce supply and the greatest options in terms of the action planning we will cover in Part Six of this book.

Turnover modelling

There are a variety of options for turnover modelling that trade speed and ease for accuracy. According to the standards for human capital reporting (International Organization for Standardization, 2018), the recommended calculation for the turnover rate is:

$$\frac{\text{Total number of workers leaving in the period}}{\text{Number of workers at the start of the period}} = \text{Turnover rate}$$

The benefit of this approach is that it avoids the outflow of workers being watered down by new hires. Though this approach is very effective for monthly and even quarterly reporting to support modelling for first and second horizon planning, it becomes problematic beyond then. A study of nearly a quarter of a million workers found that nearly 38 per cent of all turnover was attributable to those leaving within their first year (Mahan *et al*, 2020). This means that between the start and end of an annual reporting period, over a third of workers will both join and leave the organization. Using the ISO approach on an annual basis effectively counts the terminations of workers that are not recorded at the start. As a result, I recommend the most common method of calculation:

$$\frac{\text{Total number of workers leaving in the period}}{\text{Average number of workers in the period}} = \text{Turnover rate}$$

For a quick model, we can extrapolate the turnover trends and project them forward over the planning horizon. To increase our accuracy, particularly over a longer time period, then we need to model based on the correlations of the specific segments. Resignations are probably our largest group of exits and consistent across the workforce. The starting point lies in the existing trends and the rates of resignations for the workforce segments we are examining; this rate can serve as a baseline for resignations in the model. The same approach can also be taken with dismissals and death in service, unless there has been an outlier incident that has impacted the trend. Mutual severance and end of contract data need to be abstracted from those that result

TABLE 8.2 Retirement model

Gender	Age	Retirement Rate	Year					
			2020	2021	2022	2023	2024	2025
Male	59	5%	186					
	60	10%	164	177				
	61	20%	146	148	159			
	62	20%	139	117	118	127		
	63	10%	112	111	93	94	102	
	64	0%	85	101	100	84	85	92
	65	80%	74	85	101	100	84	85
	66	20%	44	15	17	20	20	17
	67	40%	37	35	12	14	16	16
	68	10%	10	22	21	7	8	10
	69	10%	9	9	20	19	6	7
	70	100%	2	8	8	18	17	6
Female	59	10%	90					
	60	60%	63	81				
	61	40%	34	25	32			
	62	60%	18	20	15	19		
	63	80%	12	7	8	6	8	
	64	100%	4	2	1	2	1	2

from redundancies, restructures and layoffs. That will calibrate the figures to account for a normal base of workforce performance. The modelling of retirement requires a different approach as, with the exception of ill-health retirement, it is a choice tied to the characteristic of age. To ensure an accurate approach, it is important to segment those workers by age and gender to understand the retirement rates at a more granular level. By applying those rates to the baseline workforce over time, an accurate forecast can be made.

In the model in Table 8.2, we have taken an example workforce from above the age of 59, split by male and female. In this example, we have taken the average retirement rate for the previous 24 months and will use that as the indicative rate for the model. On average, 5 per cent of males have retired at age 59; we apply that rate to the 186 males aged 59 in 2020, which provides a forecast of 177 males aged 60 in 2021. That group of 60-year-olds is subject to the 10 per cent average retirement rate, which results in a forecast of 159 males aged 61 in 2022.

The impact of megatrends

In a model that abstracts recruitment, the end result is a forecast of a workforce that reduces over time through turnover. The basis of all the models we have discussed is the existing internal workforce trends. However, we need to overlay this with the impact of megatrends on the demography of the labour market. Megatrends are the sustained macroeconomic forces that shape our world and our future; many of these are increasingly global in nature, such as climate change. 'The truly important events on the outside are not the trends. They are the changes in the trends' (Drucker, 1985). These trends do exist, have existed and will continue to exist: megatrends are the changes in the trend. The environmental scanning we conducted will have identified many of the external factors that will also impact the evolution of our workforce.

The effects of migration

Migration changes the size and shape of the labour supply. The impacts of migration on labour market demography depend on both the competencies of migrants and existing workers in addition to the characteristics of the home and host economies. Where immigration increases the supply of existing competencies, this can increase competition and reduce wages for existing workers in the short term (Borjas, 1995). Where immigration brings new competencies into the labour market, this can lead to economic growth through the provision of new or a higher number of goods and services (Dustman et al, 2005). The reverse can be true with emigration, with a critical issue being brain drain, the loss of high levels of competency from developing countries (Docquier et al, 2007). The most recent megatrends in the West are the increases in nationalist voting, which correlated with preceding increases in low-competency immigration (Moriconi et al, 2018). The years since the 2016 referendum on Brexit and the exit of the UK from membership of the EU, have seen a reduction in net migration from the EU to the UK whilst non-EU net migration to the UK has continued to grow since 2013 (Office for National Statistics, 2019). Meanwhile, since the election of Donald Trump in 2016, migration to the United States has slowed to its lowest level since 2008 (Tavernise, 2019). This has translated into a marked decrease in the movement of skilled labour between markets since 2015 (PwC, 2020).

The multigenerational workforce

Age demographics are a slow-moving trend, notwithstanding the impact of migration at a national level. Since the turn of the millennium, we have seen the fastest rise in global life expectancy since the 1960s, reversing declines in the 1990s that related heavily to the AIDS epidemic in Africa and the impact in Eastern Europe of the collapse of the Soviet Union (World Health Organization, 2018). If the predictions of biomedical gerontologist Aubrey de Grey are correct, the first person who will live to see 150 years of age has already been born (Kelland, 2011). Factors such as legislation to combat age discrimination, including the removal of mandatory retirement, combined with increases in life expectancy and the overall health of the population are translating into longer working lives. For the first time in western history, we are now seeing five generations in the workforce: the silent generation, baby-boomers, generation X, generation Y and generation Z (Dimock, 2019). Traditionalists, also known as the silent generation, were born between 1925 and 1945. Those who continue to play a part in the workplace were certainly shaped by the Second World War and the later Korean War. Baby-boomers, born between 1946 and 1964, were characterized by a commensurate surge in the birth rate. They were shaped by the Cold War, the assassinations of President John F Kennedy Jr and Martin Luther King Jr, the space race, the Vietnam war and the civil rights movement. Generation X was born between 1965 and 1980, a demarcation that places me in the last of the gen X and my slightly younger sister as generation Y, the millennials born between 1981 and 1996. Generation X saw both a decline in birth rates and an increase in migration, which has increased the diversity of this cohort (Markert, 2004). They were shaped by the politics of Ronald Regan and Margaret Thatcher, and the Soviet policies of perestroika and glasnost and the subsequent collapse of the Soviet Union. They were later shaped by the events of 9/11 and the subsequent War on Terror.. In the United States, this was the generation impacted by reduced state spending on social care and a rising cost of tertiary education. Millennials were born during the rise of the information age and an increase in globalization; the eldest group was shaped significantly by the wars in both Afghanistan and Iraq, and the impact of the 2008 financial crisis during their formative years in the workplace. Generation Z, born between 1997 and 2012, mark the most recent generation to enter the workplace. They are the first cohort to have had the internet readily available since their early years and are viewed as digital natives (Prensky, 2001). I expect this group will be shaped heavily by the impact of the COVID-19 pandemic as a result of losing their first job, disruption to their education and the resulting repercussions of social distancing and lockdown. Those born after 2012, who I expect will become known as generation Alpha, will start to join the workforce around the turn of 2030 when the eldest of the baby boomers will turn 85. There are certainly generational differences that have been shaped by political, economic and social factors; it is clear that these differences have been somewhat overstated (Becton el al, 2014). The biggest factor is that, even if based solely on their respective stages of life, these different generations will want and need different things from the workplace. Moreover, the fluctuations in birth rates mean that older people will account for around a quarter of the workforce in the 2020s, skewing the wants and needs in a significant degree towards the older workforce for the first time.

The changing concept of the worker

The concept of a worker has certainly evolved since the archetype of an employee. Organizations are increasingly utilizing labour from outside their pool of permanent workers in order to access key capabilities. Management consulting is 'an advisory service contracted for and provided to organizations by specially trained and qualified persons who assist, in an objective and independent manner, the client organization to identify management problems, analyse such problems, and help, when requested, in the implementation of solutions' (Greiner and Metzger, 1983). The global management consulting market is forecast to grow to US $350 billion in 2025, from around $250 billion in 2015 (Mazareanu, 2019). The gig economy is that part of the labour market characterized by freelance work or short-term contracts. Fifty-seven million Americans freelanced in 2019, an increase from 53 million in 2014, which generated an income of nearly $1 trillion (Upwork, 2019). The ubiquity of Uber is just one example of the growth of the gig economy. In 2019 it reported 99 million monthly active users globally, an increase on 76 million the previous year (Sage and Sharma, 2019). The growth in drivers is largely down to the fact that it accommodates those who wish to work alongside a permanent job elsewhere or other commitments. The self-employed are those who work exclusively for themselves, so this incorporates some of the freelance industry. Rates of self-employment in the West are much higher for older workers than for younger workers; indeed the financial crisis triggered a decade-long spike in self-employment in the UK amongst those who are over 65 (Office for National Statistics, 2018; Hipple and Hammond, 2016; Eurostat, 2019).

The talent shortage

'Arguably, one of the greatest threats facing organizations today is the talent shortage' (LaPrade *et al*, 2019). Talent shortage, or the skills gap, is the global problem of an insufficient number of workers with the competencies required to create the capabilities that organizations need. One report suggests that organizations in the UK are spending £4.4 billion a year as a result of increased recruitment costs, inflated salaries, temporary staffing and training (Open University, 2019). Projecting this through to 2029, employers in the United States are expected to face significant shortages of workers with tertiary education, leading to nearly $1.2 trillion in lost economic output (AAF, 2019). By 2030, the global demand for talent will outstrip supply, resulting in a talent shortage of over 85 million people and translating into $8.5 trillion in unrealized revenue (Korn Ferry, 2018).

This talent shortage results from three key trends, which are being compounded by demographic shifts. The first trend is the declining supply of traditional competencies, those with a long half-life, particularly in so-called blue-collar industries such as construction. Heavy industry and manufacturing have seen a steady decline in younger workers entering this field: 35 per cent of employed 18- to 24-year-olds in the United States held a blue-collar job in 1980 but by 2010 that figure had nearly halved to 19 per cent (Carnevale *et al*, 2013). This decline is certainly influenced by stigmatization of these industries as a sub-optimal career choice (IndustryWeek, 2016). This decline is certainly a contributing factor in the retention of older workers, with decades of experience in these industries, who have been able to command increasing levels of pay as a result. It is also contributing, perversely, to comparatively higher levels of youth unemployment (Ahn *et al*, 2019). A survey of 7,000 young people in the UK found a three-fold disconnect between their career aspirations and the employment market in over half of economic sectors, extending to a five-fold gap in the fields of art, culture, entertainment and sport (Rogers *et al*, 2020).

The second trend is the rapid development of new skills in the marketplace, those with a shorter half-life, where growth in demand quickly outstrips the available supply. The pace of change is being accelerated by four specific technological advances: the increasing use of automation, the expanding analytical effect of big data, the development of cloud technology, and the ubiquity of high-speed mobile internet (World Economic Forum, 2018).

The third trend is the inconsistency in demand, which is the phenomenon of organizations actively seeking and acquiring competencies that they do not need. The first aspect is tied to what I call the *omnicompetent worker*, those workers with multiple professional competencies; for example, an HR practitioner who is also a qualified accountant. In the immediate aftermath of the financial crisis of 2009, omnicompetence was highly prized; having that accountancy-qualified HR practitioner could allow a business to lay off their existing finance manager with a reduced level of risk. Organizations evolved their business operations around this omnicompetence so that, when it came to that worker leaving, the organization wanted to recruit an exact replacement. This exact competency mix would be a rare commodity in the labour market and would command a much higher price, much more than if the organization looked to hire the original set-up of a separate HR manager and finance manager. The second aspect to the inconsistency in demand trends is the tendency towards overqualification. Research suggests that whilst the competencies required to create a capability have remained largely unchanged, the competencies being demanded by organizations have grown (Warhurst and Findlay, 2012). Labour market factors such as the expansion of higher education, combined with organizational factors such as a decreasing appetite for risk and struggle to accurately quantify requirements, have led to organizations overstating the competency requirements for roles (CIPD, 2018). This talent shortage is exacerbated by the prevailing low levels of unemployment in western economies: unemployment in the EU area at the lowest level since January 2000 (European Commission, 2019), in the UK at the lowest level since January 1975 (BBC News, 2019) and in the US at the lowest level since December 1969 (pre-COVID of course!) (Olohan, 2019).

Eminence of worker expectations

Inextricably linked to the increasing shortage of talent is the rise in the eminence of worker expectations. The narrative of the 2010s was that millennials were 'flaky, lazy and in need of constant praise' (Fenzi, 2013). Concepts such as a desire for meaningful work, wanting opportunities to collaborate, seeking freedom of choice and fun in the workplace (Gross, 2012) were derided as symbols of entitlement. The quotation from Tyler Durden, protagonist and antagonist of *Fight Club*, 'you are not special, you are not a beautiful and unique snowflake' (Palahniuk, 1996) came to be ascribed to this millennial cohort. In reality, these desires for a better working environment could be applied to all generations; the difference was that talent shortages have given leverage to workers who could exercise greater choice in where and how they worked. A 2019 survey ranked the top factors in worker satisfaction as business practices in line with worker values, opportunities for growth and advancement, having ideas taken seriously, and recognition for their work (Mirabile *et al*, 2019). These are the factors becoming increasingly critical in the choices being made by workers in both their attraction to, and their retention within, organizations.

Workforce performance

The models we have discussed so far in this chapter have dealt with the quantities of the workforce. It is a key point to understand that the workforce, per se, does not service demand; demand is serviced through performance. Workforce performance is the supply side of productivity.

PRODUCTIVITY

Productivity is a measure of the efficiency of production, expressed as the rate of output that is created for every unit of input using variations of the following:

$$\frac{Output}{Input} = Productivity$$

Organizational productivity hinges upon the performance of the workforce and the efficient use of land and capital. Whilst the performance of the workforce is the key supply-side factor, processes and procedures are the key demand-side factor.

In order to calculate the level of workforce performance to compare against the demand profile, we use the workforce performance model shown in Figure 8.2. This approach is critical as the contracted time of a worker,

FIGURE 8.2 The workforce performance model

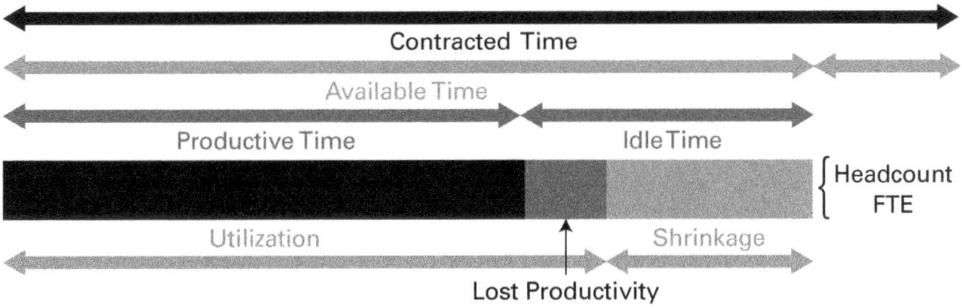

```
|<---------------------- Contracted Time ---------------------->|
    |<------------- Available Time ------------->|
    |<------- Productive Time ------->|<- Idle Time ->|
    [====================================]  { Headcount
                                              { FTE
    |<---------- Utilization ---------->|<- Shrinkage ->|
                                    ^
                              Lost Productivity
```

perhaps a 40-hour week, is not what is available to the organization; that worker does not translate into 40 hours of productive time. This model breaks down the contracted time of a worker into three corollaries: available time, utilization and productive time.

Available time

Available time is the amount of FTE hours that we have available to the organization. The starting point for available time is the contracted FTE concept described in Chapter 6, which is the sum of their individual FTE within their contracts. If we take an example of 1,000 FTE who are contracted to work a 40-hour week, we would calculate the contracted hours using the following:

$$\frac{\textit{Number of FTE} \times \textit{hours per week}}{\times \textit{weeks in the planning horizon}} = \textit{Available time}$$

In an annual planning horizon, 1,000 FTE contracted to work a 40-hour week would equate to 2,080,000 hours; however, an organization cannot plan based on this figure. It is common for contracts of employment to guarantee a number of days of annual leave, including public holidays and any additional entitlement of holiday or personal days. This time must be deducted to come to an accurate level of availability. For the purpose of this example, we will assume a common UK figure of 33 days of annual leave (8 public holidays and 25 days of holiday entitlement), or 264 hours (33 days × 8 hours); this extrapolates to 264,000 hours across the workforce. In this example, available time is 1,816,000 hours (2,080,000 hours of contracted FTE minus 264,000 hours of annual leave).

Utilization

Utilization is the act of doing something, to be utilized. Process-heavy environments tend to focus on utilization and shrinkage as key metrics, where utilization is time working on a core task and shrinkage is time not spent on a core task. Utilization is, therefore, a positive metric, whereas shrinkage is something an organization would want to avoid. It is key, therefore, that utilization and shrinkage are calculated as components of available time, rather than contracted time. Many resource planning professionals will categorize all annual leave as shrinkage. This is usually based on the practical perspective that they will often deal in a short time horizon and will abstract pre-booked annual leave and statutory holidays as part of a single calculation. Whilst sensible in approach, this miscategorization can drive poor business behaviours. Annual leave is a reduction *to* available time, as opposed to shrinkage, which is a reduction *from* available time. Shrinkage is viewed as a negative reduction in management's resources, and something to be reduced. By including annual leave within shrinkage, not only does annual leave come to be seen as a negative, but it also artificially inflates the shrinkage figures (often prompting an aim to reduce further).

Shrinkage, where a worker is not utilized, is typically regarded as a combination of two components, internal and external. External shrinkage is additional absences, for example sickness and lateness. Internal shrinkage can include system downtime, meetings, comfort breaks and additional projects. Though this definition can be helpful in understanding where shrinkage can be reduced, there are more important ways to view shrinkage when it comes to the impact on the organization: FTE shrinkage and headcount shrinkage. FTE shrinkage is those absences that impact as a percentage of planned working, such as sickness and temporary closure of premises. For example, the sickness of 0.5 FTE is half the loss of the sickness of 1.0 FTE. Headcount shrinkage is those absences and events that impact in absolute time, such as staff meetings and system downtime. For example, a one-hour meeting causes a higher rate of shrinkage to 0.5 FTE than to 1.0 FTE.

Productive time

Productive time is a component of utilization: we have to be utilized in order to be productive. However, the concept can be understood only within the concept of work: productive time is that time spent operating at or above processing speed. The processing speed, the expected time to complete an activity, can be determined in a number of different ways that will be covered in greater detail in the next part of this book. Activities may take longer than expected due to a number of different reasons: poor systems, which will be accounted in the assessment of processing speed; shrinkage, which is separately accounted; and underperformance, individually processing at a slower speed than expected. The factors of underperformance are inextricably linked to the definition of capability provided in the first chapter. Shrinkage, plus underperformance, is shown in the workforce performance model as idle time, which is time where core outputs are not achieved. Environmental factors that are not captured within shrinkage can result in subsequent underperformance. There can be multiple environmental factors that may not be considered in the calculation of the expected processing time. For example, the impact of climate change in creating hotter summers and colder winters in the future is estimated to create a productivity impact of 0.4 per cent in London, UK and 9.5 per cent in Bilbao, Spain (Costa *et al*, 2016). In addition, a review of more than 100 workplace studies found that open offices had a negative impact on attention spans and productivity for certain types of work (Davis *et al*, 2011). Finally, a toxic workplace culture can have a significant impact on worker productivity. One study has shown that ostracism, incivility, harassment, and bullying have significant direct negative effects on job productivity, while job burnout was shown to be a statistically significant mediator between the dimensions of a toxic workplace environment and job productivity (Anjum *et al*, 2018).

Underperformance is also expected where there are changes to a worker's physiology. The range of possible changes to physiology are manifold, but I will focus on a few key areas. In CIPD's 19th annual survey into health and well-being in the workplace, they calculated the average level of employee absence at 5.9 days per employee per year (CIPD, 2019). This was the lowest level they had recorded, which may point to a positive increase in the health and well-being of the workforce; however, it could also point towards a more concerning trend. Presenteeism is the act of coming to work whilst sick, a growing trend, with four-fifths of survey respondents having observed it in their organization over the past 12 months and a quarter of these reporting that it has increased over the period (CIPD, 2019). Illness affects both the quantity of work, through reduced speed and repetition of tasks, and the quality, through an increased number, or greater severity, of mistakes. Not only are sick workers less productive than healthy workers, but there is an increased likelihood of contagion and spreading that sickness to healthy workers (both in the workplace and during the daily commute).

Furthermore, increased presenteeism correlates with increases in both stress-related absence and mental health problems such as anxiety and depression (ERS, 2016). Reports on the cost to organizations of presenteeism in comparison to the cost of absenteeism vary between 1:1.5 and 1:2.6 (ERS, 2016), with the American Productivity Audit estimating an annual cost to the US economy of $150 billion (Stewart *et al*, 2003). Indeed, it has taken the transmission risks of the COVID-19 pandemic to really begin to dictate a shift against presenteeism in the workplace.

In the employment cycle of a worker, underperformance is expected in new starters; it will take time for someone starting a new role to gain the necessary skills and knowledge required to create a capability. This timeframe tends to be lower for professionals than it is for other workforce segments due to the homogeneity of professional capabilities. Timeframes tend to be lower for those workers who have moved internally rather than those who are joining a new organization, due to familiarity with the broader systems of the organization. Productivity may also dip towards the end of an employment lifecycle where, perhaps whilst working a notice period, the mindset of a worker is with *one foot out of the door*. The other factor to impact productivity, usually in the middle of an employment cycle, is that of or capability decay.

Capability decay

Capability decay, more commonly known as skill decay or fade, is the decline in the elements of capability through lack of use. The result is that, at a time in the future when that skill or knowledge is required, a worker is at best underperforming and at worst negligent. Without mitigation, there are two reasons for capability decay, the first being that the activity does not often take place. To provide an example that will resonate: in a small and stable team, the process of hiring or firing a team member may be rare for a line manager. At best, the process may have been taught many years previously so that, when such a circumstance arises, the process feels slow and cumbersome. When working out how long the process would be expected to take and how much energy a line manager would expend on the process, little account is taken of the impact of capability decay. When faced with the situation, the line manager probably has to search an online HR repository of process and policy in order to comprehend the subsequent activity; it is likely that constant reference is made to guidance at each stage. All this activity will certainly take longer than expected and, depending on the complexity of the processes or systems, carries a significant risk of error. The second reason for capability decay is time away from a role, where we are no longer practising a common activity. An industry-wide, but low-severity, example is that of password resets after a holiday. A password, ingrained in the unconscious competence and input multiple times daily, can easily fade from memory even after a short period of inactivity. Those in the West will be familiar with the rise in requests for a password reset on the first day back after the Christmas holidays and I expect the same is true the world over.

The half-life of a learned skill is five years, meaning that we are likely to have forgotten at least half of a skill if not practised within a five-year period (Thomas and Seely Brown, 2011). One comprehensive study found that after a year of non-use or non-practice, the average participant's performance was reduced by almost 10 per cent (Arthur *et al*, 1998). A range of studies point to consistencies in the nature of capability decay. Closed-looped tasks, where there is a fixed-sequence task (such as inputting a password) tend to decay faster than open-looped tasks, where there are continuous and repeated responses without a clear start and finish (such as problem solving) (Childs and Spears, 1986). Physical tasks, based on manual dexterity and muscle memory (such as sports), suffered slower capability decay than cognitive tasks requiring mental dexterity (such as problem solving) (Arthur *et al*, 1998). In addition, skill decay is over three times higher on the accuracy of completing tasks than it is on the speed to complete a task (Arthur *et al*, 1998).

This capability decay is a factor not just in the productivity of an organization, but also in the capabilities of an organization. Organizations with a significant grasp of the skills and knowledge of their workers may not be taking account of the impact of capability decay. A skill listed on a CV, evidenced at interview, may well have decayed significantly by the time it is required.

Summary

Workforce evolution is perhaps best captured in the opening line of a song from *Les Misérables*: 'At the end of the day you're another day older' (Schönberg *et al*, 1986). During our baseline of the organization, we will have identified the current levels of capability and the characteristics to segment them. In modelling and forecasting supply, we will see how that baseline evolves and changes over the planning horizon. Workers get older, their skills decay and they will leave our organization. The organization we are in is not the sum total of the organization we are planning for. Our planning is on the basis of the organization today and every day until the end of our planning horizon. In understanding our future workforce, we need to take the time to consider carefully the trends that are applicable to our workforce. We consider the factors that are specific to our geography and elements in our environmental scanning that relate to our industry. Recognize that the result of this will not be a single forecast, but a range of most-likely, best-case and worst-case forecasts of our workforce.

When you practise workforce planning, ask yourself:

- What is the level of churn in my organization?
- What does that churn look like in the future, given my planning scenarios?
- What are the possible impacts of megatrends on that forecast?
- What are the levels of productivity and productive time in my organization?
- What is the impact of skill decay on my forecast?

References

AAF (American Action Forum) (2019) Projecting future skill shortages through 2029, 18 July, www.americanactionforum.org/research/projecting-future-skill-shortages-through-2029/#ixzz6ChALg0UE (archived at https://perma.cc/L6G5-32GU)

Ahn, J et al (2019) Improving youth labour market outcomes in emerging market and developing economies, IMF Staff Discussion Note, Jan, www.imf.org/~/media/Files/Publications/SDN/2019/SDN1902.ashx (archived at https://perma.cc/VT2S-XFTP)

Anjum, A et al (2018) An empirical study analyzing job productivity in toxic workplace environments, *International Journal of Environmental Research and Public Health*, **15** (5) doi:10.3390/ijerph15051035

Arthur, W et al (1998) Factors that influence skill decay and retention: A quantitative review and analysis, *Human Performance*, **11** (1), pp 57–101, doi.org/10.1207/s15327043hup1101_3 (archived at https://perma.cc/3E8T-9X9U)

BBC News (2019) UK unemployment falls to lowest level since 1975, 17 December, www.bbc.co.uk/news/business-50820280 (archived at https://perma.cc/P8RS-4ZAA)

Becton, J B, Walker, H J and Jones-Farmer, A (2014) Generational differences in workplace behaviour, *Journal of Applied Social Psychology*, **44** (3), pp 175–89

Borjas, G J (1995) The economic benefits from immigration, *The Journal of Economic Perspectives*, **9** (2), pp 3–22, www.nber.org/papers/w4955.pdf (archived at https://perma.cc/8KZB-DH4Z)

Carnevale, A P, Hanson, A R and Gulish, A (2013) *Failure to Launch: Structural shift and the new lost generation*, 30 September, Georgetown University, https://1gyhoq479ufd3yna29x7ubjn-wpengine.netdna-ssl.com/wp-content/uploads/2014/11/FTL_FullReport.pdf (archived at https://perma.cc/Q7Q7-ZLH5)

CIPD (Chartered Institute for Personnel and Development) (2018) *Over-Skilled and Underused*, www.cipd.co.uk/Images/over-skilled-and-underused-investigating-the-untapped-potential-of-uk-skills_tcm18-48001.pdf (archived at https://perma.cc/Y5EQ-KHXH)

CIPD (Chartered Institute for Personnel and Development) (2019) *Health and Well-Being at Work*, www.cipd.co.uk/Images/health-and-well-being-at-work-2019.v1_tcm18-55881.pdf (archived at https://perma.cc/SW64-C857)

Childs, J M and Spears, W D (1986) Flight-skill decay and recurrent training, *Perceptual and Motor Skills*, **62** (1), pp 235–42, doi.org/10.2466/pms.1986.62.1.235 (archived at https://perma.cc/9GB8-8AQR)

Costa, H et al (2016) Climate change, heat stress and labour productivity: A cost methodology for city economies, London School of Economics, Working Paper 248, www.lse.ac.uk/GranthamInstitute/wp-content/uploads/2016/07/Working-Paper-248-Costa-et-al.pdf (archived at https://perma.cc/LV4Y-Q2X7)

Davis, M C, Leach, D J and Clegg, C W (2011) The physical environment of the office: Contemporary and emerging issues, *International Review of Industrial and Organizational Psychology*, **26**, pp 193–237, onlinelibrary.wiley.com/doi/10.1002/9781119992592.ch6 (archived at https://perma.cc/T3JC-NAM9)

Dill, W R, Gaver, D P and Weber, W L (1966) Models and modelling for manpower planning, *Management Science*, **13** (4), pp B142–B165, doi.org/10.1287/mnsc.13.4.B142 (archived at https://perma.cc/R5J5-59R5)

Dimock, M (2019) Defining generations: Where millennials end and generation z begins [Blog] *Pew Research*, 17 January, www.pewresearch.org/fact-tank/2019/01/17/where-millennials-end-and-generation-z-begins/ (archived at https://perma.cc/NM3R-TBJ9)

Docquier, F, Lohest, O and Marfouk, A (2007) Brain drain in developing countries, *The World Bank Economic Review*, **21** (2), pp 193–218, doi.org/10.1093/wber/lhm008 (archived at https://perma.cc/UN3R-FJNU)

Drucker, P F (1985) *The Effective Executive*, HarperCollins, New York

Dustman, C, Fabbri, F and Preston, I P (2005) The impact of immigration on the British labour market, *The Economic Journal*, **115** (507), doi.org/10.1111/j.1468-0297.2005.01038.x (archived at https://perma.cc/5XNV-NMKC)

ERS Research & Consultancy (2016) *Health at Work: Economic evidence report*, British Heart Foundation, 21 March, www.bhf.org.uk/-/media/files/health-at-work/health_at_work_economic_evidence_report_2016.pdf (archived at https://perma.cc/W587-2V8E)

European Commission (2019) Labour Market and Wage Developments in Europe – Annual Review, ec.europa.eu/social/main.jsp?catId=738&langId=en&pubId=8257 (archived at https://perma.cc/Y695-JCCV)

Eurostat (2019) *Ageing Europe: Looking at the lives of older people in the EU*, Publications Office of the European Union, Luxembourg, ec.europa.eu/eurostat/documents/3217494/10166544/KS-02-19-681-EN-N.pdf/c701972f-6b4e-b432-57d2-91898ca94893 (archived at https://perma.cc/HVF5-3H8M)

Fenzi, F (2013) Survey: What millennials really want at work [Blog] *Inc.com*, 15 May, www.inc.com/francesca-fenzi/what-millenials-want.html (archived at https://perma.cc/S63D-4R9W)

Greiner, L and Metzger, R (1983) *Consulting to Management*, Prentice Hall, Englewood Cliffs

Gross, T S (2012) *Invisible: How millennials are changing the way we sell*, Triple Nickel Press, Bloomington

Haire, M (1967) Managing management manpower, *Business Horizons*, 10 (4), pp 23–28, doi.org/10.1016/0007-6813(67)90004-3 (archived at https://perma.cc/3S7T-6PLG)

Hipple, S F and Hammond, L A (2016) Self-employment in the United States, US Bureau of Labor Statistics, 7 March, www.bls.gov/spotlight/2016/self-employment-in-the-united-states/pdf/self-employment-in-the-united-states.pdf (archived at https://perma.cc/ZQ86-J73Y)

IndustryWeek (2016) Parents have misconceptions of manufacturing careers, IndustryWeek, 9 May, www.industryweek.com/talent/article/21972720/parents-have-misconceptions-of-manufacturing-careers (archived at https://perma.cc/F5N9-BGZC)

International Organization for Standardization (2018) ISO 30414:2018 Human resource management – Guidelines for internal and external human capital reporting, ISO, Geneva

Kelland, K (2011) Who wants to live forever? Scientist sees aging cured [Blog] *Reuters*, 4 July, www.reuters.com/article/us-ageing-cure/who-wants-to-live-forever-scientist-sees-aging-cured-idUSTRE7632ID20110704 (archived at https://perma.cc/M7JG-3WVB)

Korn Ferry (2018) Future of Work: The global talent crunch, https://www.kornferry.com/challenges/future-of-work (archived at https://perma.cc/Z4JJ-RGMW)

LaPrade, A et al (2019) The enterprise guide to closing the skills gap, IBM Institute for Business Value, www.ibm.com/downloads/cas/EPYMNBJA (archived at https://perma.cc/W9TX-FSHM)

Mahan, T F et al (2020) *2020 Retention Report: Trends, reasons & wake-up call*, Work Institute, http://info.workinstitute.com/en/retention-report-2020 (archived at https://perma.cc/6T6E-8A79)

Markert, J (2004) Demographics of age: Generational and cohort confusion, *Journal of Current Affairs and Research in Advertising*, 26 (2), pp 11–25, www.sitemason.com/files/dW3ABy/articledemographics%20of%20age.pdf (archived at https://perma.cc/2L2J-YY7G)

Mazareanu, E (2019) Size of global management consulting market from 2014 to 2025, *Statista*, www.statista.com/statistics/466460/global-management-consulting-market-size-by-sector/ (archived at https://perma.cc/2XA2-8JSP)

Merck, J W (1965) *A Markovian Model for Projecting Movements of Personnel Through a System*, Air Force Systems Command, Texas, https://books.google.com/books?hl=en&lr=&id=JFpfLMjXpYEC&oi=fnd&pg=PP9&ots=pTm6avOZb-&sig=8JU3diMtSGYSTaOPbj8-pxo4sG8 (archived at https://perma.cc/9WU5-8ZQW)

Mirabile, K, Raffo, R and Thomas, C (2019) *Workplace Satisfaction Report*, Aerotek, www.aerotek.com/en/insights/what-workers-want-and-what-does-not-matter (archived at https://perma.cc/59P7-GXW4)

Moriconi, A, Peri, G and Turati, R (2018) Skill of the immigrants and vote of the natives: Immigration and nationalism in European elections 2007–2016, The National Bureau of Economic Research, Working Paper 25077, doi.org/10.3386%2Fw25077 (archived at https://perma.cc/5Y2V-WPN9)

Office for National Statistics (2018) Trends in self-employment in the UK, 7 February, www.ons.gov.uk/employmentandlabourmarket/peopleinwork/employmentandemployeetypes/articles/trendsinselfemploymentintheuk/2018-02-07 (archived at https://perma.cc/5RLU-W9XF)

Office for National Statistics (2019) Migration statistics quarterly report, 28 November, www.ons.gov.uk/peoplepopulationandcommunity/populationandmigration/internationalmigration/bulletins/migrationstatisticsquarterlyreport/november2019#there-are-different-patterns-for-eu-and-non-eu-migration-over-time (archived at https://perma.cc/UUT6-LUSB)

Olohan, M M (2019) Unemployment dips to 3.5% at 266,000 jobs added, 6 December, *The Daily Signal*, www.dailysignal.com/2019/12/06/unemployment-dips-to-3-5-as-266000-jobs-added/ (archived at https://perma.cc/ZDR4-VYJS)

Open University (2019) *Business Barometer*, July, http://www.open.ac.uk/business/Business-Barometer-2019 (archived at https://perma.cc/2554-SX94)

Palahniuk, C (1996) *Fight Club*, W W Norton, New York

Prensky, M (2001) Digital natives, digital immigrants, *On The Horizon*, 9 (5), pp 1–6, doi.org/10.1108/10748120110424816 (archived at https://perma.cc/LMJ2-7VR4)

PwC (2020) *23rd Annual Global CEO Survey*, www.pwc.com/gx/en/ceo-survey/2020/reports/pwc-23rd-global-ceo-survey.pdf (archived at https://perma.cc/32D2-4BVS)

Rogers, M, Chambers, N and Percy, C (2020) Disconnected: Career aspirations and jobs in the UK, *Education and Employers*, 22 January, www.educationandemployers.org/disconnected/ (archived at https://perma.cc/J4NZ-7AX5)

Sage, A and Sharma, A (2019) Uber loses $5 billion, misses Wall Street targets despite easing price war, *Reuters*, 8 August, www.reuters.com/article/us-uber-results/uber-loses-5-billion-misses-wall-street-targets-despite-easing-price-war-idUSKCN1UY2NG (archived at https://perma.cc/Y8NS-8D3Z)

Schönberg, C-M *et al* (1985) *Les Misérables* [Play], Cameron Mackintosh, London

Star Trek II: The Wrath of Khan (1982) [Film] Paramount Pictures, USA

Stewart, W F *et al* (2003) Lost productive work time costs from health conditions in the United States, *Journal of Occupational and Environmental Medicine*, **45** (12), pp 1234–46, www.nationalpartnership.org/our-work/resources/economic-justice/paid-sick-days/lost-productive-work-time-american-productivity-audit.pdf (archived at https://perma.cc/8ZAS-VH3K)

Styron, W (2004) *Sophie's Choice*, Random House, London

Tavernise, S (2019) Immigrant population growth in the US slows to a trickle, *The New York Times*, 26 September, www.nytimes.com/2019/09/26/us/census-immigration.html (archived at https://perma.cc/7X5U-FRSA)

Thomas, D and Seely Brown, J (2011) *A New Culture of Learning*, Createspace Independent Publishing Platform, South Carolina

Upwork (2019) Freelancing in America, www.upwork.com/i/freelancing-in-america/2019/ (archived at https://perma.cc/4JF4-J7UQ)

Vroom, V H and MacCrimmon, K R (1968) Toward a stochastic model of managerial careers, *Administrative Science Quarterly*, **13** (1), pp 26–46, www.jstor.org/stable/2391260 (archived at https://perma.cc/74FR-FBQZ)

Warhurst, C and Findlay, P (2012) More effective skills utilisation: Shifting the terrain of skills policy in Scotland, ESRC Centre on Skills, Knowledge and Organisational Performance (SKOPE), Research Paper 107, ora.ox.ac.uk/objects/uuid:b608844c-4178-4761-b283-81cc9c497b06 (archived at https://perma.cc/U6ZW-UGWS)

World Economic Forum (WEF) (2018) *The Future of Jobs Report*, http://www3.weforum.org/docs/WEF_Future_of_Jobs_2018.pdf (archived at https://perma.cc/4XW6-VWP4)

World Health Organization (2018) Global health estimates 2016: Life expectancy, 2000–2016, www.who.int/gho/mortality_burden_disease/life_tables/en/ (archived at https://perma.cc/M7TX-T8E7)

PART FOUR

Demand

How is demand structured, what drives it and what is the forecast for the future?

09

The nature of demand

Introduction

In economic theory, demand is the quantity of a good or service that consumers are willing and able to purchase during a time period (O'Sullivan and Sheffrin, 2003). In the concept of the value chain we explored in Chapter 5 (Porter, 1985), it is the marketing, sales and service components that drive consumer demand. Servicing this demand for a good or service generates subsequent demand across the rest of the value chain. The consumer demand for a loaf of sliced bread requires workers to support the inbound logistics for a bakery to receive flour from a mill, store it and manage stock levels. Workers will support the operational process of combining flour with water, yeast, and salt to create dough; further workers will engage in placing the dough in ovens to bake the bread whilst a final group will supervise the bread going through the bread slicer and the wrapping machine. At the end of the operational process worker are engaged in outbound logistics. They will move the bread from the bakery to a storage unit, from where it will be loaded onto trucks and workers will drive these to supermarkets. In addition to these primary activities, workers are engaged in procurement, technology development, human resource management and firm infrastructure to support these primary activities. The subsequent requirement for a workforce as a result of *consumer* demand is known as *derived* demand (Marshall, 1997) and is the focus of demand in the context of workforce planning.

In this chapter, we will look closely at the nature of demand, what it is and how it manifests and flows within the organization. Crucially, this will be the framework for how to calculate demand within our own organization.

What is demand?

In 1973, Russian-American economist Wassily Leontief was awarded the Nobel Prize in Economics for his research on input–output analysis. His model showed the relationships between industries within an economy so that an output from one industry would become an input to another (Leontief, 1986). This macroeconomic model is also applicable at the microeconomic level where the output from one process becomes an input to another process. Controls in the form of processes, systems and governance, and resources in the form of workers, are applied to create a subsequent output.

FIGURE 9.1 The input–output model of processes

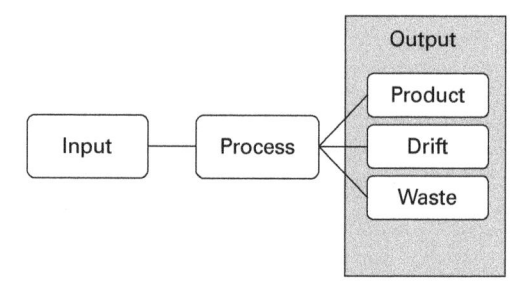

This output can take the form of one of three things: product, drift or waste. A product, in the form of a good or service, is the intended output of a process. Drift is where output is still able to become a product, but exits a standard process flow and takes greater time and resource than expected. Waste is where a process fails to produce a product at all. Drift and waste are often the results of an inadequate level of resource or control, which may be an insufficiency of resource or too many cooks spoiling the broth. One example would be the production of electronics: usually, the process creates a device, a product; sometimes in final testing the product fails to function and requires repair in order for it to function (drift); occasionally there is an accident resulting in the destruction of a device (waste). A service-related example might be the process of sales. In the best case, a sales process results in a sale. Sometimes there is drift: a buyer procrastinates, sales conversations are repeated and senior team members are utilized to convert the sale. Often, a sale does not convert, and that is waste. The nature of sales means that a higher level of waste is accepted and tolerated than in the production of electronics devices. Product, drift and waste will each create different levels of demand; the creation of a product will take place within the expected time of a process, whereas drift will always result in a higher level of demand. Waste is changeable: a potential buyer walking away mid-pitch would result in less demand than having gone through a complete sales process. In certain industries, the chasing of an unsuccessful lead might result in a higher level of demand. This model translates into two categories of demand: variable and fixed.

Variable demand

Variable, or direct, demand is derived from the upstream volume: changes in the volume of work have a direct relationship with the level of resource required. For example, a customer requirement for 2,000 loaves of bread will derive greater demand for resources than for 1,000 loaves. The nature of this demand looks quite different based on the time horizon. In a resource planning horizon, the critical timeframes are likely to be hourly, weekly and seasonally. Consider consumer demand in a shopping centre or arcade on a typical Tuesday: shops may see their busiest times in the middle of the day (when customers have a lunch break) and later in the afternoon, depending on the type of shop (schoolchildren after school and adults following work). These spikes in customer demand result in a requirement for workers, often achieved through scheduling more workers in the afternoon and planning staff breaks before and after the periods of peak demand. Over a seven-day period, shops tend to attract more customers at the weekend than they do during the rest of the week. Higher demand for workers is derived from this increased customer demand, leading to more staff in the shops at the weekend. The next time horizon tends to be seasonal, where certain industries experience spikes at particular times of the year; those shops may find their peak demand periods are around the holidays, which in turn result in a higher number of workers. The nature of demand within a resource planning horizon is also heavily dependent on processes and the nature of the supply chain. In agriculture, for example, a forecast of demand may well have dictated a level of a crop that has been sown. However, it is the success of the crop that dictates the scale of demand for workers and the harvest season that dictates the timeframe for those workers.

Demand also looks different based on the level of the organization and the impact of the marginal product of labour (MPL). In economic theory, the marginal product of labour is the change in output that results from an additional worker (O'Sullivan and Sheffrin, 2003).

$$\frac{\text{Change in output}}{\text{Change in labour}} = \text{Marginal product of labour}$$

At micro and meso levels, different elements of the value chain may have differing impacts on the number of workers. The earlier example of increasing from 1,000 to 2,000 loaves of bread would be expected to increase the number of workers required in the operational processes. However, it may make little impact within outbound logistics: a single truck driver may simply require a larger truck. At a macro level, the increase in the number of workers is simply counted at an organizational level as a product of customer demand. Within the primary activities of the organization, operations and inbound/outbound logistics are typically categorized as variable demand.

Fixed demand

Fixed, or overhead, demand is that demand that derives from factors separate from changes in customer demand. At a micro level, consider the number of one-to-one meetings between a worker and their line manager. The number of these for a line manager is dependent entirely on the number of direct reports they have, which is their span of control. The number of briefings that take place, where a line manager meets with the entire team to cascade information, is dependent on the number of management layers within the organizational hierarchy. The level of management reporting within an organization will be based far more on the way the organization chooses to manage business operations than it is on customer demand. At a meso level, consider the nature of demand for a risk and compliance function: this demand will be much higher in regulated industries, such as financial services, than it is in other sectors and will be relatively consistent between similar firms. Equally, the size of the current workforce within a research and development function will be largely based on the long-term strategy of an organization, rather than on current customer demand. The location strategy has a significant part to play in fixed demand as simply having a site or office will require an irreducible minimum level of staffing in order to simply keep the lights on. Fixed demand is commonplace within the supporting activities of an organization: procurement, technology development, human resource management, and firm infrastructure. The primary function of marketing and sales may be a fixed demand based purely on strategy, or a variable demand based on estimated customer throughput.

Budgets

A budget is the financial equivalent of a workforce plan: a clear statement of cash flow, of planned revenues and costs and of assets and liabilities. These budgets will be set at different levels of the organization and over a specific planning horizon, typically a year. As budgets restrict expenditure, they are typically viewed as a method for controlling supply. This heuristic serves us well in both the workplace and our home life in dissuading expenditure on something that we cannot afford. In reality, budgets are not a binary method of controlling supply, they are a method of attempting to control demand. Using the heuristic, a restricted budget stops us spending money on that loaf of bread. In reality, the restricted budget attempts to control our demand for the loaf of bread and results in the second-order effects of hunger, which will endure or be satiated either through a substitute within the restricted budget or theft of the loaf of bread. This is a concept we recognize when we might enquire about a service and we are asked about a budget, as they determine the end result. It is a concept that we might forget when we try and hire an experienced professional on a restricted budget. In the workplace, therefore, rigid budgets to contain variable demand may well have a detrimental impact on business performance.

Fixed demand is usually controlled by budgets, which are set regardless of customer volume. Sevices' activities are often an anomaly within the fixed and variable demand model. A service is a set of processes that provide support or assistance to a customer. As such, these processes when compared against customer volumes will provide a clear variable demand. Organizations will often use a variable demand model for services where that service generates direct revenue. Where that service is an overhead expense that does not generate revenue, such as after-sales support, then budgets are used to restrict the demand through the application of service levels.

Service levels

Service levels determine the types of services that are offered, the target levels of the performance of those services, and the rates at which those services are actually performed. These are critical determinants of demand, as it may add or remove process steps and entire processes. If an organization wished to improve quality, it may add a quality assurance process with an associated budget; if an organization was content to risk their quality standards for an immediate cost reduction, they may choose to remove a quality assurance step or process. Budgets do not reflect the types of services that are offered and their target levels, they reflect the rates at which those services are actually performed. Usually, there is a healthy tension between service levels and budgets; budgets are often set at a level just below the target standard in order to create stress that seeks to increase the productivity of workers. This approach is drawn from the notion of *ephemeralization*, where technological advance allows us to do 'more and more with less and less' (Fuller, 1973). For example, eight hours of available time might be the expected duration for a worker to produce 19 units. With a budget for one worker expected to produce 19 units, an organization may set the service level at 20 units in the hope of nudging the worker towards higher performance. In our lives we will often see this healthy tension play out in our interactions with organizations. Sometimes a worker will go the extra mile for us, for example helping to carry a purchase from the shop to our car; other times, the service falls short and we may have to wait a little longer to be served. Where the tension fails, a worker will make a unilateral decision on service levels that will either raise costs or provide a complete failure in the service provided.

Service levels are a key component of the public sector operation, for example. The public sector is typically free at the point of consumption and, rather than generating revenue, it is allocated a budget. As the following case study illustrates, public sector budgets are entirely political. Levels of overall funding are the result of the political will of the people translated into actions of elected officials, and typically seek to balance a desire to keep taxation as low as possible whilst delivering the best possible services. Public services are further afflicted by the reality that public goods fall within a wide arc where politics defines the definition. It therefore sits within the public sector to manage service levels at the macro, meso and micro levels of the organization.

LAW ENFORCEMENT

In the immediate aftermath of the financial crisis of 2009, governments in the West embarked on a series of cost-cutting measures designed to reduce fiscal deficits. Then UK Prime Minister David Cameron pledged to usher in a new 'age of austerity' (Summers, 2009). As part of these measures, there was a 19 per cent real-terms reduction in police funding over eight years (National Audit Office, 2018) and between 2010 and 2019, police numbers in England and Wales fell by around 16 per cent (Home

Office, 2019). Chief Constable Sara Thornton, head of the National Police Chiefs' Council, said that significant budget cuts and the changing nature of criminality meant that police had to prioritize and may no longer respond to burglaries (Ward, 2015a). Less than a week later, it emerged that Leicestershire police had trialled a money-saving scheme to deploy forensic police officers to reports of attempted burglary only at even-numbered houses. This change to service levels was being considered by multiple forces after an analysis showed that forensic science officers had been deployed to 1,172 attempted burglaries in the region but few scenes were found to contain any scientific evidence (Ward, 2015b). Such was the public outcry against an approach based on the arbitrary factor of a house number, the initiative was quietly shelved. Public expectations were detached from the efficacy of particular services and the politics of demand was affirmed.

Calculating demand

The purpose of calculating demand is to establish a baseline for forecasting future demand. Whereas data on workforce supply is typically in plentiful supply within an organization, data on demand is often scant and fragmented. This delta, and the complexity of the subject, is why we conduct a baselining activity as part of the demand stage rather than as part of the baseline stage. If we are operating at a macro level, there would be little disadvantage to conducting this exercise earlier. At a meso and micro level, we risk the economy of our effort by collecting and analysing too much demand data before we understand fully the nature of the workforce supply that will be servicing the demand.

In Chapter 8, the workforce performance model gave us a clear framework that a greater level of resource is required than is indicated by volumes and processes when we convert from contract time to productive time. The product of labour is based on the productivity of a single worker, not the productivity of the productive time of a single worker. This provides us with two approaches that are output based or input based.

An output-based approach

This approach seeks to identify the relationship between the workforce and the outputs they produce, which are known as products of labour and are illustrated in Figure 9.2.

FIGURE 9.2 Product of labour curves

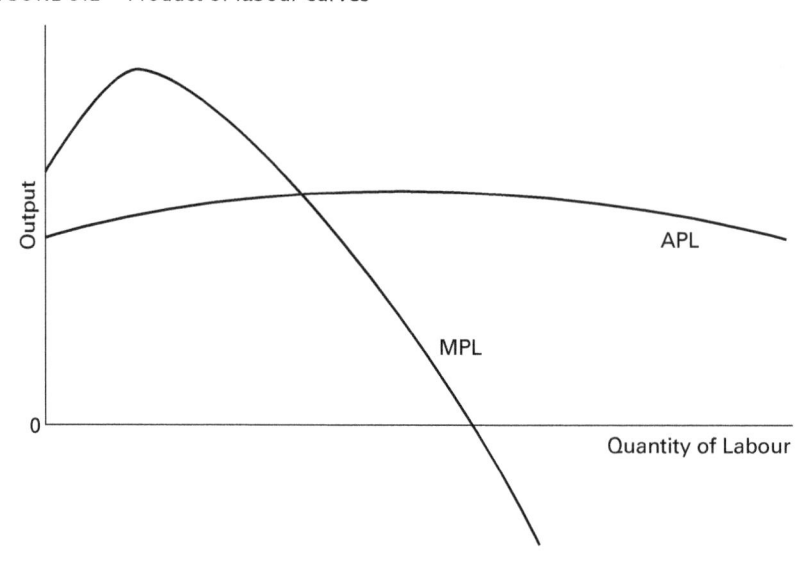

[Graph showing APL and MPL curves with Output on y-axis and Quantity of Labour on x-axis]

The *average product of labour* (APL) is the average individual output for the workforce. For 10 workers producing 100 units, the APL is 10. The APL increases at a slow rate as the organization benefits from the advantages of additional workers. These economies of scale reach a peak and then become diseconomies of scale as average output improves. The 10 workers with an APL of 10 may operate a production line where increasing hands allow the average output to increase. When that team reaches maximum capacity for space, and workers start bumping into each other on the production line, the APL starts to reduce. Whereas APL is the average, MPL is the *marginal product of labour*: the change in output from adding an additional worker. Initially, there are *increasing marginal returns*: the benefit of adding a worker is greater than the benefit of adding the previous worker. This quickly hits a peak before descending into *diminishing marginal returns* where each additional worker continues to increase the overall output but makes less of a difference than the last. There are two key factors in play at this point: communication and divisibility. As more workers are added to the process, there is a polynomial growth in lines of communication as more people need to pass information to each other. This combinatorial explosion in demand erodes the benefit created by the marginal return. The second factor, divisibility, is that some activities are not easily divided and so the addition of workers does not add the same benefit as the initial workforce. At the end of the MPL curve, we hit the worst case, *diminishing returns*, where the organization is saturated and the addition of an extra worker results in a decrease in output. This is the point, perhaps, where the organization reaches the Malthusian catastrophe of having too many workers for the number of machines or space they have, and work suffers as a result (Malthus, 1798). Aligning high-level output data with worker levels will allow us to map a number of points on both the APL and MPL curves to understand current levels of derived demand for workers and how that varies.

The benefits of this approach are that the data on outputs is often the most readily available and is much easier to calculate. The limitations of this approach are that it does not connect with input data and is less useful at meso and micro levels.

An input-based approach

The input-based approach calculates the relationship between inputs, workers and outputs. It is the most comprehensive approach to calculating demand. To do this, we need to first understand the input volumes and how those volumes translate into the derived demand for labour.

DETERMINING INPUT VOLUMES

The start point for determining input volumes is through the analysis of time series data, which is a collection of sequential data points over a time period. The source of this time series data will sit within our supply chain and be different depending on the nature of our organization. In a best case, the organization will also have data around their business operations including the flow of demand in and around the business. It is more likely, however, that we will be looking at whatever data is available. Those producing goods will have data on their inbound logistics of primary or secondary sector products; equally, there will be data on the outbound logistics of the final products going to market. Other types of organization, such as those providing a shared resource, would have data on their customers and their usage rates. The level of the organization and the planning horizons will dictate the nature of this data. Creating a calculation for a short planning horizon at a micro level can necessitate minute-by-minute breakdowns of demand data. Planning at higher levels and longer timeframes can be achieved through aggregated datasets. Analyses of the trends in this data will show not only both the initial inputs and final outputs, but also the associated inputs and outputs throughout the entire internal supply chain.

ESTABLISHING DERIVED DEMAND FOR LABOUR

A top-down method
As process systems and controls will typically remain a constant, it is the analysis of the trends in inputs, outputs and resources that will indicate the derived demand for labour. Regression analysis of those trends will indicate the causal relationship between the process steps to give an indication of the ratio of inputs and outputs in relation to the workforce.

A bottom-up method
In the absence of clear top-down information, or when planning at either a micro level or in horizon one, we may require a bottom-up approach to calculate our demand. The basis of this will require a work study to understand the nature of the process. At the lowest level, this will necessitate a *time and motion* (T&M) study, a timed review of each process step to understand the expected duration of each process step at a micro level. At a higher level, an *average handling time* (AHT) may be more appropriate; this is the time for an overall process rather than a detailed time and motion study of each specific process step. At the next level, we may look at individual workers or teams; for this group, the *day in the life of* (DiLo) may be the best approach. DiLo can be particularly useful when quantifying the activity of knowledge workers who may follow irregular processes. A DiLo is an indication over a single day (or the average of a number of days) to list the types of work and interactions and the time spent on these.

T&M, AHT and DiLo are all effective bottom-up methods for establishing derived demand based on current work. It may be the case that we are looking to calculate based on new types of work, for example a new service offering, or new ways of working following a process change. For this, looking at benchmarks can be an immensely helpful guide. Either within our own organization or across the industry in other organizations, there will be benchmarks that could be detailed or abstract. In line with the principles we discussed in Chapter 6, make and track assumptions around these benchmarks in order to establish those as the basis for the model.

CALCULATING THE LABOUR REQUIREMENT

Establishing the labour requirement, the target level of FTE, is based entirely on the workforce performance model in Chapter 8 (see Figure 8.2). We first start with the input volume levels, the quantity of input, and the processing time – how long it takes to convert that input into outputs – to establish the Productive Time:

$$Input\ Volume \times Processing\ Time = Productive\ Time$$

CAPACITY

The term capacity originates from, and still means, a volume that can be held by a vessel. This has evolved into use in relation to production: capacity is that volume that can be produced. When we have a workforce, we can use a variation of the above equation to calculate the capacity:

$$\frac{Productive\ Time\ (hours)}{Processing\ Time\ (units\ per\ hour)} = Capacity$$

As we see from this, whilst capacity is often used erroneously to mean the overall size of the workforce, it actually relates to the output that can be produced by the workforce.

The next step in calculating the labour requirement is to add to Productive Time a Lost Productivity multiple, which comprises the speed to competence and the levels of underperformance. Speed to competence is the time it takes for a new starter to become fully productive as a result of their training; underperformance is those existing workers who are not delivering at the productive level. This creates a utilization target:

$$Productive\ Time + (Productive\ Time \times Lost\ Productivity\ Multiple) = Utilization\ Target$$

A shrinkage multiple, based on the percentages of FTE and headcount shrinkage, is added to the utilization target to create an available time target. For example, if the overall impact of shrinkage on a single FTE is 8 hours, or 0.2 FTE, the multiple is 0.25:

$$Utilization\ Target + (Utilization\ Target \times Shrinkage\ Multiple) = Available\ Time\ Target$$

Next, we add a core absence multiple to available time to create the target time. The core absence multiple is based on holiday levels. If we take a standard offering within the United Kingdom of 8 public holidays and 25 days of holiday entitlement, the multiple is 0.145374449339207:

$$\frac{Available\ Time\ Target +}{(Available\ Time\ Target \times Core\ Absence\ Multiple)} = Target\ Time$$

Finally, the target time is divided by the contract hours and time in weeks, for example, 40 hours and 52 weeks, to create the Target FTE:

$$\frac{Target\ Time}{Contract\ Hours \times Planning\ Horizon\ in\ weeks} = Target\ Time$$

THE ERLANG MODEL

Agner Krarup Erlang was a Danish engineer and mathematician who invented the fields of queuing theory that enabled the predicting of waiting times in telephony. His formulae have been the standard across the telephone industry since the 1920s and have much wider applicability where customers arrive at random with an expectation of exclusive service. The Erlang C formula is a common input-based method used in contact centres to determine the levels of derived demand for labour based on a particular service level around caller waiting times (Kleinrock, 1976). Though there are some flaws in the model, in that it assumes that no caller ever hangs up or encounters an engaged tone, it remains an effective tool for calculating workforce demand.

Summary

The demand analysis we have just conducted will allow us to understand the workforce levels needed to achieve particular outcomes. Some demand is derived from a pull model, particularly in the production of goods, where output targets are predetermined. In this setting, the output requirements pull a derived demand for resources. Other demand, particularly the service sector, is a push model. In this case, it is immediate customer requirements that push a derived demand for resource throughout the organization. Being conscious of the inputs and outputs of processes will enable us to calculate derived demand for workers. This calculation, however, is on the basis of specific volumes over a specific period. Unless the genuine expectation is that our organization will not change, then the critical next step is to take that demand calculation as a baseline for forecasting.

When you practise workforce planning, ask yourself:

- What are the levels of fixed demand in my organization?
- Do I need to take an input-based or output-based approach to calculating demand?
- What is the derived demand for labour?

References

Fuller, R B (1973) *Nine Chains to the Moon*, Jonathan Cape: London

Home Office (2019) *Police Workforce*, England and Wales, 31 March 2019, 18 July, assets.publishing.service.gov.uk/government/uploads/system/uploads/attachment_data/file/831726/police-workforce-mar19-hosb1119.pdf (archived at https://perma.cc/QQ3M-J6FD)

Kleinrock, L (1976) *Queueing Systems: Theory, Volume 1*, John Wiley & Sons, Chichester

Leontief, W (1986) *Input–Output Economics*, Oxford University Press, Oxford

Malthus, T (1798) *An Essay on the Principle of Population*, 1993 reprint, Oxford University Press, Oxford

Marshall, A (1997) *Principles of Economics*, Prometheus Books, New York

National Audit Office (NAO) (2018) *Financial Sustainability of Police Forces in England and Wales 2018*, 11 September, www.nao.org.uk/wp-content/uploads/2018/09/Financial-sustainability-of-police-forces-in-England-and-Wales-2018.pdf (archived at https://perma.cc/XSE9-UAG3)

O'Sullivan, A and Sheffrin, S M (2003) *Economics: Principles in action*, Pearson Prentice Hall, Upper Saddle River

Porter, M E (1985) *Competitive Advantage: Creating and sustaining superior performance*, The Free Press, New York

Summers, D (2009) David Cameron warns of 'new age of austerity', *The Guardian*, 26 April, www.theguardian.com/politics/2009/apr/26/david-cameron-conservative-economic-policy1 (archived at https://perma.cc/2LLD-9SKR)

Ward, V (2015a) Police chief warns that officers may no longer respond to burglaries, *The Telegraph*, 28 July, https://www.telegraph.co.uk/news/uknews/crime/11767419/Police-chief-warns-that-officers-may-no-longer-respond-to-burglaries.html (archived at https://perma.cc/X6Y9-JUNK)

Ward, V (2015b) Police 'only investigate attempted burglaries at even-numbered homes', *The Telegraph*, 5 August, www.telegraph.co.uk/news/uknews/crime/11784254/Police-only-investigate-burglaries-at-even-numbered-homes.html (archived at https://perma.cc/SE5S-9KM9)

10

Forecasting demand

Introduction

In the last chapter, we were able to understand the nature of demand within our own organization. We know the inputs that come into our organization and the subsequent outputs, the successful products and the levels of wastage. We have a good comprehension of how long processes take and what takes longer than planned. We are also clear on the level of fixed demand that is inherent within our organization. In this chapter we explore the next stage. We take that information and use it as a baseline to forecast derived demand for the duration of our planning horizon. To do so, we will examine how our organization is expected to change in the future and how that translates into demand for workers. This process 'provides one of the greatest benefits in workforce planning because it offers the chance for an [organization] to reexamine its purpose and the direction of its programs in light of changes that are taking place in the external environment' (Perez, 2013).

The impact of change

The conversion of a demand calculation into a demand forecast is impacted by only one element: change.

Drivers of change

We have already identified the drivers of change to our organization during the baseline exercise we conducted in Chapter 5. This will have presented a number of internal factors that differ depending on the type and strategic alignment of the organization we are in and the business model it operates, in addition to the wider external factors that prevail.

Internal factors

The internal factors are those that emanate from our organization. The first port of call is the strategic alignment: the why, mission, goals, objectives, strategy, and execution of our organization. Does any of it result in a change in execution within our planning horizon? For example, our organization may have a growth objective of a 20 per cent revenue growth within three years. Unless our organization generates revenue through producing goods and services with high price elasticity, and can therefore simply increase prices without change to output, revenue growth typically results in a requirement to sell a higher volume of goods and services. This change in execution, a requirement to produce a higher volume, results in a change in the derived demand for labour. Our organization may be looking to change in some other way, from moving into new markets and selling new goods or services, to performance improvement and transformation. For example, our organizational strategy may be pointing towards technological innovation and increased use of automation. Automation reduces derived demand in the specific process where it is used; consider the use of robots on an assembly line that negates the need for an employee to carry out the work. However, automation generates a derived demand for new capabilities, for example, workers to maintain the machines.

External factors

The external factors lie outside our organization; they are the political, economic, social, technological, legal and environmental elements we assessed in our PESTLE analysis. Does our planning horizon take us through an election cycle or a period of political uncertainty? What impact will that have on consumer demand? If we have an ambition for revenue growth, is that against a background of wider economic growth? If not, achieving that growth may necessitate a significant increase in our need for sales and marketing resources. How are consumer demands changing, both in terms of what they buy and how they buy it? Is technology changing across the wider industry or marketplace and will we need to keep up in order to compete? An increase in regulation on our industry will likely increase our derived demand as we not only move to a more complex process, but also require additional compliance resources in order to reduce our risk of breaching the new legislation. Finally, are there direct or indirect implications of the environment? Consider, for example, the impact of societal pressure around climate change to force a shift away from single-use plastic.

The planning fallacy

1979 was a busy year for Daniel Kahneman and Amos Tversky; in March their concept of prospect theory was published (Kahneman and Tversky, 1979). This theory would conclude that people are risk-averse when facing a choice linked to gains and risk-seeking when facing a choice linked to losses. (This theory would go on to earn Kahneman the Nobel Prize in Economics, which he shared with Vernon Smith, in 2002.) Later in 1979, the pair shared the concept of the planning fallacy, where those engaged in planning fall victim to optimism bias and are prone to underestimate the cost and overestimate the benefit of an initiative (Kahneman and Tversky, 1982). This fallacy results from a tendency of those creating plans and forecasts to take an inside view, rather than an outside view.

Inside view

The inside view occurs when we focus on the specific circumstances of a situation or project and search for singular information, or case data, that it evidences the peculiarities of that situation. This might be on the basis of personal experiences, for example when we start a project and estimate the completion time. That expectation of duration tends to be based on the duration of having completed what are, most likely, the easiest elements of the project. Equally, this might be on the basis of other data, but framed far more around what makes this product or situation different and ignoring the similarities with other evidence. This results in forecasts and plans that 'are unrealistically close to best-case scenarios [and] could be improved by consulting the statistics of similar cases' (Kahneman, 2011). A famous example of this is the construction of the Sydney Opera House, which was expected to be completed in 1963 at a cost of AUS $7 million. A decade later than expected, a much scaled-down version was completed at a cost of AUS $102 million (Sanna *et al*, 2005).

CASE STUDY
High Speed Two (HS2)

In 2010, Transport secretary Lord Adonis announced plans for a high-speed rail network in the UK to connect London to Birmingham in the West Midlands and then on to cities in the north of the country at an overall cost of £30 billion (Milmo, 2010). Estimates in March 2012 placed the cost of the network at between £30.9 and £36 billion (High Speed Two Ltd, 2012) and in June 2013 Treasury secretary Patrick McLoughlin revealed the projected cost had risen to £42.6 billion (in 2011 prices) (Topham, 2013). Less than a week later it was revealed that civil servants in the Department for Transport had been using an outdated model when making their calculations and that costs were expected to be far higher than expected (Gillan, 2013). By 2015, the cost was estimated to be £50.1 billion at 2011 prices and a figure of £56.6 billion, adjusted to 2014 prices, was recognized at the realistic cost (Economic Affairs Committee, 2015). Lord Tony Berkeley, the former deputy chair of the review into HS2, produced a damning report in early 2020 that 'Parliament has been seriously misled by the failure of HS2 Ltd and by ministers to report objectively and fairly on costs and programme changes' and that the costs were expected to exceed £106 billion (Berkeley, 2020).

Outside view

Unlike the singular information, prevalent in the inside view, distributional data focuses on the outcomes of similar situations and projects. This outside view is perhaps the most significant step planners can take in improving the accuracy of forecasts. There are two key methods that can be taken to achieve an outside view: segmentation and reference class forecasting. The segmentation effect is a bias whereby the expected duration of a task is lower than the sum of its component sub-tasks (Forsyth and Burt, 2008). The solution to this is to adopt the recommended approach from the last chapter of a more detailed input-based demand calculation, rather than a wider output-based calculation. Reference class forecasting is the specific remedy proposed by Kahneman and Tversky (1982) and involves four stages. The first is to identify and select a reference class, a similar previous instance to which this situation can be referred meaningfully. The second stage is to assess the distributional data for that reference class, in terms of both the relevance and accuracy. The third stage is to make estimates based on the singular data, that which is wholly different from the reference class. The fourth stage is to consider the data in the same way we did with workforce data in Chapter 6. We assess whether we have sufficient information and where we are making assumptions, then we adjust the forecast accordingly and track the risks in the assumptions. Indeed, the insurance industry is one of a number of sectors where their entire business model hinges on taking an outside view. When they assess the risk of insuring us or one of our assets, the determination is based on the factors that make our situation similar to their reference data. When insuring a car, they will look at factors such as our age and location, how long we have been driving and if we have ever made a claim, as these are the factors they have determined are key drivers of the likelihood of a future claim. There is a growing use of telematic trackers, devices that monitor vehicle use and driver safety. This can provide an overlay of an inside view once drivers gain a demonstrable record of safe driving, which can lead to a reduction in insurance premiums.

The multiplier effect of change and crisis

On 15 January 2009, US Airways flight 1549 struck a flock of Canada geese just five miles northwest of New York City's LaGuardia Airport, just after take-off. The Airbus A320-214 lost thrust in both engines and, realizing they would be unable to reach an airport, pilots Captain Chesley 'Sully' Sullenberger and First Officer Jeffrey Skiles glided the plane to a water landing (ditching) on the Hudson River. The miracle on the Hudson saved all 155 passengers and crew and was immortalized in the memoir *Highest Duty* (Sullenberger, 2009). In that book, Sully details that the subsequent investigation by the National Transport Safety Board (NTSB) used flight simulators to test the possibility of returning safely to LaGuardia or diverting to nearby Teterboro Airport. In the Aviation Accident Report, the NTSB referred to these simulations and said 'the immediate turn [to airports by simulator pilots] did not reflect or account for real-world considerations, such as the time delay required to recognize the extent of the engine thrust loss and decide on a course of action' (National Transport Safety Board, 2010). The impact of change and crisis is not simply the sum of process steps but must account for real-world implications that create a multiplier effect on the derived demand for labour.

Inspired by work with terminally ill patients, the book *On Death and Dying* postulates the theory of the five stages of grief: denial, anger, bargaining, depression, and acceptance (Kübler-Ross, 1969). This model is equally applicable in change and crisis and often referred to as the change curve. At the first stage of a crisis, denial, the affected workforce will be in a state of shock and may be unable to fully comprehend the gravity of the situation. In the second stage, anger, the workforce may be gripped by fear of the unknown or anger at being in their current situation. In the third stage of bargaining, the affected workforce looks for a route out of the current situation; that route may not be the best outcome for either the worker or the organization. The fourth stage of depression results in a severe reduction in performance before the final stage of acceptance, where the workforce adopts a new norm of performance. During each stage, not only is individual performance impacted (supply side), but additional demand is generated in order to manage the situation (demand side). Where we are forecasting against an expected change, these factors must be considered as multiplying factors in demand levels; moreover, they must form part of any contingency planning against worst-case scenarios of change or crisis.

Changing demand trends

The fourth industrial revolution

The fourth industrial revolution is creating a new cyber-physical world that is changing the trends in demand. Autonomous technology and the catch-all of artificial intelligence are perhaps the changes that have received the most significant spotlight. This new intelligence is enabling activity without direct human intervention. Blockchain, the use of a distributed ledger over a network, is possibly a close second in publicity, primarily driven by being the enabling technology behind cryptocurrencies. Two key trends that have not quite received the same fame, but are nonetheless key shifts, are edge and quantum. Edge computing is a topology where processing power and information access is placed closer to the end-user, similar to the way RAM works on a computer. For example, rather than having millions of subscribers attempting to stream the same film from the same datacentre (with the result of people receiving the buffering screen of their chosen provider), data is placed closer to the users to provide localized data traffic and reduce latency. The analogy is that the centralized network is our bookcase, and the edge is having on our desk a small pile of the books we most commonly use. With the increased use of the cloud and the advent of 5G networks, the empowered edge is a crucial enabler. The use of quantum-mechanical phenomena to perform computation is the other major shift. In late 2019, 77 scientists at Google claimed to have achieved *quantum supremacy*, where a quantum computer has been able to carry out a specific calculation beyond the capabilities of a regular computer (Arute *et al*, 2019). The analogy is that rather than organizing our bookcase by ourselves, quantum is the equivalent of bringing our friends round to help.

The cyber-world directly intersects the physical world in advances in robotics and the ubiquitous internet of things (IoT). Advances in material science are combining with biotechnology to create new materials at a cellular and molecular level. Combining these together with 3D printing is enabling innovations such as the building of houses by Aectual using bioplastics (Molitch-Hou, 2018). Finally, the mark of all industrial revolutions, are the latest advances in not only the generation and transfer of energy but also in the storage of it.

The impact on demand

The apparent impact of the fourth industrial revolution on people is information and access to information, with various studies indicating the extent of these trends. The total number of business and consumer emails sent and received per day is expected to exceed 347 billion by year-end 2023, from 293 billion in 2019 (Radicati Group, Inc, 2019). In 2020, the site internetlivestats.com (archived at https://perma.cc/5L2M-W2VF) indicated there were 500 million tweets sent and 3.5 billion Google searches each day. Cisco's annual *Visual Networking Index* report predicts that by 2022 there will be more than 28 billion connected devices, up from 18 billion in 2017 (Cisco, 2019). All of this connectivity means that global data is forecast to grow from 33 zettabytes in 2018 to 175 zettabytes in 2025 (Reinsel *et al*, 2018). To give an indication of scale, if we were to attempt to download 175 zettabytes at an (enviable in 2020 terms) average speed of 50 megabits per second, it would take us 900 million years! Quite simply, we are generating and accessing more data than ever before and the trend is pointing upwards.

The meeting of these technological innovations with the demographic trends we explored in Part Three is resulting in a seismic shift in the expectations of humankind, both as consumers and as workers, that translates into a change in the derived demand for labour. The ubiquity of technology and greater choice has given rise to the demand for greater personalization and individuality, a demand that is both satiated and fuelled by social media. As consumers, we increasingly want goods and services that are specifically tailored to us and available at a place and time of our choosing. This is shifting demand to provide us with greater choice and allow that personal tailoring; no longer will Henry Ford's famous phrase apply, that 'any customer can have a car painted any color he wants so long as it is black' (Ford, 1922). Perhaps more significantly, it is translating to increased demand in the service element of the value chain (Porter, 1985) that many organizations are unable to directly monetize and are absorbing as an overhead cost, such as aftersales support.

In spite of the rise of individualism, this change has given rise to a new form of social justice far beyond the traditional view that stems from Saint Augustine of Hippo (Clark, 2015). The emphasis has been increasingly on 'fair and just distribution of rights, opportunities, and resources' (Cramme and Diamond, 2009). Not only has this extended into pressure for greater social mobility and reduced income inequality, but this is also transcending time in pushing the climate change agenda to ensure greater equality between current and future generations. Nowhere has this ambition been more cohesively conjoined than in the 17 goals for sustainable development created by the UN, which we explored in Chapter 3. For organizations, this change is presenting as a population that takes an increasing interest in the social and ethical credentials of the places they work and the businesses from which they buy. One famous example was the Volkswagen emissions scandal of 2015. The US Environmental Protection Agency (EPA) issued a notice of violation after they found that Volkswagen had intentionally programmed turbocharged direct injection (TDI) diesel engines to activate their emissions controls only during laboratory emissions testing, but emit up to 40 times more nitrogen oxides in real-world driving (Chappell, 2015). Sales of its cars plummeted and within a year the share price had fallen 30 per cent (Chu, 2016). As a result, organizations are progressively moving away from the Friedman doctrine that has influenced business for many decades. Economist Milton Friedman propounded the theory that an organization has no social responsibility towards general society and that its sole responsibility is towards its shareholders. In this view, the CEO is an employee of the owners of the business and has 'a direct responsibility… to conduct the business in accordance with their desires' (Friedman, 1970). This built on earlier thinkers, notably the Nobel Prize-winning economist Friedrich Hayek. He said the focus of organizations must be on the long-term maximization of returns on capital investment and that 'the fashionable doctrine that [business] policy should be guided by *social considerations* is likely to produce most undesirable results' (Hayek, 1960). There are many who still hold true to the doctrine and that shareholder value is not the enemy of social responsibility; after all, the Volkswagen scandal did impact shareholder value. However, this perspective conflates the issues; Volkswagen's shareholders benefited from the apparent start in 2008 (Ewing, 2015) of defeat device installation and different shareholders lost in 2015. As a result, organizations are placing greater effort on what was once called corporate social responsibility (CSR) and is often termed as variations of responsible and sustainable. At the basic level, there is a requirement for corporate compliance with legislation aimed at improving social justice. Examples of this at the cusp of the 2020s are global ambitions around banning single-use plastics in the short term and carbon neutrality in the long term. The next level is one of corporate philanthropy. There are certainly claims that there has been a growing practice of both deceiving the public on the credentials of a product or business approach, and of distracting the public from reputationally damaging news with some form of philanthropic gesture. One example is *greenwashing*, when related to the environment, which was claimed when Starbucks introduced a new straw-less lid that actually contained more plastic by weight than the old straw and lid combination (Britschgi, 2018). Another is *pinkwashing*, in the context of LGBT rights, which was claimed when BP launched an LGBT careers event in the wake of the Deepwater Horizon explosion and oil spill (Wilkins, 2014). Regardless of the rationale and terminology, there are certainly clear correlations between adverse negative coverage on social justice and subsequent mitigations. One study at Brown University concluded that investment in advertising and promotion by major oil companies directly corresponded to negative media coverage on climate change (Brulle *et al*, 2019). The better organizations are tending to go beyond compliance and corporate philanthropy to the third level of connecting aspects of social justice to their business model as a method of value creation. It is, perhaps, a return to the view of post-Keynesian economist John Kenneth Galbraith that 'the firm is wholly subordinate to the social edict as prescribed by the consumer. So, accordingly, are the people who comprise the firm' (Galbraith, 1967). The totality of this change continues to have a fundamental impact on the nature of demand for organizations, necessitating transformations in products, operating models and supply chains.

The future of work

A report by Deloitte defined the future of work as the result of changes affecting three key dimensions: work, workforce and workplace (Schwartz *et al*, 2019). The dimension of work is inextricably linked to the changing demand trends we have just covered. Automation and technological innovation are expected to reduce the human share of time spent on today's tasks from 71 per cent to 58 per cent by 2022, whilst creating new tasks as a result (WEF, 2018). This will mean a fundamental shift in the way work is done for a number of occupations and results in two specific outcomes. For certain types of work, it will necessitate the development of new skills in order for a worker to remain relevant in the workplace. The biggest shift we have seen is the necessity for basic digital skills as more work is migrated through technology platforms. The second outcome we will see from this innovation is the lowering of barriers to entry into certain roles as the requirement for knowledge is offset by technological changes in the environment, which we discussed in the first chapter. We have all seen that the ubiquity of satellite navigation has largely made irrelevant the essential local knowledge that was the mark of taxicab drivers. In addition to reducing the human share of tasks, technology will undoubtedly replace jobs. It is projected that around a million jobs will be lost, but another 1.75 million jobs will be gained as a result (WEF, 2018). In total, we can expect up to 14 per cent of current jobs to be eradicated and a further 32 per cent to be disrupted (Nedelkoska and Quintini, 2018). This shift will mean 'more than 120 million workers in the world's 12 largest economies may need to be retrained/reskilled [by 2022] as a result of intelligent/AI-enabled automation' (LaPrade et al, 2019).

The dimension of workforce is based on the megatrends that were detailed in Part Three of this book. The future workforce will, therefore, have a much higher average age as a result of both the extension of working lives and a historic decline in birth rates that means there are fewer younger workers than before. The workforce will be increasingly more diverse across a number of different strands. There will be greater diversity in race, that being the meshing of nationality and ethnicity, as a result of increases in migration. This will be supported by greater democratization of information that continues to enable migrants to assimilate faster into the working environment of the host nation. The pressure towards greater social justice will support greater diversity in terms of race but also across the many wider strands. The movement will dovetail into a declining working-age population that will necessitate organizations looking beyond their traditional talent pools for new workers.

This will be supported by the final dimension of the workplace and a change from work being viewed as a place, to being recognized rightly as an activity. Technology is enabling a shift in when and where work is done. The increase in connectivity will also increase diversity as it enables supply chains to transcend national boundaries with far greater ease than before. Moreover, it will allow many of those who have previously been underrepresented to now gain greater access to work. For example, those with either a disability or caring responsibilities that may have been incompatible with the traditional notions of work are now able to deliver value to organizations at a place and time of their choosing. The more prevailing aspect to the workplace is that of the evolution into new forms of organization. In *Reinventing the Organization*, Professors Dave Ulrich and Arthur Yeung talk of the market-oriented ecosystem (MOE) being adopted by leading firms. These organizations are leveraging the key capabilities of the assimilation of market information with a relentless focus on the consumers, rapid innovation and the agility to fail fast and scale at pace (Yeung and Ulrich, 2019). In order to achieve this, greater demand is emerging for a different mix of skills. Bernadette Wightman, Managing Director of BT Group, highlights that:

> Study after study shows that while technology will alter many roles directly, it's also set to have indirect effects. As demand for mathematics, computing and data analysis grows, so too will the need for human attributes like creativity, critical thinking, persuasion and negotiation' (Bernadette Wightman, Managing Director of Banking and Financial Services, BT Group, 2020).

Quantitative methods

Forecasts based on reference class are just one of a number of quantitative methods that can be used to forecast the derived demand for the workforce.

Extrapolation and interpolation

Extrapolation is perhaps the quickest and easiest method of forecasting; it involves taking the historical trends and projecting them forward. The limitation of the model is that it is based solely on historical data, so it should be saved for areas of the organization where change is not expected. Interpolation, though simple, can be an enormously powerful tool where we have a future target. If an objective is to double revenue in five years, with a strategy of increased sales of current goods and services, then interpolating the future state to the current state can provide an effective indication of the demand forecast. Indeed, a quick comparison between extrapolation and interpolation can provide a quick indication of the scale of change required to meet the target.

Moving averages

The moving average approach, occasionally referred to as a rolling average, is an effective method of forecasting on the basis of time-series data. There are a number of variations of this approach, of which we will focus on those most relevant to demand forecasting. The simple moving average (SMA) is an unweighted mean of the time series data.

$$\frac{\text{Sum of quantities in the time period}}{\text{Number of time periods}} = SMA$$

If, for example, quarterly output for a process is 300 units, then the three-month moving average would be 100 units. The limitations of the model are similar to those of extrapolation. A weighted moving average (WMA) places greater importance on more recent changes in demand. Weighting is done in line with the number of periods, so 300 units in the quarter may translate into sequential months of 95, 100 and 105. On this basis, the WMA calculation would be:

$$\frac{[(3 \times 105) + (2 \times 100) + (1 \times 95)]}{6} = 101.67$$

The exponential moving average (EMA), more commonly known as exponential smoothing, is similar to a WMA except that the applied weighting decreases exponentially over time. WMA and EMA can both prove highly valuable across all three planning horizons.

Error correction model

The error correction model (ECM) is a much more complex, but highly effective, method of forecasting workforce demand based on time series data. The model corrects for the short-term deviation from the long-term equilibrium that can exist in moving average models. One study utilizing a vector error correction model (VECM), which utilizes a multivariate approach, was able to establish a long-term relationship between economic variables and the derived demand for labour within the construction industry (Wong *et al*, 2007).

Qualitative methods

Qualitative approaches are some of the simplest to use when conducting demand forecasting. Given the prevalence of absent and fragmented demand information, qualitative methods 'are particularly useful when high-quality empirical data are not available' (Safarishahrbijari, 2018). These approaches hinge on the expert knowledge that we, and those around us, are able to bring when considering the future. As a starting point, we may well have scenarios as part of gaining buy-in, which we covered in Chapter 7. Scenarios are a qualitative approach that can be highly effective. However, depending on how we arrived at those scenarios, they are often prone to the bias of the HiPPO (highest paid person's opinion). The following are the main approaches I recommend for qualitative demand forecasting.

Delphi method

The Delphi method, also known as estimate-talk-estimate (ETE), was developed by the RAND Corporation in the early Cold War. The aim was to understand, from a Soviet perspective, how they might plan aspects of strategic atomic bombing against US industrial targets. The approach involves the creation of a virtual panel of experts who are questioned about a central problem on an individual basis. The panel is asked to respond with their forecast, the factors they have considered when reaching that conclusion, and further information they would need to make a better determination. This exercise is repeated over a number of subsequent rounds where the facilitator shares the collective factors that are being considered and any further information that has been requested. This exercise continues over several rounds until a consensus is reached (Dalkey and Helmer, 1963).

The principles of the approach are anonymity, iteration, controlled feedback and a statistical group response (Rowe and Wright, 2001). Anonymity results in better-quality responses from the experts, who are able to be more honest about their view and are not swayed by the opinions of others. The iteration of rounds, using written feedback, enables experts to learn from the wider understanding and modify their judgements accordingly. The feedback is controlled by the facilitator, who analyses responses and restates these to the panel in an aggregated form. Finally, the group response is presented in a statistical format to enable the panel to understand the extent to which they deviate from the collective view (Von der Gracht, 2012).

Business educator Clifford Neal Smith predicted a world where technology would provide rapid analysis of Delphi questionnaires and enable it to reach a consensus far quicker than a normal committee (Smith, 1972). Over 40 years later, the Defense Advanced Research Projects Agency (DARPA) funded research into this vision. In an approach known as real-time Delphi (RTD), the conventional application of iterated rounds is replaced by analysis in real time using a combination of artificial intelligence and natural language processing (Gordon and Pease, 2006). Professor Heiko von der Gracht has shared subsequently the details of over 40 studies across two platforms, from the Millennium Project and the Center for Future Studies and Knowledge Management, which demonstrate the success of the approach (Von der Gracht et al, 2011). Indeed, thinkers have utilized RTD alongside counterfactual approaches that seek to identify the key 'fork in the road' of our current lives and apply that to futures forecasting (Todorova and Gordon, 2017).

Nominal group technique

The nominal group technique (NGT) started life as a component of the programme planning model, developed by Andre Delbecq and Andrew H Van de Ven, both experts on organizational management and professors at the University of Wisconsin. The approach involves the framing of a problem to an assembled panel. The panel members then consider the problem independently and formulate their forecasts, before sharing those forecasts and discussing them collectively. The forecasts are voted and ranked and the overall process may be repeated a number of times until a consensus is achieved (Delbecq and Van de Ven, 1971).

The nominal group technique has the advantage of often arriving at a consensus far faster than the conventional Delphi method. By avoiding the delay necessary to analyse and aggregate the feedback, NGT can be far quicker at progressing thinking. In addition, unlike many other collective brainstorming approaches, NGT ensures equal participation in both sharing and discussing ideas. The key disadvantage, by comparison, is the lack of anonymity that increases the risk of consensus being swayed by factors of personality rather than the rationality of the ideas.

Crowdsourcing

Sir Francis Galton was an English polymath at the turn of the 20th century who pioneered a number of innovations in statistics and psychological theory. In 1906 he visited a livestock fair, the West of England Fat Stock and Poultry Exhibition. Whilst there, he attended a contest where participants could, for an entry fee, attempt to guess the correct dressed weight of an ox (that being the weight after being butchered). Galton examined the 800 entries and found the median estimate to be 1,207 imperial pounds in weight, a mere 0.8 per cent higher than the actual weight of 1,198 pounds (Galton, 1907). This was a remarkable level of accuracy that was entirely unexpected. In fact, what Galton observed was not a one-off event. In his book *The Wisdom of Crowds*, US journalist James Surowiecki cites numerous similar examples of collective intelligence. The criteria for this wisdom are, foremost, that those involved must have either private knowledge or an individual interpretation of the situation. Furthermore, the individual perspective must be independent of the influence of others and able to be based on local knowledge. In addition, there needs to be a way of aggregating those individual views and converting them into a collective decision that is underpinned by a collective view of fairness (Surowiecki, 2004). In spite of this, many organizations have tended towards a Platonistic approach: eschewing the views of the masses in favour of those of the management (Plato, 1955).

As Galton's example shows, the practice of crowdsourcing certainly predates the first use, in a *Wired* article, of the portmanteau (Howe, 2006). The crowdsourcing most commonly found in relation to organizational and demand planning is that of market research. Drucker recognized the importance of this when he wrote, 'true marketing starts out… with the customer, his demographics, his realities, his needs, his values' (Drucker, 1973). We may consider conducting market research as an independent exercise in forecasting demand, or as part of other qualitative approaches. In this sense, the information provided by consumers is more important than any other input.

What is important about all these approaches, both qualitative and quantitative, is that they are most effective when combined. For example, the nominal group technique can help establish the factors to be included in a vector error correction model. Alternatively, an extrapolation or moving average forecast can be fine-tuned with the Delphi method. Regardless of which approach is used, the forecast must be provided in a quantitative format. I have seen many instances of demand forecasts that indicate a need for more digital specialists, which tends to translate into a workforce plan of undefined additionality of digital specialists. This is an unhelpful metric; how is a digital specialist defined? Would success be achieved if there was just one more? How about if, to the contrary, millions were spent ensuring the entire workforce was a digital specialist? How can we possibly compare the gap between what we have and what we need now and in the future? Avoid vague definitions and qualitative measures; instead, ensure metrics are quantitative and that requirements are aligned to the aspects of the seven rights.

Determining the seven rights

The demand forecast results in a quantification of the seven rights: capability, size, shape, location, time, cost and risk. Just like concepts of *right* from ethical and moral philosophy, what is right for an organization often comes down to perspective. Joseph P Overton was a senior vice president of the Mackinac Center for Public Policy when, in the 1990s, he postulated that the viability of a political policy hinged on whether it fell within a range of acceptability rather than on personal preference (Lehman, 2003). This *Overton window* is equally applicable to the seven rights, where what is right for the organization is the most acceptable point that lies within the range of the best- and worst-case scenarios. As such, the demand forecast provides an indicative view of the seven rights. This will be calibrated during the action planning phase in order to arrive at the final view.

The right capability

As the core of the seven rights, the right capability is what many practitioners find the most complex of the rights to forecast, particularly over longer planning horizons. Part of that challenge rests on the uncertainty around the types of capability that will be necessary for the future of work. The key is to remain true to the assumptions that we made within our planning horizon. Those assumptions will likely determine that for the workforce segment we examined, over the horizon we are forecasting, there will be capabilities that remain unchanged. For areas of work that we expect will require different capabilities, then consider if there are external sources of information that give us an indication of the capabilities that are needed. Are there other organizations that have already made that change and can serve as a benchmark? Are there industry forecasts that give an indication of the emerging capability requirements? These will help reduce the aperture on the nature of capability requirements. Where we still have a known unknown, then that points towards the capabilities of a growth mindset that will enable us to develop new capabilities once they emerge. The unknown unknowns are at the edge of the best- and worst-case scenarios, for which the capability requirements will not only be the growth mindset but also the ability to respond quickly to disruption.

The right size

The right size is inextricably linked to the concept of the right capability. Our forecasts will provide a quantitative measure of the size of workforce the organization will require. That forecast is likely to be much clearer at a macro level than it is at a meso or micro level as accuracy decreases with increasing granularity.

The right shape

At this stage, the right shape for the organization may not necessarily be defined across all strands. The intra-capability strand, the mix of capabilities, will be clear as a result of having established the right size. Aspects of the inter-capability strand may be less clear, either as a result of planning at a macro level or as a result of planning across a strategic horizon. Though there may be some common elements that are clear, we should not expect to have every single inter-capability element identified. For the characteristic element, these are best defined only in relation to specific targets that have been set for the representation of groups within the workforce. For example, 50 pioneering companies at the annual meeting of the World Economic Forum in Davos committed to a framework of recruiting women into half of their top five emerging high-growth roles by 2022, across all seniority levels, and developing a system of gender-equal reward (WEF, 2020). The strand of contract, like that of characteristic, will relate only to elements that are already specified. For example, Barclays and GlaxoSmithKline are alleged to have imposed a blanket ban on the use of off-payroll contractors in the UK as a result of legislative changes that force organizations to adopt accountability for the tax status of contingent workers (Faragher, 2019).

The right location

The strand of the right location consists of two separate elements. The right size of the organization must be established based on ensuring that the right capability aligns to the locations of demand. This ensures that the right location is confirmed in relation to both the geographic and structural aspects. The geographical element will be further informed by existing plans on the location of sites, which may evolve during the planning horizon.

The right time

An accurate appreciation of the right time is often absent in demand forecasting; the crucial component is that the overarching time is the duration of the planning horizon. The common error is to focus exclusively on the demand forecast at the end of the planning horizon, for example, the workforce that the organization needs in five years. The correct question relates to the workforce that the organization needs *for* the next five years. This gap leads to the abandonment of workforce plans as the organization falters in the short and medium term due to a lack of appreciation of the impact on the first two planning horizons. Within the planning horizon, we can expect to see changes in the other rights. For example, if we are embarking on a significant transformation, we would expect to see an increase and subsequent decrease in the demand for labour that is dedicated specifically to that transformation. We may also forecast demand spikes where, during the cutover of service, we have a workforce operating on the existing model and a workforce operating on the new model. I have seen numerous plans over the years where there has been an expectation that a service can transition at the flick of a switch and a redundant workforce is forecast to disappear into the ether; that is not a feasible expectation.

The right cost

The culmination of the preceding five rights will arrive at an indication of the right cost. The primary aspect is the indicative *total cost of the workforce* (TCOW), which is a key metric to understand. The first component of TCOW is the sum of all the direct workforce costs; this will include all pay, benefits and bonuses that are associated with the workforce. It includes all costs for worker-related insurance and taxes for which the organization is liable, in addition to all off-payroll costs for contingent labour. The second component, which is slightly more complex, comprises the additional overhead costs associated with the workforce. This will include the cost of providing technology, facilities expenses and the cost of any outsourced services such as payroll, IT support, learning and recruitment. At a meso and a micro level, this second component also extends to overhead costs that are borne outside of our workforce segment, for example, the share of the cost of support functions such as HR and finance. A common mistake, however, is to forget the components of a calculation at a meso level when it is rolled up to a macro level, thus double counting the TCOW for supporting functions.

The second and often contrasting aspect of the right cost may be a budget, the desired control on the TCOW. The tension is the unsurprising rarity of a workforce budget being higher than the TCOW that results from a demand forecast. This contrast is a feature that will be addressed in detail within Part Six of this book, but the single most fatal mistake that can be made is to accept the right cost as being based exclusively on the budget. As we covered in the previous chapter, **the budget is not the demand**; the budget is simply a financial lever for controlling demand. If we have captured the aspects of the right time accurately, then opportunity cost will not feature in the demand forecast. The opportunity cost results in a choice to realign the workforce, ie the supply, from one source of demand to another.

The right risk

If we have correctly mapped the previous six rights, then we are able to move into the largest Overton window of the right risk. At this point, it is helpful to understand risk in terms of primary and secondary. Primary risks are those associated with the primary drivers of demand. In simple terms, even if the organization has a workforce that meets all the seven rights, there is a risk that the business activity still does not deliver the end result. For example, this may relate to launching a new product or expanding into new countries. By examining the drivers of change and the changing demand trends, we will be able to establish the likelihood and the impact of key factors. The detail of, and appetite for, these primary risks will be quantifiable as a result of this process. Secondary risks result from operational execution: the *choices* that are made in the management and resourcing of demand. In advance of the phase of creating an action plan, which we will cover in Part Six, this risk cannot yet be determined. However, there may be underlying appetites around the secondary risks that have been shared by stakeholders that may be captured as indicative at this stage.

Summary

This exercise aims to create a forecast of demand that can be expressed, quantitatively, in the form of the seven rights. To do that, we take the demand calculation from the previous chapter, and we consider the factors that will cause that calculation to change over time. Using a mixture of quantitative and qualitative methods, we overlay these factors on the calculation to create a forecast over time.

The former ice hockey legend, Wayne Gretzky, has often shared the advice from his father '[to skate] to where the puck is going, not where it's been' (Gretzky and Reilly, 1990). The demand calculation is where the puck has been; the demand forecast is where the puck is going. If we think of the metrics we see in the workplace, the vast majority are descriptors of the past: the equivalent of where the puck has been. The problem is not the metric; it is that businesses then make decisions on that information alone and then, figuratively, skate to where the puck has been. By creating an accurate forecast of demand, we will be able to illustrate where the puck will be at every stage of the planning horizon: that is the target.

> When you practise workforce planning, ask yourself:
> - What are the factors that will influence the forecast of demand?
> - What are the changing demand trends that are likely to impact demand?
> - What are the most appropriate methods to forecast demand in my organization?
> - How do I express this forecast against each of the seven rights?
> - Is my forecast quantitative?

References

Arute, F *et al* (2019) Quantum supremacy using a programmable superconducting processor, *Nature*, 574 (7779), pp 505–10 doi.org/10.1038/s41586-019-1666-5 (archived at https://perma.cc/4E5N-M7VG)

Berkeley, T (2020) A Review of High Speed 2, 5 January, documentcloud.adobe.com/link/review?uri=urn%3Aaaid%3Ascds%3AUS%3A8e9c8f87-2650-4aa0-8e0f-0eaf6e709640 (archived at https://perma.cc/RBC4-9YGT)

Britschgi, C (2018) Starbucks bans plastic straws, winds up using more plastic, *Reason.com*, 12 July, reason.com/2018/07/12/starbucks-straw-ban-will-see-the-company/ (archived at https://perma.cc/ML6L-LPFS)

Brulle, R J, Aronczyk, M and Carmichael, J (2019) Corporate promotion and climate change: An analysis of key variables affecting advertising spending by major oil corporations, 1986–2015, *Climatic Change*, 11 December, doi.org/10.1007/s10584-019-02582-8 (archived at https://perma.cc/8AFA-2XQY)

Chappell, B (2015) Volkswagen used 'defeat device' to skirt emissions rules, EPA says, *National Public Radio*, 18 September, www.npr.org/sections/thetwo-way/2015/09/18/441467960/volkswagen-used-defeat-device-to-skirt-emissions-rules-epa-says (archived at https://perma.cc/V9Y4-Q3SN)

Chu, B (2016) Volkswagen diesel emissions scandal: The toxic legacy, *The Independent*, 17 September, www.independent.co.uk/news/business/Leading_business_story/volkswagen-diesel-emissions-scandal-the-toxic-legacy-a7312056.html (archived at https://perma.cc/QK28-L6UG)

Cisco (2019) *Cisco Visual Networking Index: Forecast and trends, 2017–2022*, www.cisco.com/c/en/us/solutions/collateral/service-provider/visual-networking-index-vni/white-paper-c11-741490.pdf (archived at https://perma.cc/SW7M-5TUR)

Clark, M T (2015) Augustine on justice, in T Delgado, J Doody and K Paffenroth (eds) *Augustine and Social Justice*, Lexington Books, Maryland

Cramme, O and Diamond, P (2009) *Social Justice in a Global Age*, Polity Press, Cambridge

Dalkey, N and Helmer, O (1963) An experimental application of the DELPHI method to the use of experts, *Management Science*, **9** (3), pp 458–67, doi:10.1287/mnsc.9.3.458

Delbecq, A L and Van de Ven, A H (1971) A group process model for problem identification and program planning, *The Journal of Applied Behavioral Science*, 7 (4), pp 466–92 doi:10.1177/002188637100700404

Drucker, P F (1973) *Management: Tasks, responsibilities, practices*, Harper & Row, London

Economic Affairs Committee (2015) The economics of High Speed 2, 10 March, publications.parliament.uk/pa/ld201415/ldselect/ldeconaf/134/13402.htm (archived at https://perma.cc/3857-CB3E)

Ewing, J (2015) Volkswagen engine-rigging scheme said to have begun in 2008, *The New York Times*, 4 October, www.nytimes.com/2015/10/05/business/engine-shortfall-pushed-volkswagen-to-evade-emissions-testing.html (archived at https://perma.cc/U2US-P7CH)

Faragher, J (2019) IR35: Barclays and GSK impose blanket off-payroll ban, contractors claim, *Personnel Today*, 3 October, www.personneltoday.com/hr/barclays-and-others-urge-contractors-to-go-paye/ (archived at https://perma.cc/HB3F-63BC)

Ford, H (1922/2006) *My Life and Work*, Xlibris, Bloomington

Forsyth, D K and Burt, C D B (2008) Allocating time to future tasks: The effect of task segmentation on planning fallacy bias, *Memory & Cognition*, 36 (4), pp 791–98, doi:10.3758/mc.36.4.791

Friedman, M (1970) The social responsibility of business is to increase its profits, *The New York Times Magazine*, 13 September, http://www.umich.edu/~thecore/doc/Friedman.pdf (archived at https://perma.cc/78AT-U4XB)

Galbraith, J (1967) The goals of an industrial system, in H I Ansoff (ed) (1969) *Business Strategy*, Penguin, Harmondsworth

Galton, F (1907) Vox populi, *Nature*, 75 (1949), pp 450–51, www.galton.org/essays/1900-1911/galton-1907-vox-populi.pdf (archived at https://perma.cc/8ADX-BX5V)

Gillan, C (2013) The cost of HS2 just ballooned, thanks to the bungling transport department, *The Telegraph*, 2 July, www.telegraph.co.uk/news/politics/10155631/The-cost-of-HS2-just-ballooned-thanks-to-the-bungling-Transport-Department.html (archived at https://perma.cc/6ZL6-R5QK)

Gordon, T and Pease, A (2006) RT Delphi: An efficient, "round-less" almost real time Delphi method, *Technological Forecasting and Social Change*, 73 (4), pp 321–33 doi:10.1016/j.techfore.2005.09.005

Gretzky, W and Reilly, R (1990) *Gretzky: An autobiography*, HarperCollins, New York

Hayek, F A (1960) The corporation in a democratic society: In whose interest ought it and will it be won? in H I Ansoff (ed) (1969) *Business Strategy*, Penguin, Harmondsworth

High Speed Two Ltd (HS2)(2012) *HS2 Cost and Risk Model Report*, https://assets.publishing.service.gov.uk/government/uploads/system/uploads/attachment_data/file/69741/hs2-cost-and-risk-model-report.pdf (archived at https://perma.cc/CPR3-S2VU)

Howe, J (2006) The rise of crowdsourcing, *Wired*, 6 January, www.wired.com/2006/06/crowds/ (archived at https://perma.cc/NZ93-JQ7J)

Kahneman, D (2011) *Thinking, Fast and Slow*, Allen Lane, London

Kahneman, D and Tversky, A (1979) Prospect theory: An analysis of decision under risk, *Econometrica*, 47 (2), pp 183–214, doi:10.1017/cbo9780511609220.014

Kahneman, D and Tversky, A (1982) Intuitive prediction: Biases and corrective procedures, in A Tversky (ed) *Judgment Under Uncertainty: Heuristics and biases*, Cambridge University Press, New York

Kübler-Ross, E (1969) *On Death and Dying*, Routledge, London

LaPrade, A et al (2019) *The Enterprise Guide to Closing the Skills Gap*, IBM Institute for Business Value, www.ibm.com/downloads/cas/EPYMNBJA (archived at https://perma.cc/W9TX-FSHM)

Lehman, J G (2003) The Overton window, Mackinac Center for Public Policy, www.mackinac.org/overtonwindow (archived at https://perma.cc/3QQC-KHRE)

Milmo, D (2010) Adonis unveils £30bn high-speed rail plans, *The Guardian*, 11 March, www.theguardian.com/politics/2010/mar/11/adonis-high-speed-rail-blueprint (archived at https://perma.cc/3MH6-GDX7)

Molitch-Hou, M (2018) Aectual 3D prints everything from floors to walls [Blog] *Engineering.com*, 13 September, www.engineering.com/BIM/ArticleID/17639/Aectual-3D-Prints-Everything-from-Floors-to-Walls.aspx (archived at https://perma.cc/9MNU-73X4)

National Transport Safety Board (NTSB) (2010) Aircraft accident report 10/03, 4 May www.ntsb.gov/investigations/accidentreports/pages/AAR1003.aspx (archived at https://perma.cc/25AP-E8UL)

Nedelkoska, L and Quintini, G (2018) Automation, skills use and training, OECD Social, Employment and Migration Working Papers 202, OECD Publishing, Paris doi.org/10.1787/2e2f4eea-en (archived at https://perma.cc/G4N8-YTNG)

Perez, M B (2013) Strategic Workforce planning in the federal government: A work in progress, in D L Ward and R Tripp (eds) *Positioned: Strategic workforce planning the gets the right person in the right job*, AMACOM, New York

Plato (1955) *The Republic*, Penguin Books, London

Porter, M E (1985) *Competitive Advantage: Creating and sustaining superior performance*, The Free Press, New York

Radicati Group, Inc (2019) *Email Statistics Report, 2019–2023*, www.radicati.com/?p=15792 (archived at https://perma.cc/73HF-N9A8)

Reinsel, D, Gantz, J and Rydning, J (2018) *The Digitization of the World, IDC White Paper*, November, #US44413318 https://www.seagate.com/files/www-content/our-story/trends/files/idc-seagate-dataage-whitepaper.pdf (archived at https://perma.cc/5B56-D4ZY)

Rowe, G and Wright, G (2001) Expert opinions in forecasting: The role of the Delphi technique, in J S Armstrong (ed) *Principles of Forecasting: A handbook for researchers and practitioners*, Kluwer Academic Publishers, Boston

Safarishahrbijari, A (2018) Workforce forecasting models: A systematic review, *Journal of Forecasting*, **37** (7), pp 739–53, doi:10.1002/for.2541

Sanna, L J et al (2005) The hourglass is half full or half empty: Temporal framing and the group planning fallacy, *Group Dynamics: Theory, research, and practice*, **9** (3), pp 173–88, doi:10.1037/1089-2699.9.3.173

Schwartz, J et al (2019) What is the future of work? *Deloitte*, 1 April, www2.deloitte.com/us/en/insights/focus/technology-and-the-future-of-work/redefining-work-workforces-workplaces.html (archived at https://perma.cc/TKZ6-DH4C)

Smith, C N (1972) Some long-range aspects of international personnel planning, in E Burack and Walker, J W (eds) *Manpower Planning and Programming*, Allyn & Bacon, Boston

Sullenberger, C B (2009) *Highest Duty: My search for what really matters*, William Morrow, New York

Surowiecki, J (2004) *The Wisdom of Crowds*, Anchor, New York

Todorova, M and Gordon, T J (2017) Report on a study of counterfacts as a futures research technique for forecasting future developments, *World Futures Review*, **9** (2), pp 93–105 doi:10.1177/1946756717702754

Topham, G (2013) Cost of HS2 up £10bn to £42.6bn, transport secretary tells MPs, *The Guardian*, 26 June, www.theguardian.com/uk/2013/jun/26/hs2-costs-escalate-mps-told (archived at https://perma.cc/QM2H-BZ3Z)

Von der Gracht, H A (2012), Consensus measurement in Delphi studies, *Technological Forecasting and Social Change*, **79** (8), pp 1525–36, doi:10.1016/j.techfore.2012.04.013

Von der Gracht, H A *et al* (2011) New frontiers in Delphi research-experiences with Real Time Delphi in foresight, Conference Volume of the WorldFuture 2011, Vancouver, Canada www.researchgate.net/publication/292524949_New_Frontiers_in_Delphi_Research-Experiences_with_Real_Time_Delphi_in_Foresight (archived at https://perma.cc/8DQ5-3XX7)

WEF (World Economic Forum) (2018) *The Future of Jobs Report: 2018*, www3.weforum.org/docs/WEF_Future_of_Jobs_2018.pdf (archived at https://perma.cc/4XW6-VWP4)

WEF (World Economic Forum) (2020) Hardwiring gender parity in the future of work, www.weforum.org/projects/hardwiring-gender-parity-in-the-future-of-work (archived at https://perma.cc/9X3W-37TP)

Wightman, B (2020) Hundreds of millions of workers need reskilling. Where do we start? World Economic Forum, 16 January, www.weforum.org/discom?bobulate=BfuasPmflRxHYPO2MAth4%2BtNFKrJPq5E%2FmyLtB6ODoju%2F%2FAmXgjdm%2FVT2Hvl%0AFLufiMdjukoy%2FNTEARQHwAzfhw%3D%3D%0A (archived at https://perma.cc/JZH2-EFKQ)

Wilkins, N (2014) BP reach for the pinkwash with 'LGBT Careers Event', *Bright Green*, 11 November, bright-green.org/2014/11/11/news-bp-pinkwash/ (archived at https://perma.cc/C725-NL3C)

Wong, J M W, Chan, A P C and Chiang, Y H (2007) Forecasting construction manpower demand: A vector error correction model, *Building and Environment*, **42** (8), pp 3030–41, doi:10.1016/j.buildenv.2006.07.024

Yeung, A and Ulrich, D (2019) *Reinventing the Organization*, Harvard Business School Publishing, Boston

PART FIVE

Gap analysis

What is the gap between the forecasts of supply and demand?

11

Establishing the gap

Introduction

In a quotation often misattributed to Albert Einstein, a department head at Yale University said, 'If I had only one hour to solve a problem, I would spend up to two-thirds of that hour in attempting to define what the problem is' (Markle, 1966). Having established the truths of supply and demand, gap analysis is focused on defining the problem. It is unfortunate, therefore, that many contemporary thinkers give little time to this aspect of workforce planning. It is too often given lip service as an obvious outcome of forecasting needs and wants. Conducted in isolation, forecasting is academic exercise; gap analysis asks the *so what* question.

If we are unable to identify the true nature of the problem, and make it clear to others, then we cannot hope to create a plan to solve it. 'The most common source of mistakes in management decisions is the emphasis on finding the right answer rather than the right question' (Drucker, 2007).

Assessing the gap

How does the gap evolve to the future organization?

The single biggest mistake I see in the gap analysis of workforce planning hails from the traditional approach of assessing the delta between the current workforce and the future demand. These are two snapshots of distinct points in time: a photograph of today and a painting of the desired state at the end of the planning horizon. To plan against this gap is to embark on an

FIGURE 11.1 Traditional and agile gap analyses

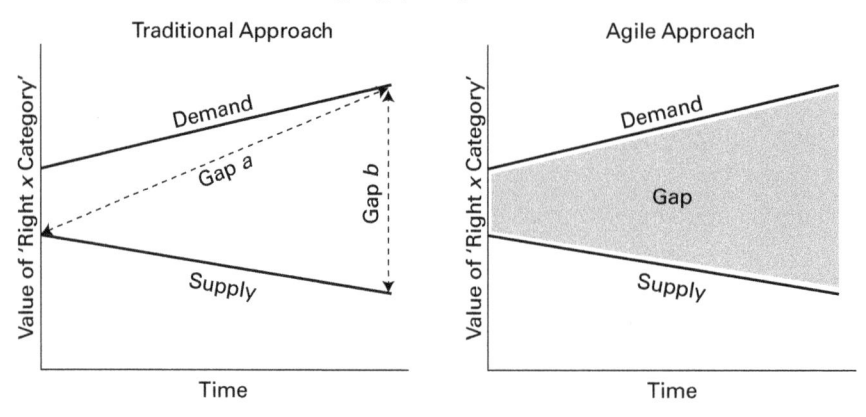

interplanetary flight, where a rocket flies through the vacuum of space until it reaches the final destination. It is an approach that ignores the necessity for an organization to conduct business throughout the planning horizon and is prevalent in horizon two and three approaches. In reality, workforce planning is like sailing a vessel to an island; setting forth on the ocean and adjusting the rudder and the sails as the winds change and the waves hit.

To illustrate the difference between the two, Figure 11.1 shows an x-axis of time and a y-axis of the value of whichever of the seven rights we are looking at. For example, in assessing the Right Size, the values on the x-axis would be either the headcount or FTE of the workforce. In an organization that aims for growth, the derived demand will translate into an increase for a higher number of workers. During the same period, the supply of workers will always decrease, as we covered in Part Three of this book. These aspects are identical in both charts. The traditional approach assesses and plans on a single variant, the gap between the current level of supply and the future level of demand (shown as Gap *a*). In this instance, the approach is ignorant of the change that will naturally take place within the workforce. This approach often results in restructures and redundancies, dismissing workers equivalent to those who would have departed anyway during the planning horizon. Contemporary thinkers have recognized this issue and recommend an approach that compares both the workforce and demand at the end of the planning horizon (shown as Gap *b*). This, unfortunately, ignores a second critical flaw of the traditional approach. By its very nature, it overlooks the demand requirements over the course of the planning horizon; no consideration is given to the achievement of organizational goals and objectives before the endpoint. Such an approach, as we can imagine, would be disastrous for an organization to implement. As a result, this traditional approach lies behind the common problem of being unable to translate workforce plans into action.

Instead, in the agile approach, we examine the gap throughout all the points in the evolution towards the end of the planning horizon. The gap is multivariant, in that it is based on every point of the supply being contrasted against every proceeding instance of the demand. The reason for this is that traditional workforce planning has treated the gap between supply and demand as a constant factor in the organization. Therefore, aiming to bridge the gap at a future point in time is clearly better than never bridging the gap. The concept that I want to introduce here is that **gaps exist only in the future** and never in the present. As soon as we reach the point of execution, the gap is immediately closed. This may seem counterintuitive: how does the gap close and, if it always closes, why plan to close the gap? Let me explain, as much of this relates to Parkinson's law that 'work expands so as to fill the time available for its completion' (Parkinson, 1955). Consider a normal working day and the demand being the meetings we need to attend and the work we need to do, the totality of which exceeds the eight hours that we are contracted to work. How do we fit it all in? What some people do is work longer hours, therefore increasing their supply; another supply method is to delegate that demand to a subordinate. It is more likely, however, that we choose to manage the demand instead. For much of the demand, for example a report we need to write, we may choose to delay completing it until a day in the future. In doing so, the demand moves from today to tomorrow and, to reference one corollary to Parkinson's law, 'in ten hours a day you have time to fall twice as far behind your commitments as in five hours a day' (Asimov, 1961). Alternatively, we may choose to exercise Horstman's corollary, that 'work contracts to fit in the time we give it' (Auzenne and Horstman, 2012). In doing so, we may spend just five minutes on a task that we would have planned to spend half an hour to complete. This may produce a perfect result, in which case the delta of 25 minutes would simply be demand that produced no additional value: a productivity issue. Alternatively, that choice of spending five minutes may be insufficient to create the necessary outcome and result in the drift and waste that we covered in Chapter 9. Another demand choice is to decline work, such as not attending a meeting. Such a choice spans both of the previous corollaries; maybe the meeting is rescheduled and the demand moves. Alternatively, the absence results in no negative impact and reaffirms the decision to decline;

worse, the absence results in drift and waste. In all instances, a supply or demand solution is found. On the supply side, spare capacity is utilized or the workforce is reallocated at the opportunity cost of an alternative source of demand. On the demand side, it can move to a later point in time, potentially generating additional demand as a result. Alternatively, the demand forecast is requalified as necessitating a lower level of derived demand. Finally, the demand may simply be cancelled and the result is a missing output, which may either generate additional demand or result in a failure to generate a successful outcome, such as revenue. This is a critical concept in workforce planning, which we will revisit in Part Six of this book.

The impact of scenarios

The longer the planning horizon, the greater the extent to which the gap between supply and demand is influenced by multiple scenarios. These scenarios, identified during environmental scanning and agreed with our key stakeholders, produce a range of possible outcomes. The extremes of these ranges are the best-case (B-C) and worst-case (W-C) scenarios, with the most-likely (M-L) scenario sitting within the range. It is essential to recognize that these apply separately to both the supply and the demand, as seen in Figure 11.2.

If we think back to our earlier example of the Right Size, considering an organization with a growth ambition, then the best-case scenario would be high consumer demand, which would lead to a high derived demand for labour. The worst-case scenario is clearly the opposite: low consumer demand and low derived demand for labour. The most likely scenario sits

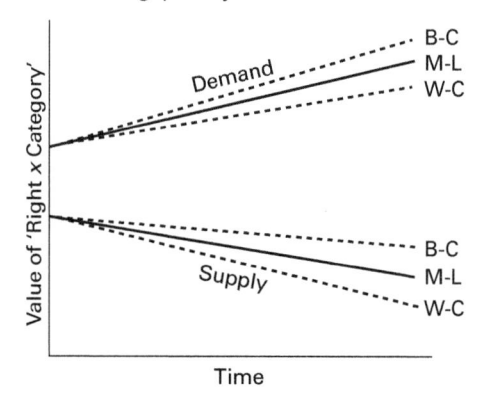

FIGURE 11.2   Scenario-based gap analysis

between these two ranges. It is, of course, possible that the most likely scenario is also either the best or the worst case. The best-case scenario, when looking at the size of the supply, is for a lower level of turnover that leads to a lesser reduction in workforce numbers and a smaller gap to bridge. In the worst case, the reverse is true with high turnover and a greater workforce reduction. As we can see from this example, the combination of a best-case demand scenario and a worst-case supply scenario results in the largest gap to overcome through planning. In an organization with poor planning, that combination is likely to be the worst-case scenario for a human resources department.

The gap in the seven rights

Unsurprisingly, the gap analysis is quantified along six strands of the seven rights: capability, size, shape, location, time and cost. As was covered in the previous chapter, the gap in the risk cannot be gauged at this stage as it relates to the secondary demand generated in the action plan. The nature of the six strands will look quite different depending on the organizational level and planning horizon. Here I will endeavour to provide the broadest steer for all practitioners.

The right capability

The right capability, as the core of the seven rights, extends into the remaining six strands; foremost that of the right size; this strand focuses on the gap in the nature of capability. A simple approach is to start with the key capabilities that exist in the workforce today. Unless our supply modelling has indicated that there is a high risk of losing the entire capability by the end of the planning horizon, such as them all being over the normal retirement age, then stick with that current supply record. Next, be clear on the nature of capabilities that are demanded now and what is expected at the end of the planning horizon. The final stage is to consider any capabilities that might be needed during the planning horizon that have not yet been captured. These are likely to be transitory in order to design or implement some element of transformation. This forecast is our most likely scenario and is likely to be no different from a best-case scenario, as more positive circumstances are unlikely to require a capability that remains to be identified. In a worst-case scenario, however, there are the unknown-unknown capabilities;

those that do not yet exist and their requirement is undetermined. As we covered in Chapter 10, this requires both a growth mindset and a base of skill in foundational areas or adjacent skills, which we will cover in Chapter 14 . For example, let us consider the possible futures in relation to digital programming. I cannot possibly imagine the specific nature of capability required in future years. However, it will certainly necessitate an understanding of programming languages, therefore, a capability that is based upon something like core Java, Python or R will certainly be a starting point. This kind of capability can be expected to follow the growing trend towards computation of bigger unstructured data across a network, so it is likely to build on those with an existing capability in NoSQL. To qualify the worst case for capability, consider the likely foundations and adjacencies.

The right size

We have given an introduction to the nature of the right size gap earlier in the chapter. We will need to look at the macro level as well as the meso level. The macro level is as has been described, with the biggest expected gap existing between the best-case demand and the worst-case supply. At a meso level, this can look quite different. Our demand forecast may have already included some form of transformation that is in progress at the time of planning. What if that transformation is unsuccessful? The change may take place, but there may be unforeseen consequences that erode the realization of benefits. These consequences would usually exist in the generation of additional demand; consider, for example, the need for a workaround because a new process does not work as expected. Therefore, the worst case for demand at a meso level can generate more derived demand than a best case at the macro level. To understand the implications of the right size fully, it must be overlaid against the right capability. That means quantifying the size of each of the capabilities that have been defined.

The right shape

Assessing the gap of the right shape is easily one of the most multi-faceted of all the seven rights. This has spurred the advice in the last chapter to avoid creating too many additional segments as part of this. On an intra-capability level, we might revisit the assessment of the right capability and apply levels of foundation, intermediate and advanced against each of these.

This can be a telling gap as our organization may be in the highly fortunate position of requiring little to no change in capability during the planning horizon. However, it would remain highly likely that capabilities would need to increase to a higher degree.

At an inter-capability level consider first the derived demand for either our critical roles, or those at the first point of contact with the external supply chain (in a pull model) or the first point of contact with the customer (in a push model). From that point, our demand calculation will enable us to calculate each other element within the internal supply chain based on the representative ratios. Therefore, we will have a clear indication, for example, of our frontline customer service staff and the associated management and support infrastructure that they would require.

The characteristic level is often the most insightful about an organization. *Nitaqat* is the Saudi nationalization scheme, commonly referred to as *Saudization*. This policy, implemented as an approach to reducing native unemployment and wage deflation, requires companies in Saudi Arabia to employ a minimum percentage of indigenous workers (Wynbrandt, 2010). There are few other examples of legally binding targets for employment based on characteristics; therefore, all other targets are organizational choices. These choices tend to be stated as a target at a particular point in time, for example, gender parity in employment numbers within five years. The flight path to this target is often not stated, so remains an *Overton window* that typically hinges on achieving the target and being able to demonstrate progress towards that target throughout the planning horizon. The best case would likely be a feasible achievement in excess of the target, providing it did not have an adverse impact on another group. For example, if the target and most likely scenario is 50 per cent of roles being occupied by women within five years, then the best case may well be parity within three years. It would be unlikely that the best case would be to achieve 60 per cent female representation as, by default, there is no longer gender parity. Similarly, the worst-case scenario would clearly be the lowest achievable level against the target. What makes this such an insightful area is that all of this is heavily intertwined. Higher levels of male turnover may present a best-case scenario for achieving gender parity as it would allow for a greater number of women to be brought into the organization. If, however, a sizeable proportion of that male workforce happen to be from an ethnic minority background, then the best case for gender parity could be the worst-case scenario for ethnicity parity.

The right location

Any gap between supply and demand at a location level must, by its nature, result from meso-level modelling. Location, be it geographic or structural, is a constituent part of the macro level. Therefore, modelling at a purely macro level will not indicate any gaps in location; at a meso level, however, various gaps will exist. If the organization is not expected to change, then at both a geographic and structural level there will be gaps through the decline of supply. If there are existing plans to open new locations, then there will be an obvious deficit as there will be no supply at that location. Conversely, if there are proposals to close an existing location then we can anticipate a surplus over a short planning horizon. The gap is reversed by having a demand of zero at an existing location, accompanied by some form of existing supply. The best scenario from a planning perspective is that such a relocation plan does not exist, unless the rationale is based on changes to the external supply chain or marketplace. For example, we may choose to create a new location in order to break into a new market; equally, we may choose to relocate in order to move closer to our suppliers. More often, location decisions are taken on the basis of reducing the cost of the estate or an upfront decision on the cost of resourcing, such as offshoring. Such decisions, taken outside a workforce planning cycle, risk a failure to achieve the desired benefits of cost reduction. For example, toy manufacturers in Germany reversed their existing offshore arrangements in China and moved their production back to Europe. Though they had benefitted from a lower total cost of workforce (TCOW), the lengthier supply chain was slower to respond to changing market requirements, which had a much more significant impact on revenue (Kastner, 2017). The characteristics of the gap are similarly true in relation to the structure if there are new capabilities we need in the future, or existing capabilities we will not require.

The right time

By the process of understanding the gap as something that evolves, we will have captured the nature of each gap based on time. Time must be the constant factor across all forecasts. The critical aspect is to recognize that this gap will evolve during the next phase, the action plan. At the end of this stage, we will have a clear gap analysis of six of the seven rights, which might incorporate a specific point in time where there is a dynamic shift in the size of the gap. This might be because a new capability is required, or one ceases to be required. If, as part of the action plan, we plan to recruit a new workforce and train them up for a month to become the new capability, then the right time for the right size is now a month earlier. The lead-in time for activity, therefore, will refine the right time as we conduct the action plan.

The right cost

This is the gap between the forecast workforce and the two dimensions of the cost of the derived demand and the budget. As has been stated, planners often look to close the gap between the workforce and the budget; this does not solve the problem of getting work done. Throughout the next part of the book, one of the golden threads is to tackle the discrepancy between derived demand and the budget.

Re-engaging stakeholders

Traditional thinkers on workforce planning record stakeholder engagement exclusively within the baseline stage. It is an unfortunate oversight that commonly leads to plans failing to translate into execution. As the father of strategic management, Igor Ansoff identified that, whilst 'strategic decisions are the basic determinants in the success of the firm', they do not receive the highest priority from senior leaders (Ansoff, 1968). The final part of establishing the nature of the gap is to establish it firmly in the minds of stakeholders, alongside the support and resource required to close it.

Three brains

This challenge is not one that is isolated to poor managers; it is, as it happens, simple biology. In his 2011 book *Thinking, Fast and Slow*, Daniel Kahneman postulated the theory of two systems of thought, which we touched upon in Chapter 3. System one thinking makes fast and almost automatic decisions, which emanate from two different parts of the brain. The oldest part of the brain sits in the brain stem and cerebellum, often referred to as the reptilian brain (MacLean, 1990). It deals with fight or flight responses and basic bodily functions, the key elements of survival for the primitive brain. Surrounding the reptilian brain is the limbic system (MacLean, 1990), comprising the hypothalamus, amygdala and the hippocampus. This is the paleomammalian brain, more popularly known as the 'inner chimp' (Peters, 2011). This part of the brain deals with habits, memories and emotions. It is habits that enable people to operate on autopilot, almost as if programmed by a computer, as we may do on the daily commute to work. Ansoff posited that operating decisions received priority over strategic ones because they are routine, automatically escalated by junior levels, frequent and familiar (Ansoff, 1968). It is habit that means stakeholders are predisposed to focus on operational matters rather than strategic ones. Memories are what provides a frame of reference for decisions in the form of biases. We have mentioned a number of these that can impact the decision making of stakeholders: a *negativity bias*, where a negative experience of a previous attempt at workforce planning can have a powerful impact over their willingness to engage in the activity again; a *planning fallacy*, where stakeholders are overly optimistic about their own ability to plan and execute; *anchoring*, where a specific factor overrides the workforce planning conversation, such as a perception of what workforce planning is or what it can solve. For example, a stakeholder view that workforce planning is a recruitment tool can anchor all conversation to devising a recruitment solution. More usually, however, it is anchored to a finite game (Carse, 2013). This means that, rather than considering success in the longer term, they are focused on a more short-term view, often on account of budgetary cycles. Another common bias is *attribute substitution*, where the complexity of the situation is substituted for a heuristic, either the anchor or some other factor, and then judgement is made based on that substitute. To evolve the previous example, a stakeholder may be under the certain misapprehension that recruitment is the cause of, and solution to, the problems of the organization. The *availability heuristic* is a mental shortcut where examples in the memory are viewed more favourably than an alternative. This is often the case when people return from conferences and are fixated on an initiative, regardless of the applicability to their own organization. As 19th-century German philosopher Arthur Schopenhauer once wrote, 'There is no opinion, however absurd, which men will not readily embrace as soon as they can be brought to the conviction that it is generally adopted' (Schopenhauer, 2009). This availability heuristic may well be solidified with a *pro-innovation bias*, where a stakeholder has such a strong bias in favour of an initiative that they are unable to see the weaknesses or the limitations when applying it in a new situation. The *segmentation effect*, where the expected duration of a task is lower than the sum of its component sub-tasks, causes stakeholders to underestimate the time to complete a task. All these biases impact decision making on the basis of memories that we all have. Emotions, on the other hand, are how people feel; these can drive a mental shortcut called the *affect heuristic*, where our feelings play a lead role in decision making (Zajonc, 1980). We can all recognize the concept of the gut feeling and the part it plays.

System two thinking emanates from the neomammalian brain, which consists of the cerebral neocortex; this is the grey matter found in higher mammals and the centre of reasoning. This logical brain will search for facts in order to come to a conclusion, rather than relying on the feelings, impressions and habits that underpin system one thinking. This may seem academic: if there are two systems of thinking, use the second system for complex decisions. This would be the obvious aim, except that cognitive function passes through the reptilian brain and the paleomammalian brain before it reaches the neomammalian brain. On a good day, this means that system one thinking can frame the search for facts in system two thinking. On a moderate day, the stress of cognitive load can diminish the energy available for system two thinking and substitute system one thinking instead in a phenomenon called *ego depletion* (Kahneman, 2011). Even something as simple as hunger can have a significant impact; a study of Israeli judges showed a peak after lunch in the proportion of parole requests that were granted, which then decreased throughout the day (Kahneman, 2011). On a bad day, an event can trigger emotions that cannot be contained and, as Professor Steve Peters would say, 'the Chimp takes over' (Peters, 2011).

Influencing stakeholders

In earlier years, I remember thinking that the key to success was to find a way of bypassing the system one brain of key stakeholders and finding passage to their system two brain. As it happens, this too is folly. Professor Antonio Damasio, the chair of neuroscience at the University of Southern California, found that 'emotion, feeling and biological regulation all play a role in human reason' (Damasio, 2006). His research on victims of brain trauma found those with impaired emotions, but otherwise unaffected reasoning abilities, struggled to make decisions. Therefore, even the most rational thinker is impacted by their system one thinking.

If humans are ruled by feelings and habit, how can a workforce planning practitioner hope to convey a logical analysis of the gap between the forecast and the derived demand for a workforce? The answer is with telling stories as, it turns out, the chimp brain likes stories. Communication expert Nancy Duarte talks about the importance of stories in her book *Resonate*.

She acknowledges that facts can allow someone to agree with the logic of an argument, but it is not enough to enable them to believe with personal conviction. Stories have conveyed meaning ever since the earliest humans sat round a fire. By learning the lessons from the stories we have read, heard and watched, we can create impact (Duarte, 2010). We make our stakeholder the key protagonist of the story, establish what the gaps we have identified will mean to them and 'communicate this information broadly and dramatically, especially with respect to crises, potential crises, or great opportunities' (Kotter, 1995). We are not simply communicating with stakeholders in order to pass information, we aim to influence them in order to gain their support for change. People analytics expert, Cole Nussbaumer Knaflic, builds on Duarte's thinking in *Storytelling With Data* (2015). It continues the theme and focuses specifically on how to use data visualization to tell that story. It is an incredible resource that brings the entire subject home with some fantastic case studies. It is certainly recommended reading as a clear and easy-to-follow guide on how to communicate our analysis to stakeholders.

Katy Bowers, people analytics senior specialist at Nestlé, set up their HR analytics capability in the UK and now designs new projects for markets across Europe, the Middle East and North Africa. She talks about the four key capabilities to enable such storytelling: coder, cruncher, comic book artist and consultant. The coder is the data scientist who has the technical ability to connect operational, finance and people data. The cruncher is the statistician who can take the work of the coder and conduct robust analysis and modelling. They are the people who can make connections within the data and spot the patterns and trends; they are the key behind describing, diagnosing and predicting based on the data. Both the coder and the cruncher are existing capabilities within most business intelligence functions. The comic book artist is the visualizer of the data and able to look at multiple datasets to 'get people excited and engage with the story'. Indeed, she goes further in recognizing the importance of overcoming what is often a low maturity of data comprehension and, at worst, a complete aversion to data. She explains, 'In lots of areas, I'd run into issues of people not being interested in the numbers and some of that is [due to their] preference. They don't want the detail, [they are more interested in] strategy.' The consultant capability needs to be linked to each of the other three elements and someone who has relationships with stakeholders and a deep understanding of the organization. They are the key component that can answer the 'so what' question and translate the data into a business problem. Moreover, once a business problem is uncovered in one area of the business, they can see how this connects to other areas where intervention may be needed (Bowers, 2020).

Summary

Rather than being a simple act of comparing two forecasts, the gap analysis is a stage to which it is essential to dedicate time and energy into getting right. We will need to assess the forecasts in terms of the seven rights of workforce planning and understand how that gap evolves over the planning horizon. Next, we will need to understand the impact of that gap and why it matters to our organization. We will need to be clear on what will happen to our organization as the gap between supply and demand continues to develop. This step moves us from the diagnostic analytics we discussed in Chapter 6, into predictive analytics. Our forecasts of supply and demand and analysis of the gap will provide a clear prediction of the future of the organization.

Critically, we also need to understand why the gap matters specifically to our key stakeholders. What is it about that gap that will cause problems for them and impact their objectives? Once we understand that problem, we need to help our stakeholders understand it too. This stage needs to conclude with stakeholders being clear on the future impact of not closing this gap and their support for us to embark on the creation of an action plan.

> Failures in talent management may be more recognizable than the concept itself. Those failures include mismatches between supply and demand: on the one hand, having too many employees, leading to layoffs and restructurings, and on the other hand, having too little talent, leading to talent shortages (Cappelli, 2008).

When you practise workforce planning, ask yourself:

- What does the gap look like across the seven rights (excluding right risk)?
- How does that gap evolve over time?
- What problems do the gaps cause for my key stakeholders?
- What is the best way to present the problem to my key stakeholders?

References

Ansoff, H I (1968) Toward a strategic theory of the firm, in H I Ansoff (ed) (1969) *Business Strategy*, Penguin, Harmondsworth

Asimov, I (1961) The machine that won the war, in I Asimov (ed) (1971) *Nightfall and Other Stories*, Fawcett Crest, New York

Auzenne, M and Horstman, M (2012) Work family balance – chapter 1 – go home [Podcast] *Manager Tools*, 2 September, www.manager-tools.com/2012/08/work-family-balance-chapter-1-go-home (archived at https://perma.cc/BMK3-QLQ6)

Bowers, K (2020) Interview by telephone, 28 February

Cappelli, P (2008) *Talent on Demand: Managing talent in an age of uncertainty*, Harvard Business School Publishing, Boston

Carse, J P (2013) *Finite and Infinite Games*, The Free Press, New York

Damasio, A R (2006) *Descartes' Error*, Random House, London

Drucker, P F (2007) *The Practice of Management*, Routledge, London

Duarte, N (2010) *Resonate: Present visual stories that transform audiences*, John Wiley & Sons, Hoboken

Kahneman, D (2011) *Thinking, Fast and Slow*, Allen Lane, London

Kastner, J (2017) German toymakers shift production from China, *Nikkei Asian Review*, 16 March, asia.nikkei.com/magazine/20170316/Business/German-toymakers-shift-production-from-China (archived at https://perma.cc/DVP5-PCJY)

Kotter, J P (1995) Leading change: Why transformation efforts fail, *Harvard Business Review*, 73, pp 259–67, hbr.org/1995/05/leading-change-why-transformation-efforts-fail-2 (archived at https://perma.cc/NED5-KPKZ)

MacLean, P D (1990) *The Triune Brain in Evolution: Role in paleocerebral functions*, Plenum, New York

Markle, W H (1966) The manufacturing manager's skills, in R E Finley and H R Ziobro (eds) *The Manufacturing Man and His Job*, American Management Association, New York

Nussbaumer Knaflic, C (2015) *Storytelling With Data*, John Wiley & Sons, Hoboken

Parkinson, C N (1955) Parkinson's law, *The Economist*, 19 November, www.economist.com/news/1955/11/19/parkinsons-law (archived at https://perma.cc/DR76-MPN5)

Peters, S (2011) *The Chimp Paradox: The mind management programme to help you achieve success, confidence and happiness*, Random House, London

Schopenhauer, A (2009) *The Art of Always Being Right*, Gibson Square, London

Wynbrandt, J (2010) *A Brief History of Saudi Arabia*, Facts On File Inc, New York

Zajonc, R B (1980) Feeling and thinking: Preferences need no inferences, *American Psychologist*, 35 (2), pp 151–75, doi:10.1037/0003-066x.35.2.151

PART SIX

Action plan

What is the best way to close the gap?

12

The planning approach

Introduction

2009 was the bloodiest year for British troops in Afghanistan, closely followed by 2010. It was over those years that I deployed on my first operational tour as part of the International Security Assistance Force (ISAF). I deployed in the role of the operational mentoring and liaison teams (OMLT, pronounced *omelette*), as part of Task Force Helmand to the province of the same name, a hotbed of insurgency. The OMLT were precariously placed teams of around 12 infantrymen that operated alongside the Afghan National Army (ANA). Our area of operations was the district of *Musa Qal'ah*, which is Pashto for the Fortress of Moses. It is a rocky desert area with an elevation of over 1,000 metres and intersected by a tributary of the Helmand river; a sharp contrast of barren plains and the lush, and treacherous, green zone. My team was located in Patrol Base Talibjan, a small isolated compound a few kilometres south of the district centre, alongside an Afghan *tolay* (company) of around 40 soldiers. This hybrid force conducted daily fighting patrols on foot, each of us carrying well over 120 pounds in equipment, to maintain the security of the local population from the Taliban of shadow governor Mullah Abdul Ghafoor.

In mid-November, we were joined briefly by a troop from the nearby cavalry battle group; their six reconnaissance vehicles, commanded by a young lieutenant, would provide us with additional firepower and manoeuvrability. Seizing the opportunity, I led a fighting patrol to push further to the south-west, my OMLT and the ANA moving on the left and the cavalry supporting on the higher ground to the right. Some hours into our patrol, in the rising heat of the late morning, my team came under fire from the machine guns of the Taliban, who were located in two compounds. The

Taliban were experienced and tenacious fighters who knew they were out of range from the weapons carried by my team. The cavalry team separated, with one half moving closer to the enemy and the other half moving to provide close support to me. I turned to my fire support element, who were charged with controlling artillery fire and aircraft support, and ordered them to neutralize the enemy in the left-hand compound. Within minutes, an EXACTOR-2 missile struck the compound with pinpoint accuracy, enabling us to move out of the killing zone and defeat the enemy.

This is an effects-based approach in practice; rather than give a prescriptive instruction, I gave them the effect to achieve. General George S Patton once famously said, 'Never tell people how to do things. Tell them what to do and they will surprise you with their ingenuity' (Patton, 2003). Neutralize, the effect of stopping a threat and rendering it harmless, could be achieved in multiple different ways. My fire support element were the experts on how to achieve it, not me; by empowering them to achieve the desired result, we were able to defeat the Taliban without sustaining any casualties. The encounter was made famous by the book *The Longest Kill* as one of the cavalry snipers was credited with the longest confirmed kill in combat during that firefight (Harrison, 2015).

This chapter will help us build the foundations of effects-based thinking, and avoid the traps of the *availability heuristic* and *pro-innovation bias*, in order to create the best outcome for our organization.

The seven Bs of action planning

The great polymath, Archimedes of Syracuse, is said to have remarked, 'give me a lever long enough and a fulcrum on which to place it, and I shall move the world.' This illustrates the mechanical advantage of a lever whereby a small force at one end can exert a far greater force at the other. It is in this way that we solve the problems of the workforce through the application of workforce levers, initiatives that deliver exponentially greater benefits to the organization and the workforce than the cost to implement them. I talk about a model of workforce levers I call the seven Bs of action planning, which I will introduce here.

As shown in Figure 12.1, the levers are buy, build, borrow, bind, bounce, balance and bot. Buy is the approach of buying and acquiring a permanent capability and build is the process of building a capability out of existing capacity. Borrow is similar to buy, but is the approach of acquiring a

FIGURE 12.1 Workforce planning levers

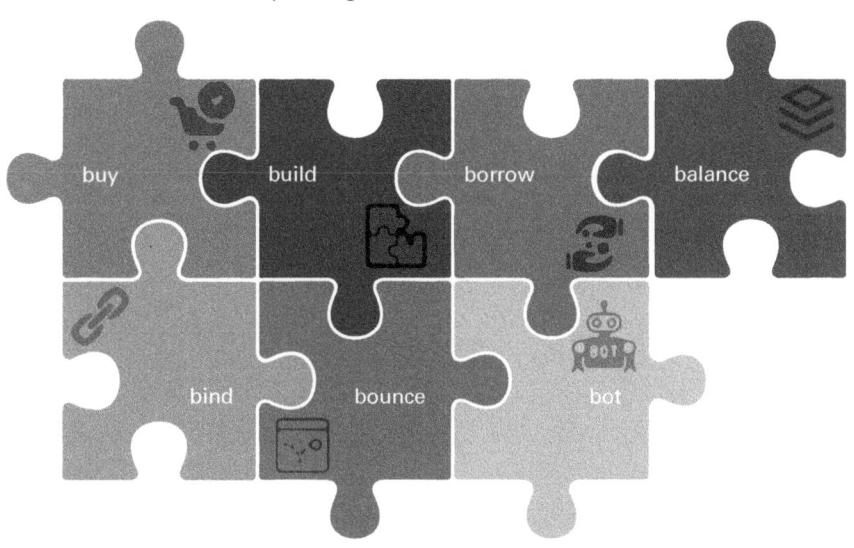

temporary capability, thereby borrowing a capability from elsewhere. Bind is where we prevent the loss of a capability by binding it in place; it is the opposite of bounce where we either move a capability around, or exit the capability from, the organization. These five levers are talent management levers and contrast to the remaining demand optimization levers. Balance, the most importance of these, is concerned with ensuring that demand drivers are correctly aligned and balanced throughout the organization and bot is concerned with automation and artificial intelligence. The lever is the effect and the method of achieving that effect is through an array of initiatives.

I will cover each of these in greater detail in the subsequent two chapters, including the elements that can form these levers. What is important to remember is to plan initially on the basis of these levers and not at a lower level. We do this for three reasons, the first of these being artificial restriction. Execution usually requires multiple levers to be pulled in sequence in order to deliver the right outcome. It can be tempting to look at one part of a capability gap and think that an initiative to recruit recent technology graduates is the solution. Such an outcome buys a specific and narrow workforce segment, which may restrict our ability to remedy the wider challenges of the organization. The second reason is that some initiatives cross multiple levers. Initiating a salary increase can help us improve our ability to recruit and is part of a buy lever. That same salary increase can also help us retain people and therefore bind them. An increase applied solely for new joiners and not applied elsewhere may have the opposite effect and drive up resignations due to perceived unfairness; this is part of a bounce lever. The impact of second-order consequences arrives once we examine the specifics of the initiatives. Therefore, we aim to remain pure during the initial planning and establish what we require at the level of the lever. The final reason is that to immediately home in on the initiative on the basis of our innate bias can rob us of potentially better solutions. During that firefight in Afghanistan, the British Army launched the EXACTOR-2 missile for the second time ever. At the time I had never heard of it and was wholly unaware we had an electro-optically guided missile with pinpoint accuracy and midcourse navigation. I empowered those with the knowledge and experience to utilize their own expertise to provide the best solution. In workforce planning neither we, nor senior stakeholders, have all the solutions to the challenges we face. Plan based on the levers, the effect we want to create, and collaborate on the detail once we have an end-to-end plan in place.

EFFECTS-BASE WORKFORCE PLANNING

An example I use in showing planning at the level of the workforce planning lever, rather than the specific initiative, is as follows. Imagine that a challenge we face is that of an ageing workforce; we have key capabilities in an older population that we forecast will retire and leave us with a capability gap. One approach would be:

- **Bind** those with essential capabilities that are scarce in the organization.
- **Borrow** essential capabilities to cover any shortfall.
- **Bot** any repeatable activity.
- **Buy** new workforce.
- **Bounce** redundant capabilities.
- **Build** capabilities in new workforce and workforce with redundant capabilities.

This allows us to bridge the gap within the planning horizon and create a sustainable solution towards the end of the planning horizon.

Collaborating with key partners

During my deployment to Afghanistan, the commander of ISAF had been General Stanley McChrystal, a veteran of over 30 years' service. From 2003 to 2008 he commanded the US Joint Special Operations Command (JSOC). In Iraq, JSOC led the task force charged with the capture of high-value targets. However, one key target, Abu Musab al-Zarqawi, remained at large. McChrystal could not understand how al-Zarqawi was able to continually evade his special forces operators with such success. One of the key limitations he identified was the lack of collaboration between the teams within the task force. 'The bonds within the squads are fundamentally different from those between squads or other units' (McChrystal *et al*, 2015). The almost tribal ethos of the military, which enables it to be so effective, equally results in frictions verging on incompatibility: 'the very traits that make teams great can often work to prevent their coherence into a broader whole'. (ibid) Across the military, groups have a view of superiority and rivalry with other groups and this view extends across all hierarchies.

What was hampering McChrystal's efforts was a phenomenological concept known as *othering*. German philosopher, Edmund Husserl, identified the concept of *the other* as a means of identifying difference from the concepts of *self* and *us*. Those who think in terms of *other* deny aspects of sameness with other people (Husserl, 1973). Othering is the reductive action of labelling people as different from themselves. The form of othering that was impacting JSOC is what Sigmund Freud called the *narcissism of small differences*, the idea that groups with close relationships are especially likely to engage in feuds and mutual ridicule because of details of differentiation (Freud, 1991).

To succeed, McChrystal needed to transform from the command of teams in silos, to a network with the same interconnectivity as the existing squads. This 'team of teams', our third principle of agile workforce planning, was effected by aligning action to capabilities rather than hierarchy. Connectivity was to those with the expertise to input and decide, rather than those simply within a machine of bureaucracy (McChrystal *et al*, 2015).

We do the same in workforce planning for two key reasons. The first is because of the way ideas are created. In a study on innovation, science author and media theorist Steven Johnson established that the best ideas are not generated in a silo. The process of ideation results from combining ideas and sharing feedback, what he calls the 'slow hunch' (Johnson, 2011).

When we consider the full range of the seven Bs of workforce planning, we can see that the expertise to develop and build on ideas will sit outside the workforce planning team. The second reason relates back to the seventh principle of workforce planning: *it's about the workforce*. The key point is that the aim of workforce planning is not to create a workforce plan, the aim of workforce planning is to create the right workforce. To create the right workforce we need to execute the plan and the best people to do that sit within the wider team of teams. As former SEAL officer Jocko Willink says, 'giving [them] ownership of even a small piece of the plan gives them buy-in, helps them understand the reasons behind the plan, and better enables them to believe in the mission, which translates to far more effective implementation and execution' (Willink and Babin, 2015).

We will talk about some of the key areas with which to collaborate. The key areas for our organizations will align to the analysis we performed in Chapter 7. This is particularly the case with RAPID®, where we assign owners to the five key roles in any decision: recommend, agree, perform, input and decide (Bain and Company, 2011). This is definitely not an exhaustive list but they will certainly be key areas for collaboration in most organizations.

Operational leads

The operational leads are the key stakeholders who sit in the primary functions of the organization. It is the part of the organization that HR practitioners often call *the business* and is typically at the front of the organizational mission. These areas are likely to be the providers of the information we used in calculating demand and, indeed, key contributors to the qualitative forecasting. Those of us operating at either the meso level, or focusing primarily on horizon one planning, are likely to sit within these operational areas. A key area of collaboration with this group is demand optimization, which we will cover in the next chapter. Demand optimization, as we will discuss, typically falls outside the remit of HR functions. As a result, it is a process that is severely neglected as a workforce planning lever. Operational leads typically have accountability for demand optimization within their areas. More importantly, such optimization goes directly to their own bottom line, either as a cost or as a profit centre, so they are directly incentivized to collaborate.

> **COST AND PROFIT CENTRES**
>
> Cost and profit centres are methods of financial management that sit within the meso level of an organization. A cost centre typically sits in the supporting functions of the organization. It is often found in primary functions focused on logistics and, more recently, it has expanded into the service area where this does not generate direct revenue. The financial focus on these areas is in the management and reduction of costs. A profit centre, also known as a profit and loss (P&L) centre, is typically found in the primary functions of marketing and sales and often within operations. These areas generate profit directly and, as a result, their focus is on the maximization of profits.

Human resources

Those of us operating at the macro level, or focusing primarily on horizon three planning, are likely to find ourselves sat within HR. In many organizations, HR is structured along variations of Dave Ulrich's model that he shared in the groundbreaking *Human Resource Champions* (Ulrich, 1996). This created four components of HR: corporate HR, centres of expertise (CoEs), business partners (HRBPs) and shared services. Corporate HR shapes initiatives at the macro level, partnering directly with the organizational executive and, increasingly, is represented on the executive board as a chief HR officer (CHRO) or chief people officer (CPO). CoEs provide specialist insights on a range of specific knowledge areas, such as policy, reward and leadership development. Where workforce planning sits within HR, it is normally found as a CoE. The HRBPs are generalists who are typically embedded at the macro levels in direct support of operational leads. Shared services are often the delivery arms of some of the CoEs. They can cover a range of activities, including administration of the HR technology systems, responding to queries from employees, and the processing of payroll. Those with a partnering role, both the CHRO and HRBPs, will play a critical part as allies in engaging operational leads; they will have trusted relationships that can help sell the benefits of workforce planning. Moreover, they will have a great deal of insight into the nature of the macro- and meso-level issues and how best to address them. The CoEs, and their extensions in the shared services, will often be the main point of execution for many of the talent management levers. As a result, they will have the deep expertise in how best to approach particular gaps between supply and demand.

Finance

Finance functions are a critical partner in workforce planning; too often I have seen finance and HR functions operating in silos despite the inextricable link between them. One report suggested that less than half of those in HR thought they collaborated with finance, and just a quarter of those in finance thought they collaborated with HR (OrgVue, 2019). I have found it can be the application of workforce planning that will bring these two functions together. They may well be arranged in a similar style to the HR function. There is likely to be a central function that conducts budgetary planning and may well be accountable for horizon two planning within the organization, and therefore we need to be joined up with them. That corporate function is likely to have CoEs that conduct reporting and analysis; they can be a key provider of data and analysis in our demand and supply forecasting. Similar to HR, these CoEs likely extend into shared services that deal with activities such as accounts payable and receivable. Finally, there is likely to be some form of macro-level partnering in the form of the finance business partner (FBP). Having both the FBP and HRBP bought into our aim will provide an extremely powerful alliance in gaining buy-in with operational leads.

Procurement

Many organizations will have some form of procurement function that manages the commercial arrangement with suppliers. This will extend to outsourced services providers and, for many organizations, may be the only function with an understanding of the levels of contingent labour that are being utilized. As a result, the procurement function is a key part of the team of teams when it comes to applying the borrow lever.

Information technology

The information technology function, increasingly referred to as the digital function, is typically accountable for the management of technology systems and data. The level of change in demand trends we referenced in Chapter 10 is often being led by these functions, under the leadership of a chief digital officer (CDO) or chief experience officer (CXO). It is key, therefore, to collaborate with these functions due to their impact on demand.

Facilities

A facilities, property or estates function will focus typically on the bricks-and-mortar infrastructure of the organization. The geographical component of the right location means that facilities have a key role to play; indeed, they are also a key element in the environment strand of the right capability. Ensuring the best balance of facilities can be an important part of optimizing demand. Even more important, facilities are an underlying component of many of the talent management levers. The ability to leverage a new estate plan can allow us to tap into talent hotspots; moreover, understanding the marketplace for skills can avoid costly mistakes in site consolidation.

Cost–benefit analysis

The final consideration as part of the action planning approach is that of the cost–benefit analysis (CBA). This is an activity we complete once we go beyond the level of the lever and into the initiative. The initiatives that we might propose to solve a workforce issue are ideas; the CBA is the application of science to ideas. It is too common for HR departments to launch an initiative that has no evidential basis and proves unsuccessful and either ends in failure or, worse, endures. The philosopher Karl Popper suggested that 'science is one of the very few human activities… in which errors are systematically criticized and fairly often, in time, corrected' (Popper, 2002). It is through the CBA that we assess, test and compare the three key outcomes. The first is that we assess if an initiative is worthwhile.

Total Benefits – Total Cost = Net Benefits

The net benefit places a metric against the initiative. Once the net benefit of an initiative is established, the second objective is to test it against our strategy. We must ask ourselves the question, does this initiative contribute towards business objectives? In Chapter 4, I introduced the concept of *stealing other people's artificial grass*, the desire to recreate an initiative from elsewhere even though it does not contribute towards the organizational objectives. The third outcome of a CBA is to compare multiple initiatives; this is key to ensuring the best outcome and is only possible if we start at the level of the lever.

To achieve this, we apply a four-stage process. The first stage is to define clearly the costs and benefits of the initiative and understand the areas that benefit and the areas that bear the cost. A key component is to identify the occurrence of transfers. This is where a benefit or cost moves from one area to another. A classic example of this is the advent of the self-service checkout in stores: the organization achieves the benefit of a demand reduction by not requiring checkout staff, which is transferred as a cost of new demand to the customer. This tends to be accompanied by having a greater density of checkouts than before, which reduces waiting times and is viewed as a greater net benefit by the customer.

The second stage is to apply metrics to those costs and benefits, which is arguably more challenging. The first thing to recognize is that benefits and costs are often differentiated as either tangible or intangible (Ward and Daniel, 2005). Tangible benefits are those where the value is quantifiable, though there is a tendency to categorize benefits as either financial or non-financial. As a result, improvements in performance and productivity are often categorized as non-financial. In reality, performance and productivity create a financial impact and, therefore, benefits of this type can be articulated as financial. Tangible benefits are best divided in terms of definite, expected and anticipated (Bradley, 2010). Definite benefits are those where the quantifiable value of a benefit can be accurately forecast. Where the forecast of value is less certain but there is still high confidence, potentially where assumptions are based on benchmarks, these may be described as expected benefits. Where the value of a benefit cannot be forecast with any degree of reliability, these may be described as anticipated. Intangibility is the inability to establish a physical aspect, where values are unquantifiable. Unfortunately, intangibility is often conflated with intractability, being complex to establish. Over many years the credibility of HR has been tarnished by the presentation of benefits that are claimed to be intangible and are therefore ridiculed as a fad: inclusion, employee engagement, employee experience and culture to cite some examples. These are complex to establish, but not impossible, and they become much clearer when precisely defined and viewed in terms of business outcomes and are more likely to move to become an anticipated tangible benefit.

The third stage is to forecast costs and benefits over time, which needs to be done in two ways. The first is to understand the life of the initiative, the end of which is the point where the initiative ceases to provide any benefit or cost. This view is critical for gaining financial approval of the initiative. The second view, which is key from a comparative perspective, is the costs and benefits during the planning horizon. If we think back to Chapter 11 and the evolution of the gap between supply and demand, many great initiatives aim to close the gap by the end of the planning horizon. If initiative only delivers at the end of the planning horizon, it is only a partial solution: 'A management decision is irresponsible if it risks disaster this year for the sake of a grandiose future' (Drucker, 1973). The initiative might be the best choice, but it must be accompanied by initiatives that close the gap *within* the planning horizon.

The final stage is to validate the assumptions. Once we have a range of initiatives to choose, revalidate the assumptions collectively. We may have decided to leverage the functional expertise in the team of teams to craft a range of solutions and provide the cost–benefit analysis. Validate the assumptions across the range of proposals to ensure costs and benefits are being recorded and calculated in the same way. Test the assumptions in the plan against the analysis of the organization and workforce that we completed in Part Two of this book.

Summary

The process of the action plan is the move beyond both the descriptive analytics we discussed in Chapter 6 and the predictive analytics we completed in Chapter 11, into the world of prescriptive analytics. We will prescribe the solution that will remedy the problem.

Workforce planning practitioners cannot act in a silo in this regard and we must collaborate with those who have the expertise to provide the best solutions and are prepared to own the execution. If we do not have a relationship with these people, then we use the leverage within our network to achieve this; HR business partners are a key component in achieving this success.

The final key aspect to appreciate is that there is rarely a solution that is absolutely perfect. As we established in Chapter 11, the gap closes at the point of execution and usually creates a second-order impact. The aim of the action plan is to create the best possible solution that balances long-term gain against short-term risk.

Over the following two chapters we will delve into the detail of each of the levers and provide examples of some initiatives that have been implemented successfully in organizations. I do not share these as a plug-and-play solution, but to illustrate what can be done to bridge the gap between supply and demand given the specific ambitions and challenges of those organizations.

When you practise workforce planning, ask yourself:

- Am I taking an effects-based approach to workforce planning?
- Which of the seven Bs, in which sequence, will allow me to close the gap?
- Have I engaged with those who are best placed to collaborate on finding the most suitable initiative?
- Have we conducted a comparable analysis of the costs and benefits of the proposed initiatives?
- Do the initiatives close the gap between supply and demand?

References

Bain and Company (2011) RAPID®: Bain's tool to clarify decision accountability, 11 August, www.bain.com/insights/rapid-tool-to-clarify-decision-accountability (archived at https://perma.cc/PE4E-SGFN)

Bradley, G (2010) *Benefit Realisation Management*, Routledge, London

Drucker, P F (1973) *Management: Tasks, responsibilities, practices*, Harper & Row, London

Freud, S (1991) *Civilization, Society and Religion*, Penguin, London

Harrison, C (2015) *The Longest Kill*, Sidgwick & Jackson, London

Husserl, E (1973) *Cartesian Meditations: An introduction to phenomenology*, Springer, New York

McChrystal, S et al (2015) *Team of Teams: New rules of engagement in a complex world*, Penguin, New York

OrgVue (2019) *Making People Count*, www.orgvue.com/resources/research-report/making-people-count-report/ (archived at https://perma.cc/ZDM7-WYBY)

Patton, G S (2003) *War As I Knew It*, Presidio Press, Novato

Popper, K (2002) *Conjectures and Refutations: The growth of scientific knowledge*, Routledge, Abingdon

Ulrich, D (1996) *Human Resource Champions: The next agenda for adding value and delivering results*, Harvard Business Review Press, Boston

Ward, J and Daniel, E (2005) *Benefits Management: Delivering value from IS and IT investments*, John Wiley & Sons, Chichester

Willink, J and Babin, L (2015) *Extreme Ownership: How US Navy SEALS lead and win*, St Martin's Press, New York

13

Demand optimization

Introduction

One of the facets of life in the military is moving home frequently. At the time of my service, officers in the British Army changed roles, on average, every two years. This ran as an overlay to units that had an 18-month gap between operational tours. As a result, I moved a lot! The practice of moving, however, is no different for any of us. One of the things that we all have in common is that we all dispose of things as part of the packing process. In my earlier years it was simply throwing items in the bin; in later years I was driving items to the refuse sites and recycling centres or offering them for sale on Gumtree or Facebook marketplace. It is something that we all do. Why? We do it because they are items that we recognize we no longer need and with a finite number of packing boxes, a finite amount of space in the removal truck and a finite amount of space in a new home, we do not want to carry unnecessary items with us. By doing so, we are conducting demand optimization.

This approach, of ensuring that demand is fully optimized before we commit the scarce resource of supply, has been noticeably absent from both the workforce planning and HR agendas. As a result, almost like trying to fill the bath without putting in the plug, there is tremendous waste of money and the endeavours of the workforce.

> I think HR for a long time was… predominantly focused on… talent management… The OD side has been rather missing and it is… HR's job now to help to understand these external pressures and trends of businesses, not just in technology, but for social demographic change and anything else… We have got to think more strategically about our workforce, capabilities, organizational

future [and] what options we've got... Hence the idea of agile... workforce planning is a fundamental business imperative and a big agenda for HR, which... I think could never be more important (Peter Cheese, CEO of CIPD, 2020).

By first optimizing the demand of the organization, we depart significantly from the traditional approaches of both workforce planning and HR and move into territory occupied by operational management. We do this through the application of two levers, balance and bot.

Balance

In the film *The Karate Kid*, Daniel Laruso is delighting in the gift of a car from his sensei Mr Miyagi:

> Miyagi: You remember lesson about balance?
>
> Laruso: Yeah.
>
> Miyagi: Lesson not just karate only, lesson for whole life. Whole life have balance, everything be better. Understand? [Hands over a photograph of Laruso and love interest Ali Mills]
>
> Laruso: [Smiling] Yeah, I understand.

Balance is the multifaceted approach of ensuring alignment between all the aspects of the organization to ensure demand is optimized and to enable the most effective use of supply. It accepts organizations as similar to all other human relationships, flows of information that regulate action. As such, the balance lever draws from the discipline of cybernetics, whose origins lie in ancient Greece (Plato, 1999 and 2004). In this section, we will take a teleological approach to the challenges of strategic misalignment, quality and organizational design.

Addressing strategic misalignment

We first introduced the concept of strategic alignment back in Chapter 5, as the framework that concerns the orientation of the why of the organization with the elements of mission, goals, objectives, strategy and execution. The purpose of understanding strategic alignment was to better understand the organization that we are in. It is a golden thread throughout workforce planning and returns at this point, as alluded to in Chapter 11, as a remedy for one of the most common issues within modern organizations: strategic misalignment. In this sense, there is a lack of alignment between these key areas. This misalignment can be the result of three factors: decay, fragmentation and overtension.

Decay is where elements of the strategic framework are no longer compatible with the world in which they operate:

> An organization which just perpetuates today's level of vision, excellence and accomplishment has just lost the capacity to adapt. And since the one and only thing certain in human affairs is change, it will not be capable of survival in a changed tomorrow (Drucker, 1985).

What may have worked successfully in the past is simply not fit for purpose in the current world and the organization suffers, often disastrously.

CASE STUDY
BlackBerry

The ubiquity of the screen-based mobile devices can make it hard to recall that, prior to Apple's release of the iPhone in 2007, the BlackBerry was the most prized in the smartphone world. Research in Motion Ltd (RIM), as the business was formerly known, dominated the smartphone market; at its peak in 2009, the BlackBerry accounted for over 50 per cent of the US market (Roy, 2011) and over 20 per cent of the global market (Richter, 2017). When Steve Jobs unveiled the first-generation iPhone with the words, 'Every once in a while, a revolutionary product comes along that changes everything' (Hicks, 2012), he disrupted the smartphone market. Jobs changed the smartphone from a business email tool into a large-screen multimedia technology platform for the mass consumer market. The response from RIM was to focus on the existing customer base, which was accustomed to the droplet-like qwerty keyboard from which BlackBerry derived its name. Their strategy was to capitalize on the government organizations and multinational businesses who relied on BlackBerry to enable connectivity for their mobile workforce.

In 2011, with the company beginning to crumble, a senior RIM executive blew the whistle in an open letter to bosses. They acknowledged the hubris in response to the iPhone: 'We laughed and said they are trying to put a computer on a phone, that it won't work. We should have made the... transition then. We are now 3–4 years too late. That is the painful truth... it was a major strategic oversight' (Geller, 2011). It was too late; by maintaining a strategic framework that did not match the marketplace, RIM could not hope to survive. The trajectory of the collapse continued and in 2013 the

BlackBerry accounted for less than 1 per cent of the global smartphone market and was declared at zero per cent in 2016 (Richter, 2017).

The second factor, fragmentation, is where elements of the strategic framework exist in different guises across an organization. This is typically the case with older strategies where it exists in one form within a strategy document, is perhaps verbally repurposed within the executive, and is then interpreted very differently at the meso level. It is also the case where the overall strategy is poor; I am always mindful of the wisdom of sales guru Rick Page: 'Hope is not a strategy' (Page, 2001). This is a vital concept, as that 'business purpose and business mission are so rarely given adequate thought is perhaps the most important cause of business frustration and failure' (Drucker, 2007). This can also happen where an organization relies on goals rather than objectives. The absence of a metric and a timeframe often leads to those goals being interpreted in different ways and not translated into execution. To quote Drucker again, 'The basic definition of the business and of its purpose and mission have to be translated into objectives' (Drucker, 1973). At best this can mean entire business areas pulling in opposite directions and failing to achieve the collective objectives. At worst, it can result in parts of the organization actively working against each other towards self-destruction.

CASE STUDY
Whole Foods Market

Whole Foods Market is a multinational grocer that operates predominantly in the United States and is known for its organic produce and, since 2017, has been owned by Amazon. In 2009 the company pledged to support the Non-GMO Project, an organization committed to 'preserving and building sources of non-GMO products, educating consumers, and providing verified non-GMO choices' (Non-GMO Project, 2020). Whole Foods committed to labelling its own products as non-GMO, which was seen as a turning point in positive engagement on the non-GMO issue (Non-GMO Project, 2009). Just two years later, the Organic Consumers Association, dressed in white hazmat suits, protested against the retailer's sale of unlabelled GMO ingredients in spite of its commitments (Eng, 2011). The following year, citizens in California launched Proposition 37, a mandatory GMO labelling initiative. Whole Foods Market was heavily criticized for its delay in supporting the proposition, criticism that spiralled after a viral video claimed that many of the company's natural products contained GMOs (Adams, 2013).

The case evidences Milton Friedman in his claim that 'the discussions of the *social responsibilities of business* are notable for their analytical looseness and lack of rigor' (Friedman, 1970). By not translating their strategy through to the way that work was being done, Whole Foods was unable to meet its earlier voluntary commitment and suffered a backlash. Following the defeat of Proposition 37, the face of growing criticism, Whole Foods announced that by 2018 all products would be labelled if they contained GMOs (Polis, 2013).

CASE STUDY
Channel 4 Television

In 1982, Channel 4 launched in the UK as its fourth terrestrial television station, following an Act of Parliament two years earlier. In the late 1990s it had a mass-market appeal, televising US hit shows such as *ER* and *Friends* and the reality show *Big Brother*. Legislative changes required the channel to shift from the mainstream to programming that 'demonstrates innovation, experiment and creativity in the form and content of programmes; ...appeals to the tastes and interests of a culturally diverse society; ... include[s] programmes of an educational nature... [and] exhibits a distinctive character' (Communications Act 2003).

The challenge for Channel 4 would be to pivot, within a commercially funded business model, to the creation of programming with more diverse appeal. Diversity consultant and original founding member of Stonewall, Simon Fanshawe, was engaged to help the commissioning teams develop a set of diversity frameworks that would work for the different TV genres. This was based on the informally articulated mission of the channel 'to take minority views and put them into the mainstream... [and] to take mainstream views and interpret them through the lens of a minority' (Fanshawe, 2020). One example was the panel show, a popular format in the UK, where celebrities compete in a quiz or series of challenges with a comedic slant. From the late 1990s in the UK, there had been a growing trend towards a *lad* culture and shows with a more crude and boisterous humour. This led to panel shows that were all-male, save for a single *ladette*, a woman who engaged in such behaviours, and attracted a largely male audience. If the channel wanted to appeal to a more diverse audience, then it would need diversity in the stories it told, which would necessitate greater diversity in the production of shows, both on-screen and off-screen. The discussions with the comedy commissions were designed to find a rationale for diversity that had its roots in how it would affect positively what ended up on screen. Male-dominated shows tended to generate a 'very competitive kind of humour'; greater female representation meant that:

> women, when they're in those kind of contexts together, tend to build rather than just tell gags... so the nature of the kind of comedy that comes out of those shows is simply different... if you're looking for a broadcast reason to bring more women on, what you're saying is you've got a different broadcast answer or result. And that in turn, of course, changes the audience figures because women are less keen on watching boys being sporty with each other, and more interested in watching that kind of show (Fanshawe, 2020).

This new dynamic had far greater appeal to female audiences, which was in line with the ambition of the legislation. With female audiences also having far greater control over spending decisions than their male counterparts (Silverstein and Sayre, 2009), this shift in programming enabled the channel to attract far greater advertising revenue. Rather than so many failed attempts to improve diversity in organizations, the discussions that happened during the work with Fanshawe helped to give the commissioners a way of aligning the diversity objectives with what appeared on screen rather than being simply an intervention based on numbers.

The third factor is overtension, where the strategic framework is well defined but is undeliverable on account of the tensions that exist within the organization. Management consultants Dominic Dodd and Ken Favaro researched the 20-year performance of over 1,000 companies to understand the challenge of overtension. Of all the competing objectives within modern organizations, three pairs stand out: profitability versus growth, short-term versus long-term, and the whole organization versus the parts. Of the companies they surveyed, just 38 per cent achieved both positive profitability and real revenue growth in the same year and 44 per cent grew earnings over the year while also being on the path toward economic profit growth over the next five years. They also found that just 45 per cent of companies were able to add value to their organization through both the improvement of the synergies between departments and improvement of the standalone performance of departments (Dodd and Favaro, 2007). We see this often in cost-cutting exercises, such as the salami slicing and penny shaving referenced in Chapter 3. I have seen many organizations who cut costs to achieve short-term profitability; this leaves departments with insufficient budget to achieve the overall objectives, which damages both revenue and long-term growth.

CASE STUDY
Kraft Heinz

Kraft Foods and Heinz Company collectively own some of the most famous household brands in the world: Heinz baked beans and tomato ketchup, Oscar Mayer meats and the many cheeses of Kraft, Philadelphia and Velveeta. In 2013 Heinz was bought by behemoths Berkshire Hathaway and 3G Capital in a deal worth over US $20 billion; in 2015 they announced a $50 billion merger with Kraft to create the fifth-largest food company in the world (Feeney, 2015). 3G's co-founder Jorge Paulo Lemman had acquired a reputation for disciplined cost-cutting and a ruthless focus on performance. In a rare interview he said, 'You're running, you're always close to a limit, you're working very hard and being evaluated all the time' (Roberts, 2013). The new company played to Lemman's strengths; in the five months following the merger, they had laid off over 5,000 employees, which was over 10 per cent of the total workforce. As a result, profits grew and the share price continued to increase.

2019 saw a change in fortunes; they announced a $15.4 billion write-down of the Kraft and Oscar Mayer brands and their stock plummeted by a third. Many of the Kraft Heinz brands were over 100 years old and consumer tastes had taken a toll on revenues, with sales declining by 13 per cent. Analysis of the strategy shows that since the merger, 3G had cut research and development by nearly two-thirds and the advertising budget by over a third (Back, 2019). The overall strategy could have been successful, but by slashing the budgets in marketing and research and development, Lemman achieved short-term profitability at the expense of longer-term profitability and growth.

The Kraft Heinz Company is just one of a number of organizations that have faltered or collapsed as a result of overtension, typically sacrificing the long term in favour of immediate gains; this is the finite game we covered in Chapter 11 (Carse, 2013). 'The bottom line is that in today's world, your organizations must respond to change and adopt new ways of doing things, even if you fail in the short term, so that you can learn and grow' (Yeung and Ulrich, 2019).

Adjusting quality

When we think back to our childhood, there are certain things that we always associate with Christmas. For me there was, of course, the tree, plastic with tinsel; and there was the TV guide, where I circled the programmes

I wanted to watch and hoped this was a year that *Star Wars* would feature. Finally, there was the food and drink; and nothing is more Christmassy than the annual tin of Quality Street. This chocolate collection, individually wrapped with different colours and shapes, was always opened up during the festive period and everyone had their favourite; mine was the Toffee Penny. In 2015, a viral post showed a collection of Quality Street tins, which had decreased in size over the years, showing that 'the latest tin weighs 780g and appears less than half the size of the tin… bought nearly two decades ago' (Sims, 2015). This activity, known as shrinkflation, is where a level of service or a feature of quality, such as size, quantity or component parts, is reduced whilst prices remain the same or increase. This reduction leads to a direct decrease in the derived demand for labour, which reduces the financial cost. It is a common practice; one study showed that over a five-year period, at least 2,500 different UK goods (typically food products) had decreased the size or quantity whilst maintaining prices (ONS, 2019). Organizations do the same with service levels, such as increasing the waiting times to speak to someone on a helpdesk or reducing the regularity of refuse collection. In some instances, the service can be added at additional cost, such a same-day delivery or a premium level of service at a carwash.

This is something that many of us do within our own lives; I have often been asked to conduct analysis and provide a report in a short time frame. In those circumstances, I often caveat that in that particular time frame the analysis may be more limited and a better standard can be achieved in more time. This allows the customer to assess their need objectively and the majority that require urgency are happy to accept a basic standard; after all, 'a good plan… now is better than a perfect plan next week' (Patton, 2003). What made the post about the chocolates go viral was that the reduction in size had largely gone unnoticed by consumers; being able to see the products side by side was a revelation of the change. It helps illustrate the sweet spot for this action; the aim is to consider the value chain and prioritize the demand that delivers the greatest value to the consumer. The start point is that activity that delivers no value, as 'nothing is less productive than to make more efficient what should not be done at all' (Drucker, 2011).

The next stage is to consider activity in line with the Pareto principle (Pareto, 1906) we discussed in Chapter 6. That principle dictates that 80 per cent of the value comes from 20 per cent of the effort, and the remaining 20 per cent of value would constitute 80 per cent of the effort. Consider the approach taken to shop security: the majority have a mix of passive cameras and some vigilant staff. Others take a greater step with alarms activated by security tags, monitored camera systems and dedicated security staff. Further still, there are reinforced doors, items in protective cases, vaults and an endless array of security. Yet, even those with the greatest security will still fall victim to criminality. To guarantee the security of a shop would require an exponential growth of measures, to the extent that trade would become impossible: 'The best is the enemy of the good' (Voltaire, 1772). Instead, organizations assess the risk and tend towards an 80 per cent solution and have sufficient insurance to cover the remaining 20 per cent. Management of these 'costs of control' (Feigenbaum, 1991), by balancing risk against the cost to prevent in advance or check afterwards, is a key activity in reducing the demand for labour.

CASE STUDY
XYZ Telco

A utilities business retained a number of complex policies from its former public sector background. One of those policies guaranteed specific considerations to different cohorts of former public sector employees if they applied for internal roles within the company. One member of staff was employed full-time in checking applications for internal roles, identifying those for whom the special considerations applied, and putting those measures in place, which all made little difference to those applications. The CHRO, looking to reduce unnecessary costs, balanced the cost of applying this preventative action against both the impact of those members of the workforce and the risk of being taken to an employment tribunal and the cost to settle. They took the decision to remove the role and their cost–benefit analysis proved to be sound.

Cost of poor quality

The process of adjusting quality is not simply a race to the bottom, the aim to achieve the golden mean, a balance between these two excesses (Aristotle, 1980). The impact of going too far is known as the *cost of poor quality* (COPQ), a concept popularized by IBM's process improvement expert H. James Harrington (1987). Harrington talked of both indirect and direct costs of poor quality. In a customer-centric organization, some of the indirect costs are the greatest concern, such as the cost of customer dissatisfaction and impact to organizational reputation through producing poor-quality goods. Often given less credence is consideration of the costs incurred by the customer, such as the time spent returning a defective product or, to take the example from Chapter 12, the effort for the customer to scan their own purchases at a self-service checkout. The direct COPQ includes not only the 'costs of control' (Feigenbaum, 1991), but also the cost that results from poor quality.

Consider, for example, the sale of a defective television set to a customer; at first, the customer calls the customer call centre helpline. The product is then returned to the store, where the customer service desk takes the faulty product and either exchanges it or provides a refund. The product is then collected by the returns team and pushed back through the supply chain to a diagnosis team who identify the fault and, if the product can be repaired, pass it back to a repair team to fix the problem. The customer call centre, the service desk, the returns team, the diagnosis team and the repair team are all dealing with 'failure demand' (Seddon, 2003). Think back to the model of demand we covered back in Chapter 9, where an output takes the form of one of three things: product, drift or waste. Failure demand occurs when we produce either drift or waste. Let us return to the example of the defective television. Providing it could be repaired, it illustrates drift; if it could not be fixed, then it would be waste. When Armand Feigenbaum first devised the concepts that would inspire the field of *total quality management* (TQM), he posited the theory of the 'hidden plant' (Feigenbaum, 1991). His analysis suggested that up to 40 per cent of capacity is wasted due to failures in ensuring that outputs do not translate into drift and waste.

CASE STUDY
123 Technologies

A medium-sized business specializing in fast-moving consumer electronics was suffering not only from decreasing profit margins, but also from declining consumer satisfaction. The CEO was candid with me that they had executed some change initiative that had failed to generate the return on investment that had been expected, which had increased their turnover of staff. A review of their processes highlighted glaring discrepancies between their process maps and the way that work was done. The operations directors had a ruthless focus on customer service; when the new initiatives resulted in an impact to consumers, managers were swift to enact workarounds and redirect sufficient resource to overcome the issue. Unfortunately, they were so stretched that no one took the time to remedy the cause of the problems. The analysis that I shared with the CEO came as a shock: 9 per cent of their TCOW was spent exclusively on resourcing these workarounds. Many of these were spiralling, as stripping out employees to focus on workarounds had left key processes perilously understaffed and was driving higher levels of drift and waste. Execution of the plan we created collectively was a key turning point in the success of the company, generating in-year savings that were refocused back into the areas of highest business value.

Managing demand

The management and control of demand is a key aspect to ensuring business success, at all three levels of the organization. Demand is rarely static and typically fluctuates, as shown in Figure 13.1.

Consider an organization that is taking steps to maintain their workforce levels, perhaps recruiting solely to replace turnover; this is shown by the solid line. Conversely, the demand for workers fluctuates in a series of peaks and troughs, shown on the dashed line. Many HR practitioners would consider the demand peaks as a workforce deficit and describe the demand troughs as a workforce surplus. This mindset is what drives an approach focused solely on talent management solutions. These are simply gaps between supply and demand, of which demand is the most prone to fluctuation. Consider an organization where, as the demand starts to increase at the first peak, they hire additional staff. By the time the staff arrive, it is too late to deal with that earlier demand. As the demand moves towards a trough,

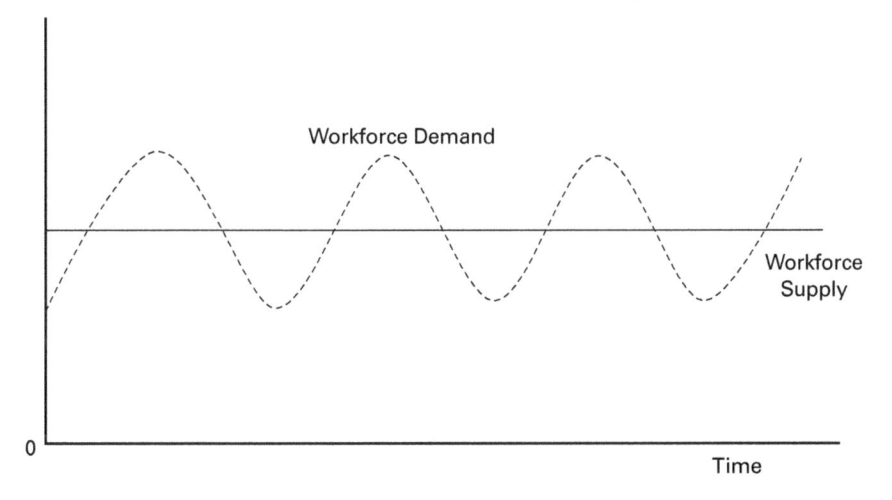

FIGURE 13.1 Demand fluctuation against maintained supply

the earlier hiring decision means they have significantly more workers than they have available work. At that point, the company may choose to lay off the entire surplus in order to reduce costs. This creates an even greater gap as the demand peaks for a second time and continues. If we make the mistake of responding to demand fluctuations immediately with a supply initiative, we are likely to suffer from a *Forrester*, or *bullwhip* effect. The pioneering computer engineer, Professor Jay Wright Forrester, established this concept in the 1960s. A small response to customer demand changes creates increasingly greater distortion further down the supply chain, almost like the wave effect from a bullwhip created by a flick of the wrist (Forrester, 1961). Operational managers will have looked at Figure 13.1 and identified immediately the opportunity to move the demand peaks into the demand troughs in order to smoothen the demand curve. At a macro level this may mean ensuring that special deals for consumers are aligned to those periods of lower demand, or adjusting the quality standards. The creation of service levels is a relatively simple way to smoothen demand, by giving greater time to complete the work, whilst reducing failure demand as customers and stakeholders will avoid calling for a progress check within the agreed service window. Businesses that provide home delivery on items purchased online do this frequently; their standard delivery terms provide a service level agreement that allows them to smoothen the demand curve and benefit from economies of scale. These same businesses may offer same-day or next-day delivery at a premium cost in order to offset the cost of being unable to smoothen demand. Another vital tool in the demand management arsenal is the use of time fences. This is the use of boundaries to separate planning horizons, which each provide different levels of governance and tolerance.

Figure 13.2 shows my favoured approach to time fences, dividing the planning horizons into three: frozen, firm and flexible. Before the first of our time fences, demand is mostly confirmed; though there may be a forecast towards the end of the period, the deviation is limited. As a result, we freeze the plan based on the confirmed demand and most-likely scenario. Let us assume, for example, that it takes a month to build a car. Imagine we have 15 orders for cars to be collected at the end of January and we plan on producing 15 cars. If a new customer calls us in January to ask for a car at the end of January, that additional demand cannot be satisfied as there is insufficient time to build the additional car; the demand is frozen at 15. Therefore, we would not accept a request to satisfy this demand and would instead agree to deliver for the end of February instead, when we are planning to build a further 15 cars, but only have 13 confirmed orders. We may be able

FIGURE 13.2 Time fences

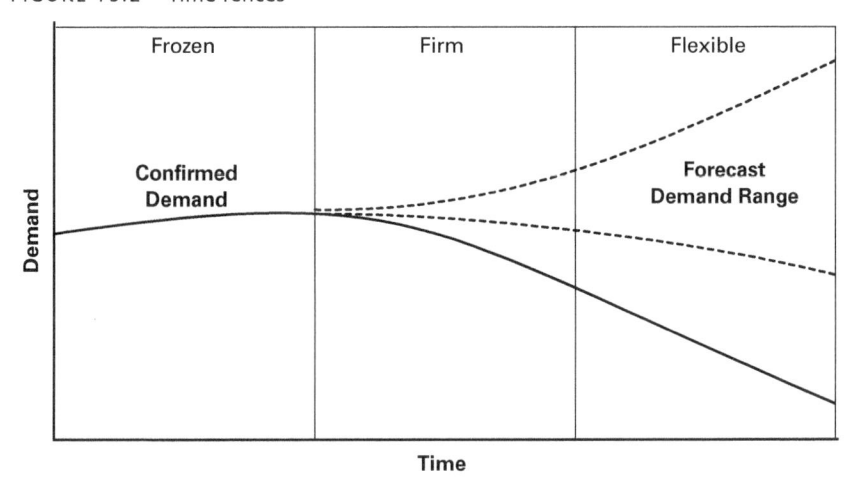

[Figure: Chart showing Demand vs Time divided into three vertical sections labeled "Frozen", "Firm", and "Flexible". A solid line labeled "Confirmed Demand" stays flat in the Frozen region then declines through Firm and Flexible. Dashed lines labeled "Forecast Demand Range" diverge into a cone of uncertainty in the Flexible region.]

to satisfy a small surge in demand for cars with a minimum of three months' notice, that being the time it would take to bring on new staff and onboard them in addition to increasing the additional resources needed from our upstream supply chain. Therefore, the first time fence would be set at three months; the time period to satisfy small demand fluctuations that can be serviced by changing the size of the workforce and the lead time for that activity.

After the first time fence, our confirmed demand begins to decline and we rely more on our forecast demand. Before the second time fence, the deviation between our forecast range (our best-case and worst-case scenario) is quite low; this period is firm. We will plan on the most likely scenario and are able to respond quickly to changes in demand that fall within the forecast range of tolerance. After the second time fence, confirmed demand declines significantly and the deviation between the forecast ranges continues to grow, creating a cone of uncertainty. To satisfy an increase in demand that would be within the best-case scenario might necessitate the procurement of new machinery or, indeed, a new factory; this might take a year or more. That determines the position of the second time fence, after which time a whole range of demand fluctuations can be satisfied, but these may necessitate a much longer lead time and significant capital investment. Identifying these time fences and adjusting governance can bring significant stability and is a vital tool in demand management as it can prevent the Forrester effect within the frozen period and limit the effect within the firm period.

Changing the organizational design

In simple terms, the organizational design is the architecture that connects the organization, both formal and informal, to the workforce and the necessary business processes that align to the strategic framework (Nadler and Tushman, 1997). The organizational design is the single biggest factor in establishing the environment component of the *right capability*. The necessity for changing the organizational design is likely to emanate from addressing strategic misalignment and considering the three factors of decay, fragmentation and overtension.

In the 1970s, Professor Larry Greiner created a model of how organizations grow and develop, which identifies and addresses the challenge of the decay factor and is adapted in Figure 13.3. He established phases of evolutionary growth, each proceeded by a revolutionary stage. During the initial phase, a start-up grows through the creativity of the entrepreneurial team, which ends with a leadership crisis as professional leadership is required for continued growth. The second phase achieves growth through the provision of clear direction, but ends in an autonomy crisis as there are insufficient workers to manage the demand. In the third phase, with a larger workforce, the business achieves growth through delegation; this ends in a control crisis as there are insufficient management processes to coordinate the growing workforce. The fourth phase achieves growth through coordination and effective management processes but ends in a red-tape crisis as bureaucracy

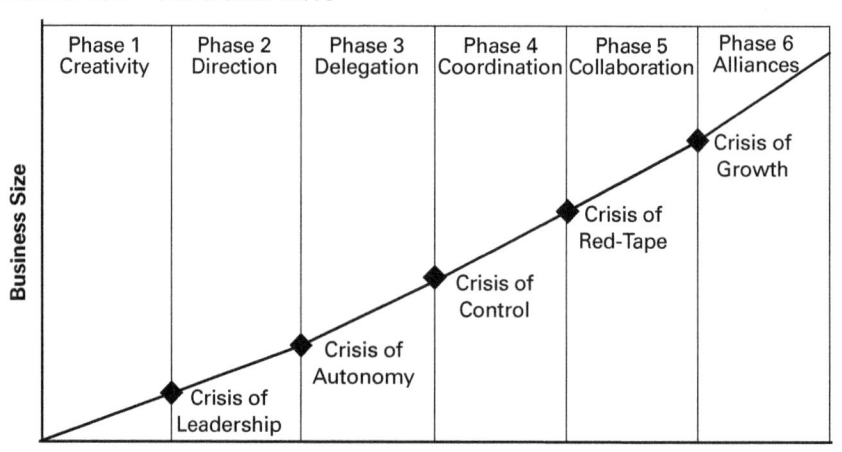

FIGURE 13.3 The Greiner Curve

SOURCE Adapted from Greiner (1998)

hinders progression. In the fifth phase, the formal and informal aspects of the organizational design are addressed and growth is achieved through collaboration. The fifth phase ends in a crisis of internal growth and prompts a shift into growth through alliances and look to outsource demand or merge with other organizations to capitalize on new demand (Greiner, 1998). Each of these crises prompts a revision of the organizational design in order to ensure growth.

Organizational structure

The formal organization is defined by its structure, of which a simple flat structure will prevail in the early stages of Greiner's model. As the organization grows in size, the most traditional structure is a hierarchical model. Political scientist Luther Gulick, who was appointed by President Franklin D Roosevelt to reorganize the executive branch of the federal government, was a leading thinker in this area. Hierarchical organizations can be structured on the basis of products, clients, geography and functions; one of these will take primacy over the others (Gulick, 1937). If we revert back to our bakery from Chapter 9, then a product-based structure may divide the organization into breads, cakes, pastries, pies and biscuits/cookies. In a client-based structure, the bakery would be divided by their clients, perhaps two divisions of major supermarkets, one division of minor supermarkets and a final division of their own smaller stores. In a geographically structured organization, the operation would be structured based on the geographies of operation, perhaps four divisions of the cardinal points of North, South, East and West. The product, client and geographic models are divisional approaches and each division would have their own bakery, logistical chain and supporting functions. In a functional design, the organization is separated by the functions, perhaps divisions of logistics, operations, sales, service and supporting activities.

As thinking on organizational design has evolved, more system-based approaches have been created and developed. Matrix structures, organized along divisional lines and incorporating a horizontal functional structure, have grown in popularity. Often these are the functional supporting activities such as human resources, finance, procurement and organizational leadership. This has enabled organizations to take advantage of some economies of scale, though often at the risk of tension between these two management hierarchies. Over time organizations have morphed into a variety of network-based structures.

CASE STUDY
Apple

A snapshot of the multinational technology behemoth shows a great deal of hierarchy. Major strategic decisions all flowed through Steve Jobs, though this has evolved under Tim Cook into a more collaborative relationship between teams and greater empowerment of subordinates. It is primarily a product-aligned structure, with vice presidents leading different outputs, and overlaid with a functional matrix (Meyer, 2019). For example, the iPhone, though designed in Cupertino in California, benefits from a wide network-based structure of secondary industries. Individual components are manufactured by a vast range of businesses from around the globe. Assembly of these components into the iPhone is conducted by Pegatron and Foxconn, technology giants based in Taiwan (Costello, 2020).

Such network approaches have spawned a variety of organizational design models, from Bill Gore's *lattice* structure (Brown, 1984) to the *holocracy* (Robertson, 2007). Perhaps the most comprehensive model for the contemporary environment is that of the *market-oriented ecosystem* (MOE), which aligns independent teams to market opportunities and connects these teams to share information and leverage customer focus, innovation and agility (Yeung and Ulrich, 2019). The MOE helps solidify the crux that we must ensure we have the most appropriate structure for organization and the marketplace within which it operates.

Discussion of organizational structure cannot conclude without mention of spans and layers. Spans of control are the number of direct reports to managers and organizational layers are the number of hierarchical levels from the CEO to the frontline employees. The standard premise is that if spans are too small and the organization will incur the cost of unnecessary managers and the greater the number of layers, the longer it will take for information to flow and decisions to be made. Analysis by Bain & Company showed the average organization has an average span of control of between six and seven direct reports and between eight and nine layers. Conversely, the 'best-in-class companies' have between 10 and 15 direct reports and no more than seven layers (Mountain and Kovac, 2010). Such benchmarks can easily give the indication that greater spans and fewer layers is always the right direction. In fact, it has long been recognized that though a larger span can reduce management costs, 'If the span of control is too large, the supervisor may not have the capacity to supervise effectively such large numbers of immediate subordinates' (Mackenzie, 1978). Business theorist and management consultant Lyndall Urwick was the first to discuss the concept of spans of control and shared the formula that each additional direct report increased the ability to delegate by 25 per cent whilst the burden to coordinate and supervise rose by 100 per cent. Indeed, he asserted that 'no superior can supervise directly the work of more than five or, at the most, six subordinates whose work interlocks' (Urwick, 1957). In my experience, I tend to start in the centre of these two extremes with 10 direct reports. If the work being executed is process work, then we can usually increase this by one or two; knowledge work will reduce the number of direct reports. We can adjust this further to account for the interlocking work that Urwick identified. Where direct reports are operating independent of each other, for example a contact centre or store managers, then the number can increase; if a supervisor has to manage the interaction between subordinates, then the number decreases. A great example is one of safety management, where spans may be limited significantly when managing overlapping work in hazardous circumstances. When we start with an assessment of spans and build them up across the organization, this provides the solution for the optimum number of layers.

Having looked at the structural location of work, one final element to consider is the geographical location of work. The location of organizations tends to evolve out of the geography of their value chain. I am always reminded of the River Irwell river, in my own hometown of Manchester in England, that was a key catalyst of the Industrial Revolution. It connects to the Mersey estuary in the west and cotton, imported through the ports at Liverpool, was brought across to Manchester and transported through its canals to the textile mills of the 18th century. Other organizations, perhaps less beholden to the geography of a supply chain, may have simply grown out of the location of the founder. The ability to be flexible around location will enhance the scope of the available workforce initiatives. If work can be done anywhere, then the available initiatives become almost limitless. The COVID-19 pandemic ignited a seismic shift in location as global supply chains were disrupted and social distancing restricted the ability of the workforce to enter their places of work. Suddenly, the aperture widened on the location lens through which work had always been viewed. As a result, homeshoring, the ability to conduct work from our own home, became possible in far more industries than before. Those organizations who had already developed their consideration around location have found themselves far more able to respond to disruption than those who had not.

Organizational culture

In the first century BCE, the great Roman statesman Marcus Tullius Cicero was perhaps the first to discuss the concept of universal crimes. These crimes are those that are so obviously recognized by all as crimes, that they do not require legislation and they circumvent local jurisdiction (Cicero, 1928). The legal concept of *hostis humani generis*, enemy of humanity, extends to those who have committed such universal crimes, from the pirates of the 17th century to Nazis sentenced during the Nuremberg trials for genocide during the Second World War. Just as there are legal rights and wrongs that are held in common by all people, there are business rights and wrongs that are held in common. Just as the legal conventions sit outside written legislation, so too business conventions sit outside written policy and process; these informal structures are the organizational culture. In the same way popular culture can override the written laws, organizational culture can override the formal structures of the workplace. As the saying goes, often misattributed to Peter Drucker, **culture eats strategy for breakfast**.

Culture comprises three key components: purpose, values and brand. Purpose, as we have covered in Chapter 5, is a way of expressing the *why* of an organization; it is the north point on the compass that provides direction to the workforce. As such, purpose is where the culture intersects with the strategic framework of the organization. Values are the core beliefs of the organization; deeply held, they shape what matters to an organization and how it acts. One great definition is that values dictate how our organization will behave to achieve its purpose (Elliot and Corey, 2018). They are often framed in a values statement; arguably the most famous heralds from the United States Declaration of Independence: 'We hold these truths to be self-evident, that all men are created equal, that they are endowed by their Creator with certain unalienable Rights, that among these are Life, Liberty and the pursuit of Happiness' (Jefferson *et al*, 1776). The values that tend to stick within an organization are those that go beyond a simple buzzword; they are described and often extend into expected forms of behaviour.

In the early 1980s, the competing values framework, illustrated in Figure 13.4, was developed from research by the University of Michigan on organizational effectiveness. The framework assesses organizations on a structural axis ranging from flexible to stable, and an axis of focus ranging from inward to outward. This four-quadrant matrix places organizations within one of four types: clan, adhocracy, hierarchy and market.

FIGURE 13.4 The competing values framework

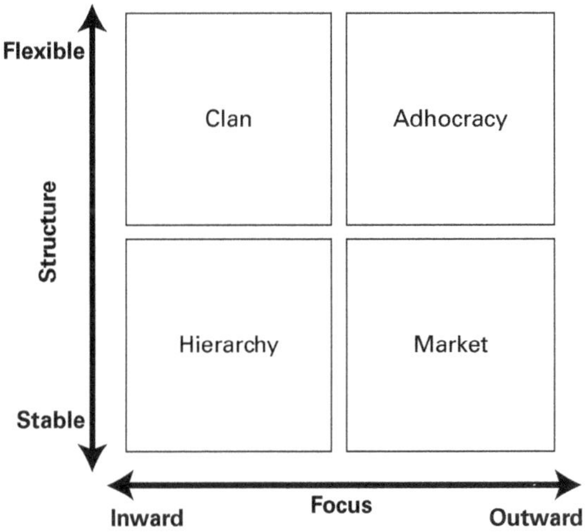

```
                    Flexible
                  ▲
                  │   ┌──────────┐  ┌──────────┐
                  │   │          │  │          │
                  │   │   Clan   │  │ Adhocracy│
                  │   │          │  │          │
         e        │   └──────────┘  └──────────┘
       r u        │
       t c        │
       u r        │
       t          │   ┌──────────┐  ┌──────────┐
       S          │   │          │  │          │
                  │   │ Hierarchy│  │  Market  │
                  │   │          │  │          │
                  │   └──────────┘  └──────────┘
                    Stable
                  ▼
                      ◄──────────  Focus  ──────────►
                       Inward                  Outward
```

SOURCE Adapted from Cameron and Quinn (2011)

The clan group is structured flexibly and inwardly focused, so oriented towards collaboration. The organization will strive to achieve a tight social network, almost like a family, and value cohesion, communication and participation.

The adhocracy group maintains the flexible structure of the clan but is outwardly focused; these tend to be dynamic businesses that are oriented towards creation. The adhocracy is more entrepreneurial and comfortable with taking risk; their values tend to be centred around innovation, transformation and agility.

The hierarchy group have stable structures and are inward facing, very much oriented towards control and ensuring stability. As a result, these organizations value efficiency, timeliness and uniformity.

Finally, the market group have a stable structure paired with an outward focus. These are oriented towards competition and aggressively focused on results. These organizations value effectiveness, profitability, increased market share and achievement of stretching goals.

The great feature of this model is that it allows us to analyse an organization and to support its reorientation based on a desired state. The final component of culture is the brand; this is the external perception of the organization. The brand of the organization can be separated into two elements: the market brand and the employer brand. The market brand relates to how the organization interacts with customers and is influenced heavily by concepts we have covered earlier in the chapter, such as quality standards. The employer brand, by the original definition, is 'the package of functional, economic and psychological benefits provided by employment, and identified with the employing company' (Ambler and Barrow, 1996).

CASE STUDY
Coca-Cola

The Coca-Cola Company is undoubtedly one of the most impressive organizations in the world; founded in the late 19th century, it has stood apart as the leading soft drinks manufacturer for over a century. It has been crowned the most powerful US brand on several occasions based on its continued familiarity with, and favourability by, global consumers. It 'continues to endure by illustrating the value of consistent brand investments, excellent execution and strategic communications to deliver stability to its brand' (Tenet, 2019). That said, Coca-Cola's use of plastic packaging and sale of sugary drinks meant it ranked ninth in a global list of the companies most criticized by non-governmental organizations (Sigwatch, 2019). In addition, from an employer brand perspective, it does not feature in the top 100 list of the best companies to work for (Fortune, 2020). These views are likely to be features that move the most powerful brand down to 13th place in 2020 in the most valuable global brands, with less than a third of the brand value of each of the top four performers: Amazon, Apple, Google and Microsoft respectively (BrandZ, 2020).

Together these three elements of purpose, value and brand compose the organizational culture. Just like wider society, culture takes time to evolve; whilst designing the desired culture is part of demand optimization, changing the culture is a talent management initiative and will be covered in the next chapter. It is important to recognize that different approaches are needed depending on whether we are building a culture in a new organization or changing the culture in a mature organization. If it is the latter, then sage advice is to honour the strengths of the existing culture: 'It's tempting to dwell on the negative traits of your culture, but any corporate culture is a product of good intentions that evolved in unexpected ways and will have many strengths' (Katzenbach *et al*, 2012). Capitalizing on these strengths will feel like more of a cultural evolution to the workforce, which garners support much easier than driving a metaphorical bulldozer over the past.

Increasing performance

When the subject of performance is raised with HR professionals, many will fall comfortably in the arms of performance appraisals, objective setting, feedback and coaching. Though there is a place for individual performance management, which we will cover in the next chapter, the starting place for performance is not the improvement of the individual worker.

In the Second World War, the American B-17 aircraft became the pinnacle of high-altitude bombing for much of the war, but not without problems. There was an alarming incidence of B-17s crashing when they came into land, an issue investigated by PhD student Alphonse Chapanis and the team of aviation psychologists at Wright Field in Dayton, Ohio. Chapanis noticed that the switches for the flaps and the landing gear on the B-17 were identical and adjacent. He identified that under pressure of a difficult landing, pilots were confusing the switches; rather than retracting the flaps to reduce speed, they retracted the wheels and crashed fuselage-first straight into the runway. This problem was overcome by improving the distinguishability of the switches with different shapes and colours. In their study of several different aircraft, all 460 'pilot errors' had their root cause in the design of the cockpit and the processes (Chapanis *et al*, 1949). These would later become known as system dynamics, another concept from Professor Jay Wright Forrester, which considers flows within complex systems (Forrester, 1961). The HR approach of assuming that performance issues are down to pilot error and therefore require individual intervention is a page out of McGregor's *Theory X*. This assumes workers are less intelligent, act only in their own self-interest and are more effective under a hands-on management approach (McGregor, 1960). Conversely, if we take a *Theory Y* approach and assume that our workers are a valuable asset who are inclined to perform at the best of their ability and take responsibility for their actions (McGregor, 1960), then we are more likely to first consider the system dynamics of any performance issues. In doing so, we will examine three key strands: process improvement, work design and operational transformation.

Process improvement

In 1939 the US engineer and statistician, Dr Walter Shewhart, devised a cycle of activity to create an iterative approach to product development. This cycle of continuous improvement comprised three steps: specification, production and inspection (Shewhart, 1959). The product specification would be designed, then the product created and inspected; this would see the specification redesigned and the cycle continue. This cycle was developed further by Dr W Edwards Deming, who split production into two stages: the testing of a prototype followed by mass production and a release to the marketplace (Deming, 1952). This approach, popularly known as the *PDCA cycle (plan, do, check, act)* is illustrated in Figure 13.5; it enables organizations to improve the efficiency of existing processes and it remains the foundation of process improvement.

In the first step, *plan*, we identify the problem or opportunity and establish clearly the objectives to be achieved. As part of this step, we devise a solution and the processes that underpin it. In the *do* step, we enact that process as a test run and gather data. In the third step, *check*, we analyse the data from the test. Did it achieve the desired outcome? Are there any unintended consequences? Only once we are happy with the results do we move onto the final stage, *act*, and implement that change. Numerous process improvement practices have grown out of this methodology and are supplemented by concepts such as the *five whys model* and the *Ishikawa fishbone diagram* that we covered in Chapter 6 (Ishikawa, 1986). Arguably the most prominent of these process improvement methodologies are kaizen, Six Sigma and lean.

Kaizen, which translates from Japanese as *change for better*, is a concept that places responsibility on all workers to improve processes (Imai, 1988). One of my guilty pleasures is watching the US version of *MasterChef*, where amateur chefs and home cooks compete in a series of cooking tests to be crowned the master chef. My favourite test is the team challenge; contestants are placed into two teams, which compete head to head against each other

FIGURE 13.5 The PDCA cycle

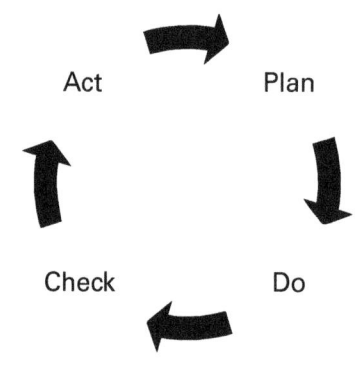

SOURCE Adapted from Deming (1952)

under the leadership of a team captain to produce meals for hundreds of waiting patrons. One of the most common failings in this test is the plating of substandard food; maybe the meat is undercooked, or possibly the potatoes are now cold. Either way, the person at the end of the production line is focused so heavily on plating the food, they forget the bigger picture and have been known to serve undercooked chicken. This failing is typically identified by the patron and addressed by an irate Gordon Ramsey, who initiates a kaizen, albeit with much swearing and shouting. In a true kaizen environment, the team would identify the failure before the substandard food was served and initiate a PDCA cycle at the time.

Six Sigma, often written as 6σ, is a quality management approach designed to minimize defects in manufacturing processes and thereby reduce variance. It was introduced in the 1980s by Bill Smith, a quality control consultant and former US Navy engineer, whilst he was working at Motorola. In process improvement it extends the PDCA cycle into a five-phase methodology, abbreviated to DMAIC. The start point is to *define* the problem and the objectives; this is followed by *measurement* of the current process and the collection of data points based on how the existing process operates. These data points are *analysed* to determine the relationships within the system and establish the root cause of any defect. It is only at this stage that options for *improvement* are considered, compared and tested. Once a workable solution is identified, the change is enacted with *controls* to ensure that any future issues are resolved before defects occur (Tennant, 2001). The ability to remove variance from a process contributes directly to a reduction of the drift and waste we discussed in Chapter 9 (see Figure 9.1). The key outcome is an increase in productivity, as a greater proportion of outputs become products. With increased productivity comes a reduction in demand to maintain production levels, which closes the gap between supply and demand. Whilst this is most commonly used across an end-to-end process, the next case study demonstrates how applying Six Sigma at the lowest level can create a significant marginal effect when compounded.

BRITISH CYCLING

Sir Chris Hoy is a six-time Olympic gold medallist and was world champion 11 times before retiring from professional cycling. In his final Olympiad, he secured two of the staggering tally of eight gold medals won by British Cycling at London, 2012. This success is a far cry from his international debut in 1996, where funding was so tight that the young Chris had to sign his tracksuit out and return it back as someone else would need to use it the following year (Slater, 2008). Fortunately, funding was secured the subsequent year from the UK's National Lottery and the Sydney Olympics in 2000 saw British Cycling's first gold medal since 1992. That Lottery funding also secured a fundamental asset in Dave Brailsford, who joined the team in 1998 and was appointed performance director in 2003. The following year, Chris Hoy and Bradley Wiggins secured their first Olympic golds at Athens; four years later, in Tokyo, British Cycling achieved a staggering eight gold medals.

Following the 30th Olympiad in London, having achieved a further eight gold medals, the concept of *marginal gains* was revealed as the secret to their success. Brailsford divulged, 'The whole principle came from the idea that if you broke down everything you could think of that goes into riding a bike, and then improved it by 1 per cent, you will get a significant increase when you put them all together' (BBC News, 2015). He took this systems-based approach to Team Sky in 2010 and, with no British cyclist ever having won the Tour de France, was instrumental in the victories of Bradley Wiggins, Chris Froome and Geraint Thomas from 2012 onwards.

Lean production, in contrast to Six Sigma, is focused on the removal of activities that do not deliver value to the customer. The term was coined by John Krafcik during his time on MIT's five-year study on the future of the automobile (Womack *et al*, 1991); more recently, Krafcik became the CEO of Waymo, Google's self-driving car project. It draws heavily on the scientific management approaches of Frederick Winslow Taylor, one of the earliest proponents of process improvement (Taylor, 1911). Taylorism relied on the optimization of detailed processes and strict supervision of the workforce to ensure standardization; with this, he eradicated the inconsistencies of the artisans. Lean expands this approach by adding the critical steps of identifying the value stream for a product and ensuring continuous flow throughout the system. The ability to remove activities from a process that do not create value also reduces the associated demand for resource and, at scale, can make a significant contribution to closing the gap between supply and demand.

Work design

A key aspect of what Taylor instigated was the practice of work design, the careful specification of the role of the worker. Whilst structures tend to look at the macro and meso levels of the organization, role design cuts to the heart of the micro level. In the 1960s, psychologist Frederick Herzberg proposed a two-factor theory of job satisfaction (Herzberg, 1966). The first factor was one of hygiene factors, extrinsic elements such as pay and benefits. These we will cover in the next chapter within the subject of the employee value proposition (EVP). Herzberg's second factor was motivators, those elements that are intrinsic to the role itself and provide *job satisfaction*. A decade later, Professors Richard Hackman and Greg Oldham would expand on Herzberg's thinking by articulating three vital psychological states. First, that work needs to be meaningful and valued; second, that people are accountable for the results of their work and, finally, that they know the result of their work (Hackman and Oldham, 1976). To achieve this, Hackman and Oldham stated that work is best designed to achieve five core dimensions: variety, identity, significance, autonomy and feedback. The most satisfying work comprises a variety of tasks and utilizes a variety of competencies. Those who are involved in a piece of work from initiation to completion will derive greater satisfaction than those who are involved only in part of the work. The most satisfied workers are involved in tasks that have significance and meaning, creating genuine value for their organization or society. As we will discuss further in the next chapter, the most satisfied workers have autonomy and discretion in their work and receive clear feedback on the impact of their performance.

By stripping the worker of many of these core dimensions, Taylor presented a classic example of McGregor's *Theory X* approach (McGregor, 1960). He asked workers to surrender these core dimensions in favour of higher reward. Though this remains a choice within an EVP, it must acknowledge the negative impact on performance. Taylorism also assumes that when we apply scientific management to a process, we will create the perfect solution the first time and there is no possibility of disruption. As both are unlikely, a workforce with autonomy and empowered to refine processes will be more successful than those who are beholden to micromanagement.

Within this concept, it is important to consider *context switch*, the ability to pause and resume processes. The term comes from computer processing and enables multitasking, a term which also has its roots in computers. The weight of evidence is that multitasking in humans is a 'mythical activity' (Hallowell, 2006). When presented with multiple tasks, the human brain is prevented from working on key aspects of both (Gladstones *et al*, 1989). What takes place is context switching; we switch our focus between multiple tasks. Computers and humans alike, the main reasons for context switching are multiple tasks or interruption during a task. The result is that, like computers, this context switching drains resources; for the human brain, that resource is time. Analysis suggests that each concurrent task adds a 20 per cent loss of time due to context switching; a significant erosion of available time (Weinberg, 2011). Though the term superseded him, the eradication of context switching was a clear ambition of Taylorism. Therefore, to take an effective approach that aligns to the *theory Y* approach and maintains efficiency, it is vital to create flow. Create a sequence of activity, rather than workers being forced to maintain focus on multiple activities. If that creates process issues, then look to enable concurrent activity across the workforce so that process flows enable each other.

The benefit of this approach is that we look specifically at the micro level of work and tasks; it opens the greatest span of workforce levers:

> [those tasks] that require strategic, proprietary, optimal, insightful, and unique solutions are more likely to be done by full-time employees who become a source of strategic differentiation. Tasks that are characterized as essential, generic, satisficing, efficient, and standardized may be done through automation with technology-enabled solutions. Part-time, consultant, and outsourced employees will perform a mix of the types of worktasks (Ulrich, 2019).

One final aspect to consider is that the design of work is a vital element in improving inclusivity and agility. Those organizations where work is designed exclusively around an office-based, 40-hour, 9-to-5 working week are less inclusive than those who are more flexible. Where work is inflexible, it excludes those who cannot work within these strict boundaries. Greater flexibility widens the possible labour market and, by doing so, can reduce the impact of the skills gap and limit the pay increases associated with a restricted labour pool. Furthermore, this flexibility provides greater agility in the face of disruption, as the COVID-19 pandemic has demonstrated.

Operational transformation

Whilst process improvement focuses on enhancement of the existing state, operational transformation is a fundamental step change to a new state. My favourite illustration of the dichotomy comes from a quotation attributed to the great mind of Professor Oren Harari: 'The electric light did not come from the continuous improvement of candles.' Transformation breaks from the past in a seismic way, often reinventing the operating model.

CASE STUDY
Procter & Gamble

Between the cities of Pargue and Plzeň, in the central Bohemian region of the Czech Republic, lies the small town of Rakovník. Located there is Rakona, the second oldest factory of consumer goods giant Procter & Gamble (P&G), which produces around 4 million cases of washing powders and liquids each year. 2010 saw a shift in consumer preference away from washing powders, which resulted in a significant reduction in demand at the site. As a result, P&G launched a rapid cost reduction programme with the ambition of attracting new business; by 2014 the plant had achieved a turnaround and needed to expand. Determined to exploit the digital environment, they embarked on an ambitious operational transformation. They designed an in-process control system, the first of its kind, which monitors quality levels during the manufacturing process and halts production in the event of a deviation. This led to a halving of reworking and complaints, a decrease in waste and a throughput time reduction of 24 hours. The implementation of a universal packing system meant that recipe changes could be enacted without having to shut down the production line; this cut the changeover time by 50 per cent and enabled a 40 per cent reduction in the minimum order quantity. Finally, a digitally enabled synchronization of the entire supply chain meant that inventory was reduced by 35 per cent whilst inventory efficiency increased by 7 per cent (World Economic Forum, 2019).

Process improvement, when embedded effectively, is a bottom-up approach that emanates from the workforce. As such, there are limits to how far upwards this improvement can progress. Operational transformation dovetails straight into the top-down direction that flows from the strategic framework. It is also characterized by an impetus for change; as the example of the Rakona plant illustrates, this is often the necessity to implement technological advancement. Without such technology, the peak of operational performance is limited and this is something we see in our daily lives. The implementation of self-service remains a great example, where the retail industry transformed the channel of interaction between the consumer and the organization. Rather than a human interface, the industry moved first to self-checkout and then augmented this with a scan-as-you-shop approach. Many of those who had operated an over-the-counter service, such as fast-food restaurants, moved the point of sale to a customer interface rather than an employee interface. Since then, some retailers have begun trialling more advanced technologies with a buy-as-you-shop approach, where purchases are made as goods are placed into the basket.

Bot

Bot is the use of automated technologies to augment or replace existing capacity or capability. The concept of automation existed in Greek mythology with the idea of automatons, moving machines that replicated the actions of sentient beings. Such automatons had been created for King Alcinous, who gave refuge to Jason and the Argonauts: 'dogs of gold and silver... forged by the god of fire with all his cunning craft' (Homer, 1996). Indeed, the god of fire, Hephaestus, had automatons in his workshop when he built new armour for Achilles before he faced Hector at Troy (Homer, 1990). Automation took on an electronic form when Henry Ford established an automation department in the late 1940s (Rifkin, 1995). Since then, automation has progressed at an exponential rate, particularly since 2015, 'driven by the vast amounts of data now in enterprises, substantially more impressive computing power delivered by the cloud and a whole host of interesting breakthroughs' (McCargow, 2020). Despite this, those in the people profession increasingly find themselves on the back foot. Just as many initiatives within the balance lever tend to be local operational activities, so too are initiatives in automation. Where automation exists at all, HR functions are often reacting to this business decision. 'HR professionals need to broaden their talent management horizon to recognize that work is not just accomplished by full-time, part-time, or contracted people, but also through automation and technology' (Ulrich, 2019). In this section we will break down the constituent elements of automation before we cover implantation.

Industrial automation

Industrial automation is the automation of material handling processes within the primary and secondary sectors of the economy. Its roots lie in the early use of the assembly line to move items between workstations, rather than operate on a static basis. Thought to have originated within the meat-packing industry in Chicago in the 19th century, the practice came to prominence in the production of automobiles. When the Ford Motor Company deployed the assembly line to their factory in Dearborn, Michigan, the impact was staggering. Production time of the Model T Ford was slashed, and output rocketed. This unprecedented move saw cost savings passed on to customers, where prices dropped by 75 per cent, and employees rewarded with a doubling of pay (Rogan, 2018).

The next leap took place in the post-war years with the rise of robotics under George Devol and Joseph F Engelberger. Founders of the Unimation company, their first robot began operation in the General Motors production line in the early 1960s. The Unimate was a robotic arm that moved and welded die castings onto automobile chassis (Menzel and D'Aluisio, 2000). The 1980s witnessed the next shift in technology as computer power combined with greater production of robotics. With this change, many business owners were striving towards the nirvana of *lights-out manufacturing*, where production could exist without human intervention, a vision that was achieved 20 years later.

CASE STUDY
FANUC

Headquartered in the shadow of Mount Fuji, the Japanese robotics company began life with Fujitsu and the development of factory automatic numerical control (FANuC) in the 1970s. Founding CEO Seiuemon Inaba invited press to an event in 1981 where 100 workers, augmented by technology, were each able to produce the output of five workers. The coverage caught the attention of General Motors CEO Roger Smith and a joint venture between the two firms was launched a year later (Hunt, 2017).

Though the venture was beset by several challenges and was eventually dissolved, FANUC has grown in strength in subsequent years to become a common name in manufacturing. Having been one of the first to successfully implement *lights-out manufacturing*, they are now one of the largest in the world where 'robots produce other robots without the presence of humans' (Wheeler, 2015). Vice president Gary Zywiol said, 'Not only is it lights-out, we turn off the air conditioning and heat too' (Null and Caulfield, 2003). In 2001 the company opened an entirely automated kitchen to prepare and serve meals to its workforce (Null and Caulfield, 2003). By 2017, 80 per cent of the assembly work was automated, with vice president Kenji Yamaguchi adding, 'only the wiring is done by engineers' (Hunt, 2017).

Data centre automation

What industrial automation does for manufacturing, data centre automation does for data processes. Data centres grew from the large computer rooms of the mid-20th century into remote facilities, *clouds*, with the growth of the internet. Automation within the data centre not only enables the maintenance of the centre itself, but from a workforce planning perspective it enables the automation of workflows and processes. Achieved typically using scripting or an application programming interface (API), it automates data flows between different software and systems; in basic terms, it allows computers and applications to talk to each other. It is this approach that allows the information on a new starter to be manually entered into one system and then populate across other systems in the organization. The benefit of this has been that new systems and software can be added into the organization without the need to replace the entire data architecture of the enterprise.

Robotic process automation

Whilst data centre automation operates at the back end of the system, robotic process automation (RPA) shifts software robotics to the front of the system. Rob McCargow, PwC's director of artificial intelligence, elaborates:

> It is relatively inexpensive, fairly rapid to implement and sits on top of your existing architecture rather than replaces it. And because of the types of tasks that it can be applied to, the more repetitive, simple, straightforward tasks will be at high volume and the ability to measure and present the ROI is very compelling (McCargow, 2020).

There are effectively two types of RPA: assisted and unassisted. Assisted RPA improves the productivity of the workforce through partial automation of tasks and acts as a desktop assistant; unassisted RPA creates automation across an end-to-end process, though still requires manual control. The leaders in this technology are UIPath, Blue Prism and Automation Anywhere (Gartner, 2019), tools that operate at the level of the graphical user interface (GUI). These have allowed repetitive activity, particularly back-office processes, to be mapped and the activity transacted by bots. This has been especially valuable for knowledge workers, who had been spending part of their time in low-value work on a cyclical basis and allows their time to be released back to high-value activity.

Though RPA has grown in popularity, it is often executed without a preceding balance lever. Rob McCargow explains that RPA:

stitches together systems running in parallel, but beyond a certain point in time, it is simply offering a kind of sticking plaster solution. You wouldn't create a long-term IT strategy on RPA alone because it's joining together inefficiency in your existing stack rather than fundamentally future proofing it (McCargow, 2020).

Those organizations, therefore, that invest in balance initiatives will likely transition to more advanced levels of automation. That said, RPA remains an effective tool for creating efficiency at a local level. Rob McCargow adds:

I think you'll see [vendors] repositioning themselves and investing a lot of money into R&D to be seen as an AI player rather than purely as an RPA player. I think the [RPA] market probably hits a certain degree of maturity in the next couple of years and they need to go a step beyond that (McCargow, 2020).

Artificial intelligence (AI)

Artificial intelligence is 'an umbrella term and operates most effectively as the catch-all brand for a very diverse set of different tools, techniques and technologies that underpin it' (McCargow, 2020). It is an academic discipline that split out of cybernetics in the 1950s and has been characterized by waves of optimism and funding, followed by criticism and defunding, known as *AI winters* (Crevier, 1993). The discipline has boomed in the 20th century, largely on account of the two most dominant approaches: machine learning and deep learning.

The appeal of this has led to a clash of language that is viewed to take place between vendors and academic purists. There is an ever-expanding range of products that are marketed as artificial intelligence and, accordingly, achieve an allure in a sales pitch. This is often challenged by practitioners, so goes the popular saying: 'If it is machine learning, it was probably written in R or python; if it is AI, it was probably written in PowerPoint.' Analytics expert Professor Max Blumberg is clear: 'The term AI is currently used too loosely in people analytics. It should be reserved only for those technologies whose decisions are indistinguishable from the decisions that a real human being would have made. This is the basis of the Turing test for AI' (Blumberg, 2020). The importance of the Turing test (Turing, 1950), whether a computer could successfully imitate a human being, is a key principle in the philosophy of artificial intelligence. Such a machine would be true AI, or artificial general intelligence (AGI), which is arguably still decades away from achievement (Grace *et al*, 2018). As a workforce planning practitioner, it is important to understand the difference between those things and that whilst contemporary products have been developed from the discipline of artificial intelligence, they do not yet demonstrate true artificial intelligence.

Machine learning

Machine learning (ML) is a strand of the AI discipline that focuses on teaching robots how to learn using algorithms, sequences of instructions that show a computer how to perform something. Whilst algorithms in traditional computer programming might be used to solve a problem directly, the algorithms in ML enable the machine to learn and thereby solve the problem independently. For example, before a bank decides to distribute loans, it assesses the customers on their ability to pay loans. Banks use machine learning to understand the correlation between loan default and factors like income, savings and financial history to create classifications of risk. This allows a bank to predict the probability of loan default and make an appropriate decision on lending (McCargow, 2020).

Rob McCargow categorizes the main uses of ML as classifying, predicting and detecting. The previous example of grouping customer financial data into risk is just one case of classifying. The use of predicting is all around us: streaming sites that predict what films we might like given those we have watched, or the social media feeds that push content that is popular with those who have similar behaviours. Detecting is the identification of anomalies in data, from underlining spelling and grammatical errors to highlighting potential fraudulent transactions.

These categories combine to produce functionality such as natural language processing (NLP) and the more advanced natural language generation (NLG). NLP is the use of computer science to understand the human language. In the early days, NLP took a rules-based approach, such as the use of a decision tree; ML has allowed machines to use statistical inference from existing text and speech to build a more natural understanding of language. NLP is being increasingly combined with NLG to create computer-generated communication with humans. Chatbots have been a long-standing example of this, the earliest being ELIZA, a rules-based machine developed in the 1960s by MIT (Weizenbaum, 1976). Chatbots are now ubiquitous within industry and are continuing to replace the need for a human workforce within many services functions of organizations. Text-based chatbots are evolving to speech-based devices, popularized by devices such as Google's Alexa, Apple's Siri and Microsoft's Cortana. Such use-cases can be expected to continue and augment the text-based services within organizations.

CASE STUDY
Legal profession

If there is one thing the legal profession has in abundance, it is data; the profession is largely rules-based, typically defined by national and international law, judicial precedent and common-law conventions. Not only does such data define the law, the profession relies on evidence from each of the involved parties; evidence that, in a digital age, can prove insurmountable.

Machine learning is not only enabling billable work to be automated, it is also enabling firms to make almost intractable challenges into solvable problems. Using NLP, firms are able to conduct legal research into all the sources of the law and review evidence at pace. NLP allows firms to review contracts, highlighting risks with greater accuracy, and uses NLG to recommend more favourable clauses. Research in 2016 suggested that, at that time, the use of machine learning could reduce lawyers' billable hours by 13 per cent (Remus and Levy, 2016).

Cognitive automation

The next step in evolution is cognitive computing, where technologies learn, improve, reason and decide. Arguably the most famous cognitive computing platform is IBM's Watson. Named after IBM's founder, Thomas J Watson, it utilizes NLP, NLG, information retrieval and automated reasoning to answer questions. Whilst machine learning may be book-smart, cognitive computing is street-smart and able to weigh the surfeit of VUCA information signals to offer a practical solution. Implementation of cognitive computing at a process level achieves cognitive automation – embedded technologies capable of independent thought.

CASE STUDY
UPS

The *travelling salesman problem* remains a perennial challenge for organizations the world over. Originating in the early 19th century and coined as a phrase in the mid-20th century, it seeks to solve the issue of plotting the quickest route from an origin point to a number of different locations and back to the point of origin (Robinson, 1949). This is no different for the drivers of the United Parcel Service, recognizable the world over in their brown uniforms. Their clockwise routes were created by their first-line managers, former drivers themselves, who had learnt to avoid unnecessary left turns; in the United States, right turns are faster, whilst left turns are into oncoming traffic and slower.

In 2003, UPS began to take the step towards a more data-driven process with the development of ORION. Standing for On-Road Integrated Optimization and Navigation, it was tested and prototyped for over a decade. Whilst ORION is still not able to solve the travelling salesman problem, it provides workable routes to the driver and continues to learn and improve its suggestions. In 2016, when ORION was fully implemented, the impact on the organization was clear: annual reductions of over 100 million miles. Not only did this reduce workforce and fuel costs, it also added up to the avoidance of over 100,000 metric tonnes of greenhouse gas emissions (BSR, 2016)

Implementation and responsible automation

Decisions around implementation of the bot lever will depend heavily on three key factors: the industry in which we operate, our business model, and our operational maturity. Our industry will determine the extent to which technology can be utilized, be it industrial automation in manufacturing or software robotics for knowledge work. Our business model is the second factor in the decision; in what way does the organization create value for its customers and does an automation solution enhance that? There are plenty of instances, for example, where chatbots have been utilized simply as navigation tools to divert customers to different sites, guides and communication channels rather than directly resolving customer queries.

Operational maturity is the final and, arguably, most important factor in this decision. If we first operate a balance lever to enhance our operational maturity, then the possibilities for automation are at their broadest; without a balance lever, ambitions of automation are likely limited to RPA. This has been one of the more unfortunate consequences of the automation agenda. Businesses have an increasing desire to introduce automation to be seen as more technologically advanced, and to do so at the quickest possible speed, so are opting for low-hanging fruit. The automation of back-office functions and low-value activity are quick wins for CTOs and CIOs, who can demonstrate a successful use case and a saving to operational expenditure. With decisions such as these being taken without a workforce planning lens, they are missing the insight of workforce segmentation. The question to ask is, what work could I automate that would generate the greatest value to the organization?

Max Blumberg advocates strongly the approach of Prahalad and Hamel (1990) when considering automation, which is to focus on those areas of core competence for the organization. By prioritizing these areas for automation, rather than the non-core activities, organizations stand to achieve much greater return on investment (Blumberg, 2020). Indeed, as RPA locks in the existing process and may continue any existing inefficiency (McCargow, 2020), subsequent transformation may eradicate the benefit realization of the initial RPA. For example, if the cost versus benefit of RPA does not break even until three years into implementation, then transformation within this horizon is likely to be limited. Whilst this is somewhat of a sunk-cost fallacy (Tversky and Kahneman, 1986) as the benefits of subsequent transformation will likely offset the lost ROI from the RPA implementation, that initial expenditure remains an avoidable cost.

With technology now at a level where not only discrete tasks, but entire workflows, can be automated in an absence of worker interaction, it naturally raises concerns around ethical considerations for our people and customers and achieving the right risk within our organizations. The first consideration is what Rob McCargow calls use-case criticality: 'You probably don't care that much about how Netflix is recommending its next movie to you. Clearly, it's got to learn your viewing habits and compare it [to those with similar] viewing habits.' Where the technology has greater consequence through advertising and micro-targeting, then there is amplified risk and the potential for regulatory oversight (McCargow, 2020). In 2018, whistle-blowers revealed that Cambridge Analytica had harvested the personal data of Facebook users to inform political advertising in the 2016 US presidential campaigns of Donald Trump and Ted Cruz (Chan, 2019). The spectre of that data scandal still looms large for those engaging in advanced automation. A further consideration is model explainability, 'how do we understand how the decision has been made with tools and the data?' (McCargow, 2020). In 2014, Amazon created a machine-learning tool to parse candidate applications and select the most promising candidates. The problem was that the machine learnt based on 10 years of applicant data, which mostly came from men. As a result, the tool came to favour male candidates over females; 'they noticed that it was penalizing CVs that included the word *women's*, such as *women's chess club captain*' (Cook,

2018). Having lost confidence in its ability to eradicate the bias from the tool, the project was abandoned.

The remedy to this is responsible automation. People analytics leader David Green has been outspoken about ethics and is a strong advocate of using such approaches for good.

> I believe ethics is the most critical ingredient... Those working in the field simply cannot afford to get it wrong. The risk to employee trust and to the reputation of the burgeoning discipline... is too high (David Green, 2018).

Such determination led to the co-creation of the People Analytics Data Ethics Charter by members of Insight222's People Analytics Programme (Petersen, 2018). As responsible automation practices have evolved, they have all coalesced around four key areas. The first is that of strategic alignment and ensuring that automation is in line with the strategic framework and culture of the organization. Second, automation projects necessitate multidisciplinary teams who are diverse in their background, thoughts and approaches. Third, these projects need to be initiated and overseen by an ethics committee who have the necessary expertise and diversity to provide assurance to the activity. Finally, there must be transparency in explaining how fairness is achieved and suitable recourse if issues arise.

Summary

Demand optimization is often a challenging concept to land with stakeholders as business practice has, in many places, turned HR into a function that simply receives and processes orders for more workers. Pivoting to demand optimization challenges operational leaders to be introspective and look at their systems first. As we have seen, however, such approaches can achieve significant returns:

> The buzz about winning the war for talent implies that it is talent alone that enables organizations to win. But talent is only part of the story. The right talent needs to be in the right place at the right time, must fully understand the mission, and must be armed with the best tools – this is what helps market-oriented organizations succeed (Yeung and Ulrich, 2019).

When you practise workforce planning, ask yourself:

- Am I starting with demand optimization levers before considering talent management levers?
- Are all aspects of the organization strategically aligned?
- What quality choices can we take that will be advantageous in achieving our goals?
- In what way does the organization design need to be adjusted in order for us to be most effective?
- In what way does the organization create value for its customers and does the automation solution enhance that?
- What work could I automate that would generate the greatest value to the organization?

References

Adams, M (2013) YouTube censors 'Organic Spies' video exposing Whole Foods employees lying about GMOs, *The Natural News*, 3 October, www.naturalnews.com/037410_Organic_Spies_Whole_Foods_censored_video.html (archived at https://perma.cc/2D7G-GFUF)

Ambler, T and Barrow, S (1996) The employer brand, *Journal of Brand Management*, 4 (3), pp 185-206 doi:10.1057/bm.1996.42

Aristotle (1980) *The Nicomachean Ethics*, Oxford University Press, Oxford

Back, A (2019) How Kraft Heinz ate its seed corn, 11 March, *The Wall Street Journal*, www.wsj.com/articles/how-kraft-heinz-ate-its-seed-corn-11552303800 (archived at https://perma.cc/8G8N-2D2G)

BBC News (2015) Viewpoint: Should we all be looking for marginal gains? 15 September, https://www.bbc.com/news/magazine-34247629 (archived at https://perma.cc/XCZ6-AF58)

Blumberg, M (2020) Interview by video, 22 April

BrandZ (2020) Global top 100 most valuable brands, www.brandz.com/brands (archived at https://perma.cc/5ZQT-82VC)

Brown, W (1984) Gore's secret is lattice structure, *The Washington Post*, 30 April, www.washingtonpost.com/archive/business/1984/04/30/gores-secret-is-lattice-structure/930b340c-ab46-4a74-ab24-cf7bfcf452b1/ (archived at https://perma.cc/P8TD-QT2Z)

BSR (2016) Looking Under the Hood: ORION technology adoption at UPS, 30 March, www.bsr.org/en/our-insights/case-study-view/center-for-technology-and-sustainability-orion-technology-ups (archived at https://perma.cc/ZGQ9-VWDH)

Cameron, K S and Quinn, R E (2011) *Diagnosing and Changing Organizational Culture*, Jossey-Bass, Hoboken

Carse, J P (2013) *Finite and Infinite Games*, The Free Press, New York

Chan, R (2019) The Cambridge Analytica whistleblower explains how the firm used Facebook data to sway elections, Business Insider, 5 October, www.businessinsider.com/cambridge-analytica-whistleblower-christopher-wylie-facebook-data-2019-10 (archived at https://perma.cc/F4UA-YKCD)

Chapanis, A, Garner, W R and Morgan, C T (1949) *Applied Experimental Psychology: Human factors in engineering design*, Wiley, New York

Cheese, P (2020) Interview in person, 8 January

Cicero, M T (1928) *On The Republic* and *On The Laws*, Harvard University Press, Cambridge

Communications Act 2003, s265, https://www.legislation.gov.uk/ukpga/2003/21/section/265 (archived at https://perma.cc/A5DH-NU3H)

Cook, J (2018) Amazon scraps 'sexist AI' recruiting tool that showed bias against women, *The Telegraph*, 10 October, www.telegraph.co.uk/technology/2018/10/10/amazon-scraps-sexist-ai-recruiting-tool-showed-bias-against/ (archived at https://perma.cc/ZN8N-CM6X)

Costello, S (2020) Where is the iPhone made? *Lifewire*, 31 March, www.lifewire.com/where-is-the-iphone-made-1999503 (archived at https://perma.cc/J7SN-8TJ3)

Crevier, D (1993) *AI: The tumultuous search for artificial intelligence*, BasicBooks, New York

Deming, W E (1952) *Elementary Principles of the Statistical Control of Quality: a series of lectures*, Nippon Kagaku Gijutsu Remmei, Tokyo

Dodd, D and Favaro, K (2007) *The Three Tensions*, John Wiley & Sons, Chichester

Drucker, P F (1973) *Management: Tasks, responsibilities, practices*, Harper & Row, London

Drucker, P F (1985) *The Effective Executive*, HarperCollins, New York

Drucker, P F (2007) *The Essential Drucker*, Routledge, Abingdon

Drucker, P F (2011) *Managing for the Future*, Routledge, Abingdon

Elliot, G and Corey, D (2018) *Build It: The rebel playbook for world-class employee engagement*, Wiley, Chichester

Eng, M (2011) With no labeling, few realize they are eating genetically modified foods, *Chicago Tribune*, 24 May, https://www.chicagotribune.com/lifestyles/ct-xpm-2011-05-24-ct-met-gmo-food-labeling-20110524-story.html (archived at https://perma.cc/Q2K9-AFN7)

Fanshawe, S (2020) Interview by video, 3 June
Feeney, N (2015) Kraft and Heinz merge to become world's 5th largest food company, *Time*, 25 March, time.com/3757678/kraft-heinz-merger/ (archived at https://perma.cc/VV4J-XS96)
Feigenbaum, A V (1991) *Total Quality Control*, McGraw-Hill, New York
Forrester, J W (1961) *Industrial Dynamics*, Martino Fine Books, 2013 reprint, Eastford
Fortune (2020) 100 best companies to work for, fortune.com/best-companies/ (archived at https://perma.cc/TNM8-CM3K)
Friedman, M (1970) The social responsibility of business is to increase its profits, *The New York Times Magazine*, 13 September, http://www.umich.edu/~thecore/doc/Friedman.pdf (archived at https://perma.cc/78AT-U4XB)
Gartner (2019) Magic quadrant for robotic process automation software, 8 July, www.gartner.com/en/documents/3947184/magic-quadrant-for-robotic-process-automation-software (archived at https://perma.cc/MG4J-V4ZY)
Geller, J S (2011) Open letter to BlackBerry bosses: Senior RIM exec tells all as company crumbles around him, BGR, 30 June, bgr.com/2011/06/30/open-letter-to-blackberry-bosses-senior-rim-exec-tells-all-as-company-crumbles-around-him/ (archived at https://perma.cc/MHR4-V3SG)
Gladstones, W H, Regan, M A and Lee, R B (1989) Division of attention: The single-channel hypothesis revisited, *The Quarterly Journal of Experimental Psychology Section A*, **41** (1), pp 1–17, doi:10.1080/14640748908402350
Grace, K *et al* (2018) Viewpoint: When will AI exceed human performance? *Journal of Artificial Intelligence Research*, **62**, pp 729–54, doi.org/10.1613/jair.1.11222 (archived at https://perma.cc/F52R-NHV3)
Green, D (2018) Don't forget the 'H' in HR: Ethics and people analytics [Blog] *LinkedIn*, 19 March, www.linkedin.com/pulse/dont-forget-h-hr-ethics-people-analytics-david-green/ (archived at https://perma.cc/4PU7-VL5J)
Greiner, L E (1998) Evolution and revolution as organizations grow, *Harvard Business Review*, May–June, hbr.org/1998/05/evolution-and-revolution-as-organizations-grow (archived at https://perma.cc/D64Z-VTZ4)
Gulick, L H (1937) Notes on the theory of organization, in L H Gulick and L F Urwick (eds) *Papers on the Science of Administration*, Institute of Public Administration, New York
Hackman, J R and Oldham, G R (1976) Motivation through the design of work: Test of a theory, *Organizational Behavior and Human Performance*, **16** (2), pp 250–79, doi:10.1016/0030-5073(76)90016-7
Hallowell, E M (2006) *Crazy Busy*, Ballantine, London
Harrington, H J (1987) *Poor-Quality Cost*, Marcel Dekker, New York
Herzberg, F (1966) *Work and the Nature of Man*, Ty Crowell Co, New York
Hicks, J (2012) Research, no motion: How the BlackBerry CEOs lost an empire, *The Verge*, 21 February, www.theverge.com/2012/2/21/2789676/

rim-blackberry-mike-lazaridis-jim-balsillie-lost-empire (archived at https://perma.cc/TG3C-75BU)

Homer (1990) *The Illiad*, The Bath Press, Bath

Homer (1996) *The Odyssey*, The Bath Press, Bath

Hunt, J (2017) This company's robots are making everything – and reshaping the world, *Bloomberg Businessweek*, 18 October, www.bloomberg.com/news/features/2017-10-18/this-company-s-robots-are-making-everything-and-reshaping-the-world (archived at https://perma.cc/63EP-R2G8)

Huxley, A (2007) *Brave New World*, HarperCollins, New York

Imai, M (1988) *Kaizen: The key to Japan's competitive success*, McGraw-Hill, New York

Ishikawa, K (1986) *Guide to Quality Control*, Asian Productivity Organization, Tokyo

Jefferson, T *et al* (1776) United States Declaration of Independence, Second Continental Congress, Philadelphia

Katzenbach, J R, Steffen, I and Kronley, C (2012) Cultural change that sticks, *Harvard Business Review*, July–August, hbr.org/2012/07/cultural-change-that-sticks (archived at https://perma.cc/JD3T-CF3R)

McCargow, R (2020) Interview by telephone, 25 April

McGregor, D (1960) *The Human Side of Enterprise*, McGraw-Hill, 2005 reprint, New York

Mackenzie, K D (1978) *Organizational Structures*, Harlan Davidson, Wheeling

Menzel, P and D'Aluisio, F (2000) *Robo Sapiens: Evolution of a new species*, MIT Press, Cambridge

Meyer, P (2019) Apple Inc's organizational structure and its characteristics (an analysis), *Panmore*, 14 February, panmore.com/apple-inc-organizational-structure-features-pros-cons (archived at https://perma.cc/YBT9-XAVD)

Mountain, D and Kovac, M (2010) How to streamline spans and layers to avoid organisational bloat, *Bain & Company*, 30 July, www.bain.com/insights/how-to-streamline-spans-and-layers/ (archived at https://perma.cc/BD9T-J2G8)

Nadler, D A and Tushman, M L (1997) *Competing by Design: The power of organizational architecture*, Oxford University Press, Oxford

Non-GMO Project (2009) Whole Foods Market displays commitment to non-GMO project in Times Square and Las Vegas, 16 July, www.nongmoproject.org/blog/whole-foods-market-displays-commitment-to-non-gmo-project-in-times-square-las-vegas/ (archived at https://perma.cc/B9GA-RE4X)

Non-GMO Project (2020) Mission, www.nongmoproject.org/about/mission/ (archived at https://perma.cc/SU3B-WU3Q)

Null, C and Caulfield, B (2003) Fade to black, *Fortune*, 1 June, archive.fortune.com/magazines/business2/business2_archive/2003/06/01/343371/index.htm (archived at https://perma.cc/2GKK-P3AH)

ONS (Office for National Statistics) (2019) Shrinkflation: How many of our products are getting smaller? 21 January, www.ons.gov.uk/economy/inflation andpriceindices/articles/theimpactofshrinkflationoncpihuk/howmanyofour productsaregettingsmaller (archived at https://perma.cc/G3Q9-7HCF)

Page, R (2001) *Hope Is Not a Strategy: The 6 keys to winning the complex sale*, Nautilus Press, Oxford

Pareto, V (1906) *Manual of Political Economy*, 2014 reprint, Oxford University Press, Oxford

Patton, G S (2003) *War As I Knew It*, Presidio Press, Novato

Petersen, D (2018) 6 steps to ethically sound people analytics [Blog] *My HR Future*, 20 November, www.myhrfuture.com/blog/2018/11/19/six-steps-to-ethically-sound-people-analytics (archived at https://perma.cc/3SXC-RBUL)

Plato (1999) *Phaedo*, Oxford University Press, Oxford

Plato (2004) *Alcibiades I & 2*, 1st World Library Literary Society, Fairfield

Polis, C (2013) Whole Foods GMO labelling to be mandatory by 2018, *Huffington Post*, 3 March, www.huffingtonpost.com/2013/03/08/whole-foods-gmo-labeling-2018_n_2837754.html (archived at https://perma.cc/84ZK-2YP3)

Prahalad, C K and Hamel, G (1990) The core competence of the corporation, *Harvard Business Review*, May, hbr.org/1990/05/the-core-competence-of-the-corporation (archived at https://perma.cc/G33D-7A8C)

Remus, D and Levy, F S (2016) Can robots be lawyers? Computers, lawyers, and the practice of law, *SSRN*, 27 November, http://dx.doi.org/10.2139/ssrn.2701092 (archived at https://perma.cc/C2JZ-WHH4)

Richter, F (2017) The terminal decline of BlackBerry, *Statista*, 26 June, www.statista.com/chart/8180/blackberrys-smartphone-market-share/ (archived at https://perma.cc/6CDU-CYQW)

Rifkin, J (1995) *The End of Work: The decline of the global labor force and the dawn of the post-market era*, Putnam, New York

Roberts, D (2013) Carlos Brito: (Brew)master of the universe, *Fortune*, 15 August, fortune.com/2013/08/15/carlos-brito-brewmaster-of-the-universe/ (archived at https://perma.cc/5GL9-U5Y4)

Robertson, B (2007) Organization at the leading edge, *Integral Leadership Review*, 7 (3), integralleadershipreview.com/5328-feature-article-organization-at-the-leading-edge-introducing-holacracy-evolving-organization/ (archived at https://perma.cc/65V5-Q86G)

Robinson, J (1949) On The Hamiltonian Game: A travelling salesman problem, RM-303, *The Rand Corporation*, https://www.rand.org/pubs/research_memoranda/RM303.html (archived at https://perma.cc/L5YK-NAPV)

Rogan, F (2018) What can the assembly line teach us about innovation? *RTE*, 12 March, www.rte.ie/brainstorm/2018/0312/946759-what-can-the-assembly-line-teach-us-about-innovation/ (archived at https://perma.cc/2MAP-7JPF)

Roy, S (2011) Blackberry's falling marketshare explained in five charts [Blog] *Online Marketing Trends*, 24 September, www.onlinemarketing-trends.com/2011/09/blackberry-losing-marketshare-explained.html (archived at https://perma.cc/6ND5-YK2G)

Seddon, J (2003) *Freedom From Command & Control*, Vanguard Press, Buckingham

Shewhart, W A (1959) *Statistical Method from the Viewpoint of Quality Control*, 2003 reprint, Dover Publications, Mineola

Sigwatch (2019) 2019 NGO praise and criticism rankings, 16 January, www.sigwatch.com/news/2019s-most-praised-and-criticised-corporations/ (archived at https://perma.cc/ANG8-FFV8)

Silverstein, M J and Sayre, K (2009) The female economy, *Harvard Business Review*, September, hbr.org/2009/09/the-female-economy (archived at https://perma.cc/L2NJ-77GJ)

Sims, A (2015) Nestle responds to 'shrinking Quality Street tin sizes' after backlash from outraged customers, *The Independent*, 17 December, www.independent.co.uk/life-style/food-and-drink/news/nestle-responds-to-shrinking-quality-street-tin-sizes-after-backlash-from-outraged-customers-a6776536.html (archived at https://perma.cc/8HTY-DPHT)

Slater, M (2008) How GB cycling went from tragic to magic, *BBC*, 14 August, news.bbc.co.uk/sport1/hi/olympics/cycling/7534073.stm (archived at https://perma.cc/2AY6-WF8H)

Taylor, F W (1911) *The Principles of Scientific Management*, 1997 reprint, Dover Publications, Mineola

Tenet (2019) *2019 Top 100 Most Powerful Brands*, www.rankingthebrands.com/PDF/Top%20100%20Most%20Powerful%20Brands%202019,%20Tenet,%20CoreBrands.pdf (archived at https://perma.cc/ERX5-D3RZ)

Tennant, G (2001) *Six Sigma: SPC and TQM in manufacturing and services*, Gower Publishing, Aldershot

Turing, A M (1050) Computing machinery and intelligence, *Mind*, 59 (236), pp 433–60 doi.org/10.1093/mind/LIX.236.433 (archived at https://perma.cc/C4V8-CR46)

Tversky, A and Kahneman, D (1986) Rational choice and the framing of decisions, *The Journal of Business*, 59 (4), pp S251–S278, doi:10.1086/296365

Ulrich, D (2019) From workforce to worktask planning [Blog] LinkedIn, 12 March, www.linkedin.com/pulse/from-workforce-worktask-planning-dave-ulrich/ (archived at https://perma.cc/E8TJ-FSLF)

Urwick, L F (1957) The span of control, *Scottish Journal of Political Economy*, 4 (2), pp 101–13, doi.org/10.1111/j.1467-9485.1957.tb00223.x (archived at https://perma.cc/ZQ4A-3GKE)

Voltaire, ed (1772) *La Bégueule*, 2014 reprint, Arvensa Editions, Paris

Weinberg, G M (2011) *Quality Software Management*, Dorset House Publishing, New York

Weizenbaum, J (1976) *Computer Power and Human Reason: From judgement to calculation*, W H Freeman, San Francisco

Wheeler, A (2015) Lights-out manufacturing: Future fantasy or good business? [Blog] *Redshift*, 3 December, www.autodesk.com/redshift/lights-out-manufacturing/ (archived at https://perma.cc/L6UN-3V84)

Womack, J P, Jones, D T and Roos, D (1991) *The Machine That Changed theWorld*, Simon & Schuster, New York

World Economic Forum (WEF) (2019) *Fourth Industrial Revolution: Beacons of technology and innovation in manufacturing*, January, www3.weforum.org/docs/WEF_4IR_Beacons_of_Technology_and_Innovation_in_Manufacturing_report_2019.pdf (archived at https://perma.cc/KB9Z-WQFS)

Yeung, A and Ulrich, D (2019) *Reinventing the Organization*, Harvard Business School Publishing, Boston

14

Talent management

Introduction

Once the optimization of demand is complete, we can be assured that any change we make to our workforce is able to deliver the most effective outcome. Talent management is the approach to make changes to our workforce, which Dr John Boudreau frames as understanding the responses we need from the workforce and the 'employment elements [that] induce those responses at the optimum cost' (Boudreau, 2010). Professor Peter Cappelli notes that talent management approaches have tended to fall into 'two equally dysfunctional camps'. The first, and most common camp consists of those that are entirely reactive to the workforce needs of the organization and rely almost entirely on outside hiring. The second camp are those with complex and bureaucratic models of succession planning that have existed since the 1950s (Cappelli, 2008).

The approaches we will cover in this chapter – buy, build, borrow, bind and bounce – are proactive and holistic, utilizing, and aiming to advance, the original ideas of Professors Dave Ulrich and Wayne Brockbank (2005). This will enable us to implement the most effective initiatives and to extract greater value from any existing approaches we have in current operation.

Buy

Buy is the approach of purchasing and acquiring a permanent capability. Alongside borrow, buy is one of only two additive talent management levers available: they are the only means to bring into the organization a capability that we do not have. The greater permanence and security for the worker in 'buy' rather than 'borrow' approaches is typically leveraged against a lower level of total reward. They are also easier to *bind*, but with that security comes limitations; those that are easier to bind become harder to *bounce*. By its very nature, the processes of the buy lever usually take longer and it is rare to buy without also having to *build*. Not only is buy the most common workforce lever, but recruitment is also the most common approach. That said, when we consider the *capability segmentation framework*, it is only criticals that tend to be a necessity to buy.

Recruitment

The action of hiring new people from outside is firmly within the DNA of most organizations and their recruitment approach is inextricably linked to their build lever, which we will cover in the next section. The approach is demarcated by experience hiring and progressive hiring initiatives.

EXPERIENCE HIRING

Experience hiring is the recruitment of those who have both the skills and knowledge to be able to perform in the role immediately, albeit with a modicum of onboarding. Such recruitment is undertaken because we want to recruit people who already know how to do the job, rather than train people and build that capability ourselves. Assessment and selection in experience hiring tends to be based primarily around the ability to demonstrate the required levels of skill and knowledge, either through previous employment in a similar role or from undertaking training and education. The potential of an individual may be considered, both longer term for a career and in the short term if the role is a step up; this does not override the necessity that the new hire must be able to perform the new role. As a result, experienced hiring is typically limited to the professional and the critical roles within the capability segmentation framework, introduced in Chapter 6 (Lepak and Snell, 1999).

PROGRESSIVE HIRING

Progressive hiring is the recruitment of those who do not have the skills and knowledge to be able to perform in the role immediately; they are therefore hired on their potential. This hiring is split into three types: basic, career and fast-track. Basic recruitment typically relates to the operator roles within the capability segmentation framework (Lepak and Snell, 1999), hence the phrase entry-level positions. Such roles require more than simple onboarding, including being trained to perform the role; selection decisions tend to be based on an assessment of the individual being able to be trained.

Career recruitment is primarily for specialist roles within the capability segmentation framework, where a high level of initial training is required. Due to the high level of investment required at the start of a career, greater importance is placed on longer-term potential and the temperamental suitability for the work.

Fast-track recruitment is an extension of career recruitment, identifying those who are suitable for a career in the organization, but also the potential to reach a more senior level quickly. Fast-tracking can be achieved to different levels of the organization, such as junior, middle or senior management and can span across specialist, professional and critical roles.

ATTRACTION

Many operational leaders have believed that if they build an organization, and advertise vacancies, then suitable new hires will follow at the point of need. Few organizations are so fortunate to even achieve this with most of their vacancies, and that fortune results from the painstaking effort to build an attractive brand, as we covered in the previous chapter. In reality, we all need to attract to our organizations the right capability that we need.

The success of the recruitment sector rests on the leverage of a key strategic position: cost. Quite simply, recruitment businesses make their money from their ability to provide the right size and right capability of recruitment professionals who can deliver candidates in the fastest possible time at a lower price point than an organization could do itself. The recruitment process outsourcing (RPO) industry exists for those organizations that have recognized this up front and have chosen to outsource their entire operation, which we will discuss later with the *borrow* lever. Where an RPO is not utilized, and instead recruitment agencies are solicited, the cost position has its roots in three factors: capacity, capability and speed:

- Agencies provide additional capacity, which is especially useful for managing seasonal spikes in recruitment activity. If the recruitment function is not the right size, however, that capacity is used on a routine basis.
- Recruitment capability is useful for an area we do not typically hire in, such as executive search and other one-off and unique hires.

- Speed is perhaps the main reason that agencies are hired. The time between a recruitment need being identified, and when a new hire is required to start, is too short for an organization to deliver themselves.

Having followed the agile workforce planning approach this far, we will have learnt that it is possible to accurately forecast demand for workers, and therefore we are enabled to do something that recruitment agencies do exceptionally well: curate talent.

Those whom we may want to hire into our organizations exist in three places. Talent lakes are the broad areas where we can find potential candidates, such as educational institutions, colleges and universities, and competitors or geographic hubs of capability, such as the technology hub of Silicon Valley. With no direct relationship to these candidates, hiring directly from talent lakes can take a lot of time. Talent pools are smaller collections of potential hires where, as a minimum, competency and contact details for individuals are available. The edge that the best agency recruiters have is their curation of increasingly smaller talent pools, with candidates they will have spoken to on a regular basis, knowing what they want from a job and what they have to offer; it is highly likely these people are also ready for a new role immediately.

Talent streams make the process of talent pooling much easier and typically return the edge from agencies and back to organizations. All organizations have access to two key talent streams: alumni and applicants. Alumni have previously worked in an organization; providing they were not dismissed, they had both the right capability and an affinity with the strategic framework. Applicants have applied for other roles in the organization, providing details on their suitability, and have been assessed on this basis. This

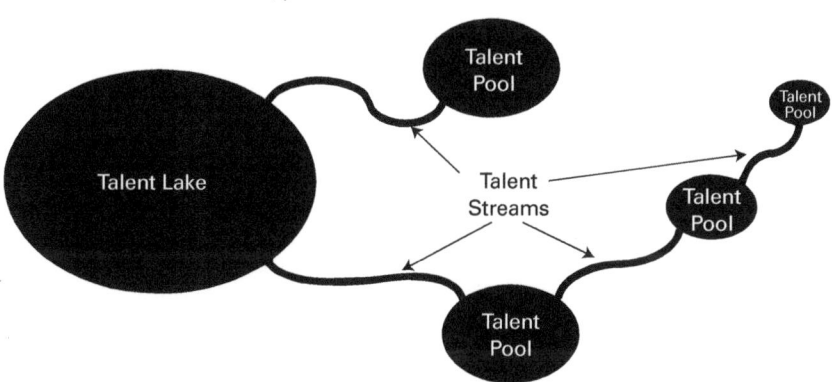

FIGURE 14.1 Talent lakes, pools and streams

stream can flow into the creation of two valuable talent pools: silver medallists who narrowly missed out on being appointed into a role, and runners who may not have been contenders for the role for which they originally applied but have competencies that may be suitable for a different role.

The sponsorship of external training and education can be a highly effective talent stream and is vital for organizations who want to recruit specialists through this method. The nature of a specialist role is that they have limited value outside of a specific industry or organization, so there is little incentive for an individual to pay for this training themselves. At one end of the spectrum, an organization can fund training and living expenses; at the other, they can guarantee a job.

Whilst the main use of talent pooling is to curate the right capability, it also provides a key advantage when we are trying to achieve the right shape of workforce. Where an organization aims to recruit greater numbers of those that may be underrepresented in the workplace, talent pooling is a vital activity. Looking in the same places for talent will not allow us to achieve the diversity that organizations need to be effective. When agile workforce planning with an effective use of talent pools, a successful organization could avoid ever needing to advertise a vacancy.

Employee value proposition

In the previous chapter we discussed the concept of the organizational brand being composed of two elements: the market brand and the employer brand. The employer brand not only attracts permanent workers (buy), it attracts temporary workers (borrow) and retains both (bind). As such, though the employer brand is shaped by the organization, it is defined by the marketplace of workers. Platforms like Glassdoor act as windows into an organization, rating it and the CEO out of five stars. The employee value proposition, or EVP, is a vital tool to help shape that employer brand. EVP can be segmented into the following aspects: reward and recognition, culture and climate, work, opportunity, and personal brand.

REWARD AND RECOGNITION

When most of us think about reward, and indeed the value of employment, it is common to think only about the salary. However, base pay is the foundation of reward and is the non-variable income we receive for trading our time. Overtime and performance-related pay are the next levels from this. The other side to the reward coin is the benefit structure, be it monetary benefits (equity, provision of payment for life events, such as sickness or becoming a parent, and retirement) or non-monetary benefits (provision of health insurance, free parking at the work place, an onsite gymnasium).

In one survey, the failure to recognize employee achievements was ranked as the top complaint from workers about their leaders (Solomon, 2015). Recognition is often conflated with the idea of reward, particularly when it comes to performance-related pay that recognizes good work. However, reward follows a structure and is established in advance, while recognition tends to be much more ad hoc. Praise of staff for great work, saying 'well done' or 'thank you' is the most inexpensive form of recognition, but it may go beyond this in the form of spot awards for individuals or teams, or even business- and industry-level annual awards.

CULTURE AND CLIMATE

In the previous chapter we discussed in detail the concept of culture, comprising three key components: purpose, values and brand. The climate, which we will discuss in greater detail within the next section on *build*, is how culture manifests in behaviours. Most obviously, the culture and climate create a sense of belonging between workers. Less obvious is the criticality of culture and climate in achieving the safety and esteem needs of the individual. The culture and climate are key in not only ensuring the physical safety of workers against accidents in the workplace, but also in the emotional and psychological safety that underpins the health and well-being of the workforce. In a post-Friedman world, the ability to articulate the culture and positive climate of our organization to potential employees is vital.

WORK

Culture captures part of *why* we work; this section will cover the *what, when, where* and *how* of work.

What: the specific tasks involved in a role and how it connects into the wider organization.

When: relates to the speed and innovation of the work. Different companies may attempt similar work, but one might achieve rapid success whilst the other moves at an almost glacial pace.

Where: this cuts across a few different areas ranging from the office location and its impact on commuting, to the environment both inside and outside. A modern working environment or premises in need of renovation?

A thriving urban centre or an isolated industrial estate? *Where* also speaks to the flexibility of working practices which is of increasing importance in a time with both the technology and business practices to support remote working.

How: this concerns role and work design, articulated in terms of people, process and technology. People considers the team at micro level. Is the role part of a broad team that allows staff to specialize, part of a small team where the expectation is to be more of a generalist? At a management level, this will indicate the ability to delegate work or prioritize the highest value activity. For an executive, this might indicate whether an assistant can provide administrative support and diary management. Process examines the way that work is done, whether it is a repetitive process or knowledge work. Are processes effective enough that a worker can be proactive or is the reality one of reactive firefighting? Technology enables those processes and is increasingly important to workers. In one survey of UK employees, more than half (51 per cent) reported that they will choose to leave their organization if they do not effectively transition to a digitally enabled way of working (Capita, 2019). Does the technology exist to do work in the most effective way, or is it much more basic and necessitates low-value activity?

Great work leads to a feeling of accomplishment and leads into achieving one's full potential; poor work, on the other hand, can leave us frustrated and limit our motivation.

OPPORTUNITY

Opportunity is how we evolve in employment and is therefore hinged upon the stability of the organization. Once the financial security of the worker is established, opportunity branches into two areas: development and progression. Development is how each of us improves in our abilities, whereas progression is how we move around the organization in increasingly progressive steps. Both development and progression are inextricably linked to our *build* approach, which we will cover in the next section.

ENHANCEMENT

Whilst opportunity is what happens within the organization, enhancement is what happens outside the organization. The foundation of enhancement is the brand of the organization and its impacts during employment (pride in working there) and post-employment (how working there may improve our prospects).

BALANCING AND DIFFERENTIATING

Establishing an EVP is critical as many organizations do not think beyond the salary of the worker. By articulating the value of employment, the EVP serves as a 'psychological contract' between the worker and the organization (Rousseau, 1995), a mutual and unwritten agreement, which is often more important than the written contract (Ulrich and Brockbank, 2005). If aspects of the EVP are lacking in comparison to competitors, organizations are likely to focus on higher pay. One example is budget supermarket Aldi, which consistently pays higher graduate salaries than their competitors. In 2018, entry-level positions for graduates joining Aldi in Australia were offered at $87,000, much higher than the average graduate starting salary of $54,000 (Polychronis, 2018). The opposite is also true. The voluntary sector has consistently demonstrated the ability to generate a workforce without recourse to pay; they do so because they provide and articulate far greater benefit to the individual than the cash nexus. This is the same reason that, particularly in the uniformed organizations, service personnel sacrifice their basic needs in favour of the greater good. In response to the COVID-19 pandemic, more than 750,000 people signed up to join the 'volunteer army' to support the health service in England, over three times the original target (BBC, 2020).

It is equally critical to differentiate the EVP as it is to balance it. Many aspects of an EVP will be consistent across an organization, but many HR departments make the mistake of failing to create differentiation. For example, the EVP that attracts someone to volunteer for a charitable organization is not the same EVP that attracts their paid staff. This has its roots in the *capability segmentation framework* that was introduced in Chapter 6. At a basic level, operators, professionals, specialists and criticals all seek a different psychological contract from the organization (Lepak and Snell, 1999 and 2002; Kang *et al*, 2003). A specialist, for example, is much more unique to the organization that a professional. Therefore, a specialist will tend to foster a greater degree of loyalty than the professional, who is able to develop their career across different employers. Equally, for most organizations the relationship with an operator is much more transactional than it is with a critical who will tend to have a much tighter psychological bond with their employer.

CASE STUDY
123 Inc

As a result of growing consumer demand, a popular global logistics and e-commerce retailer had challenges with its ever-increasing labour pool requirements across the UK. Its supply chain operations were renowned for target and productivity-driven standards in order to meet consumer expectations, and adverse publicity had tarnished their employer brand.

Partnering with multi-sector specialists PMP Recruitment, part of Cordant, a collaborative focus was put on improving their employment market position and ability to attract candidates. Candour around culture and working practices enabled them to not only challenge some myths, but also ensure they were attracting a workforce that could meet those high-performance expectations.

They were clear that productivity targets were objective, based on previous achievement, and tied these clearly to employee reward and benefits. By telling a story of a holistic working environment, a culture of teamwork and open conversation where hard work was rewarded fairly and downtime was subsidized, the company was able to meet its recruitment targets. Indeed, during the COVID-19 pandemic, its ability to articulate the prioritization of worker safety and social distancing meant that it was able to respond to a growth in recruitment needs brought on by the lockdown (Porter, 2020).

SELECTION

The aim of selection processes is to choose the workers that best achieve the seven rights, doing so in line with the organizational values and in the most cost-effective way. For many organizations, the process involves various stages, so is usually recognized by the corollary of deselection, using different grades of filter to sift out those who are unsuitable. This will typically align to the following: screen, list, choose, check and confirm.

Screening aims to deselect those who are fundamentally unsuitable for the role often based on essential criteria, though I would advise caution over making this too stringent. One impact of the skills gap in the UK is that nearly one third (31 per cent) of employers hired new workers at a lower level of competency than they had intended (Open University, 2019). Be conscious of how the role benchmarks against the wider labour market and adjust your screening criteria accordingly.

Listing is the ordering of applicants based on desirable and capability factors of knowledge, skills, accreditation and mindset and is often an adjunct to the screening process. Increasingly, technology is used; at a basic level, most applicant tracking systems (ATS) will parse applications for key words or include so called *knockout* or *killer* questions to rule out candidates. At a more advanced level, supplementary assessment tools are used, from psychometric testing to artificial intelligence video interview (AIVI), which analyses speech and facial expressions. Increasingly, and where legislation permits, diversity factors could be included at this point to ensure sufficient representation on long and shortlists that will contribute towards achieving the right shape of our organization. The result of listing is the shortlist of those to go forward for choosing. If the screen and list stages are effective, and combined with a successful attraction approach, then the choose stage should make the most efficient use of hiring manager or assessor time by examining the extent of knowledge, skills and mindset in detail. Claude Silver, the Chief Heart Officer at VaynerMedia, says 'we hire for skillset fit and culture addition, because that leads to greater diversity and helps grow the culture' (Silver, 2019). This is a valuable approach as the reverse, focusing on achieving a fit with a current culture, often carries bias that continues to disenfranchise those groups who are underrepresented in the workplace.

Once a hiring manager or assessor selects their chosen candidate, compliance checks are conducted on a candidate's background and references. There may also be a requirement for medical checks or some form of official vetting to be completed. The depth of these checks, and the organization's appetite for risk, will determine when final confirmation takes place. From a workforce planning perspective, the lead time for this process can catch many by surprise when seeking to fill a vacancy. It reinforces the importance of planning recruitment in advance based on forecast changes in supply and demand, ensuring the right attraction strategies are in place and streamlining recruitment activity to deliver the right outcome.

CASE STUDY
Rentokil Initial

When Alan Brown took over as CEO of international business services company, Rentokil Initial, in 2008, he began to examine the operational performance of the organization and its 30,000 employees. He focused on the 700-strong sales function where performance in targets and revenue was highly variable; there was a gap between what the business needed and the workforce it had. He brought in people analytics expert Max Blumberg, who conducted detailed analysis of the workforce and the processes. Whilst some sales leaders hypothesized that the issue could be resolved by changing the reward and recognition to incentivize stronger performance, others suggested it necessitated more effective sales training (both build levers, which we will cover in the next section).

Blumberg and his team studied 270 sales staff; their multinomial logistic regression identified that mindset was the most significant factor in performance. Using a personality assessment, they could identify those who would be the most effective salespeople. They implemented the assessment as part of recruitment processes that, based on machine learning, separated candidates into three pools: those most likely to be successful, those least likely to be successful, and those who fell statistically between the two. With the addition of new interview techniques to align all hiring managers with the new approach, roll-out was achieved within a year. The project was a clear success with sales improving by over 40 per cent, generating additional revenues of over $70 million (Blumberg, 2020).

SHORES

Shoring is a broad strategy on the right location of a workforce that defines three types of shore: onshore, nearshore and offshore. Onshore is where the workforce is based in the same country, for example a workforce all located in Britain. Nearshore is when part of the workforce is based in a nearby country, for example most of the workforce in Britain and a team in the Republic of Ireland. Offshore is when part of the workforce is located in a more distant country, for example most of the workforce in Britain and a team in India.

Decisions around shores rest heavily upon cost, specifically the cost of living in certain locations (known as purchasing power parity) and supply versus demand, the postulation that the cost of labour will be lower where the supply is greater than the demand (Marshall, 1997). This has led many organizations to take the decision to offshore their workforce, often as part of an outsourced arrangement, which we will cover in greater detail in a later section on the borrow lever. Whilst this decision might achieve many of the seven rights there are many aspects to be considered. Areas of the world with some of the greatest opportunities for wage arbitrage are also those with some of the greatest levels of instability. Working across different time zones can allow work to take place whilst most of the workforce is asleep but decisions may have to wait because the workforce is not available at the right time. Language and cultural differences may exist that hamper efficiency, leading to the cost benefits of the offshore being eroded.

As offshoring has often taken place through outsourcing, onshoring decisions are typically accompanied by insourcing. As we will discuss with the borrow lever, critical roles are better placed within the buy and build levers of the organization. Where workforce segmentation identifies critical roles in an outsourced arrangement, then insourcing is a highly effective activity. This has happened a great deal with technology; IT functions had been viewed as back-office functions and both outsourced and offshored. As organizations have woken up to the fact that technology is a key source of competitive advantage, such arrangements are being ended and the work is being insourced.

MERGERS AND ACQUISITIONS

Mergers and acquisitions (M&A) are changes in ownership; either two organizations, often similar in size or value, become one new organization (oil and gas giants Exxon and Mobil in 1999) or one organization becomes part of another, such as the acquisition of the messaging service WhatsApp by Facebook in 2014 for just under US$22 billion (Deutsch, 2020). In both instances a new workforce is bought as well as the market demand. As a result, M&A necessitates a supplementary *balance* lever as the two organizations will have differing strategic frameworks and organizational designs which can be a key source of friction when implementing this lever (Serapio and Cascio, 1996). Whilst M&A is a buy lever, it is usual for the initiative to result in over-buying due to a duplication of demand and supply. Once the balance lever has identified duplications and allowed the organization to benefit from new economies of scale, it is usual that the M&A initiative necessitates a subsequent bounce lever, which we will cover later in this chapter.

Though the majority of M&A decisions result from strategic decisions to enable entry into a new market or to improve financial leverage, as workforce planning practitioners we must be cognisant of this as an option to create the right capability at pace and scale.

Build

This is the process of building a capability out of the existing workforce. Training requirements may be driven by business signals related to deficiencies in either process execution or business outcomes, or change related to new products, processes, opportunities or regulatory requirements (Stone, 2008). In our own experiences, this is often how we will have seen this work; either there is a clear, new and identifiable requirement or there is a failure. As we have covered throughout this book, workforce planning allows us to think much more holistically about the most appropriate lever to pull that creates the right workforce for the organization. The build lever can be utilized across all workforce segments but is particularly important for the creation of criticals and vital in the case of specialists.

In this section we will cover the primary build interventions of learning, development and progression. We will then move into the more complex, but increasingly prioritized areas of building culture, climate. No discussion on build is complete, however, without considering talent and potential.

Talent and potential

Though used often within the HR profession, talent is challenging to define. In her bestselling book, *Grit* (2016), Professor Angela Duckworth defines talent as the rate at which, through the application of effort, an individual is able to develop a new skill:

$$Talent \times Effort = Skill$$

If we maintain consistency with our earlier terminology, then we might substitute the word 'skill' for 'competency'; that being the combination of skills and knowledge that are not yet a capability. Similarly, the word 'effort' can be replaced with 'mindset' as this is a key factor in determining effort. However, we also know that the environment has a multiplier effect on our mindset; a great environment can improve it and a negative environment can degrade it. That allows us to evolve the equation as follows:

$$(Mindset \times Environment) \times Talent = Competency$$

Where there are deficiencies on one of these factors, the others must increase to compensate. Therefore, where learning and development interventions are being created, consideration must be given to all three of these elements.

Throughout this book, I have also used the term talent in the broader context as a synonym for the workforce. The term becomes more challenging where talent is used as a noun to describe a specific segment of the workforce, which may imply judgements that rarely account for the impact of mindset and environment.

Potential is challenging to define; Aristotle viewed potentiality as the opposite of actuality (Aristotle, 1980). Whilst actuality is the current state, potentiality relates to a possible future state. For example, the actual state of water means it has the potential to be steam or ice. Therefore, potential is more than a possible future; it requires something innate. This connects to talent; those with the potential to achieve something will likely have the talent to achieve it at a faster rate than others. Equally, the mindset and environment remain a key component; without a change in the environment, water will remain liquid. Therein lies the problem for many HR practitioners; potential tends to be viewed either as a nebulous future state, or otherwise as a narrow road to the CEO's job.

As potential can refer to anything, it makes sense for us to align it to the separate strands of build. In that way, we can assess people on their potential for learning and development, both from an onboarding and an upskilling perspective. In addition, we also assess people on their potential for progression, either via promotion or in-role. In that way we can create workforce plans based on the way the workforce learns, develops and progresses through the organization.

Learning and development

Think back to some of the components of capability we discussed in the first chapter: knowledge, skills, mindset and physiology (Matthews, 2014). In simple terms, learning is the acquisition of knowledge and development is the acquisition of skills. The contemporary wisdom is that learning and development follow a 70:20:10 model (Lombardo and Eichinger, 1996). This suggests that 70 per cent of learning and development will come from trying new things and undertaking challenging assignments, 20 per cent will come from coaching and feedback, and 10 per cent will come from teaching and training. There are certainly contrary opinions to this popular model; one survey of over 13,000 business leaders suggested 55:25:20 was a more accurate reflection of reality (DDI, 2015) and others are clear that there is no evidence the approach is optimal (Jefferson and Pollock, 2014). I lean more towards the ratios espoused by Dave Ulrich of 50:20:30 (Ulrich, 2020), which takes a sizeable percentage of the on-the-job learning and repositions it in formal education. Despite the differences between these models, they remain helpful guide rails that will be qualified throughout this section as we move into the specifics.

Onboarding

Onboarding is the suite of interventions we make when bringing a new worker into the organization, which create the right capability. The chapter 'No more non-boarding' in Katrina Collier's ground-breaking book *The Robot-Proof Recruiter* details the exquisite pain felt by new starters where such interventions are missing. 'You take a deep breath, pull your shoulders downs and back. Head held high, you grab your phone, your keys, your bag and you head out the door into the unknown. You hope they are as ready for you as you are for this new chapter in your life. But no…' (Collier, 2019). The importance of onboarding cannot be understated; studies have shown that the onboarding experience has a significant impact on employee retention (Filipkowski *et al*, 2018). Fundamentally, however, onboarding needs to create capability out of the worker competencies they buy and borrow. A poor onboarding experience can seriously damage the speed to competence of the worker, the time it takes for a new starter to become fully productive because of their onboarding (see Chapter 9).

Line *b* of Figure 14.2 shows what would be expected from a credible onboarding package to create the required level of competence in workers. Line *c*, however, is the impact of poor onboarding; it takes longer for new starters to become productive. The opportunity is line *a*, to improve the onboarding experience and achieve a productive workforce in a faster time.

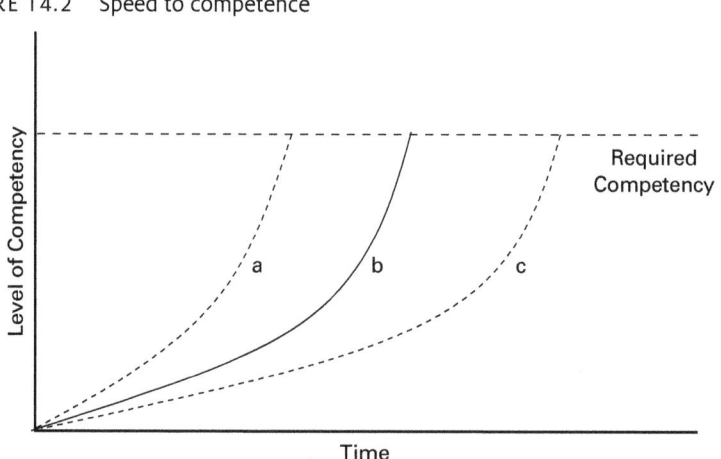

FIGURE 14.2   Speed to competence

CASE STUDY
The Co-op

Co-op Food is the sixth-largest food retailer in the UK and the most significant business within the Co-operative Group. In the early stages of the COVID-19 pandemic, food retailers were faced with the convergence of three distinct challenges. There was complexity in relation to the virus and uncertainty around how COVID-19 would spread; this necessitated rapid changes to business operations to ensure the safety of the staff. The second challenge was that the available workforce shrank. Ambiguity around who was infectious meant a government requirement to self-isolate if family members showed symptoms of the virus. This precluded many workers from coming to the workplace, alongside a rise in sickness levels as the pandemic spread. The final challenge was that the wider uncertainty around the impact of the virus resulted in a sharp rise in demand as early hoarding by customers sparked panic buying.

The Co-op realized their existing approach to buying and borrowing labour would be unable to achieve the necessary speed to competence to bridge the substantial and volatile gap between supply and demand. Recognizing the need for rapid support to over 150 stores in the London area, Keith Halliwell, Co-op's operational lead, sought help from Blue Arrow, one of its strategic national labour partners. Rather than take a broad approach to filling vacancies, Blue Arrow targeted specifically those with the right experience and behaviours that would align to great customer service. Having used skill matching to bridge part of the capability gap, they created a 'rapid induction' to create a great onboarding experience. The new starters blended seamlessly with the existing staff and the enhanced speed to competence ensured the Co-op was able to keep its local customer communities safe and well-served through the crisis (Halliwell, 2020).

At the most basic level, those joining the organization will require orientation and familiarization with their working environment; beyond that will be determined by the recruitment initiative (experience hiring or progressive hiring) and their workforce segment (see Chapter 6). Operators tend to be the lowest cost to onboard as these roles tend to require a more basic level of competency and are common amongst many sectors. For professionals who join through an experienced hire route, like operators, they too require lower levels of onboarding than other roles as their capabilities cut across industry.

As the uniqueness of the role increases, so too does the cost to onboard. As a result, criticals who come through an experienced hire route will require much more comprehensive onboarding than operators and professionals to be successful. It is more likely that, in order to build specialists, a progressive hiring approach is taken. Combining the buy and build levers in this way is the most sustainable way to create specialist capability.

There is always a risk that a critical or professional worker, brought in as a progressive hire, may leave for a competitor following completion of training and as a result, it is wise to consider a bind lever, which we will cover later in this chapter.

Upskilling

Upskilling is any learning and development initiative that proceeds the onboarding process. There are three types of upskilling: adjacent, complimentary and distant. Adjacent upskilling is the increasing of skills and knowledge in fields that have shared or similar characteristics and tends to be done on a self-directed basis in order to enhance the employability of a worker. An obvious example is you, reading this book, developing your knowledge of workforce planning. Even more important, leverage of skills adjacency can prompt a build lever when a more expensive lever is the most attractive to a stakeholder, such as if a capability gap arises. For example, if an organization had a new need for Linux network engineers, it may appear to be such a big capability gap that it would warrant the buying or borrowing of such a capability. If, however, the organization had Windows network engineers, then upskilling them in Linux may well be a more cost-effective and sustainable solution than bringing in the capability from outside.

Complementary upskilling is where we increase our skills and knowledge in areas that can be beneficial to our current roles, but our experience confers little advantage to the process of learning. Routine examples are where the workforce needs to understand new legislative or regulatory changes, for example, changes in data privacy laws. Though these may take longer to acquire than an adjacent skill, the right complementary skill or knowledge can be a capability multiplier for an organization. When looking at complementary upskilling, it is important to approach this on the basis of strength rather than weakness. Though a complementary skill may be beneficial on paper, if it is at odds with the mindset and talent of an individual, then compelling such learning may prove damaging. This might explain the reluctance found within some of the HR community to upskill in data literacy.

Distant upskilling is the acquisition of skills and knowledge that have little relation to those already possessed by a worker. This is actually relatively common; those of us that have a regular sport, hobby or pastime are all conducting distant upskilling. This presents an interesting challenge of hidden capability: without a detailed understanding of the capabilities of our workforce, we are likely to miss the true understanding of skills adjacency. The office junior, who codes in their spare time, could be a missed opportunity for upskilling to create a new capability. Distant upskilling often comes into play when used in conjunction with a bounce lever and a role is made redundant. Often known as reskilling or retraining, which unfortunately emphasizes the redundancy of the existing skills and knowledge, distant upskilling can be applied to avoid layoffs. One study by the World Economic Forum, in conjunction with Boston Consulting Group, emphasized the benefits of such an approach. Even if we were to ignore the obvious benefits to an organization of avoiding a layoff and subsequent hiring process, and the societal benefits of retained employment and new skills, reskilling has a clear incentive. The study found that a quarter of workers in roles expected to be disrupted by new technology could be reskilled into new jobs with an 'overall positive cost–benefit balance' (World Economic Forum, 2019).

CASE STUDY
Allianz

With a global workforce of around 150,000, Allianz SE is one of the world's largest financial services businesses. Antony Ebelle-ebanda led workforce planning and analytics across Europe, Africa and the Middle East. In order to ensure resilience of capabilities within the workforce across longer planning horizons, they focused on upskilling their workforce in adjacent skill areas. All areas had six core skills, in addition to competencies that were aligned to their main role. These were recorded on action plans and additional training was made available to enable them to create broader career opportunities for their people. Creating this additional capability affords them far greater flexibility than before, enabling them to both develop and 'cross-pollinate' their workforce (Ebelle-ebanda, 2020).

Return on investment (RoI)

Return on investment for learning and development is typically based along two lines: efficiency and effectiveness. Determining the efficiency necessitates a review of the process in achieving the objectives of a new competency, be it an assurance that the process delivers the new competency on a systemic, collective or individual level, or that, if necessary, accreditation is achieved for a role.

Effectiveness, on the other hand, necessitates a review of the outcomes of the intervention in relation to business objectives. HR functions have often struggled to articulate the true business impact of L&D interventions, either due to the difficulty of doing so, or the ease of reporting the metrics of 'assessment in L&D'. The limit that many will stretch to is an articulation of volumes, the numbers that have gone through an L&D process. However, assessment of L&D can provide the real RoI to organizations. 'For technical and skill training, objectives may be set for improved performance back on the job, in terms of quality, rework, waste reduction, speed, or cost' (Walker, 1992). Utilizing this as a lever within a workforce plan enables us to not only demonstrate the RoI from the intervention, it allows us to articulate that to stakeholders in advance and secure the necessary funding.

CASE STUDY
IBM Global Business Services

The professional services arm of the technology giant IBM Global Business Services provides a great example of how to demonstrate the RoI from build interventions. Mark Lawrence, now the global head of organization and people analytics at GSK, was IBM's learning intelligence leader at the time. He describes how they conducted a baseline on their consultancy practice; a process of workforce segmentation highlighted the 15 key projects. These were large multi-year transformations, many up to a decade long, with the greatest complexity and the highest cost category. Their assessment of supply and demand established a key gap in five of these projects. Organizational performance metrics showed those projects were dipping into poor health, which would impact not only IBM's objectives but also be disastrous for their clients. The team collaborated with the project leadership teams, HR colleagues and a wide variety of others to understand the factors impacting the workforce supply. It was identified that leadership and management capabilities on these projects needed some remedial support: 'There was a problem with outdated leadership and problems in managing the large, complex nature of these projects' (Lawrence, 2020). Within their Smarter Learning Analytics project, they agreed a build approach and designed interventions to bridge the gap; face-to-face learning and development focused on building these missing capabilities. This was focused on a tight cohort of leaders and project managers, no more than 50 in total.

The requirement had started from a business need, which allowed the team to demonstrate success in a different way. Rather than the traditional approaches of judging build interventions based on volumes, they utilized their learning analytics to demonstrate the impact and value of the interventions. Following the intervention, the performance metrics of each of the five projects began to improve.

Not only did the interventions successfully deliver the right capability, the impact went far beyond that. Mark elaborates that, in many organizations, there is a certain degree of scepticism around the impact of learning and development. Indeed, some of the learning tools were already available within IBM, but these were not taken up because many saw it as a 'dent in their productivity' (Lawrence, 2020). Smarter Learning Analytics was able to demonstrate clearly the value of interventions to the organization and led to a greater number of build interventions across the organization that achieved the seven rights.

Progression

Progression is a change in role that enhances the career of the worker, either as a promotion, or a less formal job enlargement. It is a valuable tool in the arsenal of an employee value proposition and, for many organizations, may be the only way to increase the salary of a worker. Whilst learning and development interventions tend to begin with teaching and training and are supported by coaching and feedback, progression falls firmly into the category of trying new things and undertaking challenging assignments. Progression initiatives are popular as they do not require capital expenditure, nor do they result in an abstraction from the workplace, unlike teaching and training that entail both. The caveat, of course, is risk: progression, without the accompaniment of learning and development, may never create a genuine capability.

More so than learning and development, progression tends to be viewed as a direct alterative to recruitment because, in most organizations, these activities are centred around the creation of roles rather than the creation of capability. There are advantages and disadvantages to both approaches; through workforce planning we can achieve greater assurance around the capabilities within our workforce and be clear on the most appropriate approach. One interesting study of a US financial services company found that internal staff who were progressed had stronger performance and lower levels of turnover in their first two years than external hires. However, those same external hires tended to have higher levels of experience and education and were paid an average of 18 per cent higher (Bidwell, 2011).

Whilst progression is an important tool, and it is rare to find organizations without it, there are mitigations that must be considered. The first of these is to avoid *the Peter principle*, the management approach where 'every employee tends to rise to his level of incompetence' (Peter and Hull, 2009). This means that many roles within an organization will be filled by those who lack the competence to execute the work. This results from both selection processes that do not accurately assess the potential of a worker in line with capability requirements, and those where insufficient activity has taken place to genuinely build capability. A common example of this is what the UK's Chartered Management Institute calls the 'accidental manager' (Chartered Management Institute, 2019). This is where successful performance by a worker, often combined with limited opportunities for recognition and reward, leads to them being promoted into a management position without the necessary skills and knowledge to execute that role. To avoid this, there must be a clear view of the gap between the capabilities of the individual and the capabilities required, and a clear plan to bridge that gap. Progression to a first management role certainly necessitates a learning model closer to Ulrich's 50:20:30 approach than Lombardo and Eichinger's 70:20:10 model. The second mitigation to consider is that of return on investment. Learning and development initiatives have an up-front cost that requires that a return on investment and building capability must always account for the speed to competency, therefore, stacking these negative effects. Avoid learning and development initiatives that build capability in those who are expected to promote into a new role where such capability is redundant. Take care not to progress someone on a temporary basis where the speed to competency is longer than the duration of the opportunity and will not add to longer-term advancement.

Performance management

Many view performance management as 'creating expectations and inspecting against those expectations' (Becker *et al*, 2009). In reality, great performance management is more than simply inspection, it is about maintaining and improving performance to the required standard. For most organizations, the improvement of performance remains a challenge. In the previous chapter, we discussed the systemic approaches to improved productivity. As we discussed in Chapter 8, once all efficiencies have been eked out from the work, workforce performance is the remaining factor in the productivity conundrum. How do we understand the components of workforce performance? Let us return to Professor Duckworth (2016) who, following her equation on the acquisition of skill, expanded to consider the attainment of achievement with the following equation:

$$Skill \times Effort = Achievement$$

To build on this, if we extend skill to include knowledge and accreditation, then we can combine this as competency. Finally, if we use achievement as a heuristic for performance, then the equation converts to the following:

$$Competency \times Mindset \times Environment = Performance$$

With this in mind, learning and development can achieve competency, whilst demand optimization and interventions around culture and climate can achieve the environment. This leaves mindset as the remaining piece of the performance puzzle that is yet to be resolved; the mental aspect that enables both skills and knowledge to become action. Mindset comprises three distinct elements: emotional, how we feel about something; cognitive, how we think about something; and behavioural, how we react to something. At the core, shifting mindset is what performance management seeks to achieve and exists through three streams: motivation, feedback and well-being.

MOTIVATION

The town of Marjah is a fairly non-descript collection of villages in the south of Afghanistan. In early 2010, it was the last remaining Taliban stronghold in Helmand province and the target of Operation Moshtarak (Dari for *together*); with over 15,000 troops, the largest offensive by the International Security Assistance Force (ISAF) under General Stanley McChrystal. Whilst the bulk of Afghan forces would come from the 205th Corps, which I had been serving alongside in Helmand, a *kandak* would come from the 201st Corps, based in the capital of Kabul. Helmand was a centre of Taliban activity and was renowned for some of the most bitter fighting of the campaign in Afghanistan. In a matter of weeks, with a small mentoring team, I had to upskill that kandak for the operation. I remember the faces on those Afghan warriors as they arrived in Helmand: some stoic, some eager and some terrified. With the same environment and similar skills and knowledge, the mindsets of those warriors were diverse. How we act is a matter of personal choice and, confronted with the same circumstances, some will shy away and others will rise up. That is the nature of motivation, the willingness of action.

In the 1960s, Professor Victor Vroom developed expectancy theory; the view that that people are motivated to behaviour based on the expected result of that behaviour. The theory is based upon three specific components: expectancy, instrumentality and valence (Vroom, 1995).

Expectancy

Expectancy is the extent to which a worker expects their efforts will achieve the expected level of performance. Does a worker believe, for example, that they can complete the volume of work to the right standard in the given time? This expectancy hinges on three elements: confidence, difficulty and control. Confidence is a self-assessment on our own efficacy; the ability to create the right outcome at that time. Much of this will hinge on an appreciation of our own competency, whether our skills and knowledge are sufficient for the task.

Difficulty pertains to how we view the general achievability of the task. Professor Vroom established that where performance expectations were viewed as unreasonable, or the goal was too difficult or unachievable, then motivation suffered as a result (Vroom, 1995). As covered throughout this book, the accurate assessment of our supply and demand helps avoid creating tasks that are unachievable with the available capability and highlights the importance of connecting the workforce plan across all levels and horizons.

Our *locus of control* is the third element of expectancy. Developed by psychologist Dr Julian Rotter, it is the extent to which we believe we have influence over the final outcome (Rotter, 1966 and 1975). This locus has a direct relationship on our behaviour; as the locus increases and decreases, so too does our motivation. The single biggest factor in adjusting this locus rests with the balance lever. From the organizational design at a macro and meso level, to the role design at a micro level, balance initiatives determine the locus of control for our workforce. Whilst many choices may achieve structural efficiencies, they risk reducing the locus of control and demotivating the workforce. This is certainly a key factor in the gradient of the average product of labour (APL) and marginal product of labour (MPL) curves we saw earlier in Figure 9.2; as more people get involved, the locus contracts and productivity suffers. Hence it should come as no surprise that organizations with informal structures and heavy promotion of collaboration will then struggle with their productivity.

Instrumentality
Instrumentality is the belief that the effort of the individual will be instrumental to the achievement of personal value. No individual engages in work without reason; we are individually driven by intrinsic and extrinsic factors that govern our willingness to work. The worker who believes the work will directly result in personal value, be it an extrinsic factor like a financial bonus, or an intrinsic factor such as a feeling of accomplishment, will have a higher level of motivation than those who do not.

Valence
Valence is the personal level of value that we place on the result of the outcome or, as the popular idiom goes, *is the juice worth the squeeze?* For example, in both the financial crisis and the COVID-19 pandemic, businesses were able to speak to the social, esteem and self-actualization needs of individuals and solicit pay reductions from their workforce to secure the survival of the organization and the jobs of their colleagues. As we referenced in relation to EVP, each worker has a different perspective on personal value. Therefore, an EVP cannot hope to be successful by operating as a catch-all proposition. As a minimum, we would aim for our EVP to be aligned by each of the four segments of the capability segmentation framework: specialists, professionals, operators and criticals.

FEEDBACK

Feedback occurs when our outputs return to us as inputs. Many of us have experienced the pain of stepping on Lego. I have done it so often that I often assume it's Lego, only to discover it's a different angular toy. 'Simple causal reasoning about a feedback system is difficult because the first system influences the second and second system influences the first, leading to a circular argument' (Åström and Murray, 2008).

Feedback is framed by our perspectives and experiences and may require multiple sources to provide the truth. Even the absence of direct feedback is, itself, feedback. What becomes critical is understanding that points of view become critical in influencing behaviour:

> Obi Wan Kenobi: So what I told you was true, from a certain point of view.
>
> Luke Skywalker: A certain point of view?
>
> Obi Wan Kenobi: Luke, you're going to find that many of the truths we cling to depend greatly on our own point of view.
>
> (*Star Wars: Return of the Jedi*, 1983)

Providing feedback to the workforce provides an additional point of view and is vital for changing perspectives of impact; by doing so, we can improve both accuracy and motivation. Let us imagine one of our direct reports has produced work that is not to the required standard. Provision of feedback can bridge that performance gap by going to the heart of the issue. Does the worker lack the skills or knowledge to complete the task? Does the worker have the right competencies, but there are mindset or environmental issues preventing that performance? Alternatively, is it simply that the worker did not understand the required standard to be achieved? By providing feedback, the cause can be remedied; without direct feedback, that worker may continue to produce poor-quality work, which will create feedback elsewhere; perhaps a colleague must step in, or a stakeholder reacts badly. Now the worker has feedback that their efforts did not result in the right outcome, yet they do not understand how to remedy the issue. This results in a worker who is not achieving the required standard and is demotivated as they have an expectancy that they cannot achieve the required standard. The same happens when the feedback given to a worker is not specific enough to correct an action. The workplace is complex, so feedback must be treated as more than the hot and cold game, where children shout 'hotter' or 'colder' to guide someone towards a hidden object.

Feedback needs to be more specific to highlight the action of the individual, the impact of that action and a solution to maintain or improve that behaviour. Moreover, the feedback must be timely if it is to influence behaviour. 'Reviewing someone's performance annually from a single perspective… The timeframe is woefully inadequate as a feedback loop' (Dignan, 2019). Performance conversations that fall outside a suitable timescale are, like a bulb illuminating months after the switch was used, a sign of a faulty system. Embedded across an organization, feedback becomes a powerful and cost-neutral initiative to clarify expectations, improve skills, increase motivation and positively contribute towards the management of performance.

WELL-BEING

Well-being is the maintenance of the mindset and physiological components of capability. Though there is symbiosis in living well and being well, the concept of well-being is more aligned to our daily state of health.

The mindset component of capability comprises three distinct elements: emotional, how we feel about something; cognitive, how we think about something; and behavioural, how we react to something. As we covered in Chapter 11, emotions play an essential part in the way we make decisions and are intrinsically linked to motivation. If our well-being has an adverse impact on our emotions, our performance will suffer. Ego depletion (Kahneman, 2011), which we also covered in Chapter 11, is stress on the cognitive aspect of our capability, and therefore productivity. Indeed, the working of longer hours has been shown to decrease productivity for this very reason. When the scrum approach was introduced to venture capital firm OpenView, they found the optimal point for productivity was 40 hours (Sutherland, 2015). It's important to note too that motivation can overcome well-being, but at a cost: burnout (Gibson, 2015). Not only does burnout impact our cognitive function, it impacts our emotional state, which results in a shift in behaviours. Moreover, occupational burnout results in a direct impact on our physiology, mental and physical (Morgan et al, 2002).

Well-being is far more than the avoidance of workplace accidents; it is assuring the safety of the mindset and physiology of the workforce. By ensuring that well-being is considered from a workforce planning perspective, an organization can both manage performance and avoid the loss of capability through deterioration of the mindset and physiological components of capability.

CHANGING CULTURE AND CLIMATE

The culture, which we discussed in detail in the previous chapter, can act as a foundation of the climate. Whilst the culture is the purpose, values and brand of the organization, the climate is how the culture manifests in the behaviours of the workforce. There is interplay between culture and climate that enables them to influence each other. An organization with a strong culture that is aligned to its strategic framework will typically find a convergence between its culture and climate. Equally, where a strong climate is left to endure with a weak culture, then there will be convergence to create a strong culture based on that climate. On the other hand, weak cultures that are not aligned to the strategic framework, or organizations going through change or disruption, will typically find divergence of culture and climate.

CASE STUDY
Enron

In the late 1990s, the foyer of 1400 Smith Street, the 50-floor skyscraper in downtown Houston, Texas, was emblazoned with banners proclaiming RICE. The headquarters of the Enron Corporation, RICE stood for its values of respect, integrity, communication and excellence. The energy and commodities company was a paragon of corporate America, receiving plaudits and awards from top business publications.

Under the guidance of chief operating officer, Jeffrey Skilling, Enron instituted a 360-degree performance review based on its RICE values. Recognized as one of harshest employee-ranking systems in America, it was an *up or out* approach that rewarded and promoted the top performers and sacked the lowest performers. The biggest issue was that associates felt that profit generation was given far greater weighting by Skilling's performance review committee than the RICE values. This created a climate of fierce internal competition and secrecy that incentivized short-term behaviours.

Skilling became CEO in 2001 as its short-termism began to unravel. Skilling would oversee a halving of the share price before he resigned after six short months. Three months later, Enron restated its financial position back to 1997, adding over a billion dollars in losses and liabilities over the four-year period; in December 2001, the corporation filed for bankruptcy (Thomas, 2002; Dobson, 2006). The scandal resulted in jail sentences for top executives and initiated the demise of its auditor, Arthur Andersen.

Although the purpose, values and brand of Enron spawned a culture that was held in high regard, it was completely at odds with the way that work was done. The performance management approach incentivized behaviours that created a toxic climate for the organization.

The key to creating the right climate is to create the foundation of a right culture and support this through the performance management structures we implement. In the previous chapter we discussed how to design the right culture that is aligned to the strategic framework of the organization, part of the balance lever. To create cultural and climate change we need to define clearly the expected behaviours, ensuring they embody the culture and identifying dependencies. Successful cultural change necessitates a mix of both formal and informal interventions, from performance management mechanisms to assess and reinforce the new culture, to role modelling of behaviours by senior leaders.

Borrow

Borrow is the approach of acquiring a temporary capability, thereby borrowing from elsewhere and typically attracting a higher rate of operational expenditure than more permanent workforce levers. The key difference is that, with a borrow lever, we typically only pay for what we need. 'One should only have on a team the knowledge and skills that are needed day in and day out for the bulk of the work. Specialists that may be needed once in a while, or that may have to be consulted on this or on that, should always remain outside' (Drucker, 1985). With the exception of criticals, all segments of the *capability segmentation framework* may be acquired through a borrow lever.

The borrow lever has been traditionally seen as an opposite to the buy and build levers, which have sat firmly within the domain of HR functions and are viewed as the least expensive approaches to build capability. The borrow lever is often applied when the buy and build levers fail to provide the right workforce. It is unsurprising, therefore, that in many organizations the choice to pull the borrow lever lies between operational management and procurement functions and excludes those from HR. Indeed, many organizations still exclude many elements of their contingent workforce from their HR information systems (HRIS). The borrow lever is not a substitute for other levers, it is a viable lever as part of a wider workforce plan.

In this section we will cover the primary borrow interventions of contingent labour and professional service firms before we move on to the complex interventions of alliances and outsourcing.

Contingent labour

Contingent labour, or contingent workers, are those who offer themselves to organizations on a non-permanent basis. These workers are freelancers within a gig economy; they comprise 20 to 30 per cent of the working-age population in Europe (Manyika *et al*, 2016) and around 35 per cent of the labour market in the US (Upwork, 2019). Contingent labour is challenging to define and measure due to differences in national taxation codes and labour laws, which shape the groups and determine nomenclature. To better understand this cohort, we will segment the contingent labour market based on payroll status, duration and choice.

PAYROLL STATUS

On-payroll workers are those who are brought into the organization as an employee; unlike permanent employees, they have a contract of employment that stipulates conditions for its conclusion. These terms are typically duration-based, where a contract would have a fixed term of a number of months, or purpose-based, where a contract would end at the achievement of a specific target. The employee status of a worker on the payroll typically entitles access to a wider range of benefits and rights. As such, this allows the organization to convey many of the broader aspects of their EVP. This makes on-payroll workers, typically, the least expensive form of contingent labour. This approach is most beneficial for resource requirements of between six and twelve months that either support

Off-payroll workers are those who are paid from the accounts payable expense account, rather than the payroll expense account, on the basis of invoices, the most common being either a *time and materials* basis of an hourly or daily rate plus expenses, or a *flat fee*, much like a restaurant menu. Off-payroll workers include the self-employed, personal service companies (micro-organizations) and managed workers who are contracted from a larger company. The benefit of managed workers is one of scale; where we wish to use different varieties of contingent workforce, the use of a single managed provider can reduce significantly the administrative demand.

CASE STUDY
Serco

Serco Group specializes in the delivery of essential public services across five sectors: defence, justice and immigration, transport, health, and citizen services. Headquartered in the UK, its workforce of over 55,000 operates across Europe, North America, Asia Pacific and the Middle East. The COVID-19 pandemic resulted in a sharp increase in demand across its healthcare business. Across 16 hospital locations in the UK, employee absences met with a surge in demand from increased patient numbers, resulting in a tripling of headcount requirements in less than two months. In addition, Serco was awarded government contracts for two new services: the running of COVID-19 test centres and the management of call handling for contact tracing.

Philip Knight, HR director for Serco's UK and Europe division, explains that, to overcome this challenge, they partnered with their managed service provider, Comensura, part of Impellam Group. With three different projects and a multitude of roles, they were able to acquire and onboard nearly 2,000 contingent workers at pace to sites across the UK. When faced with the challenges of achieving a diverse capability requirement at scale and within a short timeframe, the use of managed workers enabled Serco to achieve its aims and serve the public during a time of crisis (Knight, 2020).

DURATION

Temporary workers are the most common concept of the contingent worker, brought into the organization on a limited basis for a specified duration. The alternative is sessional workers who have a more enduring relationship with an organization, but a less formal contract, so called because they are paid by the sessions that they work. Sessional workers exist across multiple industries; in the professional workforce segment are locum doctors and substitute teachers; in the operator workforce segment are seasonal fruit pickers and support staff who work only during sporting events or music concerts. The defining feature of sessional workers is that there is no guarantee of ongoing work, and therefore they can be utilized at the right time whilst achieving the right risk, which may be avoidance of cost when demand is low.

CHOICE

The question of choice is the subject of a valuable study of the contingent labour market workforce in the United States and Europe by McKinsey & Company (Manyika *et al*, 2016). They divided the contingent labour market into four segments based on their choice and necessity: free agents, casual earners, reluctants and the financially strapped. Thirty per cent of the contingent workforce can be described as free agents who actively choose working on a contingent basis and for whom it is their primary source of income. These workers will likely have a clear business model with a value proposition that maximizes the benefits of contingent work. A larger 40 per cent of the contingent labour marked are casual earners where contingent work provides a supplemental income and, like free agents, they choose to work in this way. Casual workers are often financially leveraging a personal passion or hobby. As contingent working is a choice, both free agents and casual workers report not only the highest levels of satisfaction of all contingent workforce segments; their satisfaction is higher than those in permanent roles by choice.

The final two segments are those who undertake contingent work through necessity. There are the reluctants who, like free agents, derive their primary income from contingent work. Comprising 14 per cent of the contingent labour market, these workers would rather be in permanent employment. The final segment consists of those who are financially strapped and derive supplemental income from contingent work through necessity. Sixteen per cent of the contingent workforce are in this category and exist, typically, because the pay from their main source of employment falls below their needs. Reluctants and the financially strapped report similarly low levels of job satisfaction and their yearning for job security places them firmly within the definition of the precariat this group of nearly 60 million workers in the US and Europe. McKinsey's study found that around half of low-income households participate in the contingent labour market, with nearly 40 per cent doing so out of necessity. The opportunity for workforce planning practitioners, business leaders and policy makers is to enhance the security of reluctants and the financially strapped in order to enhance the mindset and performance of our people.

CASE STUDY
National Health Service (NHS)

The NHS comprises the collective publicly funded healthcare systems within the UK. With a combined workforce of over 1.7 million (Office for National Statistics, 2019), it is the nation's largest employer. Early forecasts were that the COVID-19 pandemic would result in an unparalleled surge in demand for medical staff and facilities. With a short timeframe until the virus would take hold, a contingent workforce would provide a vital source of capability. The NHS took two critical steps that would see it endure the crisis: the first was to secure nearly 20,000 clinical staff from the UK's private healthcare sector; the second was to look to its alumni. Speaking in March 2020, England's chief nursing officer, Ruth May, announced that they would be writing to more than 50,000 former nurses and over 15,000 doctors to return to the NHS on a temporary basis (NHS, 2020). Within 10 days, this call to action had secured 20,000 retired NHS staff (Johnson, 2020).

Regardless of the scale, the alumni networks of our own organizations can provide a valuable source of contingent labour, particularly those who have retired. Such initiatives are used by organizations across sectors as a way of generating tried and tested capability. This can be vital if the requirement is to create specialist capacity in a short timeframe. Cultivating and maintaining that network can prove invaluable at the point that capability is desired.

Professional services firms

Whilst contingent labour is a borrow initiative for individual workers, the use of professional service firms (PSFs) enables the borrowing of a collective capability. Business strategy professor, Andrew von Nordenflycht, describes four types of professional services firm. The classic PSFs are law and accounting firms, whilst the neo-PSFs are management consultancies. Then there are technology developers, such as research and development firms, and professional campuses, such as private medical hospitals (Von Nordenflycht, 2010).

Though some PSFs may provide a managed worker service as part of their market offering, we would tend to utilize PSFs for larger and more specific projects rather than a contingent labour pool. As a result, PSFs are typically commissioned through a statement of work (SoW) that articulates the requirements of the project, including deliverables and timelines. In doing so, whilst a PSF may still use a time and materials or a fixed price charging model, they may utilize pricing models that are either value-based or performance-based. As with a fixed price model, the cost in a value-based model is agreed beforehand; however, the latter charges different fees to different clients for the product. For example, a project that could increase profits by 5 per cent will generate far greater value for a billion-dollar company than it will for a million-dollar company. Therefore, a PSF would charge the billion-dollar company more under a value-based pricing model. Whilst a value-based model is based on completion of a project, performance-based pricing is based on achieving a specific business outcome. To adapt the example above, if payment occurs only when the 5 per cent increase in profits is achieved, that would be performance-based. Whilst performance-based pricing will typically incur the highest level of capital expenditure, this expenditure is mitigated against benefit realization. Therefore, particularly in high-risk projects, performance-based pricing may be the most prudent approach within the borrow lever.

Alliances

Alliances are agreements between organizations for mutual benefit, of which the most common are the vertical agreements both upstream and downstream in our existing supply chains. From a workforce planning perspective, however, there are three key forms of alliance to consider as initiatives within a borrow lever: strategic alliances, retained services and business process outsourcing.

STRATEGIC ALLIANCES

Strategic alliances and partnerships are agreements that extend beyond a basic alliance to include the sharing of knowledge and resources. These are commonplace within the public sector, even between departments operating in fundamentally different sectors of the economy. Within the private sector, the most common of these are on a vertical basis, and go beyond the standard relationship between a vendor and a client, which has existed between McDonald's and Coca-Cola since 1955. For example, it was Coca-Cola executives who suggested the idea of bundling together burger, fries and a soft drink as part of McDonald's promotion of the movie *Jurassic Park* (Gelles, 2014). At that moment in 1993, the Extra Value Meal was born; a concept that remains ubiquitous within fast food restaurants.

Horizontal strategic alliances are those between organizations in the same industry, such as the partnership between German automaker Volkswagen (VW) and the Detroit-based Ford. In early 2019, they announced a global alliance to develop commercial vans and medium-sized trucks. Later in the year, the companies took an equal equity stake in artificial intelligence company, Argo AI, to partner in the creation of self-driving vehicles (Abuelsamid, 2019).

Alongside mergers and acquisitions, the creation of strategic alliances is often the only route to accessing the critical capabilities of other organizations. This can be vital if those capabilities are niche, allowing an alliance to generate a critical mass of capability. Strategic alliances are best utilized for tasks that have high strategic importance but a low contribution to operational performance (Snell *et al*, 2000)

Strategic alliances can also enable a further borrow initiative, secondments, which we will discuss further within the bounce lever.

RETAINED SERVICES

Retained services are a form of alliance where an organization pays a fee in advance, a *retainer*, for the option to utilize a service in the future and within a given timeframe. Retained service arrangements are common with classic professional services firms, such as those in the legal and accountancy sectors. For example, we may retain the services of a law firm and pay a monthly fee that entitles us to 20 billable hours of legal work. That retainer may also specify a rate for additional billable hours of work or more specific services.

The benefit to retained service providers is not only a guaranteed income, but also income for services that are not utilized. On that basis, a mature workforce planning function with accurate forecasting may find that retained services are highly advantageous in creating the seven rights for the organization. Retained services can serve as a useful island in the gap between a strategic alliance and outsourcing, and can be valuable for activities that are a mid-point in strategic importance and their contribution to operational performance.

BUSINESS PROCESS OUTSOURCING

Peter Drucker's famous refrain was, 'do what you do best and outsource the rest' (Drucker, 2011). His reference was to the broader activity of outsourcing: handing any form of work to someone outside the organization. Whilst in a retained service, tasks are handed over on an ad hoc basis, in a business process outsourcing (BPO) model, processes are transferred on an enduring basis.

Drucker's logic began with the balance lever and the approach of work design. In his famous article, 'Sell the mailroom', he advocated a process of 'unbundling', stripping out the 'clerical, maintenance and support work' and handing this over to another organization (Drucker, 1989). His target for BPO is those operator capabilities that are low in both uniqueness and value. The opportunity is that, with low uniqueness, a BPO provider can service multiple clients and achieve economies of scale that would otherwise elude the original organization. We discussed in Chapter 6 that the operator workforce segment has a distribution of performance on a Gaussian bell curve, shown in Figure 6.2. With processes limiting the value that can be generated from high performance, there is a limited opportunity cost to the outsourcing of appropriately optimized businesses processes; little additional margin could be generated from greater individual performance. This has meant that BPO is often synonymous with offshoring, which we covered earlier in the chapter within the buy lever. Processes have simply moved to locations where wage arbitrage provides a cost advantage.

BPO agreements are typically arranged under a master service agreement (MSA), which agrees the majority of the terms and conditions and provides a framework for future transactions.

BPO is best utilized where strategic importance of the activity is low, but the contribution to operational performance is high. Not only can outsourcing be applied to the operator workforce segment, it extends to other non-critical segments. The significant benefit from a workforce planning perspective is that BPO is likely to be the most robust borrow approach for the specialists. With low competitive advantage, specialists with capability that is common across industry may find a natural home. The key issues with BPO are the same as those with any capability; outsourcing typically goes wrong because an organization does not fully understand either their business model or their demand. An organization may make the mistake of outsourcing a core function, a source of its competitive advantage. More often, an organization may underestimate the complexity of the transition, have poor demand forecasts that risk spiralling costs, or agree contractual terms that do not incentivize the desired outcomes. However, when utilized as part of an agile workforce planning approach, BPO remains a highly effective approach to creating the capability an organization needs.

Bind

Bind is to prevent the loss of a capability by binding it in place. Once we invest in the buying or building of permanent capabilities, the obvious aim is to avoid losing that capability. In this section we will discuss the importance of the bind lever and its two main elements: contractual initiatives and EVP initiatives.

Impact of organizational churn

In Chapter 8 we discussed the concept of organizational churn. Much like our own circulatory systems, maintaining a sensible level of churn is vital for the health of the organization. Capability coming into the system is a necessary life blood to either offset what is lost, or to supplement when we need more. The churn that results in the loss of capability consists of internal movement at a meso level, and turnover at a macro level.

The benefits of internal mobility were articulated earlier in this chapter within the build lever and will be reinforced within the bounce lever. Not only does internal mobility allow us to move capability to where it is needed, it can be a vehicle to enable the building of capability. Indeed, restricting internal mobility can be a catalyst for an increased rate of turnover. When it is easier to leave an organization than to progress within it, those looking for progression will be more likely to choose to leave than stay. That said, turnover is beneficial to an organization; without turnover, it becomes more difficult to bring in new capability without increasing the size of the organization. With new hires come new ideas and greater diversity of thought; without new hires, it is highly challenging to change the shape of the workforce. Unless people are leaving at all levels of the organization, it becomes more difficult to build capability through progressive routes. The more insidious impact of low turnover is that it can mask performance problems.

Flawed processes and poor management are common triggers for turnover. When turnover is normal, outliers in voluntary turnover can highlight these issues. Where turnover is low, either through strong bind levers or high levels of unemployment, these issues may not obviously come to the fore.

There are, however, considerable costs that come from churn. As we have said before in this book, internal movement is an enabler of many development initiatives within the build lever. Not only is such internal movement and promotion-from-within seen as the panacea for many organizations, but individual expectations around career management almost demand it. The fundamental factor is that all churn has a performance impact. Earlier in this chapter, within the build lever, we discussed the performance element of speed to competence, shown in Figure 14.2; this concept is developed further in Figure 14.3.

As a new worker develops their competence, they will generate greater levels of value, shown on the solid line. The first key marker, point a, is the tipping point, where the weekly value being generated by the worker is greater than their cost of wages, benefits and employer taxes.

The second key marker, point b, is where that worker achieves the required level of competence and begins to generate a level of value in line with their peers. One study, conducted by global forecasting and quantitative analysis firm Oxford Economics and sponsored by employee benefits provider Unum, found that the average time to hit point b for 'new workers from elsewhere in the same industry' was around 15 weeks. This compared against '32 weeks for a worker from another sector, 40 weeks for a new

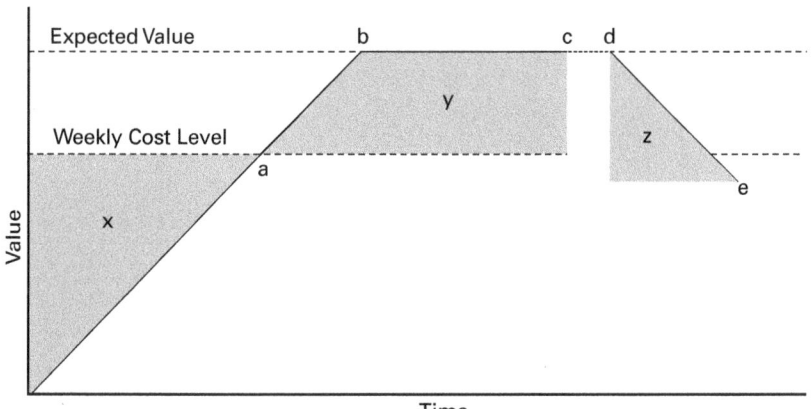

FIGURE 14.3 The performance to value model

graduate, and a full calendar year for a person coming out of unemployment or inactivity' (Rogers and Saider, 2014).

It is not until point c that an organization achieves break even and the excess value generated by the worker, area y, is greater than the initial investment, area x.

When a decision is made to leave a role, point d, performance will fall back down; part of this will be driven by time spent handing over work, rather than being productive. For a number, the decision to leave a role will see a commensurate decrease in motivation, exacerbating the performance impact until the individual leaves the role, point e, and a resulting loss of value in area z.

With a speed to competency of up to a year (Rogers and Saider, 2014), churn early in the employee lifecycle may never break even and generate a return on investment. If there is also a gap before they can fill that vacancy, this may result in a loss of revenue. The totality of this is the *performance cost of churn*, an impact that is often missed by organizations as it is an opportunity cost, rather than a direct cost.

The second factor is the *administrative cost of churn*. These are the costs incurred through the lost time of other workers who need to support churn. In Figure 14.3, between points d and e, performance falls as work is handed over. This impacts on peers, who will need to spend their time taking over the work, and also affects the line manager, whose time will be spent examining and partitioning the soon-to-be-vacant portfolio of work, managing stakeholders and conducting final interviews. When a new worker joins to fill that vacancy, the same will happen, as whilst competence is being learned and developed, there is additional cost to administer the specific build intervention, through teaching, coaching, feedback and mentorship. This may fall on dedicated learning and development staff, and will certainly fall upon those same peers and line manager. Again, as it is an opportunity cost, rather than a direct cost, it is often missed by organizations, though always felt by the team who has to support it.

The final factor is the *replacement cost of churn*, which is the total direct and indirect costs incurred to find a new worker to fill the vacancy. Examples of the direct costs may be advertising the role or the use of an agency or search firm to find suitable candidates. Indirect costs will be the time spent by the in-house recruiter, the original line manager and others, including HR business partners, to screen and select the right candidate. As the replacement cost is the aspect with direct costs, this is the area often given scrutiny by finance departments; this reinforces the idea that internal movement is the panacea of capability building as it is seen to be cost neutral. In reality, an organization that is maintaining its headcount must recruit if a vacancy arises. Internal mobility allows us, perhaps, to backfill a senior vacancy with an existing worker and therefore recruit a more junior backfill. However, each move is churn; though an internal move incurs lower replacement costs, it still generates performance and administrative costs.

A study of reports over a 15-year span indicated the typical cost of turnover in the United States for positions earning less than $30,000 annually was 16 per cent, while 'very highly paid jobs and those at the senior or executive levels tend to have disproportionately high turnover costs' ranging up to 213 per cent (Boushey and Glynn, 2012). This resonates with Josh Bersin, whose estimates place the cost of churn as ranging from tens of thousands of dollars to one-and-a-half or even twice annual salary (Bersin, 2013). With such a financial impact, utilizing the bind lever alongside the most appropriate other choices of lever becomes essential to cost avoidance whilst creating the right workforce. We will now look in detail at the two main elements of the bind lever: contractual initiatives and EVP initiatives.

Contractual initiatives

Stipulated within policy or legislation and reinforced through contracts, contractual bind initiatives create structural binding of our workforce within the organization. Contractual initiatives tend to add cost to the workforce; a worker with greater restrictions will rightly expect a higher level of compensation than one with fewer restrictions, as we discussed previously with contract theory.

There are a number of considerations for an organization to help it determine the most appropriate contractual initiatives for its workforce, the first of those being workforce segments. The operator workforce segment and specialists whose capabilities are specific to our organization will typically attract the least restrictive contracts as the cost of turnover is low. Criticals incur the highest turnover costs and therefore must have the most restrictive contracts within the workforce. For the professional segment, I advise a more variable approach to their contract that is based on the value of the work, for though they are plentiful within the marketplace, their input to high-value work may incur performance costs should they leave.

Beyond this, market availability is a common consideration, with fewer restrictions being considered during high unemployment and the reverse during low unemployment. I would always guard against being guided too strongly by this consideration as employment levels tend to be transitionary and an organization many find itself with an inappropriate level of safeguard as the employment market fluctuates. Turnover rates tend to be another consideration, with more restrictions placed on roles that are less attractive and have traditionally higher levels of turnover. Though this approach makes sense from a planning perspective, this increases significantly the performance cost of churn. Those who are desperately unhappy with their work and subject to a bind initiative will fall from point d to point e on the performance to value model (Figure 14.3), which is steeper and lower than all other groups. As an approach it is unsustainable and organizations are urged to instead look at balance and bot levers to improve the work, and supplement these with EVP initiatives from the bind lever, which we will discuss later.

Let us look at the main contractual initiatives: notice periods, tenure, restrictive covenants, vesting benefits and return of service.

NOTICE PERIODS

This specifies the duration between a termination decision, either from the employer or employee, and the last day of employment. As such, it can be seen as a double-edged weapon; it provides safeguards to employees through restrictions to the organization and also provides safeguards to the organization through restrictions to employees. Organizations may tweak these to offset poor planning and forecasting, with lower notice periods designed to provide greater latitude to lay off their workforce when desired.

TENURE

Tenure is a notice period applied at the meso level of the organization. Whilst a notice period binds a worker to the organization, tenure binds a worker to a role. The term is most common in academia, where tenure determines the permanence of a role as a buy initiative. In business circles, the term determines an end date to the duration of an individual in a specific role. Though this initiative would be part of a build lever to develop capability, it also has some very valuable bind properties. By determining an end date, an organization can have greater assurance of a suitable return on investment from new starters and internal moves. The downside of tenure is that whilst it can better manage internal mobility, it can increase turnover as it is easier to leave than to move internally. Therefore, it is an approach best utilized alongside macro-level bind initiatives.

RESTRICTIVE COVENANTS

Restrictive covenants are contractual devices to protect the interests of an organization. They prevent a worker from unduly leveraging the circumstances of their current employment to gain future employment and safeguard against malpractice by individual workers. These covenants typically restrict the activities of a worker for periods of up to a year once they leave an organization. There are four main types of restrictive covenants used by organizations, which govern competition, solicitation, dealing and poaching. Competition covenants restrict employees from working in similar employment, therefore mitigating the risk of inside knowledge reaching a competitor. Solicitation covenants prevent former workers poaching clients or suppliers of the former worker, whilst dealing covenants prevent any form of interaction between a former worker and clients or suppliers. The latter is commonplace for senior officials in the public sector in order to avoid impropriety. Of all restrictive covenants, the most common are poaching covenants, which prevent a worker from poaching former colleagues.

VESTING BENEFITS

Vesting is a period of time before an individual benefit is fully realized, after which time a benefit becomes vested. Vesting may be done on a cliff basis or a graduated basis. A cliff basis means that benefits become fully vested at a specific point in time; for example, in bonus schemes, a short-term incentive plan (STIP) involves a bonus paid annually on the basis of overall performance. More senior roles may attract a long-term incentive plan (LTIP), where such bonuses may be paid one every few years. A graduated basis is often used for equity, stock held in the organization, where a portion becomes vested each year. For example, an award of 100 shares, which vests at a rate of 25 per year, takes four years of employment to become fully vested. This creates *loss aversion* (Kahneman and Tversky, 1979); a worker would want to avoid leaving before all shares have become vested, even if taking a higher-payed role and sacrificing those shares would leave them better off.

An extension of vesting is where a benefit such as a golden handshake or training is realized immediately, but it is contingent upon remaining with the organization for a minimum duration, a *return of service*. Though legislative recourse for organizations will vary in different countries, a return of service will allow an organization to recoup some or all of their initial investment if a worker chooses to terminate their employment early. Such contractual initiatives are the norm for military pilots, where there may be a temptation to join a commercial enterprise for higher levels of pay. As a result, returns of service of anywhere between five and ten years are commonplace. Such initiatives have been considered further afield, including within the UK's National Health Service (NHS). The NHS funds the bulk of training costs for junior doctors in the UK, unlike many countries where this is borne by the medical students. But in such countries this personal investment is offset by much higher salaries. As a result, the NHS has suffered from junior doctors capitalizing on this wage arbitrage and departing overseas once they are trained. Notably, Niall Dickson, the head of the NHS Confederation, called for the institution of a four-year return of service to safeguard £220,000 worth of training costs that are borne by the British taxpayer and bind their junior doctors (Dickson, 2018).

EVP initiatives

The EVP not only provides a valuable asset for recruitment, it also plays a vital role in retention. Research by Gartner indicates organizations that deliver effectively on their EVP can decrease annual employee turnover by just under 70 per cent (Baker, 2019). The key elements are to understand both why people leave and why they stay, and then deliver an EVP that capitalizes on that.

CASE STUDY
Apple Inc

In 2014, having spent the previous eight years as the CEO of Burberry, Angela Ahrendts joined Apple as the senior vice president of retail and online stores. Whilst average turnover in the United States sits at around 15 per cent, turnover in the retail sector trends just above 60 per cent (Wells, 2018). With such a climate, the challenge for Ahrendts to motivate a workforce of over 60,000 staff was formidable. How did she do it? Ahrendts says:

> In the first six months I was able to hit 40 different markets and spend time with the leaders. An amazing culture was already built and an amazing foundation. I would first of all just listen and learn. And then you start in your own mind to think where you can add value – you're uniting people, you're getting them to collaborate. You're building trust. That alone is empowering (Tetzeli, 2016).

Ahrendts treated the staff in her stores as 'executives' who bring Apple's products direct to customers, rather than as simply retail employees. The impact was staggering;

at the end of Ahrendts' first year they reported a turnover rate of just 19 per cent, their highest ever rate of retention (Tetzeli, 2016).

Studies have shown that 'the characteristics of pay and promotion… are, as might be expected, the lead drivers of voluntary turnover' (ADP, 2019). It should come as no surprise, therefore, that in many organizations their primary bind lever is salary increases. Indeed, one survey found that just over half (55 per cent) of organizations with staff retention difficulties had increased salaries (Chartered Institute of Personnel and Development, 2018). For organizations to utilize EVP elements to bind their workforce, it is vital the approach is appropriately tailored based on different workforce segments. At a minimum, this needs to be aligned to the capability segmentation framework that was introduced in Chapter 6.

Bounce

Bounce is where we either move a capability around, or exit the capability from, the organization. We bounce when the actual capability within the workforce satisfies two key criteria: a capability is redundant in a particular area of the business, or a capability gap cannot be bridged successfully with a balance, bot or build lever. The bounce interventions we take are, therefore, demarcated on the basis of the first criterion. Is a capability redundant in the whole organization, the macro level, or is it solely redundant in a specific part of the organization, the meso level?

Macro level

If a capability cannot be utilized in any area of the organization, the following initiatives may be considered:

FURLOUGH

This is where workers are placed on a temporary leave of absence by the organization. Contingent workers could be furloughed for a number of weeks, for example during holiday seasons until customer demand increases. For permanent workers, the use of furlough is typically used as a means to avoid or delay layoffs, particularly during heightened VUCA activity. Fundamentally, furlough can be implemented when there is a temporary reduction in demand or a temporary inability to utilize capability.

Furlough took on new meaning for organizations during the COVID-19 pandemic. The imposition of lockdowns meant that production ground to a halt in many sectors, resulting in a supply shock to global economies. With reasonable expectations that production could restart once the lockdowns were eased, and ambiguity around the nature of markets once this happened, many organizations took the decision to furlough workers rather than exit them. Furlough is an extreme measure, but highly valuable in horizon one planning in response to extreme VUCA events.

CASE STUDY
Honeywell

Honeywell International is a global conglomerate that provides engineering services and produces aerospace systems and industrial products. As the 2009 financial crisis hit, they began to struggle. Their CEO, David Cote, explains, 'The only businesses in our portfolio that held up well were defense, aerospace, and energy efficiency. Everything else was down' (Cote, 2013).

Though many organizations began layoffs to exit their people, Cote realized this was a false economy: 'Most managers underestimate how much disruption layoffs create… [and] overestimate the savings they will achieve' (Cote, 2013). Cote's logic is clear: because of the cost of layoffs, it takes six months before saving are made. With recessions typically lasting between 12 and 18 months, organizations will typically start rehiring as demand picks up. Cote provides a helpful analogy, that layoffs during a recession are like spending millions of dollars on a new factory that takes six months before it breaks even, then running the factory for a further six months before shutting it down.

As a result, they decided on a furlough approach rather than have layoffs. In the first half of 2009, Honeywell asked each worker to take a series of unpaid weeks of leave. This allowed them to preserve cash and retain the workforce so that, when demand started to pick up in early 2010, they were able to respond.

SECONDMENT

In this case, one organization's borrow lever is enabled by another organization's bounce lever. Secondments allow us to bounce our capability on a temporary basis with linked benefits of offsetting salary costs during times of reduced demand and potentially enabling an alliance. As part of a build or bind lever, secondments can be inordinately invaluable from a workforce planning perspective. Secondments provide almost limitless variety to career development, which is especially important in smaller organizations where opportunities for progression may be more limited.

EXIT

If a worker no longer fits in the seven rights of the organization, they may be bounced permanently from the organization. This is a standard occurrence for temporary workers at the end of their contract. For permanent workers, an exit may take one of two forms: dismissal or mutual severance. Dismissal is where the organization chooses to terminate a contract of employment, whilst mutual severance is where both the worker and the organization agree to sever the contract of employment.

Exits of permanent workers take place chiefly because a capability is no longer required in the current form, so a role is made redundant. The negative connotations of restructures and downsizing have been brought about through immature workforce planning and strategies that have viewed workers as costs to be cut rather than as assets to be developed (Cascio, 2002). My plea to all workforce planning practitioners is that we aim to make the exiting of a worker because of redundancy a last resort, where we are unable to bounce a worker in any other way. The beauty of agile workforce planning is that it affords us time to make the right decisions that will create the best outcome for both the organization and the individual. A study of over 300 businesses that have undertaken layoffs recorded a productivity decline in nearly three-quarters (74 per cent) of workers, coining the term 'layoff survivor stress' (Murphy, 2008).

The second reason for exit, performance, is where a capability is required and a worker has proven unable to deliver it. This may take the form of persistent underperformance or a specific instance of misconduct. For such approaches to work, the organization must have an effective build lever that creates the right capability through onboarding and reinforces it through performance management. If, with that in place, we are faced with underperformance, then exiting the worker is not only the best option for the organization, it is often the best option for the worker.

DIVESTMENT

Divestment is where part of the organization is sold, often as a means to generate revenue or as a regulatory requirement. From a workforce planning perspective, it is the exact opposite of mergers and acquisitions (M&A); rather than permanently buying a capability in the form of another business, we are bouncing capability in the form of a business. As part of a workforce plan, we may choose to divest primarily for one of two reasons: strategic alignment or capability change. If elements of our demand are not aligned to the strategic framework it would make more sense to sell that capability alongside the demand, rather than eradicate the demand and bounce the capability. Secondly, if we wish to fundamentally change the lever we use for our workforce, we may choose to bounce that entire capability rather than individual workers. In 2013, the UK's Cabinet Office launched a joint venture with technology consultancy Sopra Steria to provide back-office services to the public sector. As part of the move, the Cabinet Office divested a workforce of around 1,200 from government departments to the new entity, Shared Services Connected Limited (SSCL).

Meso level

When we bounce capability at the meso level, it is because the actual capability that we have can be utilized in a different area to provide greater value. Unfortunately, meso-level bounce approaches are vastly underutilized within businesses. A lack of workforce planning maturity can lead to utilizing a macro-level approach that denies available capability to other areas of the organization.

REASSIGN

Reassignments take place when a worker moves to another business area, or is assigned to a new project, but the nature of their role does not change. This is relatively common for professional capabilities where, for example, a project manager may conclude a project in one area of the organization and commence a new project in a different part of the organization.

REALLOCATION

Reallocation is when there is a fundamental change in the nature of a worker's activities on a temporary basis, but their role does not change. Reallocation typically occurs during change and crises where certain activities are deprioritized, and workers are reallocated to support key areas of the organization. Reallocation is standard practice during industrial action; during strike action on public transport systems, it is common to find back-office staff reallocated to front-line activities to maintain key safety requirements. When we consider contingency requirements for worst-case scenarios, it can be helpful to use a build lever to upskill a portion of the workforce in order to enable reallocation at a later date.

REDEPLOY

Redeployment occurs when there is a fundamental change in the nature of a worker's role and is usually accompanied by a move to a different business area, either on a longer temporary basis or permanently. Temporary redeployment was utilized by organizations to support demand increases triggered by the COVID-19 pandemic. Whilst demand for certain business activities was disrupted, others increased. As an alternative to furlough or layoff, workers were redeployed on an indefinite basis, accompanied by a temporary change to their role title and reward levels.

Executed on a permanent basis, redeployment is a useful mechanism for bouncing capability around the organization. Where a worker is unable to demonstrate the necessary level of competency for a role, redeployment to a role of similar standing may afford a new opportunity for the individual. It must be recognized, however, that this approach is often utilized instead of effective performance management.

A common use of redeployment is within cross-functional job rotation initiatives, facilitating progression with a fundamental change in the role, for example, a move from finance to marketing. Not only can this build capability and provide greater flexibility, it fosters better collaboration between departments and cultivates higher macro-level thinking in the workforce. This means that workers are more likely to think of the wider organizational impact of issues and be more effective at resolving problems. In addition, organizations may rotate workers between demanding, high-tempo roles and ones that are less stressful, to support the well-being of the workforce (Mourdoukoutas and Roy, 1994).

A major and unfortunately underutilized approach to redeployment is as an alternative to layoffs. If demand for a capability is declining in one area and growing in another, we must consider redeployment before layoffs and rehiring. The challenge, however, is often that there is also a capability gap between that being lost in one area and that needed in another.

CASE STUDY
Standard & Poor's

In 2011, the McGraw-Hill Companies announced that they would divest their education division, McGraw-Hill Education, and arrest a three-year-long decline in its share price (Blackden, 2011). This would allow them to bounce a capability that was no longer aligned to their strategic framework, which was focused on credit ratings and market intelligence. Success would be to execute a divestment and restructure that would necessitate job losses, but without having to resort to layoffs.

John Berisford, the forward-thinking CHRO of what was then McGraw-Hill Financial, created a cross-functional team to execute the challenge under Mark Sullivan (head of HR operations and planning), Christine Dolan (head of learning and development) and Antony Ebelle-ebanda (director of human capital planning and analytics.)

There were two possibilities for the workforce: to follow McGraw-Hill Education or to stay with what would later become S&P Global. For some who wished to stay, it would necessitate redeployment supported by upskilling. In order to map the workforce to redeployment opportunities and to establish the upskilling gap to be bridged, they needed to understand fully the competencies of their workforce. This exercise had to go beyond the capture of skills that people used daily in their current roles. For example, there might be someone who used Excel and PowerPoint skills in their job who also happened to be multi-lingual in Spanish, English and French. This unlocked far greater opportunities for capabilities than they had before.

The exercise enabled sensible conversations with people to say, 'In a new world there is this job where we think you have already 65 per cent of the requirements, would you be interested in that job?' (Ebelle-ebanda, 2020). This initiated a partnership between the business and the HR function to bridge that gap and work with people to achieve those training needs. In our example of the multi-lingual worker, they might be a great match to be a credit rating analyst. These analysts need to speak two languages and be good at sales and statistics. If the key competency gap was statistics, they would work with learning providers to create a solution that would bridge the gap and allow them to create a credit rating analyst capability within 12 weeks.

They executed this as an experiment that allowed them to assess these capabilities following go-live and, having demonstrated its success, scaled the approach across the business. In addition to enabling the successful spin-off and restructure, they successfully avoided redundancies (Ebelle-Ebanda, 2020).

DEMOTE

The opposite of promotion, demotions are a reduction in status to a level of lesser seniority within the hierarchy of an organization. Demotions are typically the result of underperformance and often a last resort before an exit. As a result, its use most often relates to a realization of the *Peter principle*, which we discussed earlier in the chapter, the tendency for employees to rise to their level of incompetence (Peter and Hull, 2009). For many, demotions are usually associated with a corresponding redeployment to circumvent many of the relational issues that may have contributed to the demotion.

In reality, demotion is much broader and associated with any reduction in a permanent accountability or responsibility. This is much more common in organizations and, whilst pay and status may remain unchanged, demand is reallocated from an individual even though the design of the role may expect it.

Summary

The talent management levers of buy, build, borrow, bind and bounce enable us to intervene in the flow of our workforce in, around, and out of our organization. These levers, the traditional territory of HR professionals, are all choices that impact our organizational churn.

Whilst most of us use the buy lever, we can do this much more effectively and in a planned way. We recognize that the buy lever is essential for our critical roles. The build lever is essential whenever we are bringing new capabilities into the organization. Where we are planning on a longer time horizon, build can allow us to create new capabilities much more effectively than other levers. Our understanding of workforce segmentation highlights the opportunities for the borrow lever, providing significant value for those capabilities that we do not require on a regular basis. Finally, the bind and bounce levers can fundamentally change the churn of the workforce and complement the remaining levers to deliver the workforce that we need.

> When you practise workforce planning, ask yourself:
> - Have I started with demand-optimization levers before now considering talent-management levers?
> - Am I using the most appropriate lever for this workforce segment?
> - Am I utilizing the benefits of multiple levers to create the best outcome?
> - Do any of these approaches necessitate revisiting demand optimization levers?

References

Abuelsamid, S (2019) Ford and Volkswagen partner on self-driving and electric vehicles, Forbes, 12 July, www.forbes.com/sites/samabuelsamid/2019/07/12/ford-volkswagen-and-argo-partner-on-autonomous-and-electric-vehicles/ (archived at https://perma.cc/VMY8-G6CE)

ADP Research Institute (2019) Revelations from workforce turnover, www.adp.com/-/media/ri/pdf/adp_predictingturnover_white_paper.pdf (archived at https://perma.cc/6ZLQ-JJ5D)

Aristotle (1980) *The Nicomachean Ethics*, Oxford University Press, Oxford

Åström, K J and Murray, R M (2008) *Feedback Systems: An introduction for scientists and engineers*, Princeton University Press, Oxford

Baker, M (2019) The latest Global Talent Monitor shows discretionary effort and intent to stay increased for the third consecutive quarter in 1Q19, *Gartner*, 12 June, www.gartner.com/smarterwithgartner/gartner-quarterly-update-on-global-workforce-trends/ (archived at https://perma.cc/8FVY-Y72A)

BBC (2020) Coronavirus: NHS volunteers to start receiving tasks, 7 April www.bbc.co.uk/news/uk-52196459 (archived at https://perma.cc/XMA7-PMFV)

Becker, B, Huselid, M and Beatty, D (2009) *The Differentiated Workforce*, Harvard Business Press, Boston

Bersin, J (2013) Employee retention now a big issue: Why the tide has turned [Blog] *LinkedIn*, 16 August, www.linkedin.com/pulse/20130816200159-131079-employee-retention-now-a-big-issue-why-the-tide-has-turned/ (archived at https://perma.cc/MWB8-ALU8)

Bidwell, M (2011) Paying more to get less: The effects of external hiring versus internal mobility, *Administrative Science Quarterly*, **56** (3), pp 369–407 doi.org/10.1177/0001839211433562 (archived at https://perma.cc/M273-HBBQ)

Blackden, R (2011) Standard & Poor's owner McGraw-Hill to split itself in two, *The Telegraph*, 12 September, www.telegraph.co.uk/finance/newsbysector/banksandfinance/8758711/Standard-and-Poors-owner-McGraw-Hill-to-split-itself-in-two.html (archived at https://perma.cc/4DTJ-C7X5)

Blumberg, M (2020) Interview by video, 22 April

Boudreau, J (2010) *Retooling HR: Using proven business tools to make better decisions about talent*, Harvard Business School Publishing, Boston

Boushey, H and Glynn, S J (2012) There are significant business costs to replacing employees, *Center for American Progress*, 16 November, www.americanprogress.org/wp-content/uploads/2012/11/CostofTurnover.pdf (archived at https://perma.cc/DX62-ZH8E)

Capita (2019) Human to hybrid: The next workforce frontier, 9 April, content.capitapeoplesolutions.co.uk/whitepapers/wp-human-to-hybrid (archived at https://perma.cc/SMC4-Z335)

Cappelli, P (2008) *Talent on Demand: Managing talent in an age of uncertainty*, Harvard Business School Publishing, Boston

Cascio, W F (2002) *Responsible Restructuring*, Berrett-Koehler, San Francisco

Chartered Institute of Personnel and Development (CIPD) (2018) *Labour market outlook: Summer 2018*, www.cipd.co.uk/Images/lmo-survey-summer2018_tcm18-45850.pdf (archived at https://perma.cc/RDE5-85SJ)

Chartered Management Institute (2019) *CMI Manifesto 2019*, November, www.managers.org.uk/~/media/Files/insight-policy/cmi-manifesto-2019.pdf (archived at https://perma.cc/EBR4-SM9U)

Collier, K (2019) *The Robot-Proof Recruiter*, Kogan Page, London

Cote, D (2013) Honeywell's CEO on how he avoided layoffs, *Harvard Business Review*, June, hbr.org/2013/06/honeywells-ceo-on-how-he-avoided-layoffs (archived at https://perma.cc/3NBH-RCWT)

DDI (2015) Global leadership forecast 2014/2015, www.ddiworld.com/research/global-leadership-forecast-2015 (archived at https://perma.cc/JW3Q-FMLU)

Deutsch, A L (2020) WhatsApp: The best Facebook purchase ever? Investopedia, 18 March, www.investopedia.com/articles/investing/032515/whatsapp-best-facebook-purchase-ever.asp (archived at https://perma.cc/UCZ9-TAYR)

Dickson, N (2018) We could ask junior doctors to give a certain number of years' service back to the NHS in return for £220,000 training, *The Telegraph*, 20 January, www.telegraph.co.uk/news/2018/01/20/could-ask-junior-doctors-give-certain-number-years-service-back/ (archived at https://perma.cc/X6CG-AVQP)

Dignan, A (2019) *Brave New Work*, Penguin, London

Dobson, J (2006) Enron: The collapse of corporate culture, in P H Dembinski *et al* (eds) *Enron and World Finance*, Palgrave Macmillan, London

Drucker, P F (1985) *The Effective Executive*, HarperCollins, New York

Drucker, P F (1989) Sell the mailroom, *The Wall Street Journal*, 25 July

Drucker, P F (2011) *Managing for the Future*, Routledge, Abingdon

Duckworth, A (2016) *Grit: The power of passion and perseverance*, Scribner, New York

Ebelle-ebanda, A (2020) Interview by video, 3 June

Filipkowski, J, Heinsch, M and Wiete, A (2018) *New Hire Momentum: Driving the onboarding experience*, Kronos, 23 January, www.kronos.com/resource/download/23166 (archived at https://perma.cc/2X6Y-H7L8)

Gelles, D (2014) Coke and McDonald's, growing together since 1955, *The New York Times*, 15 May, www.nytimes.com/2014/05/16/business/coke-and-mcdonalds-working-hand-in-hand-since-1955.html (archived at https://perma.cc/Y8EG-VG9F)

Gibson, A (2015) *A Mind for Business*, Pearson, Harlow

Halliwell, K (2020) Correspondence with author, 13 July

Jefferson, A and Pollock, R (2014) 70:20:10: Where is the evidence? [Blog] *Association for Talent Development*, 8 July, www.td.org/insights/70-20-10-where-is-the-evidence (archived at https://perma.cc/B2RC-CSZ5)

Johnson, B (2020) Thanks to everyone who has been staying at home, Twitter, 29 March, twitter.com/BorisJohnson/status/1244339182690066433 (archived at https://perma.cc/9KKV-DLXA)

Kahneman, D (2011) *Thinking, Fast and Slow*, Allen Lane, London

Kahneman, D and Tversky, A (1979) Prospect theory: An analysis of decision under risk, *Econometrica*, **47** (2), pp 183–214, doi:10.1017/cbo9780511609220.014

Kang, S-C, Morris, S S and Snell, S A (2003) Extending the human resource architecture: Relational archetypes and value creation, Center for Advanced Human Resource Studies, Working Paper 03 (13), Cornell University, Ithaca http://digitalcommons.ilr.cornell.edu/cahrswp/36 (archived at https://perma.cc/CT35-SA92)

Knight, P (2020) Correspondence with author, 13 July

Lawrence, M (2020) Interview by telephone, 3 April

Lepak, D P and Snell, S A (1999) The human resource architecture: Toward a theory of human capital allocation and development, *The Academy of Management Review*, **24** (1), pp 31–48, http://citeseerx.ist.psu.edu/viewdoc/download;jsessionid=D5C8E5DF0DD496B2AA84FE07F0196FD2?doi=10.1.1.469.8661&rep=rep1&type=pdf (archived at https://perma.cc/3HJP-F94F)

Lepak, D P and Snell, S A (2002) Examining the human resource architecture: The relationships among human capital, employment, and human resource configurations, *Journal of Management*, **28** (4), pp 517–43, doi.org/10.1177/014920630202800403 (archived at https://perma.cc/M7FC-5DFN)

Lombardo, M and Eichinger, R (1996) *Career Architect Development Planner*, Lominger, Minneapolis

Manyika, J et al (2016) Independent work: Choice, necessity and the gig economy, *McKinsey & Company*, 10 October, www.mckinsey.com/featured-insights/employment-and-growth/independent-work-choice-necessity-and-the-gig-economy (archived at https://perma.cc/P7YA-WMA3)

Marshall, A (1997) *Principles of Economics*, Prometheus Books, New York

Matthews, P (2014) *Capability at Work: How to solve the performance puzzle*, Three Faces Publishing, Milton Keynes

Morgan, C et al (2002) The impact of burnout on human physiology and on operational performance, *Yale Journal of Biology and Medicine*, **75** (2002), pp 199–205, www.ncbi.nlm.nih.gov/pmc/articles/PMC2588792/pdf/yjbm00008-0021.pdf (archived at https://perma.cc/3YB3-5QYT)

Mourdoukoutas, P and Roy, U (1994) Job rotation and public policy: Theory with applications to Japan and the USA, *International Journal of Manpower*, **15** (6), pp 57–71, doi.org/10.1108/01437729410065353 (archived at https://perma.cc/TK6Z-A8MW)

Murphy, M (2008) Don't expect layoff survivors to be grateful, Leadership IQ, 16 December, www.leadershipiq.com/blogs/leadershipiq/29062401-dont-expect-layoff-survivors-to-be-grateful (archived at https://perma.cc/PCL5-YFD9)

NHS England (2020) Former docs and nurses told 'Your NHS Needs You' to tackle greatest global health threat in history, 19 March, www.england.nhs.uk/2020/

03/former-docs-and-nurses-told-your-nhs-needs-you-to-tackle-greatest-global-health-threat-in-history/ (archived at https://perma.cc/5753-3V2D)

Office for National Statistics (2019) Public sector employment, UK: September 2019, 17 December, www.ons.gov.uk/employmentandlabourmarket/peopleinwork/publicsectorpersonnel/bulletins/publicsectoremployment/september2019 (archived at https://perma.cc/5N3G-JJDZ)

Open University (2019) Business barometer, July, http://www.open.ac.uk/business/Business-Barometer-2019 (archived at https://perma.cc/2554-SX94)

Peter, L J and Hull, R (2009) *The Peter Principle*, HarperBusiness, London

Polychronis, J (2018) Who said graduates don't get paid well? *Mail Online*, 13 March, www.dailymail.co.uk/news/article-5487043/ALDI-graduates-making-87K-nations-highest-starting-salary.html (archived at https://perma.cc/3KX8-VQN3)

Porter, K (2020) Interview by video with Kevin Porter, Director of PMP Recruitment's National Resource Centre, 7 July

Rogers, T and Saider, M (2014) *The Cost of Brain Drain*, Oxford Economics, resources.unum.co.uk/downloads/cost-brain-drain-report.pdf (archived at https://perma.cc/CS82-TAPW)

Rotter, J B (1966) Generalized expectancies for internal versus external control of reinforcement, *Psychological Monographs: General and Applied*, **80** (1), pp 1–28, doi:10.1037/h0092976

Rotter, J B (1975) Some problems and misconceptions related to the construct of internal versus external control of reinforcement, *Journal of Consulting and Clinical Psychology*, **43** (1), pp 56–67, doi:10.1037/h0076301

Rousseau, D M (1995) *Psychological Contracts in Organizations: Understanding written and unwritten agreements*, Sage Publications, London

Serapio, M G and Cascio, W F (1996) End-games in international alliances, *Academy of Management Executive*, **10** (1), pp 63–73, doi.org/10.5465/ame.1996.9603293209 (archived at https://perma.cc/4B5F-7MJZ)

Silver, C (2019) Empathy wins: Unlocking people performance and human potential by emotional awareness [speech], 19 November, HR Congress

Snell, A A, Shadur, M A and Wright, P M (2000) Human resources strategy: The era of our ways, Center for Advanced Human Resource Studies, Working Paper 00 (17), Cornell University, Ithaca, http://digitalcommons.ilr.cornell.edu/cahrswp/95 (archived at https://perma.cc/63F8-XMXN)

Solomon, L (2015) The top complaints from employees about their leaders, *Harvard Business Review*, 24 June, hbr.org/2015/06/the-top-complaints-from-employees-about-their-leaders? (archived at https://perma.cc/M8WG-6E6S)

Star Wars: Return of the Jedi (1983) [Film] Lucasfilm, USA

Stone, R D (2008) *Aligning Training for Results*, Pfeiffer, San Francisco

Sutherland, J (2015) *Scrum*, Penguin, London

Tetzeli, R (2016) Apple's Angela Ahrendts on what it takes to make change inside a successful business, *Fast Company Magazine*, February, p 63

Thomas, C W (2002) The rise and fall of Enron, *Journal of Accountancy*, April, pp 41–48, www.journalofaccountancy.com/issues/2002/apr/theriseandfallofenron.html (archived at https://perma.cc/9MSJ-2R6Q)

Ulrich, D (2020) Reimagining learning and development [webinar] 14 May, Hexa

Ulrich, D and Brockbank, W (2005) *The HR Value Proposition*, Harvard Business School Press, Boston

Upwork (2019) Freelancing in America 2019, www.upwork.com/i/freelancing-in-america/2019/ (archived at https://perma.cc/4JF4-J7UQ)

Von Nordenflycht, A (2010) What is a professional service firm? Toward a theory and taxonomy of knowledge-intensive firms, *Academy of Management Review*, 35 (1), pp 155–74, doi.org/10.5465/amr.35.1.zok155 (archived at https://perma.cc/TG25-45QQ)

Vroom, V H (1995) *Work and Motivation*, John Wiley & Sons, San Francisco

Walker, J W (1992) *Human Resource Strategy*, McGraw-Hill, New York

Wells, M (2018) Retail turnover rates in 2018, DailyPay, 17 December, www.dailypay.com/business-resources/employee-turnover-rates-in-retail (archived at https://perma.cc/V3PN-C62C)

World Economic Forum (WEF) (2019) *Towards a Reskilling Revolution*, http://www3.weforum.org/docs/WEF_Towards_a_Reskilling_Revolution.pdf (archived at https://perma.cc/T3MD-2HRS)

15

Creating the plan

Introduction

In essence, the workforce plan is a formula to change the future, or a number of possible futures, and create the right workforce. Once we have established the best combination of workforce levers and the most appropriate initiatives to execute those levers, we need to combine this into the plan. In this chapter we will cover the key steps to create a workforce plan.

Tasting the plan

In addition to providing a great example of kaizen (see Chapter 13), the programme *MasterChef* shares other sage advice. High amongst these is to taste the food during preparation and cooking. We are the chef of the workforce plan and, before we serve it, we need to conduct four key steps in order to ensure it tastes right: establishing the right risk, remodelling, ensuring strategic alignment, and providing options.

Establishing the right risk

In Chapter 10, we discussed how demand forecasting would allow us to establish the risk around primary drivers of demand, but not the secondary risks that result from execution. As a result, we established in Chapter 11 that the gap analysis did not extend to risk. It is when we taste the plan that we make decisions around risk.

In an organization with low maturity in workforce planning, the cost to bridge the gap between supply and demand is often greatest. There is no workforce that we cannot create to bridge the gap between supply and demand, but the less time we have, the greater the cost. In this vein, a first workforce plan could lay out a perfect approach to bridge the gap between supply and demand across all planning horizons, but the costs are likely to be prohibitive. The right risk for the organization is likely to become one of balancing: profitability versus growth, short term versus long term, and the whole organization versus the parts. These are business choices where I recommend the option that leads an organization closest to its *why*.

Remodelling

A common criticism from the judges on *MasterChef* is not the ability of a contestant to cater to those five basic tastes of sweet, salty, sour, bitter and umami. More likely, the contestant's error is to not taste the combination of flavours.

In the same way, each workforce lever generates effects that have additional effects. Some effective meso- and micro-level initiatives may get lost in a larger macro-level initiative. Moreover, when we pull multiple workforce levers, either simultaneously or in sequence, we compound the effects we are generating.

For example, imagine that the Acme Corporation wishes to reduce the size of the workforce by around 30 per cent. Their modelling of workforce supply has highlighted annual turnover of 16.335 per cent. This prompts them to shut an existing buy lever, recruitment, and allow turnover to reduce the workforce over a two-year period to 30 per cent of the current size. Our insight would be that such a plan at a macro level could be disastrous, as the organization may lose the capabilities it needs, so it may achieve the right size but it would be the wrong shape. Putting that liability to one side, this plan is unlikely to deliver the right size of workforce as it has failed to account for the second-order effects of these initiatives. As Nassim Nicholas Taleb famously puts it, 'Never cross a river if it is on average four feet deep' (Taleb, 2017); an average depth of four feet will mask points where the depth is six feet and we risk drowning. Similarly, an average turnover rate masks variable rates from different workforce segments, particularly new starters. A study of nearly a quarter of a million workers found that nearly 38 per cent of all turnover was attributable to those leaving within their first year, and over 17 per cent to those leaving in their second year (Mahan *et al*,

2020). Assuming a similar trend to the marketplace, then the lack of recruitment in the two years of the plan would deprive Acme Corporation of this high-turnover workforce. This gives an adjusted turnover figure of around 10 per cent in year one and just over 7 per cent in year two. This would result in them shedding just less than 17 per cent of the workforce, rather than the target of 30 per cent.

It is critical, therefore, that we remodel our supply and demand to account for the compounding effects of the initiatives within our action plan. Revisiting the steps in Parts Three to Five of this book enables us to see the true extent of each initiative as the cumulative effects close the gap. Change initiatives often fail because the contributing factors to benefit realization have not been understood fully (Bartlett, 2002).

Ensuring strategic alignment

Following the discussions of strategic alignment in Chapters 5 and 13, we revisit this golden thread of workforce planning again as we conclude our planning to ensure that our own plans are aligned within the strategic framework, illustrated in Figure 5.2.

Our plans form part of the execution level within the framework: the business-as-usual (BAU) activities and ad-hoc initiatives that will create the right workforce to achieve the desired business outcomes. Whilst the formulation of the strategic framework begins with a *why* and cascades down to execution, we ensure alignment of plans by starting at the execution level and reaching back up towards the *why*. The first stage, therefore, is to ensure alignment at the execution level. Not only must the plans fit within the operating model of the organization, but they also need to complement the way that work is done. Though this can be shaped through the balance lever, initiatives are unlikely to be successful if they jar against wider execution.

The next stage is alignment with strategy, the first of these being the workforce strategy, the blueprint or design for our people to accomplish our organizational strategy. Utilization of the balance lever will provide the assurance that the workforce strategy is aligned to the organizational strategy. Once that alignment exists, our check is twofold: first, that nothing within the plan sits contrary to the strategy and, second, that all facets of the strategy are achieved through the workforce plan. For example, there may be a strategy to reduce the use of contingent labour. Modelling may indicate that the seven rights cannot be achieved whilst maintaining this position as the cost to create the capability through other levers is too high within the timeframe. Therefore, with high levels of maturity, this stage can serve as a feedback loop back into the chief human resources officer and an adjustment of the strategy. The second element of the strategic check is alignment with the appropriate meso-level strategies and the organization's macro-level strategy. The workforce plans need to both complement at the meso level and deliver at the macro level.

The third stage is a check against the goals, the broad aims to be achieved, and the objectives – those goals framed in specific metrics to measure achievement within a timeline. The workforce plan must contribute to the achievement of the goals and objectives that are within the planning horizon. This element is key in gaining support and funding to implement our workforce levers as we are creating a workforce to achieve the organizational strategic objectives. Therefore, it is essential that we are able to articulate how these changes to the workforce will contribute to the success of the organization. The next stage is a check alignment to the mission and the *why* of the organization. Not only must the plan align fully to what the organization does, but it also needs to be attuned to the spirit of the organization's why.

In Figure 15.1 we can see an example of this in practice with a business strategy of reduced costs and the delivery of better services that are aligned to the business goal to improve customer outcomes. Better services will create a better experience for customers and reduced costs, if passed through, will improve the outcome for the customer.

The workforce strategy is similarly aligned to the business strategy:

- Increasing retention can lead to a direct reduction in the turnover costs we discussed in the last chapter.
- Reducing contractor use would be expected to lead to a direct reduction in costs as contingent labour typically incurs a higher rate of operating expense than a permanent workforce.
- Improving diversity can provide two improvements to customer outcomes. For many services, a customer-facing team that better reflects the diversity of the consumer base will not only improve the brand of the organization but is more likely to create a stronger connection with the customers (Herman, 2010). Secondly, services are more likely to provide the best value to a diverse customer base if there is diversity of thought during the design. Rather than tweaking the service, the design can fundamentally reflect the diverse needs and lived experience of different

sections of the population. As Simon Fanshawe says, 'it's not about adding spice to the stew, it's about changing the recipe' (Fanshawe, 2020).

If we look at the level of the workforce plans within Figure 15.1, we see how each of these contributes to the workforce strategy, in turn contributing to the business strategy and the achievement of business goals. At the lowest level, a balance initiative of process improvement not only increases retention as fewer people leave through frustration with poor processes, but this same improvement enables automation. Through reducing demand, automation allows an organization to reduce its workforce supply, potentially in its use of contractors; similarly, a reduction in repetitive and lower-value

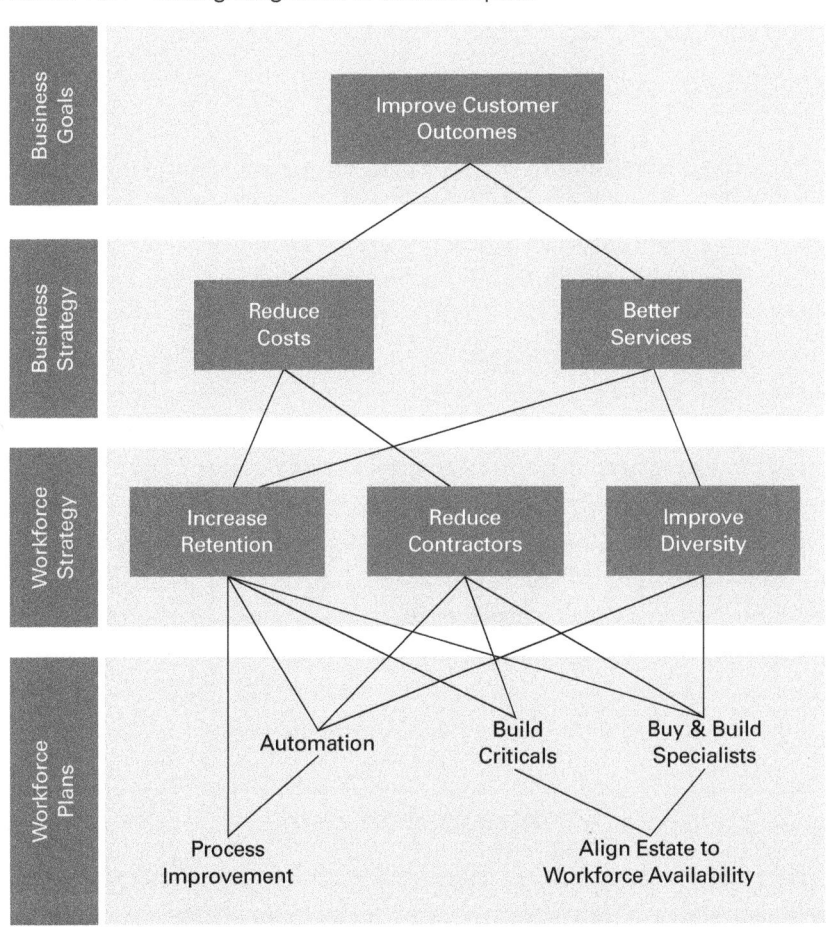

FIGURE 15.1 Strategic alignment of workforce plans

work within a role, resulting from automation, can increase retention. Finally, automation changes the environment of the workplace and can augment roles in a way that allows a different mix of capabilities to be utilized, which can be provided by a more diverse workforce. In the same way, we see that by starting with a balanced approach that aligns the organizational estate to the available workforce, we can build critical capability, and both buy and subsequently build specialist capability. By building criticals we can not only take the vital step of reducing contractor usage in our critical roles, but we can also increase retention within this segment of the workforce. Equally, if we start to buy and build our own specialists, we can tap into a more diverse talent pool rather than relying on the existing talent pools. This not only increases retention in this workforce segment, it also means we can reduce contractor usage in that segment as well. Just five initiatives align into the workforce and business strategies to contribute directly to the CEO's priority to improve customer outcomes.

Providing options

In organizations of high maturity in workforce planning, the plan may stand clearly as the approach to be taken. As we grow towards this maturity, there is a likelihood that stakeholders will want options, mainly to help manage risk and budgets. Some may hold a *confirmation bias* and be more likely to favour ideas that support their existing views and discount evidence that is contrary to their experience (Nickerson, 1998). They may view workforce planning as a risk, hence the importance of the stakeholder interaction we cover in detail within Chapters 7 and 11. Providing options that allow them to make a determination on risk can ameliorate this issue.

The second reason for needing options is to overcome budgetary conflict. Arguably the most obvious challenge to implementing workforce plans is that they make the costs of the workforce clear. As we discussed in Chapter 9, budgets are created on a different basis and may not align to the demand expectations of the organization. Therefore, it can be helpful to present an option that falls within the budgetary constraints and articulates the shortfall that will create in the gap between supply and demand.

Aspects of the plan

Once we have tasted the plan and ensured it is right for the audience, the next step is to consider what needs to be included within the workforce plan. For a workforce plan to be effective, there are a number of key aspects for us to include.

Articulating the baseline

It is vital that the workforce plan begins by articulating the key elements from our baseline of the organization. Many stakeholders will have primary accountabilities at the meso level, so providing a macro-level understanding will provide an essential context for them. Chief amongst these contextual elements are the scenarios and time horizon that we are planning within; just like telling a story, we need to set up the background to the narrative. An important inclusion for the scenarios is specific direction that has been provided, perhaps by the executive board or the chief human resources officer. This provides authority to the foundations of the plan.

Outcomes and timelines

Using the cost–benefit analysis (CBA), it is valuable to highlight early the high-level outcomes that result from the plan and to articulate all outcomes alongside the timelines. By not framing a timeline, many stakeholders can be left with an assumption that benefit realization is imminent; this unrealistic expectation can generate unfair criticism that plans are not working. Leave stakeholders with a clear understanding of what outcomes will be achieved and when.

Describing the journey

When formal orders are given in the army, a key final stage is the summary of execution. This is the point where the commander breaks down the entire mission as a story, detailing the move out from the current location, the action on target, and any subsequent onward movement. The quality of this summary is critical: poor orders can be recovered through a great summary and comprehensive orders can be lost through a poor summary. The summary satisfies necessary elements for those involved, explaining important details that may have been lost in the more formal briefing, allowing for mental and physical preparation, and enabling them to track the progress of the operation and avoid any surprises for those involved.

These same elements remain true for describing a workforce plan. It needs to speak to senior stakeholders to enable them to understand the plan and also provide sufficient detail for people to execute the plan. Workforce plans deal in the realm of change, which can be stressful for those involved and impacted; the clear description can enable people to prepare themselves to safeguard their well-being. As workforce planning practitioners, we will be experts on our own plan. Other stakeholders may not be in receipt of the detailed progress of that plan; therefore, the summary makes it far more accessible for people to understand the events they will see that will allow them to understand that progress is being made as intended. The final, and arguably most vital, aspect is that it avoids any surprises. The effective execution of great plans can quite easily be derailed by a senior stakeholder who is surprised by the impact of change. Unless it has been articulated clearly, a sudden change in the metrics of a stakeholder's HR dashboard can result in the programme grinding to a halt and additional work to allay the concerns that something is going wrong. Take the time to describe, both in writing and verbally, the journey that stakeholders are about to undertake.

Assigning responsibility

In Chapter 7 we discussed how decisions are made, utilizing Bain & Company's RAPID® approach (Bain & Company, 2011). Once a decision is made to proceed with the action plan, execution must be supported by responsibility assignment. It is equally important that we provide clarity on the responsibilities in relation to executing each of the initiatives of the plan. We can do this using a RACI matrix, the most common responsibility assignment model, detailing those who are:

- Responsible – who will execute the task?
- Accountable – who is overseeing the work and has to ensure execution is completed?
- Consulted – those who can provide expertise in the event of a deviation.
- Informed – those updated on progress, either on a routine basis or on completion of the task.

When it comes to specific initiatives then, as we discussed in Chapter 12, it is prudent to ensure those accountable and responsible are those with the greatest incentive for its success. It is wise for us, or an element of the workforce planning function, to be recorded as consulted on each of these, rather than informed, to ensure a two-way conversation is maintained.

The plan of plans

The idea that workforce planning results in a singular plan, a glossy publication, has perhaps been one of the more damaging concepts to the craft. Instead, the more effective workforce plans are a combination of plans; we will walk through the most common plans within this plan of plans.

Demand management

Just as demand optimization levers are the first port of call for workforce planning, so too the demand management plan is a vital document to ensure that capability and capacity gains are not frittered away on uncontrolled demand. The demand management plan, which we discussed in Chapter 13, will articulate the enduring elements from our balance lever to ensure that demand fluctuation remain within expected tolerance levels. This will see approaches to either smoothen spikes in demand or to respond with increased capacity, including determination of the time fences (see Figure 13.2). The plan will also identify the upstream signals that will indicate increases in demand that fall outside these tolerance levels and indicate clearly the necessary steps to manage that demand so that the organization deviates from its strategic objectives.

Recruitment and procurement

The recruitment and procurement plan articulates the ongoing plan to buy and borrow capability over the duration of the planning horizon. Over longer horizons, this plan may well articulate just the broad numbers and capability types. Over shorter horizons, it will provide a much more detailed view of the specific roles to be bought or borrowed and when they are needed. Given the necessary lead-in time required for these activities, particularly permanent recruitment, it is important that this too is guided by time fences.

Redeployment and promotion

The recruitment and procurement plan is complemented by the redeployment and promotion plan, which details the lateral and vertical movement of our workforce around the organization. Where we utilize formalized processes either in redeployment or promotion, the plan will detail the approach, criteria and timelines that are forecast for these.

Learning and development

Some organizations may find it unusual to consider learning and development as business-as-usual activity. However, not only will the learning and development plan articulate the onboarding requirement for the new workforce, it will also detail the plan for upskilling the existing workforce, including support to the redeployment and promotion of our people. Following stretching analysis of its future capability requirements, Lloyds Banking Group implemented an enterprise-wide learning and development plan to both upskill the workforce and begin to create a powerful culture of continuous learning (Papworth and Scott, 2019).

Change projects

The most common element of the workforce plan is the range of ad-hoc initiatives that will help deliver the right workforce. Unlike the plans we have already discussed that will form part of an ongoing portfolio of work for a specific function or business area, these ad-hoc initiatives will launch as a range of projects and programmes. As a result, the workforce plans are likely to articulate the high-level costs, benefits, timelines and accountabilities. These can then reference more detailed programme and project plans that, though run separately, still form part of the overall workforce plan.

Contingency

Contingency plans are an important inclusion within the workforce plan as it details the activities related to impacts to supply and demand forecasts that fall outside the planned tolerances. Separate areas of business and workforce activity are likely to have different contingency plans, which will have further distinction based upon different time fences. It is worth noting that a key element of these contingency plans is to articulate the circumstances for halting activity before the first of our time fences. The contingency plans will articulate clearly three elements: the decisions that can be taken by an organization; what will signal disruptions to supply or demand; and the effects that each of these decisions will create.

The contingency plan may also detail where there are opportunities or risks that present themselves outside the tolerance levels but within a manageable range. This will be discussed further in the next chapter.

Summary

This chapter has focused on pulling the last two chapters together to create our workforce plan. It is more than simply an articulation of decisions, but a 'commitment of resources' (Rosenhead et al, 1990). Done well, these plans succeed in 'specifying what behaviours are expected of particular units and individuals in order to realize strategy' (Mintzberg, 1994). Crafting these plans in the right way is, therefore, a critical success factor in the strategic success of the organization. In traditional workforce planning, we would smile at our success and pat ourselves on the back at our achievement. In agile workforce planning, we recognize that the plan is a success factor, not success in itself; next we must deliver the plan.

When you practise workforce planning, ask yourself:

- Does the plan align to the strategic framework and balance benefit against risk?
- Have I examined the plan in a holistic way to ensure that any stacked effects are remodelled?
- Do I need to provide options?
- Have I articulated all the necessary aspects of the plan?
- Which elements will form my plan of plans?

References

Bain & Company (2011) RAPID®: Bain's tool to clarify decision accountability, 11 August, www.bain.com/insights/rapid-tool-to-clarify-decision-accountability (archived at https://perma.cc/PE4E-SGFN)

Bartlett, J (2002) *Managing Programmes of Business Change: A handbook of the principles of programme management*, Project Manager Today, Sutton

Fanshawe, S (2020) Interview by video, 3 June

Herman, R P (2010) *The HIP Investor: Make bigger profits by building a better world*, John Wiley & Sons, San Francisco

Mahan, T F et al (2020) *2020 Retention Report: Trends, reasons and wake-up call*, Work Institute, http://info.workinstitute.com/en/retention-report-2020 (archived at https://perma.cc/2XJX-V4VL)

Mintzberg, H (1994) *The Rise and Fall of Strategic Planning*, The Free Press, New York

Nickerson, R S (1998) Confirmation bias: A ubiquitous phenomenon in many guises, *Review of General Psychology*, **2** (2), pp 175–220, doi:10.1037/1089-2680.2.2.175

Papworth, A and Scott, S (2019) Workforce planning at scale at Lloyds Banking Group, *People and Strategy*, **42** (4), pp 10–11, www.thefreelibrary.com/Workforce+Planning+at+Scale+at+Lloyds+Banking+Group.-a0604847446 (archived at https://perma.cc/8S2N-DVAC)

Rosenhead, J, Elton, M and Gupta, S K (1990) Robustness and optimality as criteria for strategic decisions, in R G Dyson (ed) *Strategic Planning: Models and analytical techniques*, John Wiley & Sons, Chichester

Taleb, N N (2017) Medium: The logic of risk taking [Blog] 25 August, nassimtaleb.org/2017/08/medium-logic-risk-taking/ (archived at https://perma.cc/FPV4-92X6)

PART SEVEN

Deliver

How do we execute a successful workforce plan that delivers?

16

Implementing the plan

Introduction

Hollywood provides scant examples of well-executed plans. The world of fiction would have us believe that planning is wholly unnecessary in the achievement of success. Indeed, if a story has a scene where the plan is revealed in advance of execution, then we can be certain that something will go wrong. In the arc of storytelling, heroism necessitates adversity; often there is faulty intelligence, or the villain has outwitted the protagonist, possibly through taking a relative hostage. We know this because there is no reward for the reader or viewer to tell the same story twice, first as a plan and subsequently as execution. That is why the only cinematic device to allow this is where we hear the narration of the plan whilst we watch its execution.

In the real world, successful execution relies on great planning, just as a plan relies on great execution to be successful. In this chapter we will cover the key elements that will enable us to implement the plan to deliver the right workforce for our organization.

> The question that faces the strategic decision maker is not what his organization should do tomorrow. It is, what do we have to do today to be ready for an uncertain tomorrow? (Drucker, 1973)

Managing a living plan

Unlike more traditional approaches to workforce planning, we are now executing a living plan that must remain both flexible and antifragile in a VUCA world. This means that, whilst specific projects will be initiated and concluded to deliver incremental moves toward the right workforce, the workforce plan requires management for the duration of the planning horizon.

Communication

It is important to remember that the workforce plan is the vehicle for delivering the right workforce; it is not the sole means of communicating elements of the plan. In Chapter 7 we discussed how to map and engage with the various stakeholder groups within our organizations. At this stage, we must now communicate the plan to these same stakeholder groups. As before, the key to this is the stakeholder mix in relation to their power and interest. Our first priority is to those stakeholders of high interest and high power: the promoters and detractors. We need to communicate the plan so that we can ameliorate detractors and aim to convert them towards promotion. If the collective power of detractors outweighs that of the promoters following this communication, I strongly recommend extending communication towards latents to build a greater number of promoters.

The next areas to consider are those of high interest and low power: the defenders and attackers. Communicate clearly with the defenders but consider clearly the aim of communicating with attackers. Often, I have seen effort wasted and antagonism raised by simply transmitting a *fait accompli* to this group. The aim is to convert them to being defenders or move them towards apathy. To achieve the former, we must listen to and acknowledge the concerns and grievances that are fuelling their resistance to this change. Then we must focus on creating a solution. The solution may be that there are facets to execution that, though they lack material impact on the plan, can be meaningful to that cohort. If such accommodations cannot be made, then moving them towards apathy is often the best solution. One of the challenges of the plurality of perspectives on workforce planning is that it can it evoke strong emotions. Staff groups may well see workforce planning as an approach to reduce their power or, worse, to initiate layoffs. Providing the plan will not reduce their power or initiate layoffs, and it is beneficial to clarify that. As they are likely to be generally resistant to change, it is vital to focus on the elements that will not change. Reinforcement of the areas where the workforce plan is simply supporting the continuation of the current state can often quickly ameliorate negativity and convert it to apathy.

A final and important element is to consider how those perspectives may change throughout the execution of the workforce plan. Whilst we prioritize maintaining existing levels of support, we cannot lose sight of those latents and apathetics who may develop interest as reality bites. Whilst we execute, we must be conscious of the workforce segments and stakeholder groups who will start to go through change. Though change management and communication steps will be built into individual initiatives, it is important that we workforce planning practitioners take additional steps in advance to prepare these groups accordingly. Moreover, it is vital that we utilize those promoters and defenders with the highest levels of interest to create a 'guiding coalition' (Kotter, 1995) to create and maintain advocacy throughout the execution.

Managing quality

Whilst the workforce plan will be comprehensive, it is not expected that implementation of the plan is dependent upon the completion of detailed planning at the lowest level. When we execute the plan, we should expect that work packages within projects will still require more detailed planning as part of the overall workforce plan. As we discussed in Chapter 15, the accountability for this will sit with those with the greatest capability and incentive. At an initiative level, they will be accountable for the more detailed planning and execution.

As this is done by project and BAU teams, we need to ensure that the governance is in place to maintain quality. Each initiative is a dependency of the plan; this means initiatives need to be executed successfully and realize the expected benefits for the workforce plan to achieve the seven rights. Moreover, certain initiatives may be dependencies of other initiatives. For example, an initiative to implement a new learning management system (LMS) may be a key dependency of upskilling the workforce. Unless the LMS is implemented to the right level of quality, we will be unable to upskill the workforce to achieve the seven rights. When we talk about quality in this context, we are talking about the balance of three key constraints on the initiative: scope, time and cost. The first constraint is the scope of the initiative, which is the work needed to be done to create the expected effect and benefits. Next, there will be specified timeframes around the creation of effects and benefits. Taking an agile approach, we will be looking to create a minimum viable product for many of our initiatives to begin early accrual of benefits and allow us to test the initiative. Though this means that the scope will be phased, this should not be confused with scope creep. With scope creep, the constraints are exceeded in such a way that it impacts both our timelines and the final constraint, cost. Each initiative will be costed in such a way that not only does the project have a budget to deliver the expected benefits, but it also safeguards the return on investment. Increased costs and delayed benefits can result from both scope creep and impacts on the assumptions, which we will discuss shortly. As a result, we must ensure that we have sufficient monitoring in place to manage the quality of these initiatives. Though this is important with specific projects, it is equally important for BAU activities that often run independently. These must be controlled within the same governance to ensure that quality is maintained throughout the planning horizon as these are all dependencies on creating the right workforce. In creating these plans it is important to have a tight handle on monitoring and realistic expectations of delivery. Charlotte Brownlee, the former head of workforce planning at Public Health England, said, 'The maturity journey looks very different in different organizations'. She recognized that a small gain could not only make a significant difference to the workforce, but it could also build rapidly the advocacy of stakeholders (Brownlee, 2020).

Managing risks and assumptions

Risks and assumptions are linked concepts: risks are those events we hope will not take place and assumptions are those things we expect to happen. Risk is concerned with two things: the potential impact of a negative event and the likelihood of that event taking place. As potential and likelihood are both future-focused concepts, our assessment of risk is an assumption: we assume a level of potential impact and a likelihood of occurrence. Therefore, for our purposes, I shall take us back to assumptions. Our assumptions are those things we have accepted as true, based on our analyses and forecasts, and have influenced our plan. These assumptions create two types of risk: explicit and implicit. Explicit risks are those that are stated as a result of an assumption. For example, we may assume that the impact of industrial action by our workforce may be high, though we assume the likelihood of that to be low. In an explicit risk, the assumption forms the basis of the risk. Implicit risks are those that result from assumptions within our plan. For example, we may assume a voluntary turnover rate of 14 per cent during our planning horizon and have created a workforce plan on that basis. As a result, there is a risk that our assumption does not transpire. Our assumption of a turnover rate carries a risk that the turnover rate will be different. The likelihood of that risk will depend on our confidence in the forecast.

Clearly, we would want a high level of confidence and a low level of likelihood; what matters is that we record it accurately. The impact of the risk will depend on the variance; a turnover rate higher than expected will incur the costs we discussed in Chapter 14 and discussion of the bind lever. Conversely, a turnover rate that is too low will not only increase the cost of the workforce but may also impact our ability to bring in new capabilities.

With each of these risks we must consider the following: ownership, tolerance, indicators and proximity. Ownership comes down to responsibilities and accountabilities, identifying the most appropriate individual to manage the risk and their chain of accountability. This chain is supported by tolerance, where we determine in advance the tolerance thresholds within which the likelihood and impact may move before it must be reported, and the ownership moved up a level. The indicators are those data points that will support or counter the original assumption. For our assumption on turnover, the indicators are the monthly turnover data that will indicate whether we are on target or tracking at a higher or lower rate. The proximity, therefore, is twofold: the proximity of the indicator and of the impact. We need to establish the point where we will be clearer on the validity of our assumptions and the lead time we have to implement any additional mitigations in the event of deviation. I recommend strongly that we, as workforce planning professionals, are at least responsible for managing these risks, if not accountable.

Information flow

In some organizations there is a thirst for information; in other organizations the opposite is true. Regardless of the maturity of workforce planning within our organizations, it is valuable to consider information flow in terms of the following: reporting, escalation and feedback loops.

REPORTING

Reporting is a routine flow of updated information to stakeholders and typically executed in one of two approaches: highlight and milestone reports. Highlight reports are the most common form of reporting that we see within organizations, and provide a regular update on the status of performance against the plan. Those from a project management background may be tempted to become internally focused and become the purveyor of the team's progress. Instead, focus on the progress of the workforce and update how the workforce is evolving in relation to the plan. This will draw upon updates to the data sets that we have collected throughout the planning cycle. I would recommend is Scott Berinato's book *Good Charts* (2016), which is packed full of tips on visualization to help present this data to our stakeholders. The highlight report is likely to serve multiple stakeholders where it is unfeasible for us to present it with an accompanying verbal narrative. Utilizing HR and finance business partners, particularly in larger organizations, can reap dividends in them cascading this information directly to their own stakeholders. As we provide them with the relevant information that enables their work, they will cascade the highlight report and present the progress of the workforce to their own stakeholders.

Whilst highlight reports must be focused on the workforce, milestone reports are the opportunity to update on the specific achievements of those involved. Milestones are significant points within execution, for example the conclusion of specific projects or significant work packages, which are agreed in advance. This is likely to be presented directly to a group of key stakeholders verbally, alongside a visual accompaniment. Whilst the initiator is the programme milestone, remember to frame this around the workforce. Draw upon the lessons about storytelling that we covered in Chapter 11 in order to embed the key messages for our stakeholders.

ESCALATION

Whereas the schedule for reporting is agreed in advance, escalation is an event-driven activity. Reporting is aimed at informing and maintaining support and confidence. Escalation is focused on initiating action from stakeholders. Within project management circles there is a similar practice of reporting by exception; however, this activity is still framed around reporting rather than seeking action. As a result, we draw a clear distinction between the two. We escalate when risks and issues fall outside tolerance levels that have been agreed in advance. As a result, we must be clear on the actions that need to be taken and our recommendations for action.

FEEDBACK LOOPS

Just as important as the information we pass to stakeholders is the information we receive back. All action results in feedback; as we discussed in Chapter 14, even the absence of direct feedback is, itself, feedback. Feedback is what allows us to see the impact of our actions; in a closed system, like the flick of a light switch, the presence of light highlights our success. In open systems, like the workplace, the feedback may be less obvious. This is amplified by the greater need for feedback that results from an agile approach.

If we have launched an initiative in the hope of improving it, but are not obtaining feedback, we are 'playing golf in the dark' (Syed, 2016). To combat this, we must prioritize two key areas. The first is the proactive pursuit of feedback from stakeholders. With senior stakeholders, utilize the reporting mechanism to solicit feedback. For those stakeholders with less influence and power, consider engaging in employee listening. The second area to prioritize is the identification of error signals. The check engine light in our motor vehicles is the ubiquitous example of an error signal, an indicator within a system that indicates a fault. Look carefully at our workforce metrics and identify what changes would indicate an error signal for the initiatives within the workforce plan.

Embedding the process

Author on leadership and former US Navy SEAL commander, Jocko Willink, admits that 'early in my career as a SEAL officer, there was a time when I felt that... planning was needless and burdensome... But I was wrong. Establishing an effective and repeatable planning process is critical to the success of any team' (Willink and Babin, 2015). To deliver the seven rights, we must embed our agile workforce planning process as part of the normal business rhythm. To do that, we must deliver in line with our agile principles, to which these next activities are aligned: iterating the plan and workforce challenge sprints.

Iterating the plan

In order to iterate, our plan must be built in a way that retains flexibility. Without flexibility, we are treating our assumptions as fact and our forecasts as prophecy. Indeed, as we discussed in our third chapter, it is the rigidity of more traditional workforce planning approaches that has damaged the perspective on our craft. To iterate effectively requires commitment to learn from and respond to the qualitative and quantitative feedback that we receive during the execution of the plan. This is where, when sailing to our destination, we adjust the sails and the rudder as the winds change and the waves strike. It is wise to agree the tolerances for iteration in advance of execution. Tolerance for change allows us to keep a constant hand on the tiller and respond immediately to keep the organization moving in the right direction. Without these tolerances, any deviations in our assumptions that necessitate change will require escalation and delay execution. As maturity in workforce planning grows, such tolerances are likely to extend.

As we do this, we must ensure that we have clear change controls in place. For the BAU activities, it is helpful to enable a range of deviation to be able to adjust these plans in real time in accordance with the time fences. This means that we can avoid having to recast the entire plan with such regularity.

Workforce challenge sprints

As we execute our first workforce plan, opportunities begin to present themselves. Our focus on a specific workforce segment may highlight wider issues. Our agile workforce planning approach enables us to solve these problems on an incremental basis, in line with our agile principles. The most effective approach I have found is the use of workforce challenge sprints, boxed periods of time to apply the scientific method to solve problems on an incremental basis. There are two variations of workforce challenge sprint that we can launch: issue-focused or lever-focused.

ISSUE-FOCUSED SPRINTS

Issue-focused sprints are centred on causal analysis, which we covered in Chapter 6, where we have identified an issue within the workforce and are seeking to identify the cause. For example, our workforce plan may have included pulling a bind lever for our critical roles, which is successfully achieving our goal to reduce turnover by 5 per cent. However, our feedback may highlight a difference in the levels of outcome depending on length of service. Perhaps those with lower lengths of service have experienced a much greater increase in retention than those with much greater tenure within the organization.

Our first step is to define the problem; in this case, our initiative is not having the desired effect on a specific workforce segment. The next stage is to hypothesize on a cause. Do we think an initiative has been communicated less well to a particular segment, or perhaps we may consider that something about the initiative has been less appealing? We must now test this hypothesis through analysis. A common mistake is to begin searching through existing workforce data. Instead, we ask ourselves what information we would need to solve the problem. Ideally, we have that information available; if not, we must consider if there is an available heuristic. We might have a hypothesis that a bind lever might have a tax implication based on pension levels. Though we might not have that information available, we may be able to make assumptions based on salary levels and ages and use that as a heuristic for pension data. With our analysis identifying a causal relationship, we now have clarity on a new baseline. With this, we can execute the agile workforce planning cycle again to adjust the forecasts of supply and demand, creating a new gap analysis against which we can action plan and deliver. This aligns with the 'probe first, then sense, and then respond' approach from the Cynefin framework that we covered in Chapter 4 (Snowden and Boone, 2007).

LEVER-FOCUSED SPRINTS

Even in the 15th century and Vasco da Gama's expedition, citrus fruits had been widely purported to be a cure for scurvy, a disease that particularly afflicted sailors. This was an issue with a hypothesis of a cure, which was not proven until Scottish doctor, James Lind, conducted the first ever clinical trials in 1747 (Lind, 1753). In a lever-focused sprint, we are focused on testing the causal relationship between a specific initiative and the workforce. Once we have successfully implemented our workforce plan, we may find that a lever pulled for one workforce segment could also be pulled for a wider element of the workforce. Indeed, it is unsurprising that stakeholders may wish to increase the return on an investment in a particular initiative by increasing the scale and rolling it out to a wider audience. In the Cynefin framework, this is the 'sense–analyse–respond' (Snowden and Boone, 2007).

Again, we take a similar approach to before by first defining the problem statement. To do this, we must return to our stakeholder with a *why* question. We must establish what business problem we aim to solve through applying this solution to a different workforce segment. This is a vital first step to avoid spending resources and increasing costs to fix things that are not broken. Once we have the problem clear, our hypothesis is that our existing initiative will solve that problem. In Chapter 11, we highlighted that **gaps exist only in the future**. Therefore, our hypothesis will be that our initiative solves a future problem (either a new problem, or one that endures from today), and so we must conduct our analysis in two stages. First, we execute the agile workforce planning cycle to create a baseline of this new workforce segment and forecasting supply and demand to create a gap analysis. We then test that gap analysis against the problem statement to provide the evidential basis for the problem. In the next stage, we apply a suggested solution within an action planning phase to test whether that solves the problem. If our analysis successfully tests the problem and hypothesis, we can add this into the plan and deliver the solution.

Summary

In Chapter 4 we highlighted the principles of agile workforce planning; amongst those is one often absent from traditional workforce planning: *it's about the workforce*. I will reiterate that **the aim of workforce planning is not to create a workforce plan, the aim of workforce planning is to create the right workforce**. Without delivery, a plan is just an idea, a hypothesis that has meant workforce planning has been viewed by many as a purely academic exercise. Success is taking that workforce plan, the culmination of analysis and problem solving, and executing it effectively to deliver the workforce that the organization needs. That is what enables us to demonstrate the value of the workforce planning process.

When you practise workforce planning, ask yourself:

- What is the best way for me to communicate the plan to stakeholder groups?
- Do I have the right governance in place to ensure I can manage the quality of delivery?
- Am I accurately tracking my risks and assumptions?
- Have I enabled the flow of information into and outwith the workforce planning team?
- What are the opportunities for me to integrate the workforce plan and incrementally solve workforce problems?

References

Berinato, S (2016) *Good Charts*, Harvard Business Review Press, Boston
Brownlee, C (2020) Interview by telephone, 11 May
Drucker, P F (1973) *Management: Tasks, responsibilities, practices*, Harper & Row, London

Kotter, J P (1995) Leading change: Why transformation efforts fail, *Harvard Business Review*, **73**, pp 259–67, hbr.org/1995/05/leading-change-why-transformation-efforts-fail-2 (archived at https://perma.cc/NED5-KPKZ)

Lind, J (1753) *A Treatise of the Scurvy*, Sands, Murray and Cochran, Edinburgh

Snowden, D J and Boone, M E (2007) A leader's framework for decision making, *Harvard Business Review*, November, hbr.org/2007/11/a-leaders-framework-for-decision-making (archived at https://perma.cc/LRY8-C28F)

Syed, M (2016) *Black Box Thinking*, John Murray, London

Willink, J and Babin, L (2015) *Extreme Ownership: How US Navy SEALS lead and win*, St Martin's Press, New York

PART EIGHT

Conclusion

How do we make this work?

17

Becoming a workforce planning professional

I love agile workforce planning as it enables organizations to create the best-quality work that will enable its success. Successful organizations with meaningful work create prosperity for the workforce. It is prosperity that can lift people out of poverty, change lives and provide a sense of purpose and value that is vital to our mental and physical well-being. When we think about work and workforce in a different way, we can draw upon those people and communities that have been historically underrepresented. As we create a diverse and inclusive workforce, we create a better society. Connecting engaged people with meaningful work – that is why agile workforce planning matters.

I started this book by introducing workforce planning, its history and both its benefits and limitations. I hoped to both explain the value of workforce planning and my passion for the craft, whilst also presenting the case for change to a more agile approach. We have subsequently progressed through each of the six stages of the agile workforce planning methodology: baseline, supply, demand, gap analysis, action plan and deliver. That journey has allowed us to better understand our organization and the context within which it operates. We have learnt how to both calculate and forecast supply and demand, and then to analyse the gap between the two. Armed with this knowledge we now know how we can collaborate in a team of teams across the organization to create effective action plans, and then we have seen how these can be delivered. Throughout the book, we have developed our understanding of how to engage stakeholders to make them advocates of agile workforce planning; defenders and promoters of each of us as we deliver the workforce of the future. And as we deliver, as we execute the workforce plan, we begin the cycle again. We iterate, adjusting the plan to respond to the latest insights and changes within the marketplace and our workforce. We incrementally solve the problems of the organization as they present themselves, looking for opportunities to support additional segments of the workforce and create greater value. We look to the next planning horizon, further into the future, to support the infinite possibilities of our organization.

I wish you well on what will be a rewarding and challenging journey that will enable you to make a difference to your organization and, in doing so, improve the lives of your workforce and all the many people they touch. It will require inner resilience and, through applying this methodology, will make you antifragile; each experience will progressively increase your confidence and capability to make a difference. This will balance against the deep sense of reward that comes from being able to create meaningful change, the many watershed moments where you will discover the true difference you can make.

It is likely that many of those within your organization, even within leadership roles, will recognize the challenges and be making the best of the cards they have been dealt. They will lament on the past and what it means for the organization and its workforce, now and for the future. **As workforce planning professionals, we think and act differently.** We cannot alter the past to change our current situation, but we can act now to create the workforce of the future.

INDEX

Page numbers in *italic* denote information contained within figures or tables.

A Positions 91
absenteeism costs 128
   see also core absence multiple
acceptance 155
accidental manager 268
accidental specialists 90–91, 100
accomplishment 12, 207, 254, 271
accountability 229, 308, 310, 317, 319
   see also RAPID® matrix
accounting cost 12
accreditation 6, 7, 8, 87, 91, 256, 266
achievement measure 269, 304
act-sense-respond 52
action planning 32, 61, 184–85, 191–312, 329
activity-based budgeting 39
actuality 261
ad-hoc initiatives 75, 281, 303, 310
ad-hoc plans 75
additional overhead costs 167–68
adhocracies 223
adjacent upskilling 264
administrative cost of churn 284
Adonis, Lord 153
advanced capabilities 8, 9
advocacy 106, 317, 318, 329
Aectual 156
affect heuristic 187
after-sales support 141, 157
age demographics 113, 120–21, 159
   see also Baby Boomers; older workers
agencies 69, 70, 251, 284
aggregated data (feedback) 145, 162
AGI 236
agile gap analysis *178*, 179–80
Agile Manifesto 48–50
agile principles 56–59
   see also flexibility; incremental problem solving; iterative planning; 'team of teams'; 'why' question; workforce planning, defined
agile workforce planning framework 59–61
   see also action planning; baseline organization; delivery (execution); demand; gap analysis; supply

agility 46–47, 160, 220, 223, 230
agreement 98
agriculture sector 68, 139
Ahrendts, Angela 288–89
AI (artificial intelligence) 9, 155, 159, 163, 195, 235–36, 257, 280
   see also machine learning
AI winters 235
AIVI 257
Aldi 255
alliances *218*, 219, 279–81
   see also partnerships
Allianz 265
alumni 251, 278
'always be learning' mantra 58–59
Amazon 208, 224, 239–40
ambiguity 26, 105, 263, 290
analysis 82
   see also gap analysis; PESTLE analysis; regression analysis
analytics 26–27, 33, 42, 82, 94
anchoring 101, 186
anger 155
animal characteristics 9
annual leave 86, 125, 126
annual performance reviews 51
annual planning limitations 40, 125
anonymity 162, 163
anticipated benefits 202
antifragility 33, 315, 330
apathetics 100, 101, 317
apathy 316–17
APL 144, 145, 270
Apple 207, 220, 224, 237, 288–89
applicant tracking systems 257
applicants 251–52
application programming interface 234
apprenticeship levy 38
Argo AI 280
Arthur Andersen 274
artificial general intelligence 236
artificial intelligence (AI) 9, 155, 159, 163, 195, 235–36, 257, 280
   see also machine learning
artificial intelligence video interviews 257
assisted RPA 234

INDEX

assumptions 83–85, 154, 165, 202, 203, 318–19
attackers 100, 101, 316
attribute substitution 101–02, 186
audience aggregation 70
authority 10, 100
automation 9, 35, 123, 151, 159, 195, 232–40, 305–06
Automation Anywhere 234
automobile industry 228, 232–33
    see also Ford, Henry (Ford Motor Company); General Motors
autonomous technology 155
autonomy 53, *218*, 229
availability 100, 125, 285–86, *305*
availability heuristic 102, 186
available time 125–26, 142, 147–48, 230
available time target 147
average handling time 146
average product of labour (APL) 144, 145, 270
average turnover rates 288, 302–03
averages 85

Baby Boomers 34, 120, 121
balance lever 195, 206–32, 238, 259, 270, 303
banking sector 25, 236, 310
    see also Barclays
Barclays 166
bargaining 155
base pay 252
baseline organization 59–60, 65–108, 266, 307
basic recruitment 249–50
BAU (business as usual) plans 75, 303, 310, 317, 318, 322
Bear Scotland ruling (2014) 86
behavioural mindset 6
bell curve distribution 89–90, 281
benchmarking 51, 85, 146, 165, 202, 220, 256
benefits 201–02
benefits packages 252–53
    see also annual leave; pensions; vesting benefits
Berisford, John 294
Berkeley, Lord Tony 153
Berkshire Hathaway 211
best-case scenarios 31, 58, 152, 166, 180–82, 183, 217
best practice 51
bias 31, 101–02, 186–87, 196, 239–40, 257

confirmation 306
negativity 20, 186
optimism 50–51, 152
pro-innovation 102, 186, 194
    see also HIPPO; planning fallacy; segmentation effect
bind lever 195, 196, 249, 264, 282–89
biotechnology 105, 156
black swan events 25
Blackberry 207–08
blockchain 155
Blue Arrow 263
blue-collar industries 122
Blue Prism 234
borrow lever 194–95, 196, 274–82
bot lever 195, 196, 232–40
bottom-up resource planning 16, 146
bounce lever 195, 196, 249, 259, 265, 289–95
Bowers, Katy 188–89
Brailsford, Dave 228
brain science 185–87
brain stem 185
brand 223–24, 250–52, 254–55, 256
British Cycling 227–28
Brown, Alan 257–58
Brownlee, Charlotte 102
budgetary slack 40
budgeted FTE 86
budgeting 39–41, 42, 141–42, 168, 185, 186, 200, 306
    see also cost cutting (reductions)
build lever 194, 196, 249, 254, 258, 259–74, 275
bullwhip effect 216
bundling 71, 280
    see also unbundling
burnout 127, 273
business as usual (BAU) plans 75, 303, 310, 317, 318, 322
business insights 33
business model canvas 72–73
business models 70–73, 154, 158, 209, 238, 277
business partners (HRBPs) 54, 199, 200, 284, 320
business problem focus 53–54, 59, 188–89, 323
business process outsourcing 279, 281–82
buy lever 194, 195, 196, 248–59, 264, 275

Cabinet Office 292
Cambridge Analytica 239
Cameron, David 142

Canada 36
capability 5–14, 41, 90–91, 165–66, 181–85, 188–89, 218, 250
  critical 264, 285, 306
  duration of 277
  location of 11, 140, 166–67, 184, 201, 221, 253–54
capability change 292
capability deficit 6, 13, 14, 184, 215
capability gap 196, 264, 268, 293
capability loss 13
capability segmentation framework 89, 249, 255
capability shape 8–11, 13, 166, 182–83, 252, 257
capability size 7–8, 166, 178, 180–81, 182
capability surplus 13–14
capability timing 11–12, 14–17, 167, 184–85
  see also operational workforce planning (horizon two); resource planning (horizon one); strategic workforce planning (horizon three)
capacity (capacity models) 38, 147, 250
  see also resource planning (horizon one)
capital 20, 71
car insurance 154
career recruitment 250
Cartesian theory 52
casual workers 277
causation 92, 322, 323
centralization 22, 155
centres of expertise (CoEs) 199, 200
cerebellum 185
cerebral neocortex 187
certification 7, 87
change (change management) 34, 75, 109, 150–55, 310, 316–17, 321–22
change controls 322
change curve 154–55
change plans 75
change projects 310
Channel 4 Television 209–10
chaos theory 51–52
characteristics 9–10, 166, 183
charts 82
chatbots 236–37, 238
checklists 32
Chief Digital Officers 200
Chief Experience Officers 200
Chief Human Resources Officers (CHROs) 199, 213, 294
chief of the gang 21

Chief People Officers 199
choose stage (recruitment) 257
churn 101–14, 282–85
clan organizations 223
classic PSFs 278–79
classical economic theory 20
classification 236
client-based structures 219
cliff basis vesting 287
climate 253, 269, 273–74
  see also culture (culture change)
climate change 127, 152, 157, 158
closed-looped tasks 129
cloud technology 123, 155, 232, 234
Co-op Food 263
Coca-Cola 224, 280
coders 188
CoEs 199, 200
cognitive automation 237–38
cognitive biases 101–02
cognitive mindset 269
cognitive skills 6
cognitive tasks 129
  see also problem definition
collaboration 49, 197–201, 219, 220, 223, 293
  see also alliances; coordination
collective intelligence 164
Comensura 276
comic book artists 188
command states 10–11
communication 49, 144, 316–17
  see also feedback; storytelling; summary of execution
competencies 6, 87–88, 122, 260
competing values framework 222–23
competition 41, 223, 287
complementary upskilling 264
complexity 25, 50–51
compliance (compliance functions) 140, 152, 158, 257
complication 51, 52
confidence 270
confirmation bias 306
confirmed demand 217
connectivity 11, 156, 160, 197, 207
consultancies 41, 42, 89, 121, 188–89, 230, 279
consumer demand 137, 139, 151, 156–57
context switching 229–30
contingency plans 58, 310
contingent workers 166, 275–78, 304
continual workers 277
continuous delivery 49, 53, 56, 57

continuous improvement 225–28
contract extension (renewal) 113
contracted FTE 86
contracts 10–11, 13, 88, 89, 113, 125, 275–76, 285–88
    see also psychological contract
contractual initiatives 285–88
control 32, 77, 138, 218, 223, 270
    see also budgeting; governance; processes
Cook, Tim 220
cooperation 49
coordination 31, 218, 221
core absence multiple 147–48
core competence automation 239
Corporate HR 199
corporate philanthropy 158
corporate social responsibility 158
correlation 92–94
cost-benefit analysis 201–03, 307
cost centres 39–40, 87, 198–99
cost cutting (reductions) 39–40, 142–43, 184, 210–11, 212
cost of poor quality 213–15
costs 12–13, 32, 128, 167–68, 185, 250, 258–59, 268, 283–86, 304
    indirect 213–14
    metrics for 202
    see also cost-benefit analysis; cost centres; cost-cutting (reductions); cost of poor quality; costs of control; external costs; total cost of workforce
costs of control 213, 214
counting rules 103
Covid-19 121, 221, 230, 255–56, 263, 271, 276, 278, 290, 293
creativity 160, 218
criminality 14, 143, 213
critical capabilities 91, 264, 285, 306
cross-functional job rotation 293
cross-functional teams 53, 294
crowdsourcing 163–64
crunchers 188
culture (culture change) 41, 127, 222–24, 253, 256, 269, 273–74
customer-centricity, (satisfaction) 49, 53–54, 213–15
customers 54, 145, 183
    see also consumer demand; customer-centricity (satisfaction)
cybernetics 206, 235
cyberspace 11
Cynefin framework 50–53, 56, 323

data 27, 80–85, 82, 87, 143, 156, 188, 320
    time series 145, 161
    see also assumptions; distributional data
data centre automation 233–34
data gaps 83–84, 85
data gathering 81–85
data quality (reliability) 82–83
data sets 83, 84–85, 320
data visualization 82, 188
day in the life (DiLo) studies 146
dealing covenants 287
decay 128–29, 207–08
decentralization 22
decision making 22, 31, 50–53, 98–99, 101, 186–87
Declaration of Independence (United States) 222
decomposition tree technique 92–94
defenders 101, 316, 317, 329
Defense Advanced Research Projects Agency 163
definite benefits 202
delegation 10, 99, 179, 218, 221, 254
delivery (execution) 32, 61, 75–76, 195, 198, 303, 307–08, 313–25
    continuous 49, 53, 56, 57
Delphi method 162–63, 164
demand 60, 123, 135–73, 183, 198, 205–47, 269, 309
    derived 178, 180
demand calculation 143–48, 183
demand inconsistency 123
demand management 215–18, 309
demand optimization 198, 205–47, 269
demand peaks 215, 216
demand spikes 139, 167, 309
demand troughs 215–16
demographics 34, 87, 113, 120–21, 122
    see also older workers
demotions 112, 114, 294–95
denial 154
depression 128, 155
derived demand 137, 146, 148, 156, 178, 180, 183, 212
descriptive analytics 94
detection 236
detractors 101, 316
development 254, 261, 264–68, 269, 310
diagnostic analytics 94
diamond operating model 75
Dickson, Niall 288
differentiation 255
difficulty 270
digital natives 121

digital programming 182
digital skills 13, 91, 159
digital specialists 164–65
digitalization 231
    see also Chief Digital Officers; digital natives; digital programming; digital skills; digital specialists; Information Technology (IT) function
diminishing marginal returns 144
diminishing returns 144–45
direct demand (variable demand) 139–40, 141
direct workforce costs 167
direction phase 218
dismissal 112–13, 291
disorder 52–53
disruption 41, 105, 230
    see also Covid-19
distant upskilling (reskilling) 35, 159, 265
distributional data 153–54
diversity 34–35, 83, 87, 159–60, 209–10, 240, 252, 257, 304–05, 329
    see also inclusion
diversity data 83, 87
divestment 291–92, 293–94
divisibility 144–45
DMAIC method 227–28
documentation 50
Dolan, Christine 294
drift 138–39, 179, 180, 214, 215, 227

Ebelle-ebanda, Anthony 265, 294
economic cost 12
economic factors 76
    see also global financial crisis
economic mission 74
economic sectors 68–70
economic theory 20, 70, 137, 138, 139
ecosystems 72–73, 160, 220
edge computing 155
effectiveness 38, 39, 266
effects-based approach 194, 196
efficiency 38, 39, 265–66
ego depletion 187, 273
electronics production 138, 214
ELIZA 236
email 156, 207
emigration 119
emotions (emotional mindset) 6, 187, 269, 272–73
employee engagement 55, 61, 88, 185, 202
employee value proposition (EVP) 252–59, 271, 288–89

    see also hygiene factors
employer brand 224, 250–52, 254–55, 256
employment 14, 183
    see also unemployment
empowerment 155, 194, 196, 220, 229, 288
end of contract 113, 117
enemy of humanity concept 222
energy sector 22, 37, 156, 274, 290
engagement
    employee 55, 61, 88, 185, 202
    stakeholder 101–02, 185–89
enhancement 254–55
Enron 273–74
entry-level positions 91, 250, 255
environmental factors 6, 127, 260, 261, 269
Environmental Protection Agency (US) 157
environmental scanning 76–77, 99, 119
ephemeralization 142
equality 36, 37, 87, 157
    see also gender parity
Equality Act (2010) 87
Erlang C formula 148
error correction model 161, 164
escalation 320
estimate-talk-estimate (Delphi method) 162–63, 164
ethics 76, 157, 165, 239, 240
ethics committees 240
ETPS 76
Europe 25, 120, 184, 188, 265, 275, 276, 277, 278
European Union (EU) 24, 119, 123
EVP *see* employee value proposition (EVP)
execution (delivery) 32, 61, 75–76, 195, 198, 303, 307–08, 313–25
    continuous 49, 53, 56, 57
exits 291
    see also dismissal; mutual severance
expectancy 270
expectancy theory 270–71
expected benefits 202
experienced hires 249, 263, 264
experimentation 51, 56, 209, 294
explicit risks 318
exponential moving average 161
external costs 12–13, 14
external disruptions 41
external factors 76–77, 151–52, 205
external hires 267–68
external shrinkage 126
external training 252
extrapolation 117, 125, 160–61, 164

extrinsic motivation 229, 271
ExxonMobil 259

face-to-face conversations 49
Facebook 205, 239, 259
Facilities function 167, 201, 278
failure, learning from 56, 227
failure demand 214, 216
Fanshawe, Simon 209, 210
Fanuc 233
fast-track recruitment 250
feedback 162, 229, 261, 271–72, 304, 320–21
feedback loops 272, 304, 320–21
female representation 92, 93, 114, *118*, 183, 210, 239–40
50:20:30 learning model 261, 268
55:25:10 learning model 261
fight or flight responses 185
Finance Business Partners 200, 320
Finance function 16, 39, 123, 168, 200, 219, 284, 320
financial FTE 86
financial services sector 69, 140, 265, 267–68
financial workforce structure 87
financially strapped contingent workers 277–78
fire and evacuation capability 11
firm forecast plans 217
fishbone diagram 92, 226
five Ds 41
five whys model 92, 226
5W1H model 92
fixed costs 12
fixed demand (overheads) 140, 141
fixed price (flat fee) model 276, 279
fixed-term contracts 89, 275–76
flexibility 49, 57, 58, *217*, 221, 223, 230, 254, 321–22
flow 87, 220, 228, 230, 319–21
Ford, Henry (Ford Motor Company) 157, 232–33, 280
forecast FTE 86
forecast range 217
forecasting 27, 53, 60, 114–19, 150–73, 217
Forrester effect 216
foundation capabilities 8, 9, 182
fourth industrial revolution 89, 155–60
Foxconn 220
fragility (antifragility) 33, 315, 330
fragmentation 208–10, 218
fraud 14, 76, 236
free agents 277

freelancers 121, 122, 275–78
Friedman doctrine 157
frozen forecast plans 216–17
FTE (full-time equivalent) 85–86, 88, 125, 126, 146–48
FTE shrinkage (full-time equivalent shrinkage) 126
functional organizations 219, 220
furlough 289–90
future-focus 31
future of work 158–60

Galton, Sir Francis 163–64
gangs 21
gap analysis 60, 175–90, 323–24
gaps in data 83
gaps of data 83
Gaussian distribution 89–90, 281
gender parity 166, 183
  see also female representation
General Electric 22
General Motors 22, 233
Generation Alpha 34, 121
Generation X 34, 120
Generation Y (Millennials) 34, 120, 123–24
Generation Z 34, 120–21
geographic workforce location 11, 167, 221, 253–54
  see also shoring
geographically structured organizations 219
gig economy 121, 275–78
Glassdoor 252
GlaxoSmithKline 166
global data 156
global financial crisis 23–25, 33
Global Goals for Sustainable Development (UN) 36, 37, 157
goals 36, 37, 74, 76, 157, 208, 270, 304
gold collar workers 69
Google 90, 155–56, 224, 228, 237
governance 101, 138, 216, 217, 317, 318
graduated vesting 287
greenwashing 158
Greiner Curve 218–19
growth mindset 56, 166, 182
growth strategy 151, 178, 210–11, 218–19
G7 24, 25
Gulick, Luther 219

habit 31, 186, 187
hard factors 6, 76
  see also processes; resources; technology

headcount approach 36, 85, 126
Heinz Company 211
heuristics 85, 87–88, 101–02, 141, 186–87, 194, 269, 322–23
hidden plant theory 214
hierarchical organizations 98, 219–20, 223
hierarchies 87, 140
high potential talent groups 87
High Speed Two 153
higher education 123
highlight reports 319–20
HIPPO 80, 162
holocracy models 220
home delivery service 216
homeshoring 221
Honeywell 290
horizon one (resource planning) 14, 16, 38, 103–04, 146, 198
horizon two (operational workforce planning) 16, 38–41, 103, 178, 200
horizon three (strategic workforce planning) 16–17, 23, 32, 41–42, 104, 178, 199
horizons 14–17, 103–04, 145, 151, 167, 202–03
  see also horizon one (resource planning); horizon two (operational workforce planning); horizon three (strategic workforce planning)
horizontal movement (mobility) 114
horizontal strategic alliances 280
Horstman's corollary 179
Hoy, Sir Chris 227–28
HR analytics 26
HR business partners (HRBPs) 54, 199, 200, 284, 320
HR function (human resource management) 22–23, 33, 72, 82, 140, 168, 199–200, 232
  see also Chief Human Resource Officers (CHROs)
HR metrics 33, 88, 266–67
human capability 9, 12
human capital facts 82–83
Human Resource Planning Society 22
Human Resource Planning (Walker) 22
hunger 36, 37, 141, 187
hygiene factors 6, 229

IBM 213, 237, 266–67
ideation 197–98

idle time *125*, 127
ill-health retirement 113, 118
illness 127
immigration 119
implicit risks 318
in-process control methods 231
inanimate capabilities 9
inbound logistics 72, 137, 140, 145
inclusion 10, 34–35, 202, 230, 329
  see also LGBT rights
increasing marginal returns 144
incremental budgeting 39, 42
incremental problem solving 56, 58, 322, 330
indicators 319
indirect costs 213–14, 284–85
industrial action 292, 318
industrial automation 232–33
influence 100, 187–89, 270
information access 6, 156, 159, 160
information flow 319–21
Information Technology (IT) function 200, 259
infrastructure 72, 76, 137, 140, 183
  see also Facilities function; Finance function; HR function (human resource management); Information Technology (IT) function
initiative life 202
'inner chimp' (paleomammalian brain) 185–86, 187
input 98
input-based demand calculation 145–48, 153
input-output model 21, 138–39
input volumes 145
Inquiry into the Nature and Causes of the Wealth of Nations (Smith) 21
inside view 152–53
Insight222 240
insourcing 259
instrumentality 271
insurance (insurance industry) 71, 85, 154, 213, 253
intangible benefits 202
intelligence preparation of the battle space 97
inter-capability mix 9, 166, 183
interest vs power 100–01
interlocking work 221
intermediate capabilities 8, 182
internal demand factors 151
internal disruptions 41

internal mobility (movement) 112, 114–17, 282, 283, 285
    see also progression
internal shrinkage 126
internet 81, 121, 123, 156, 234
interpersonal skills 6
interpolation 160–61
interviews 257
intra-capability mix 8, 166, 182–83
intra-national workforce location 11
intractability 50, 202
intrinsic motivation 229, 271, 273
investments 40
iPhone 207, 220
Ishikawa fishbone diagram 92, 226
issue-focused sprints 322–23
iterative planning 58, 162, 321–22

job rotation 293
job satisfaction 229, 278
Jobs, Steve 207, 220

Kaizen 226–27, 301
key leader engagement 97
knockout (killer) questions 257
knowledge 5–6, 8, 159
knowledge economy 69
knowledge workers 90, 91, 146, 221, 234
known knowns 51
known unknowns 51
Krafcik, John 228
Kraft Foods 211

labour requirement calculation 146–48
    see also average product of labour (APL)
latents 100–01, 316–17
lattice structures 220
law of the customer 53–54
law of the network 54
law of the small team 53
layoff survivor stress 291
layoffs 12–13, 23, 74, 112–13, 189, 265, 290–91
leadership 97, 218
lean production 228
learning 56, 58–59, 87, 261, 264–69, 310
leasing 70
legal environment 41, 76, 151
legal professions 69, 237, 280
legislation 113, 120
    see also Equality Act (2010)
Leontief, Walter 138
lever-focused sprints 323–24
levers 194–96, 206–40, 248–95, 303

LGBT rights 158
life expectancy 34, 120
lights-out manufacturing 233
limbic system 185
listing 256–57
Lloyds Banking Group 310
loans 70, 236
locale workforce location 11
location 11, 140, 166–67, 184, 201, 221, 253–54
locus of control 270
logistics 72, 137, 140, 145
long-term abstraction 89
long-term incentive plans 287
loss aversion 287
low turnover 282–83

machine learning 235, 236–37, 239–40, 258
macro organization level 4, 9, 12, 140, 143, 182, 199, 216, 289–92
macroeconomics 119, 138
macroscenarios 104
Malthusian catastrophe 145
management 30, 87, 140
    see also accidental manager
management by objectives 51
mandatory retirement 113, 120
manpower planning 20, 22
marginal gains 228
marginal product of labour (MPL) 139–40, 144, 145, 270
marginal returns 144
market brand 223–24
market organizations 223
market-oriented ecosystem 160, 220
market research 160, 164
market shocks 41
marketing 11, 72, 137, 140, 199, 211
master service agreements 281
material requirements planning 21–22
matrix organizations 10, 219, 220
McChrystal, General Stanley 58, 197, 269
McDonald's 280
McGraw-Hill Companies 293–94
McKinsey & Company 23, 42, 76, 277–78
McLoughlin, Patrick 153
meaningful work 55, 61, 74, 123, 229, 329
megatrends 119–24, 159
memories 20, 186–87
mental health 128
    see also burnout
mergers and acquisitions 259, 291

meso organization level 4, 9, 12, 140, 143, 167–68, 182, 184, 198, 199
  bounce capability 292–95
metrics (measurement) 33, 88, 202, 208, 266–67
  achievement 269, 304
  see also shrinkage; total cost of workforce; utilization
micro organization level 4, 9, 140, 143, 145, 146, 167–68, 229–30, 254
microeconomics 138
Microsoft 224, 237
migration 119–20, 159
milestone reports 320
Millennials (Generation Y) 34, 120, 123–24
mindset 6, 56, 166, 182, 258, 260–61, 269–70, 272–73
minimum viable products 317
missing output 180
mission 74, 208, 304
mission statements 57
mixed bundling 71
modelling 114–19
modern agile 54–56
most-likely scenarios 31, 58, 104, 105, 130, 180–81, 183, 216, 217
motivation 229, 269–71, 273
moving averages 161, 164
MPL 139–40, 144, 145, 270
multidisciplinary teams 240
multigenerational workforces 34, 120–21
multiple sector organizations 69
multiplier effect 154–55, 260
multitasking 229
mutual severance 112–13, 291
MyoKardia 105–06

narcissism of small differences 197
National Health Service 278, 288
national workforce location 11
nationalist voting 119–20
NATO 10–11
natural language generation (NLG) 236–37
natural language processing (NLP) 163, 236–37
nearshoring 258
negative mindset 6
negativity bias 20, 186
neo-classical economic theory 70
neo-PSFs *see* consultancies
neomammalian brain 187
Nestlé 188–89
net benefit 201–02

network-based organizations 54, 219–20
new skills development 122–23
Nintendo 71
Nitaqat 183
nominal group technique 163, 164
non-delivery 13, 14
non-financial benefits 202
Non-GMO Project 208
non-physiological characteristics 9–10
notice periods 13, 128, 286

objectives 74, 208, 304
OECD countries 24, 36
off-payroll workers 166, 167, 276
off-the-job training 38
offshoring 12–13, 184, 258–59, 281
older workers 121, 122, 159
omnicompetent worker 123
on-payroll workers 275–76
onboarding 32, 262–64, 276, 291
onshoring 258, 259
OODA loop 46–47
open-looped tasks 129
open offices 127
OpenView 273
operating models 75–76
operational command 10
operational control 10
operational leads 198–99
operational maturity 238–39
operational transformation 230–32
operational workforce planning (horizon two) 16, 38–41, 103, 178, 200
operational workforce structure 87
operations 72
operators 91, 255, 263, 277, 281, 285
opportunity 254
opportunity cost 12, 168, 284
optimism bias 50–51, 152
options 71, 306
Organic Consumers Association 208
organization 3–4, 68–73, 219–21, 232, 270
  baseline 59–60, 65–108, 266, 307
  culture of 41, 222–24, 253, 256, 269, 273–74
  hierarchical 98, 223
  internal demand drivers 151
  macro 9, 12, 140, 143, 182, 199, 216, 289–92
  market 223
  matrix 10
  meso 9, 12, 140, 143, 167–68, 182, 184, 198, 199, 292–95

micro 9, 140, 143, 145, 146, 167–68, 229–30, 254
network-based 54
public sector 142, 213, 279–80, 287, 292
secondary sector 145
voluntary sector 255
see also churn; hierarchies; infrastructure; strategy
organization design 218–19, 270
organizational layers 220–21
ORION 238
othering 197
outbound logistics 72, 137, 140, 145
outcomes 307
output-based demand calculation 143–45
outputs 138, 180
outside view 153–54
outsourcing 167, 200, 219, 250, 258, 259, 281–82
overqualification 123
overtension 207, 210–11
Overton window 165, 183
ownership 319
paleomammalian brain 185–86, 187
panel shows 209–10
Paretian distribution (Pareto principle) 89–90, 212–13
Parkinson's law 179
part-time working 88
partial retirement 114
partnerships 98, 105, 279–80
pay 252
PDCA cycle 226, 227
Pegatron 220
penny shaving (salami slicing) 40, 210
pensions 113, 323
people analytics 26
People Analytics Data Ethics Charter 240
performance 98, 124–28, 202, 225, 258, 269, 270, 291
performance-based pricing model 279
performance cost of churn 284
performance management 90, 225, 268–74, 291
performance reviews 51, 274
performance to value model 283–84, 286
permanent workers 113, 252, 289, 291
personal circumstance change 114
personal value 271
personality assessments 258
personalization 26, 156–57
PERT 31, 104
PESTLE analysis 76, 151

Peter principle 268, 294
phyles 21
physical tasks 129
physiology 6, 9–10, 127, 273
PIIGs countries 25
pinkwashing 158
pivoting 36, 102, 209
planned FTE 86
planned specialists 90
planning fallacy 51, 152, 186
poaching covenants 287
policy 75
political environment 76, 104, 142, 151, 239
positive mindset 6
potential 261, 268
power law relationship (Pareto principle) 89–90, 212–13
power vs interest stakeholder map 99–101, 103
predictive analytics 203, 236
presenteeism 127–28
pricing 276, 279
primary risks 168
primary sector organizations 68–69, 232
primary value activities 72, 137, 140, 145
priority workforce segments 91
pro-innovation bias 102, 186, 194
problem definition 322–23
problem solving 56, 58, 322, 330
process improvement 225–28, 231
process workers 90
processes 47–48, 57, 75, 137, 138–40, 225–28, 231, 254
see also business process outsourcing
processing speed 126–27
Procter & Gamble 231
procurement 72, 140, 200, 309
product-based organizations 219, 220
production 21
productive time 126–28, 143, 147
productivity 35–36, 124, 143, 202, 227, 268–69, 273, 291
products 70, 138–39
products of labour 143–45
professional campuses 279
professional services firms 278–82
professionals 91, 255, 263, 277, 285
proficiency 88
profit centres 39–40, 87, 198–99
profitability 35, 210–11, 223
programme evaluation and review technique 31, 104
programming languages 182

progression 254, 267–68, 293
  see also internal mobility (movement)
progressive hiring 249–50
promoters 101, 316, 317, 329
promotions 114, 309
Proposition 37 208-09
prospect theory 152
proximity 319
psychological contract 255
public sector organizations 69–70, 142, 213, 279–80, 287, 292
pure bundling 71
purpose 74, 208, 222, 276
purpose-based contracts 276

qualifications 7, 87, 123
qualitative methods 162–64, 165
quality adjustment (management) 82–83, 141–42, 211–15, 216, 231, 317–18
  see also Six Sigma
Quality Street 212
quantitative methods 160–61, 164–65
quantum supremacy 155–56
quaternary sector organizations 69
queuing theory 148
quinary sector organizations 69

RACI matrix 308
RAPID® matrix 98–99, 198
rationality 31
real-time Delphi 163
real-time resource management 16
reallocation 292
reassignments 12, 292
recognition 124, 252–53, 258, 268
recommendations 98
recruitment 112, 113, 114–15, 166, 249–52, 256, 309
  experienced hire 263, 264
  external hires 267–68
  see also selection process
recruitment agencies 250–51
recruitment process outsourcing 250
red-tape crisis 218–19
redeployment 114, 293–94, 309
redundancies 113, 114, 178, 265, 291
reference class forecasting 153–54
regression analysis 146
regression to the mean 8
regulated professions 7
regulation 7, 151–52, 239
reluctants 277–78
remodelling 302–03

Rentokil Initial 257–58
replacement cost of churn 284–85
reporting 82, 319–20
reptilian brain 185, 187
requirements 13
resale 71, 72
Rescorla, Cyril Richard ('Rick') 52
resignation 112–13, 117, 196
resilience 33, 265, 330
reskilling (retraining) 35, 159, 265
resource planning (horizon one) 14, 16, 38, 103–04, 139, 146, 198
resources 100, 138
responsibility assignment 308
responsible automation 240
restricted budgets 141
restrictive covenants 287
restructuring exercises 114, 178, 291, 294
retained services 280–81
retirement 92, 113–14, 118–19, 120
return of service 286, 287–88
return on investment 56, 91, 103, 239, 265–67, 268, 284, 286, 318, 323
reward 252–53
  see also benefits packages; salary increases
RICE values 273–74
right (concept) 165
rightsizing 7–8
risk 13–14, 40, 123, 152, 168, 236, 257, 301–02
Risk function 140
risk management 318–19
River Irwell 221
robotic process automation (RPA) 234–35, 238, 239
robotics 156, 233, 234–35, 238, 239
roles of interest 16, 85, 88–91, 92, 103
rolling averages *see* moving averages
rotas 16
run plans 75
runners 252

safety 7, 32, 55–56, 154, 221, 253, 256, 263, 273, 292
salami slicing 40, 210
salary increases 195–96, 289
Sales function 72, 138, 140, 199
Saudization 183
scenario planning 31, 58, 104–06, 162, 180–82, 307
  best-case 152, 166, 183, 217
  most-likely 130, 183, 216, 217
  worst-case 31, 58, 104, 155, 165–66, 180–82, 183, 217

schedules 16
scope creep 317–18
screening 7, 256–57
scrums 273
seasonality 139, 250, 277
secondary risks 168, 301
secondary sector organizations 68, 69, 145, 220, 232
secondments 89, 103, 280, 290–91
sector experience 87
security clearance 7
segmentation 85–91, 118, 153, 186, 239
    see also capability segmentation framework
segmentation effect 153, 186
selection process 256–58
self-employment 121–22, 276
self-organizing teams 50
self-service checkouts 202, 214, 231–32
self-service data 82
sense-analyse-respond approach 51, 323
sense-categorize-respond approach 51
sentient workforce characteristics 9
Serco Group 276
service 70, 72, 137, 141, 157
    see also shared services
service levels 141–43, 148, 212, 216
    see also master service agreements
sessional workers 277
seven Bs of action planning 194–96
seven rights of workforce planning 5–14, 49, 81, 165–68
    see also capability; capability timing; costs; location; risk; shape; size
7-S operating model 76
70:20:10 learning model 261
severance pay 113
shape 8–11, 13, 166, 182–83, 252, 257
shared resources 70, 145
shared services 199, 200, 292
Shared Services Connected Limited 292
shareholders 157–58
shoring 258–59
    see also offshoring
shortlisting 257
shrinkage 126, 127, 147
shrinkflation 212
significance 229
silent generation 34, 120
silver medallists 252
simple moving average 161
simplicity 50, 51
Six Sigma 227–28
size 7–8, 166, 178, 180–81, 182

skill (skills) 6, 88, 122–23, 260
    digital 13, 91, 159
    see also influence; reskilling (retraining); skills gaps (shortages); upskilling
skill decay 128–29
Skilling, Jeffrey 274
skills gaps (shortages) 34, 35, 256
small gains 318
small teams 53
Smarter Learning Analytics (IBM) 266–67
smartphones 207–08
    see also iPhone
social environment 34, 76, 151
social justice 157, 158, 159
social media 156, 236
    see also Facebook
social responsibility (considerations) 157–58, 209
soft factors 6
    see also culture (culture change); leadership
soft S factors 76
software 40, 48–49, 50, 53, 56, 71, 234, 238
solicitation 287
Sopra Steria 292
spans of control 220–21
specialists 90–91, 100, 164–65, 250, 252, 255, 264, 275, 285, 306
speech-based devices 237
speed to competence 147, 262, 263, 283, 284
stagflation 22
stakeholder mapping 99–101
stakeholder power 103
stakeholder theory 100
stakeholders 20, 49, 54, 97–108, 185–89, 307–08, 316–17, 321
    see also operational leads; shareholders
Standard & Poor's 293–94
standardization 228, 230
Starbucks 158
statement of work 279
statistical group responses 162
stealing other people's artificial grass 54, 102, 201
storytelling 187–89
strategic alignment 73–76, 151, 206–13, 240, 292, 303–06
strategic alliances 279–80
strategic disconnect 41–42
strategic misalignment 207–11, 218
Strategic Staffing (Bechet) 23
strategic workforce planning (horizon three) 16–17, 23, 32, 41–42, 104, 178, 199

strategy 32, 67–79, 104, 140, 151, 208
   growth 151, 178, 210–11, 218–19
   location 11, 140, 166–67, 184, 201, 221, 253–54
   workforce 303–06
   see also strategic alignment; strategic alliances; strategic disconnect; strategic misalignment; strategic workforce planning (horizon three)
stress 128, 142, 187, 273, 291, 293, 308
subscriptions 70
Sullivan, Mark 294
summary of execution 307–08
sunk-cost fallacy 239
superordinate goals 76
supply 60, 109–34, 155, 180
support activities 72
   see also after-sales support; infrastructure
sustainability 36–37, 49, 55, 157, 158, 264
Sydney Opera House 152
synergies 210
system dynamics 225–32
system one thinking 31, 185, 187
system two thinking 31, 187

tables 82
tactical command 10
tactical control 10–11
talent, defined 260
talent groups 87–88
talent lakes 251
talent management 33, 189, 199, 201, 205, 215, 240, 248–300
   see also automation; bind lever; borrow lever; bounce lever; build lever; buy lever; culture (culture change)
talent pools 159, 251–52, 306
talent shortage (skills gap) 122–23, 124
talent streams 251–52
tangible benefits 202
target FTE 86, 148
target time 148
tax legislation 166
Taylor, Frederick Winslow (Taylorism) 228–30
'team of teams' 57–58, 197, 198
teams 50, 53, 57–58, 197, 198, 240, 294
technical skills 6
technology 34, 76, 81–82, 123, 151, 155–56, 159–60, 254, 259
   cloud 127, 152, 157, 158

   and location 11
   overreliance on 42
   recruitment and selection 257
   see also AI (artificial intelligence); application programming interface; automation;biotechnology; chatbots; cybernetics; digitalization; email; speech-based devices
technology development 72, 140, 270
temporary workers 113
tenure 87, 286, 322
terms of reference 102–06
tertiary sector organizations 68–69
Theory X 225, 229
Theory Y 225, 230
third sector see voluntary sector
360-degree performance reviews 274
three laws of Agile 53–54
3D printing 156
3G Capital 211
time see available time; average handling time; capability timing
time and materials 276, 279
time and motion studies 146
time fences 216–17
time series data 145, 161
timelines 307
tolerance 319
top-down demand analysis 146
total cost of workforce 167–68, 184
toxic workplace culture 127
traditional competencies 122
traditional gap analysis 177–79
traditionalists (silent generation) 34, 120
training 7, 13, 38, 87, 252, 259–60
transfers occurrences 202
transformational work 167, 182, 230–32
transition probability matrix 115–16
transparency 54, 240
travelling salesman problem 237–38
Troubled Asset Relief Program 25
Trump, Donald 119–20
trust 49, 240, 288
Turing test 235–36
turnover 112–13, 117–19, 282–83, 286, 288–89, 302–03, 304, 319
turnover modelling 117–19
turnover rate calculation 117
12 standard forms of value 70–71

Uber 121
UIPath 234

UK 36, 38, 122, 127, 166, 254, 256, 292
  unemployment 24, 123
UN (United Nations) Sustainable Development Goals 36, 37, 157
unassisted RPA 234
unbundling 281
uncertainty 25, 105, 165, 263
under-hiring 40
underperformance 127–28
unemployment 22, 23–24, 35, 122, 123, 183, 283–84, 285
Unimate 233
universal crimes 222
universal packing systems 231
unknown unknowns 50, 166, 181–82
unresponsiveness 40, 41
up or out performance management 274
UPS 237–38
upskilling 35, 264–65, 269, 294, 310, 317
US (United States) 23–25, 26, 36, 120, 122, 123, 128, 157, 222, 285
USAID 23
utility 70
utilization 16, 126, 147
utilization target 147

vacancies 13
valence 271
value (value creation) 70–73, 80–96, 271
  see also primary value activities; social justice
value-based pricing model 279
value chain 72, 137, 212
value proposition 72–73
  see also employee value proposition (EVP)
values 222–23, 273–74
values statements 222
variable costs 12
variable demand 139–40, 141
variety 229
vector error correction model 161, 164
vertical movement see demotions; promotions
vertical strategic alliances 280
vesting benefits 287–88
vices 6
virtues 6
vision 74

vital talent segments 91
vitality curve see Gaussian distribution
volatility 25, 263
Volkswagen 157–58, 280
voluntary redundancy 113
voluntary sector 70, 255
VUCA world 25–26, 33, 237, 289–90
  see also ambiguity; complexity; uncertainty; volatility

war for talent 23
waste 138, 139, 214, 215
waterfall process 47–48, 57
Watson 237
Waymo 228
weighted moving average 161
well-being 127, 272–73
WhatsApp 259
Whole Foods Market 208–09
whole-time equivalent 85–86
whole workforce approach 89–91
'why' question 57, 74, 102
work 158–60, 253–54
  see also meaningful work
work design 228–30, 254, 270
work results 229
workforce 59, 80–96
  costs of 167
  evolution of 111–34
  expectations of 123–24, 156
  future of 159
  strategy 75, 303–06
  see also location; segmentation; whole workforce approach
workforce analytics 26–27, 42, 82, 92–94, 103
workforce challenge sprints 322–24
workforce performance model 124–28, 143, 146–47
workforce planning, defined 3, 59, 198
workplace 127, 159–60
World Economic Forum 166
worst-case scenarios 31, 58, 104, 155, 165–66, 180–82, 183, 217

youth unemployment 122

zero-based (zero-sum) budgeting 39

CPSIA information can be obtained
at www.ICGtesting.com
Printed in the USA
JSHW050304250321
12876JS00001B/19